Hollywood Dance-ins and the Reproduction of Bodies

Hollywood Dance-ins and the Reproduction of Bodies

ANTHEA KRAUT

OXFORD
UNIVERSITY PRESS

Oxford University Press is a department of the University of Oxford.
It furthers the University's objective of excellence in research, scholarship,
and education by publishing worldwide. Oxford is a registered trade mark of
Oxford University Press in the UK and certain other countries.

Published in the United States of America by Oxford University Press
198 Madison Avenue, New York, NY 10016, United States of America.

© Oxford University Press 2025

All rights reserved. No part of this publication may be reproduced, stored in a retrieval system, transmitted, used for text and data mining, or used for training artificial intelligence, in any form or by any means, without the prior permission in writing of Oxford University Press, or as expressly permitted by law, by license or under terms agreed with the appropriate reprographics rights organization. Inquiries concerning reproduction outside the scope of the above should be sent to the Rights Department, Oxford University Press, at the address above.

You must not circulate this work in any other form
and you must impose this same condition on any acquirer.

CIP data is on file at the Library of Congress
ISBN 978–0–19–778967–4 (pbk.)
ISBN 978–0–19–778966–7 (hbk.)

DOI: 10.1093/oso/9780197789667.001.0001

Paperback printed by Marquis Book Printing, Canada
Hardback printed by Bridgeport National Bindery, Inc., United States of America

The manufacturer's authorized representative in the EU for product safety is
Oxford University Press España S.A., Parque Empresarial San Fernando de Henares,
Avenida de Castilla, 2 – 28830 Madrid (www.oup.es/en).

For my dance teachers

Contents

Acknowledgments	ix

Introduction: Bodies, Reproductive Labor, and Research at the Margins	1
Hollywood's "Golden" Age and Midcentury Racial Formations	5
"The Body" in Dance Studies	9
Fanon, Spillers, and Racial Embodiment	11
The "Bodily Turn" across Academia	15
Screen Bodies	18
Reproducible Bodies/Reproductive Labor	20
Archival Sleuthing and Research at the Margins	24
Coming Attractions	30

1. "Doing Angie": Betty Grable, Surrogation, and the (Non) Indexicality of Whiteness	34
Whiteness, Surrogation, and Privileged Embodiment	38
The Ambivalence of the Index	41
"Doing Angie"	43
"Bogus Brunettes"	51
The Other Betty	54
Marie Bryant and Betty's Buns	58

2. Marie Bryant, Black Reproductive Labor, and White Parasitism	66
Remembering Bryant	68
Bryant's Early Flights	71
Trying to Crash the Movies	73
"He Still Calls Her Pocahontas"	76
White Women and the Black Reproductive	86
Helping Vera-Ellen Fall Up	89
Polishing Black Acts	95

3. Female Reproductive Labor and White Corporeal Debt in *Singin' in the Rain*	100
Corporealizing Credit and Debt	103
Modes of Accounting	105
Reproductive Labor	106
Passing and White Credibility	114

viii CONTENTS

Disclosing White Debts and Ethnicizing Whiteness	116
Rita Moreno and Sidelined Labor	122

4. "Cool It, Alex": Queering the Dance-in — 127
Romero as Double and Mirror — 131
Romero and Erotic Triangles — 134
Romero as Queer Mode of Reproduction — 143
Romero as Dark Copy — 148

5. Racial Dis/Orientations and the Ambivalence of
Nancy Kwan's Dancing Body — 156
Cold War Orientalism and the Paradoxes of Integration and
Assimilation — 160
The (False) Indexicality of the Mirror — 163
White Voice/Yellow Face? — 167
Inscriptions of the Flesh — 170
Triangulated Orientations — 173
Panethnicity and Patrick Adiarte's Rock 'n' Roll Aesthetic — 174
Anonymous Chorus Dancers and the Asian Space of "Grant Avenue" — 178

Coda — 186
Hollywood's Corporeal Ecosystem in the Age of Television — 189
Female Pairings and Homosociality — 190
Cross-racial Pairings and Not-Quite-Synched Unison — 192

Notes — 197
Bibliography — 245
Index — 267

Acknowledgments

Over a decade ago, during a work dinner with my colleagues in UC Riverside's Department of Dance, Wendy Rogers off-handedly mentioned that her physical therapist's mother had been Debbie Reynolds's dance double. That's odd, I remember thinking. The female lead of *Singin' in the Rain*, one of my favorite childhood movies, had a dance double?[1] My curiosity piqued and many rabbit holes later, I wrote a book that is not about dance doubles at all (though it is partially about Debbie Reynolds) but about a related and even more obscure figure, the dance-in. It is only appropriate, then, that my first thanks go to the department that has been my academic home for over twenty years. The labor of running a small, multiple-degree-granting department in an underresourced public university facing perpetual budget cuts has never been easy and has often felt overwhelming. Just as consistent, however, have been the intangible rewards of working alongside brilliant colleagues and students, who have enriched my intellectual life and shaped my thinking in more ways than I can name. Thank you to Wendy Rogers, Linda Tomko, Luis Lara-Malvacías, Jacqueline Shea Murphy, Joel Smith, taisha paggett, Imani Kai Johnson, José Luis Reynoso, Anusha Kedhar, María Regina Firmino-Castillo, Sage Whitson, and Heather Rastovac Akbarzadeh. Thank you especially to Joel Smith and taisha paggett for the mostly thankless labor of serving as chair during periods when I worked on this book, which enabled me to step away from the department, and also for sharing in the dark humor of being chair. Thank you to the students who have enlivened my seminars and the advisees who have taught me as much as I have taught them. I am especially grateful to the members of my spring 2023 seminar Theorizing Corporeality: Mariia Bakalo, Rotem Herrmann, Mallory Peterson, Jorge Poveda Yánez, Surmani Sanford, Sammitha Sreevathsa, Andrew Ssebulime, and Kevin Wong. Thank you also to the incomparable Lily Szeto, my work wife during my last stint as chair.

Beyond my department, I have had the great luck of belonging to the Performing Difference Faculty Commons, an interdisciplinary group of scholars and artists supported by UC Riverside's Center for Ideas and Society. The colleagues I got to know through this group are the most caring and

X ACKNOWLEDGMENTS

critically astute I have had the pleasure of working with in my time at UCR, and they continue to model for me how to move through academia with integrity and heart. A number of them, including Liz Przybylski, Tammy Ho, Katherine Kinney, Judith Rodenbeck, Stephen Sohn, and Deborah Wong, offered feedback on an early version of Chapter 5, and Crystal Baik, Donatella Galella, Emily Hue, and Liz Przybylski helped me think through some critical issues along the way. Much of the book was drafted in writing zooms with members of the group. I am thankful to Deborah Wong for initiating those zooms and to those who showed up to write alongside me at key periods in the book's development. Liz Przybylski's friendship, writing companionship, and encouragement were integral throughout the drafting and revising of this book, and Liz and Imani Kai Johnson cheered me on through the last push.

Other friends and colleagues listened to my ideas as I worked on this project and responded enthusiastically enough to keep me going. Imani, Rebecca Chaleff, Susan Manning, Susan Foster, Clare Croft, and José Luis Reynoso all expressed support early on. Invitations from Harmony Bench at the Ohio State University, Mark Franko at Temple University, and Susan Manning at Northwestern University allowed me to present some of my initial ideas about dance-ins, and feedback from attendees at those presentations proved extremely valuable, including from Hannah Kosstrin and Laura Vriend. Yumi Pak, Julia Walker, Tara Rodman, and Soo Ryon Yoon also offered critical feedback on early iterations of parts of this project. Conversations (often via text) with María Regina Firmino-Castillo on the body, corporeality, and the human have helped sharpen my thinking. Cindy Garcia has consistently made me feel like my work matters. I am grateful for Stephanie Batiste's generous engagement with my ideas in the project's later stages. Brynn Shiovitz wrote a review of John Franceschina's book about Hermes Pan, which is where I first learned about the existence of dance-ins, and has been a superb audience for my ideas as I worked on this book. Clare Croft, Anusha Kedhar, and Liz Przybylski generously read drafts of portions of the manuscript in its later stages and offered enormously helpful suggestions for revision. Special thanks to Clare, whose friendship, humor, and wisdom have been life-sustaining, especially through a pandemic and especially for an introvert like me.

Dipping my toe into film studies waters for the first time was daunting, but I was fortunate to find intellectual community with a small group of scholars working at the intersection of dance studies and film studies, including

Pamela Krayenbuhl, Brynn Shiovitz, Colleen Dunagan, Hilary Bergen, Sylvia Vitaglione, Melissa Blanco Borelli, and Cara Hagan. Thanks to Pam for initially bringing us together and inviting me. I am grateful, too, for the intellectually rich experience of presenting at my first Society of Cinema and Media Studies conference alongside my astute and receptive co-panelists, Curran Nault and Ani Maitra, as well as for feedback at that conference from Linde Murugan. Other film scholars, including Matthew Solomon, Kristen Hatch, Tien Jhong Zhang, Kevin Wynter, and Bliss Cua Lim, provided encouragement and/or shared their expertise with me.

Given the challenges of researching dance-ins, especially while holding down administrative duties and raising my kids, I benefited enormously from several research assistants, a number of colleagues who passed along tips and resources, and many helpful archivists and librarians. My thanks to Theresa Goldbach, Ania Nikulina, Steven Romero, Sara Ferguson, and Anna Robinson-Sweet for research assistance. Daniela Blei is a fabulous permissions sleuth and indexer extraordinaire. Thanks as well to Sherrie Tucker, Debra Levine, Harmony Bench, Heather Castillo, Jennifer Fisher, and Rita Marks Penrod for such kindness in sharing resources with me. I remain astounded by the generosity of John Franceschina, who made his Hermes Pan materials available to me. My gratitude to Tracy Kadlec for lending me her family photo of the Blue Sisters, to Leigh Barbier for permission to publish photographs taken by Larry Barbier, to Michelene Laski for permission to use the photos from the collection of Vasso Pan Meade, and to Barbara Plunk for permission to use the photo of Eugene Loring's American School of Dance. Thanks to Helice Koffler at the Rochester Institute of Technology Libraries; Derek Davidson at Photofest NYC; Stacey Fott in Special Collections at the University of Nevada, Las Vegas; Scott Stone, the research librarian for the Performing Arts at UC Irvine; Josie Walters-Johnston at the Moving Image Research Center at the Library of Congress; Faye Thompson at the Margaret Herrick Library; Jim Hardy, the audiovisual archivist at Bob Hop Enterprises; Sandra Garcia-Myers at the University of Southern California's Cinematic Arts Library; Michael Mery in the New York Public Library's Schomburg Center for Research in Black Culture; Mimmo Bonanni at the Arizona State University Library; and Sabrina Simmons, Ronnie DeRosier, and Sahra Missaghieh Klawitter in the Interlibrary Loan Unit of UC Riverside's library. My never-ending thanks to Finis Jhung, Patrick Adiarte, Katie Kahn, Barrie Chase, and Lennie Bluett for being willing to speak with me about their experiences in Hollywood.

xii ACKNOWLEDGMENTS

I had the extreme, almost unfathomable good fortune of receiving both a John Simon Guggenheim Memorial Foundation fellowship and a National Endowment for the Humanities fellowship in support of this project, which enabled me to complete the book. I am forever grateful for the generosity and support of my letter writers, Susan Manning, Judith Hamera, Rebecca Schneider, and Melissa Blanco Borelli. My debt to Susan is bottomless; she has championed my work from the very beginning, and I would never have found my way into dance studies without her.

I am deeply grateful for the support of Norm Hirschy, who remains the most responsive and enthusiastic editor one could hope for, as well as for Zara Cannon-Mohammed's guidance through the publication process. The feedback of anonymous reviewers helped strengthen the book. Any and all errors are mine alone.

Thank you to all my jazz and tap dance teachers who planted other seeds that led to this book, most of them long before I had any idea I would become a dance scholar. They include Jeannie Willhite, Kim Tunstall, Debbie and Nan Giordano, Wilfredo Rivera, Toni Sostek, Danny Buraczeski, Fred Benjamin, Billy Siegenfeld, Fred Strickler, Joel Smith, and my current beloved tap teacher, Miki Amen.

I am so grateful for my Claremont village, who took care of my family when I couldn't. Thank you to my amazing women friends outside of work, especially Jo Hardin, Ilsa Lund, Margaret Metz, and Susannah Pratt. I have the most unbelievably supportive family and owe so much to my parents, Richard and Susan; my brother, Jonah, and his wife, Mylla; and my sister, Naomi, who is forever and always my ride-or-die. My last and most lasting thanks go to Dave, Avie, and Luna (and Pandi), the loves of my life.

An early version of Chapter 1 appeared in the *International Journal of Screendance*, https://screendancejournal.org/index.php/screendance/index. An early version of Chapter 4 appeared as "The Hollywood Dance-In: Abstract and Material Relations of Corporeal Reproduction" in *Arts* 8, no. 4 (2019), doi:10.3390/arts8040133. An early version of Chapter 3 appeared as "Female Surrogate Labor and White Corporeal Debt in *Singin' in the Rain*" in *Camera Obscura* and is republished by permission of the publisher, Duke University Press.

Introduction

Bodies, Reproductive Labor, and Research at the Margins

In 1940, a journalist for the *Winnipeg Free Press* identified what he believed to be "Hollywood's first dancing stand-in." Writing about the film musical *Love Thy Neighbor* (1940), which starred the white actress and singer Mary Martin, he reported that a woman named Irene Devoe "is rehearsing all the steps and routines Mary will perform ... because it will be necessary to have cameras and lights tested before the fast action scenes are shot."[1] Movie industry watchers had begun to take notice of "dancing stand-ins" in the 1930s, when musicals became a staple of film production,[2] but this 1940 account registers their most basic function: enabling cinematographers to prepare to shoot dance sequences without requiring stars to expend extra energy. This only partially captures the nature of a dance-in's labor, though. In a 2019 interview, Barrie Chase, who danced for several of Hollywood's celebrated "Golden" Age choreographers, partnered movie star Fred Astaire in his television specials during the 1950s and 1960s, and had experience as a dance-in, clarified that, because stars were so busy with other aspects of production, "the choreographer choreographs on you, then you teach the star." The star then "tries to do it like the dance-in."[3] More than just placeholders for stars in the final hour before filming, dance-ins were key to the creation and transmission of choreography, their bodies serving as models for both choreographers and stars.

As these initial descriptions should begin to indicate, dance-ins have a rather peculiar status. They are analogous to actors' stand-ins, but they perform specialized dance skills. They are akin to dance doubles, but they don't replace stars' bodies on screen.[4] They are ubiquitous during rehearsal and production and are lit and viewed through camera lenses, but they aren't recorded on film. They replicate choreography, but they also help create it. They impersonate stars, who in turn impersonate them. For all their dualities, dance-ins might be regarded as "compelling disturbances"[5] who

---

Hollywood Dance-ins and the Reproduction of Bodies. Anthea Kraut, Oxford University Press.
© Oxford University Press 2025. DOI: 10.1093/oso/9780197789667.003.0001

2 HOLLYWOOD DANCE-INS

are nonetheless completely ordinary features of film production. However fascinating these contradictions are in and of themselves, they render dance-ins ideal figures for reexamining certain foundational concepts across the fields of dance studies, performance studies, and film studies. Dance-ins, this book proposes, help us rethink our understandings of the body by forcing us to attend to the multiplicity of bodies and the multiple kinds of reproduction that give rise to images of bodies that appear singular.

While dance-ins are not a relic of the past, this book takes a historical approach to them. Focusing on dance-ins in Hollywood during the 1940s, 1950s, and early 1960s, the book tells the stories of a handful of uncredited dancers whose labor supported some of the most iconic stars of midcentury film musicals in the United States. *Hollywood Dance-ins* turns a spotlight on Angie Blue, a white chorus dancer who became an assistant to the prolific white film choreographer Hermes Pan and served as the long-term dance-in for the white actress and pin-up star Betty Grable. Averse to rehearsals, Grable was reportedly "doing Angie" in many of her filmic dance numbers. The book also features Carol Haney and Jeanne Coyne, a pair of white women dancers who worked behind the scenes on the famous 1952 film musical *Singin' in the Rain* as assistants to the film's white choreographer, director, and star, Gene Kelly, and as the dance-in for its white female star, Debbie Reynolds. Together, Haney and Coyne gave Reynolds a crash course in dancing that helped launch her into stardom. On several of Kelly's other films, he collaborated with Alex Romero, a Mexican American jazz dancer who was similar in size and stature to Kelly but whose training and ethnic background differentiated him from the star. Romero helped Kelly generate choreography and danced in his place during rehearsals, raising questions about the relationship between their exchanges and Kelly's filmic image.

Though this is a book about dance-ins, not all of its protagonists held that role. In the course of my research, I kept coming across an incredibly talented jazz dancer named Marie Bryant, reportedly the first African American to serve as an assistant dance director in Hollywood, who coached a staggering number of stars in the mid-twentieth century. Her off-screen work was, like dance-ins', critical to the shaping of stars' bodies and is no less deserving of recognition. Indeed, one of the chief values of attending to dance-ins is that they expand our awareness of the various kinds of reproductive labor on which the creation of choreography and the making of star images depend. Dance-ins invite us into an entire history of marginalized dancers

INTRODUCTION   3

in Hollywood who made possible the film musicals now hailed as classics. Chorus dancers are part of that history, too; as I show by the book's end, they not only danced alongside stars but at times took stars' place on screen. While the roles of an assistant dance director, a dance-in, and a chorus dancer were by no means identical, neither were they always discrete, and I hope the book leaves readers with a sense of how much overlap and interchange there could be in the functions they performed.

Even as *Hollywood Dance-ins* recovers the histories of unsung dancers in Hollywood (while keeping one eye on the limits of recovery projects, as I return to below), it rejects artificial divisions between history and theory. The chapters that follow are devoted to specific material histories, but the book is invested equally in history that makes theoretical claims and in theory that is rooted in history. Subsequent sections of this introduction offer historical, theoretical, and methodological overviews that lay the groundwork for the book's microhistories, but it is worth stating here that the book's argument revolves around three interrelated historical and theoretical premises: that the dance-in's reproductive labor, like other forms of reproductive labor in the United States, was structured by race and gender; that, in a U.S. context, white privilege has been sustained by repressing reproductive bodily labor and upholding the coherence and autonomy of "the body"; and that Hollywood dance-ins are uniquely situated to highlight the simultaneous dispersion and suturing of "the body" that has helped perpetuate U.S. racial and gender hierarchies.

It has by now been well established that U.S. movie stars are overwhelmingly white and that Hollywood has, since its inception, disseminated images that glorified whiteness.[6] Yet while most of the dance-ins who appear in this book supported white stars, the network of dancers whose interactions and exchanges fueled the construction of film stars' dancing bodies at midcentury was more racially diverse than the whiteness of those star bodies would suggest. I refer to this network as Hollywood's "corporeal ecosystem."[7] Viewed through the lens of the film industry's distinction between "above-the-line" and "below-the-line" work—a reference to the "bold horizontal line on a standard production budget sheet" that separates so-called creative from so-called craft labor—Hollywood's corporeal ecosystem emerges as a racially and gender-stratified division of labor and credit that depended on reproductive mechanisms to manufacture the seeming coherence of white stars' dancing bodies.[8] Attention to the intercorporeal relationships between film musicals' above-the-line white stars and the below-the-line white, Black,

4 HOLLYWOOD DANCE-INS

and Latinx dancers who served as their proxies, assistants, and coaches lays bare the acts of doubling, imitation, and substitution that have propped up idealized images of whiteness.

Hollywood stars were predominantly but not exclusively white, and in its last chapter the book considers the relations of reproduction between the biracial Chinese and English star Nancy Kwan and her white dance-in, her white vocal double, and the Asian/American cast members she danced with in the film musical *Flower Drum Song* (1961). In contrast to the white stars this book covers, Kwan was not granted the privilege of assumed bodily coherence, and the ambivalence that has plagued her image helps illustrate the assigning or withholding of corporeal integrity as a racialized operation.

Foregrounding dance-ins' labor also challenges the privileging of choreographers as the sole or primary behind-the-scenes shapers of stars' dancing bodies. Like the whiteness of stars, the fact that dance directors of midcentury Hollywood musicals were overwhelmingly male is not news. But shifting our focus to some of the women dancers who assisted men choreographers allows for a more nuanced picture of the gender structures that buoyed this patriarchal system. Performing as surrogates for stars, women dance-ins brought dance directors' conceptions to life and served as vital genealogical links in the transmission of jazz dance from its multiracial sources to the screen, even as the feminization of their reproductive labor all but guaranteed their erasure. In the case of Alex Romero, the sole male dance-in I examine, the gendered relations between star and proxy complicated the heteronormative masculinity that Kelly worked so hard to cultivate.

Written at the intersection of dance studies and film studies and drawing on critical race theory and feminist materialist approaches to labor, *Hollywood Dance-ins* regards filmic images of dancing bodies as particularly rich sites for exploring the interface between racial and gender ideologies and material conditions of production.[9] As mediated representations that are, especially in Hollywood's "classical period," designed to conceal their means of production, filmic images exemplify the tensions between heterogeneous technologies of reproduction and the projection of seemingly unified images. Parsing these tensions as they apply to images of star dancing bodies allows us to deepen our understanding of *bodies* as similarly forged out of tensions between heterogeneous forms of reproductive labor and idealized projections of homogeneity. Dance-ins exist in the seams of these tensions. As such, they can illuminate the fissures in ideas of unity that structure both filmic images and fantasies of white racial embodiment in a U.S. context. Dedicated to investigating these fissures, *Hollywood Dance-ins* argues that midcentury Hollywood's reliance on dance-ins activated one notion of bodies—as interdependent, relational, and reproductive—that filmic images of and discourse about white stars' dancing bodies worked to suppress.

Hollywood's "Golden" Age and Midcentury Racial Formations

As indicated, the scope of this book coincides with Hollywood's classical period and the "Golden" Age of the Hollywood musical, demarcations whose precise dates vary but generally extend from the advent of sound in film in 1927 to around 1960.[10] This temporal frame allows me to probe the reproduction of star bodies at a time when dance on screen and the movie studio system were at their height in the United States and to survey Hollywood's dance landscape during a time of both "classic Hollywood, classic whiteness"[11] and shifting U.S. racial formations.

According to film scholars, "continuity" and "integration" were the defining characteristics of Hollywood in this era.[12] Formally, these terms refer to modes of filmmaking that preserve a film's apparent unity and integrity. "Continuity" describes a style of "invisible" filmmaking in which "mise-en-scène, cinematography, and editing" are subordinated "to a coherent, character-driven system of storytelling."[13] More closely associated with musicals, the term "integration" denotes the "seamless" coming together of music and dance numbers with plot and character development.[14] Economically, "integration" also describes the market conditions in which five of the major motion picture studios—Warner Brothers, Metro-Goldwyn-Mayer (MGM), Twentieth Century-Fox, RKO, and Paramount—owned the production, distribution, and exhibition of their films.[15] This "vertical" integration enabled "a Ford-like studio system" with "astonishingly efficient business practices" to flourish.[16] Among this system's notable features were a "star machine" that manufactured stars like commodities and a "streamlined . . . filmmaking process" in which studios contracted employees to carry out specialized tasks in specialized units.[17]

Crystallizing as a film genre with the transition to sound, musicals reached the height of their popularity between the early 1930s and the 1950s.[18] The studio system was the musical's "*sine qua non*," as Jerome Delameter

6 HOLLYWOOD DANCE-INS

explains, for "without the cooperation engendered by that system, the 'repertory company' associations of contract musicians, dancers, designers, and technicians" would not have been possible.[19] Musicals, in turn, became "one of the industry's most prestigious and reliable products."[20] With profits booming, the major studios competed to discover and groom their own performers for stardom and to develop their own distinctive "look": Warner Brothers became known for its "backstage musicals" (musicals about the making of musicals) and the mobile camera of director Busby Berkeley, RKO for a string of musicals featuring Fred Astaire and Ginger Rogers, Twentieth Century-Fox for Betty Grable and Carmen Miranda, and MGM for "perfecting the integrated musical" and spending so lavishly on production that its initials were said to stand for "More Great Musicals."[21] A 1948 government ruling that ordered the studios to divest their movie theater holdings, known as the Paramount Consent Decrees, dealt a blow to the studio system and eventually to the ascendency of the film musical, though studios continued to make musicals with regularity until the mid-1950s.[22]

As Arthur Knight observes, there is a perverse irony to the use of the term "integration" to describe midcentury Hollywood musicals, for "the so-called integrated musical . . . was manifestly not integrated" for African American performers, nor for performers of color more generally.[23] Thanks to the whiteness of the major movie studios, "white audiences' disproportionate economic power," and the Hollywood Production Code (essentially a system of censorship that forbade depictions of cross-racial romance), racial segregation in Hollywood was the norm.[24] So it was that, despite the profound influence African American dance and dancers had on "what was understood as 'American' dance during the mid-twentieth century," film dancing remained "almost exclusively a white dancer's field."[25] Whiteness also permeated film-making styles in classical Hollywood—from an approach to movie lighting that took "the white face as the touchstone" to the use of a "soft style" of cinematography that relied on "gauze filters, mesh screens, and special lenses" to render "the body of the star . . . hyperbolically white."[26] With their hold on mainstream culture, movie studios in the classical era "systematized the popularization of whiteness."[27]

At the same time, developments at home and abroad made Hollywood's "Golden" years a period of transformation for U.S. racial relations. In the 1930s, racial segregation and discrimination pervaded every sector of society, lynchings of African Americans were still commonplace, and national immigration laws restricting Eastern Europeans and excluding

INTRODUCTION 7

Asians were in effect, as were state antimiscegenation laws targeting African Americans, Native Americans, and Asian/Americans.[28] Across the country, local deportation programs forcefully "repatriated" Mexican Americans, classified as "nonwhite" for the first time in the 1930 census. In 1934, Congress reclassified Filipinos living in the United States as "aliens." These same conditions led to burgeoning efforts in the years before World War II, both within and across racialized groups, to organize opposition to U.S. racial structures.[29] The war itself triggered more significant changes, as the contradictions of a nation relying on a segregated military to combat a fascist and racist regime became evident to a wider swath of Americans.[30] While "[e]ntry into the war increased employment and political opportunities for many African Americans, Mexican Americans, and women," so too did it stoke concerns about whether nonwhite communities "posed threats to the stability of the home front."[31] The war years saw African American undertakings like the Double V campaign, which promoted "a simultaneous victory over foreign fascism and domestic racism" and helped usher in a broader civil rights movement.[32] But they were also marked by the mass internment of Japanese Americans and the eruption of racial violence in cities across the United States, including the 1943 "zoot suit" riots between white servicemen and Latinos/as in Los Angeles.[33]

The "restructuring of the global political economy" in the postwar era, brought about by the U.S. "displacement of Britain as the leading world economic power," prompted additional changes to U.S. racial formations.[34] A Cold War policy of "internationalism and communist containment" spurred a drive to integrate racialized minorities into American society and to expel anyone perceived as a threat to the U.S. political system.[35] This translated to national desegregation efforts as well as to "new patterns of migration and immigration," facilitated in part by the repeal of a number of Asian exclusion acts, even as Asian/Americans continued to be racialized as "foreigners-within."[36] Meanwhile, the response to World War II and the agitation for civil rights led to a minimization of "racial differences *within* the white community," as ethnic white Americans, including Irish Americans and Jewish Americans, were "extended the privileges offered to white members of the middle class."[37] Mexicans, Puerto Ricans, and Cubans, by contrast, "were segregated from the . . . midcentury expansion of whiteness as a racial category."[38] The result was the "solidifi[cation of] whiteness as a monolith of privilege."[39]

8 HOLLYWOOD DANCE-INS

Film historians have thoughtfully addressed how these racial politics played out on Hollywood screens across the 1930s, 1940s, and 1950s: from the rise of the "Latin number" in the 1930s, which presented a spectacularized "fantasy of Latin American peoples, places, and traditions" and corresponded with the movie industry's efforts to exploit Latin American markets during the so-called Good Neighbor Era, to the "uncertain or mixed raciality of Latina/o performers" in the 1950s;[40] from the declining prevalence of visible blackface to the "representational gains" African American performers made in response to pressure from Black actors and organizations like the National Association for the Advancement of Colored People (NAACP);[41] from the turn away from filmic depictions of "Oriental villainy" in the 1930s and 1940s to the "fascination" with Asia and the Pacific in the 1940s and 1950s;[42] to the "postwar cycle of social problem films" that sought to tackle "pressing social issues concerning race, ethnicity, gender, class, and national identity."[43] Scholars have additionally demonstrated how Hollywood films of this era, especially in the wake of the Red Scare, sought to manage anxieties about race and ethnicity by "stress[ing] conformity to white patriarchal capitalist ideals."[44]

Attention to dance-ins during Hollywood's classical period and Golden Age contributes new insights into the era's industry practices and its racial politics. Created for the purpose of saving a star's labor and energy, the dance-in exemplifies the studio system's pursuit of efficiency in its manufacturing of stars. The reproductive labor of the dance-in also prompts us to consider how the period's signature style of "continuity" and "unity" was achieved via corporeal as well as filmmaking techniques— smoothing over bodily substitutions and edited shots alike—and to raise questions about when and to whom the "seams" of filmmaking and stars' multiple corporeal referents have been visible. Approaching the manufactured integrity of a star's body as a key axis of white privilege allows us to see how classic Hollywood managed racial anxieties and upheld white supremacy in ways that exceeded narrative devices, lighting styles, and revised forms of minstrelsy.[45] Then, too, as intermediaries between choreographers and stars, dance-ins help us chart more closely how Africanist dance styles wound up on white stars' bodies. In all of these ways, making room in our histories of Hollywood for dance-ins reveals the coexistence of a racially variegated and gendered ecosystem that operated behind the screen and a filmic surface that perpetuated the myth of white corporeal unity.

"The Body" in Dance Studies

While *Hollywood Dance-ins* is written for audiences across the fields of dance studies, performance studies, and film studies, the book is also motivated by a disciplinary-specific concern: dance scholars cannot continue to rely on "the body" as an analytical category without taking seriously the critiques of racialized embodiment that Black scholars have advanced for decades.[46] I rehearse some of the most prominent of these critiques below, for they have informed my thinking about dance-ins, about bodies, and about whiteness in profound ways. What I want to stress from the outset is that critical race approaches to embodiment cannot be isolated to studies "about" race nor applied only to discussions of bodies of color.[47] Not only must we acknowledge that our invocations of "the body" may be mobilizing a racialized construction; we must confront the ways in which white embodiment has been structured by antiblackness.

Insofar as dance is understood to be an "embodied social practice" and a medium that is "*of* the body,"[48] the body might be dance studies' most fundamental unit of analysis.[49] While the claims U.S.-based dance scholars make about bodies vary, they generally share a conviction that bodies are not empty vessels but are both reflective of and active producers of knowledge, meaning, culture, and identity. Over the past three decades, dance scholarship has demonstrated that bodies are political and economic agents,[50] migrants and citizens,[51] archives of history and memory,[52] catalysts of pleasure and sources of pain,[53] and locuses of racial, ethnic, gender, class, and national formations.[54] U.S. dance studies bears the influences of poststructuralism's refusal of essentialism, Foucauldian approaches to power, and Judith Butler's theory of gender performativity.[55] But it has also argued forcefully that bodies "initiate . . . as well as respond" and that somatic and kinesthetic experiences give bodies the capacity "to move for or against . . . authority" and "to know . . . the world differently."[56] In dance studies, bodies are key sites for the negotiation of power.

From a certain angle, however, dance scholars' emphasis on the body as full of agentive potential feels at odds with recent warnings about the violence the term "body" can do. In a 2021 online presentation, Alice Sheppard, a multiracial Black dancer and choreographer who uses a wheelchair, took issue with the title of the event, "Bodies at Risk," at which she had been invited to speak. In a probing dialogue with dance artist Emily Johnson, Sheppard asserted, "[T]he recognition of me as a body . . . is part of the problem. . . . I mean, it is part of the notion that I am a pile of flesh that can be transacted—just a pile of flesh that can be transacted." "This understanding of dancers as bodies," Sheppard continued, "is one of the things that's wrong with the dance world."[57] Sheppard's critique—that risk is not inherent in her body but "inheres in the systems that [she has] to live in and around," and that it is "harmful" to approach her *as* a body—resonates with the concerns several leading Black scholars have articulated about a focus on bodies.[58] In a 2016 essay in the *Boston Review* on Black student activism in the wake of Michael Brown's murder in Ferguson, Missouri, historian Robin D. G. Kelley cautioned, "In the argot of our day, 'bodies'—vulnerable and threatening bodies—increasingly stand in for actual people with names, experiences, dreams, and desires."[59] That same year, likewise in response to Brown's killing and the hours his body was left lying in the street, theorist and poet Fred Moten stated, "The idea that there is such a thing as a discrete, individuated body is a fiction that we seem to live by, but I don't really believe in it." "When I hear that phrase, 'the black body,'" Moten explained, "I kind of want to say, 'Well there's no such thing,' or, if there is such a thing, it's something that is imposed upon and conferred upon us at the moment of our death. The moment of death is also the moment of individuation."[60]

These admonitions about the hazards of framing persons as bodies should give pause to those of us who make claims about bodies so routinely and so assuredly. If the term "body" pulls focus away from structural systems, away from the dreams and desires of the living, and away from collectivity, (how) can it also be regarded as a site of liberation?[61] How should we reconcile the objectifying effects of the term with dance scholars' embrace of the body's "open potentiality"?[62] Might our habitual reliance on the term perpetuate harm despite our faith in bodies' abundant capacities? And what should we make of the suggestion that our most basic unit of analysis is a fiction?

As should by now be clear, *Hollywood Dance-ins* does not avoid the term "body" or "bodies." While I frequently use the word "corporeality"—generally to denote a body's materiality as it has been constructed through repetition and rehearsal—this is just another way of centering bodies in my analysis.[63] My point is not that dance studies needs to jettison these terms. Neither do I advocate indiscriminately importing Black studies critiques of the body into dance studies. What I do maintain is that such critiques warrant much greater scrutiny of the ideological work the term "body" has done and continues to do, regardless of disciplinary location, but especially for those of us who lean on it so heavily.

Even as I seek to put pressure on what dance scholars take for granted about "the body," *Hollywood Dance-ins* insists on the value of attending to bodily practices—and not just representations of bodies (filmic, literary, or otherwise)—when we theorize corporeality.[64] Adopting one of the hallmarks of dance studies, the book treats bodies as concrete, material beings rather than chiefly as abstract, conceptual figures, though I am interested throughout in how the material and the conceptual interact. The book also builds on the dance scholarship truism that choreographing constitutes an act of theorizing and that different choreographic works enact different theories of or about bodies,[65] though I join other dance scholars who have pushed against the elevating of choreography and choreographers over dancing and dancers.[66] I hope to show that even the most unremarked-upon of conventions in the most middlebrow and capitalist of arenas enacts a theory about bodies. In fact, it is the very unremarkableness of dance-ins that makes it all the more urgent that we examine the assumptions on which they rest and the racial ideologies they support.

Fanon, Spillers, and Racial Embodiment

In her 2019 book *Ornamentalism*, Ann Anlin Cheng names "two primary frameworks through which many of us conceptualize racial embodiment: Frantz Fanon's 'epidermal racial schema' and Hortense Spillers's 'hieroglyphics of the flesh.'"[67] For Cheng, these two frameworks are points of departure for the alternative theory she develops to account for the racially gendered corporeality of Asian women, which I turn to in Chapter 5. Rizvana Bradley, however, has recently asserted that, *contra* Cheng, "the difficult substance and implications of [Fanon's and Spillers's] respective interventions have yet to be thought, to say nothing of reckoned with."[68] Bradley's critique arguably holds even more true for dance studies, where considerations of Fanon and Spillers are predominantly found in work by Black dance scholars. While I draw on a number of critical race theorists and attend to multiple racial formations across this book, the challenges that Fanon and Spillers present to the idea that the body exists outside of structures of racialization drive my argument. With Bradley, I believe it is pressing that far more of us grapple with their "difficult substance and implications."

In "The Fact of Blackness," first published in 1952 in *Black Skin, White Masks*, the Francophone Afro-Caribbean philosopher Fanon offers a searing description of his experience of embodiment under the white colonial gaze. "In the white world," Fanon writes, "the man of color encounters difficulties in the development of his bodily schema. Consciousness of the body is solely a negating activity." Assaulted by the white man's gaze, Fanon's "corporeal schema"—his sense of his body in the world—crumbles, leaving in its place a "racial epidermal schema" woven by the white man "out of a thousand details, anecdotes, stories."[69] Fanon's analysis of the "somatics of Blackness"[70] has been influential among dance scholars attending to Black bodies living under colonialism and its aftermath.[71] But his account of experiencing his body "solely as a legible surface without depth" should provoke more wide-reaching questions about whether or when we can speak about somatic experience in neutral or universal terms.[72]

Three decades after Fanon, Black feminist theorist Hortense Spillers published "Mama's Baby, Papa's Maybe: An American Grammar Book," a scathing rejoinder to the 1965 Moynihan Report and its problematic casting of the "Negro family" as pathological due to the prevalence of female-led households. Spillers demands that we approach the intersection of gender and race through a different genealogical lens: the "socio-political order of the New World" and the "willful and violent . . . severing of the captive body from its motive will" for capitalist purposes.[73] For the enslaved, the resulting "American grammar" of reproduction both disrupted the patriarchal order (since children born to enslaved women inherited the condition of their mother) and evacuated "kinship" of its meaning "*since it can be invaded at any given and arbitrary moment by the property relations.*"[74] In one of Spillers's most cited passages, she distinguishes between "flesh" and "body" and identifies this distinction as "the central one between captive and liberated subject-positions." "In that sense," she proposes, "before the 'body' there is the 'flesh,' that zero degree of social conceptualization that does not escape concealment under the brush of discourse, or the reflexes of iconography."[75]

Though Spillers can be read as suggesting that flesh constitutes "a temporal and conceptual antecedent to the body," that is, a prediscursive materiality,[76] both Bradley and Zakkiyah Iman Jackson interpret Spillers's "before" in a more complicated sense. Where Jackson asserts that the *before* in Spillers's "before the 'body'" holds "spatial as well as temporal significance,"[77] Bradley maintains that "flesh is before the body in that it is everywhere subject to the body as racial machinery, violently placed at the disposal of those who would claim the body as property."[78] In their respective readings of Spillers, meanwhile, both Alexander Weheliye and Hershini Bhana Young remind us that flesh is neither a "biological occurrence" nor a "natural substrate"; instead, flesh is the result of a "rupture" brought about by "the calculated work of iron, whips, chains, knives, the canine patrol, the bullet."[79] In Spillers's piercing analysis, it is this violent and violently racialized rupture that enables the "body" to assume form as "a categorical coherence," or what Ashon Crawley describes as "a theological-philosophical concept of enclosure, a grammar and logic producing something like bodily integrity."[80] The "improper body of black enfleshment," in short, is "the body's condition of (im)possibility."[81]

Theorized "from the vantage point of black women," Spillers's emphasis on the twin impositions of property status and "kinlessness" on enslaved Africans underscores gender's constitutive role in racial formations.[82] The U.S. "regime of captivity" relied on the "genetic reproduction of the enslaved" while (or rather by) denying enslaved African women claims of belonging to their offspring. The result, as Spillers writes at the end of "Mama's Baby," was a "play of paradox," in which "only the female stands in the flesh, both mother and mother-dispossessed."[83] The centrality of gender to Spillers's flesh/body formulation guides this book's treatment of the gendered structures of reproduction as pivotal to the racialization of corporeality.

Spillers's work is canonical in Black feminist studies,[84] but with some exceptions, dance scholars have not responded to her discussion of embodiment in any thoroughgoing way. Among those exceptions,[85] Jasmine Johnson's essay "Flesh Dance" takes Spillers as its starting point to ask "[w]hat . . . black feminist theories [can] teach dance scholars about black bodies in motion" and to argue for an approach to Black women's performance in sexually explicit Hip Hop music videos that "loosen[s] our fidelity to sight."[86] In "Haunting Gathering: Black Dance and Afro-Pessimism," Mlondolozi Zondi considers whether performance studies' and dance studies' reliance on "assumptions about the body's sentience as evidence for subjectivity" may reify the same Western conceptions that Spillers identifies as organizing the logic of chattel slavery. "Instead of theorizing from performance studies' presumption that there is a body endowed with (restricted) agency and capacity," Zondi wonders, "what can be gained from taking seriously Spillers's assertion that 'the "body" is neither *given* as an uncomplicated empirical rupture on the landscape of the human, nor do we ever actually "see" it.'"[87] In his study of the career of Black choreographer Len Fontaine, Barry Brannum takes Spillers's flesh/body distinction as an impetus to shift away from more narrow questions about racial representation and agency and toward investigations of presence and "ways of 'doing' the body."[88] Crucially, Brannum argues for the wider relevance of Spillers's theories to critical dance studies: "within a discourse so thoroughly dedicated to the body's workings," Brannum writes, "a body/flesh conversation should be par for the course."[89]

This book echoes Brannum's contention that Spillers's argument has implications far broader than dance studies has yet accounted for, and that we must understand the racialization of corporeality to extend beyond the violent rendering of Blackness as flesh. If the founding of the U.S. nation state rested on a racialized opposition between flesh and body; if "body" took shape as a coherent, bounded site of sovereignty in a U.S. context only in opposition to nonindividuated, dispossessed, gendered Black flesh; and if both emerged in an antiblack matrix that enabled white supremacy to thrive, it would seem incumbent upon us to start from an approach that considers "the body" as a racial project and to query the ongoing legacies of that project, not only for Black bodies but for all bodies living in slavery's afterlife and wake.[90] After Spillers, taking "the body" as self-evident is a failure to recognize "the constitutive imbrications of raciality and embodiment within the modern world,"[91] just as after Fanon, taking the "corporeal schema" as phenomenologically universal is a failure to reckon with the bodily effects of racialized colonialism.

As much as my thinking in *Hollywood Dance-ins* is indebted to Fanon and Spillers and to scholars in Black studies who have so compellingly elucidated and engaged with their ideas,[92] I am cognizant of the dangers of extrapolating from Black scholars' interventions. As a white scholar, my employment of Spillers in particular may well raise the kind of questions that Jennifer C. Nash has pointed to, about "whether [non-Black] scholars' mobilization of Black feminist theory is genuine or predatory, embedded in political commitment or rooted in gaming a hyper-competitive academic marketplace."[93] In dance studies, there is certainly a risk that, as more non-Black scholars attend to Black thought, we will reproduce the patterns of racialized extraction and appropriation that have long structured the field of dance, including dance in Hollywood.[94] It is important to acknowledge, too, the disparate stakes between the star/dance-in relations that I examine in this book and the relations that motivate Fanon's and Spillers's theorizing. The manufacturing of star bodies took place in an ecosystem that exploited Black reproductive labor, both via white stars' parasitical relationships to African American dancers like Marie Bryant (as I explore most directly in Chapter 2) and via more diffuse chains of cross-racial imitation and substitution by which African diasporic dances found their way onto non-Black Hollywood dancing bodies (as I explore throughout the book). But the exchanges and substitutions that enabled the making of film musicals were far from a matter of life and death and far removed from the violence that underpins Spillers's analysis.[95]

My goal is not to collapse the different stakes of racialized embodiment across time, space, and context, nor to "lay claim"[96] to Black critical thought, nor to treat it as free for the taking. Neither do I mean to imply that Fanonian and Spillersian models of racialized embodiment are applicable across all racial formations. This book's history of Hollywood dance affirms the multiracial sources of jazz dance and the multiracial dancers who shaped star bodies, and I rely throughout on scholars of Latinx and Asian/American racialization to contextualize that history. I nonetheless believe that dance scholars have much to gain from more sustained reflection about the implications of Black scholars' critiques of embodiment for the arguments we make about bodies. This is no less true—and arguably is more true—for those of us who write about white bodies, often without considering how whiteness as a racial formation and "the body" coproduce and reverberate off one another. Listening to Black scholars and artists should mean grappling with the racial ideologies that have infused our assumptions, categories, and concepts, including our assumptions about the body.[97]

The "Bodily Turn" across Academia

In her survey of understandings of bodies in the field of theater studies, Soyica Colbert identifies the ripple effects that Black, feminist, and queer scholarship on nonnormative bodies have had in fields like environmental studies, transgender studies, and disability studies. Across these fields, she sees a flourishing of "theories of the body as part of an ecology rather than a singular closed-off entity."[98] Lisa Blackman's *The Body: Key Concepts* likewise notes the impact of "new developments across the life and biological sciences" on approaches to bodies as "entangled processes rather than separate distinct categories."[99] Indeed, scholars in multiple disciplines increasingly acknowledge the complex materiality of bodies by emphasizing their "porosity" and relationality to other beings. Gender and sexuality studies scholar Chikako Takeshita, for example, turns to biology and immunology to develop alternatives to individualized notions of corporeal autonomy with respect to pregnant bodies; she proposes the scientific term "holobiont" as a way to recognize that the gestational parent is an "integrative symbiotic system" that, like all human bodies, "relies on millions of microbes to co-function."[100] Margrit Shildrik's work on "visceral prostheses" weaves together critical disability studies, transplantation studies, and bioscience to move us "towards a new imaginary in which the traditional closure of the embodied self against the putative threat of external otherness gives way to an acknowledgment that the self is never pure or internally immune but is always shot through with otherness within."[101] Also citing the influence of cultural studies of biosociality, Rachel C. Lee situates the Asian Americanist literary canon "in relation to the question of the biological" in order to consider how race scholars might straddle a "humanist, organismal" and "distributed, multiscalar" approach to embodiment.[102]

There are parallels between these biologically and ecologically oriented understandings of the body and the work of French philosophers Gilles Deleuze and Félix Guattari, particularly their conceit of the "body without organs," often shorthanded as the "BwO." In their 1987 book *A Thousand Plateaus*, Deleuze and Guattari write, "The BwO is opposed not to the organs but to . . . the organic organization of the organs." In place of the totalizing order suggested by "the organism," the "BwO reveals itself" as a "connection of desires, conjunction of flows, continuum of intensities."[103] Scholars in a number of fields have taken up their call to "open . . . the body to connections that presuppose an entire assemblage, circuits, conjunctions, levels and thresholds, passages and distributions of intensity."[104] In its refusal "to subordinate the body to a unity or a homogeneity," its insistence that "the organism itself cannot be represented as an ordered system," and its deconstruction of "the contours of the organic body," Deleuze and Guattari's BwO has particularly served scholars invested in theorizing minoritized corporealities in feminist studies, trans studies, and disability studies.[105]

Despite the concerns I have articulated about what dance studies takes as a given about the body, dance scholars, too, have offered thoughtful challenges to conceptions of the body as an enclosed, self-governing unit. Two and a half decades ago, Randy Martin proposed a "composite body" that is "not one but multiple" and asserted, "Even solo dancing implicates other bodies and assumes that the expressivity of what circulates as interiority is not confined or contained to that edge or boundary we attribute to the skin."[106] Similar proposals can be found across much subsequent dance scholarship. Halifu Osumare, Priya Srinivasan, Ben Spatz, Selby Schwartz, and

Rosemary Roberts posit understandings of bodies as "intercultural," as collective and relational, and as forged out of and containing multiplicities.[107] Anurima Banerji, Kate Elswit, and Elisabeth Motley present views of the body as "distributed," as extending beyond its perceived edges by the exhalation of breath, and as "excessively ooz[ing] outside of containment."[108] María Regina Firmino-Castillo distinguishes between a colonial ideology that contends "some persons are only bodies" and an Indigenous Mesoamerican "acknowledgment of our inextricable relationality with and in a living, agentive material world."[109] Thinking with Deleuze and Guattari, dance philosophers such as José Gil and Erin Manning proclaim the body to be "a cluster of forces, a transformer of space and time" that is "inhabited by—and inhabiting—other bodies and other minds" and "an ecology of operations that straddles the flesh of its matter and the environmentality of its multiple takings-form."[110]

Notwithstanding such examples, Rizvana Bradley's critique of the "bodily turn" in the humanities could be applied to many (though certainly not all) of these more expansive approaches to corporeality. Too often, theorizations of the body as plural, permeable, and a "node of relational processes" do not "begin . . . from an interrogation of [the] quintessentially racial foundations" of the "body proper."[111] Instead of replacing notions of the body as bounded and individuated with notions of the body's multiplicity, we need more analyses of how conceptions of the former are entangled with histories and legacies of antiblackness and white supremacy, and how they may continue to wield influence.[112]

To be sure, for all the wealth of perspectives that dance scholars have offered on the body, including those that emphasize its porosity, liberal ideas of the body as an autonomous site of truth and "self-expression" that emerged with the development of Euro-American modern dance in the early twentieth century have not exactly disappeared from contemporary dance milieus. As Doran George's work makes clear, even the ascendance of somatics training among dancers in professional and educational institutions has not retired modernist notions of the truthful, expressive body, for somatics, too, recycles ideas of the body as a "natural" site of "individual creative freedom."[113] How should we make sense of the staying power of formulations of the dancing body as the organic container of the self—arguably still the reigning "body proper" in many U.S. dance settings—alongside the proliferation of alternative theories?

Hollywood Dance-ins does not directly answer that question. But it does offer insight into an earlier historical moment in which conflicting beliefs about bodies worked in tandem. Participating in academia's "bodily turn" in its resituating of Hollywood bodies within a larger "corporeal ecosystem," the book also follows Bradley in approaching "the body" as a racialized fiction and in probing how that fiction has been sustained via specific material practices. Querying those practices reveals that conceiving bodies in relational terms may not undermine structures of racial dominance at all. As this study of Hollywood dance-ins shows, a codified system predicated on bodies' plurality and co-constitutive materiality could and did operate in service of an ideology that promoted white star bodies as singular and self-referential.

Screen Bodies

Though I hope an examination of dance-ins' reproductive labor is useful to readers thinking critically about corporeality in multiple contexts, the dance-in's most immediate implications are for theorizations of screen bodies. *Hollywood Dance-ins* thus also enters into a more disciplinary-specific set of conversations about bodies in the subfield of screendance studies. As Douglas Rosenberg has written, while the term "screendance" can refer to "any and all work that includes dance *and* film or video as well as other screen-based software/hardware configurations,"[114] histories of dance on screen tend to be divided into two "intertwined but differently rooted . . . narratives": one devoted to "mainstream films" with "high entertainment values," and the other associated more with "the visual arts and the avant-garde" and with "auteurs, amateurs, and outsiders."[115] In general, both lineages reinforce the idea that, as Sherril Dodds asserted in her 2001 book *Dance on Screen*, "the presentation of a 'live body' is unavoidably transformed when it becomes a 'screen body.'"[116] Because of that transformation, a process that Rosenberg calls "recorporealization," screendance has the potential to shift our understanding of bodies, including by "unmooring" them "from somatic and corporeal absolutes."[117] Scholars of digital media have been especially attuned to the ways in which, in a postfilm era, as Addie Tsai argues, screendance "has irrevocably shifted our sense of the real body."[118] Yet in light of Black critical thought on how "the body" has functioned as a "racial apparatus,"[119] it seems imperative to ask what notion of "the real body" screendance studies might be upholding. Relatedly, as a live body that is part of the cinematic apparatus, the dance-in pushes us to nuance our thinking about the relationship between the live and the filmic.

Hollywood Dance-ins complicates the accepted wisdom about that relationship in two somewhat contradictory ways. First, rather than insisting on ontological differences between live and screen bodies, the book proposes that filmic images of white star dancing bodies are not so far removed from racialized notions of "the body" as a discrete and bounded site of individuality; both entail a presumption of coherence and credibility that covers over (or "sutures," in the parlance of film theory)[120] the mediations and displacements that give rise to them. Counterintuitively, studying the reproductions that undergird and are concealed by two-dimensional images of stars' dancing bodies yields insights into the reproductions that undergird and are concealed by live bodies, or at least hegemonic notions of them.[121] Even as I hope to blur the divisions between live and screen bodies, however, I also contest assumptions of the inverse: that there is an isomorphic or one-to-one correspondence between the live body and its technologically mediated projection. Put differently, the book challenges the idea that the filmic body of the dancing star was "moored" to its apparent material referent (their live dancing body) in any straightforward, unproblematic way.

My argument thus engages with the film studies concept of indexicality, which, as I elaborate in Chapter 1, holds that celluloid images, like their photographic antecedents, bear a relationship of proximity to and the direct material traces of the "original" that they represent.[122] As trace, film scholar Mary Ann Doane writes, the index implies a relation between image and referent that is physical as well as temporal: "The trace does not evaporate in the moment of its production, but remains as the witness of an anteriority."[123] While film scholars point to animation and digital manipulation as modes of reproduction that subvert this relationship, indexicality is typically considered "the primary indicator of cinematic specificity."[124] Yet the mediating presence of the dance-in suggests that even in analog mediums like film, and even in genres like the midcentury film musical, a star's bodily image also indexed unseen or less visible corporealities. As my language here betrays, I am not arguing against the idea of indexicality. Instead, my contention is that we must interrogate rather than presuppose whose material traces and which anterior moments filmic bodies index. Destabilizing the indexical certainty of filmic images of dancing bodies in turn opens up space for reconsidering the presumed self-referentiality of live bodies. The

20 HOLLYWOOD DANCE-INS

assumption that bodies are self-indexical—that they point transparently and directly to themselves—must be recognized as a site of racialized privilege.

Situated between the live and the filmic and raising questions about indexicality, dance-ins have much to contribute to discussions of corporeality in film studies, where scholars tend to focus on the semiotic meanings of filmic representations of bodies or on spectators' embodied, affective experiences of the movies.[125] There are, to be clear, film scholars and scholars working at the intersection of dance and film who offer keen analyses of bodies by foregrounding their material conditions of production. This includes the work of Adrienne McLean, Jennifer Bean, Ann Chisholm, Eva Cherniavsky, Brynn Shiovitz, Pamela Krayenbuhl, and Usha Iyer, all of which has informed my own.[126] Chisholm's 2000 essay "Missing Persons and Bodies of Evidence," which historicizes and theorizes the paradoxical functions of body doubles in the Hollywood film industry, was particularly helpful early in my research on dance-ins, while Iyer's 2020 book *Dancing Women: Choreographing Corporeal Histories of Hindi Cinema* was a source of inspiration in the later stages of this project. Like Iyer, who examines the gendered relations of labor that underwrite the construction of screen dancing bodies in the context of Hindi film, I strive to provide "a complex intermedial, corporeal history of film dance production,"[127] though with a focus on midcentury Hollywood. Building on these works and compelled by the dance-in's intermediary status to think about live and filmic bodies in analogous rather than oppositional terms, *Hollywood Dance-ins* turns to the most overlooked of dance figures to shed fresh light on the relations of reproduction that have supported white Western notions of corporeality in the United States.

Reproducible Bodies/Reproductive Labor

While dance-ins are not technologically reproduced bodies in the conventional sense, they are, unmistakably, figures of reproduction. Taking their reproductive functions seriously aligns with Jane Gaines's claim that the body is a "technology of reproduction" not wholly dissimilar from "the motion picture machine." It is "not only that the body has the capacity to reproduce itself," she writes, "but that it produces bodies in the image of itself, that are like and not-like itself."[128] While Gaines is referring to the body's uncanny but taken-for-granted mimetic abilities via biological reproduction, those same mimetic capacities are what enable the transmission of dance across and between the bodies of choreographers, dance-ins, and stars. The dance-in's very raison d'être was to replicate (or prefigure) a star's physicality and movement, as is evident in reports that the film star Betty Grable was imitating her dance-in Angie Blue when she performed some of her most Grable-like moves (see Chapter 1), and in records of Alex Romero and Gene Kelly's mirroring of one another to create film choreography (see Chapter 5). Rather than emphasizing the differences between modes of reproduction, *Hollywood Dance-ins* asks how reproductive acts bind dancing bodies to one another even when those acts are hidden behind bodily images.

In the field of dance studies, issues of reproduction come to the fore in scholarship on how dance circulates, the politics of appropriation, and the transmission of embodied knowledge. Claims of dance's ephemerality notwithstanding, dance scholars, like the performance studies scholars I cite below, have pointed to the multiple ways in which dance participates in economies of reproduction.[129] There is an entire Oxford *Handbook* dedicated to dance and reenactment.[130] The discourse of appropriation, meanwhile, has been key to critical dance studies efforts to analyze the reproduction of dance styles across lines of class, race, ethnicity, nationality, and caste and to call out the histories of colonization and dispossession that have shaped many dance histories.[131] Imani Kai Johnson has argued, however, that if appropriation names "one type of cross-cultural performance" that involves "staking a claim to a culture," it is limited in its ability to limn a fuller "spectrum of cross-racial performances."[132] As I've written elsewhere, the "vacillating terminology" that both scholars and dancers use to refer to the reproduction of one dancer's or group of dancers' moves by another ("copying," "borrowing," "mimicry," "stealing," to cite a few) suggests the highly variable and context-specific ways the reproduction of dance is understood.[133]

Though dance scholars tend to describe the oral and embodied process by which dance is passed on from one body to another with the more neutral-sounding "transmission," they routinely identify emulation and mimesis as fundamental to the transmission process.[134] Jasmine Johnson frames this emulation in particularly forceful terms. "A guiding philosophy of any dance class," she writes, "is to reproduce: reproduce an instructor's choreography, reproduce an obedience to rhythm, reproduce a social order. In a class, we dancers pay, in part, for an occasion to mime."[135] Dance scholars are equally insistent, however, that this reproduction can never be exact, for

22 HOLLYWOOD DANCE-INS

as any dancer knows, one's body seems "constantly to elude one's efforts to direct it."[136] Sometimes the elusion is deliberate.[137] The transmission process is thus rife with minute negotiations of power, as authority can oscillate between teacher and student and between one student and another.[138] Hired by studios, subordinate to choreographers, and frequently more skilled dancers than the stars they stood in for (as was true for Grable's dance-in Angie Blue, Debbie Reynolds's coaches Jeanne Coyne and Carol Haney, and Marie Bryant and most if not all of the white stars she coached), dance-ins encourage us to reckon with both the macro and micro power dynamics that govern the reproduction of dance and that trouble distinctions between original and copy.

The discourse of reproduction and mimesis is arguably more conspicuous in the field of performance studies. As Soyica Diggs, Douglas Jones, and Shane Vogel write, "repetition is axiomatic in performance studies," owing to "the term's centrality in the field's founding theories and documents."[139] Those theories include Richard Schechner's famous definition of performance as "twice-behaved behavior"[140] and Judith Butler's theory of gender performativity as iterability.[141] Performance studies also has a long tradition of asserting, *pace* Peggy Phelan,[142] that "performance is a reproductive machine"[143] and that "the *conjunction* of reproduction and disappearance is performance's condition of possibility."[144] Given the dance-in's role as a substitute for the star, theories of performance as a form of surrogation are especially relevant to my study. In his 1996 book *Cities of the Dead*, performance studies scholar Joseph Roach explores how "culture reproduces and re-creates itself by a process that can be best described by the word *surrogation*."[145] As I return to in Chapter 1, in the case of the dance-in the "vacancies" that require filling through surrogation are caused not by the deaths and departures that Roach considers but by the exigencies of film production, the needs of choreographers, and the demands of stars.

Roach's notion of surrogation has not been without criticism. Performance studies scholar Diana Taylor argues that because as a model, surrogation depends on an assertion of cultural continuity enabled by the erasure of antecedents, notions of performance as "doubling, replication, and proliferation" are more apt.[146] Yet as I hope to demonstrate, among the many lines the dance-in blurs are those between surrogation and doubling. Even while the dance-in's labor must be forgotten in order for the star to assume the appearance of coherence and originality, in many of the examples I cover, the surrogate's dancing bleeds into and helps mold the corporeality of the star. In other words, surrogation not only propels the *re*production and *re*-creation of culture writ large; it also propels the production and creation of a star's bodily image, which, in the case of the white stars I examine here, cohered around the fantasy that their filmic image was a technological but not a corporeal reproduction.

In addition to highlighting the absences and substitutions that are constitutive of stars' corporealities, conceptualizing the dance-in's labor as a form of surrogation underscores its convergence with biological modes of reproduction and thus its gendered dimensions. Asking why "the vocabulary of maternal reproduction" is largely missing from the "range of vantage points and host of (often economistic) metaphors" through which performance theory has explored reproduction, Joshua Chambers-Letson proposes centering performance's capacity to "appropriate . . . the reproductive function of the mother" in our analyses.[147] The lexical overlap between performance theory's "surrogation" and the assisted biological reproduction technology known as "surrogacy" is especially hard to ignore. Because surrogacy generally refers to a form of contracted reproductive labor that allows for procreation outside of the male/female dyad, regarding dance-ins as surrogates can direct us toward both the maternal-like and the non-heteronormative nature of their reproductive labor. This book focuses on the gendered relations between dance-ins and stars in several chapters, but I hope it also spurs further investigations of the various forms of gendered reproductive labor that make possible the transmission of dance and the construction of bodies.

Just as crucially, approaching the dance-in as a surrogate calls attention to what Alys Weinbaum calls the "race/reproduction bind": an "ideological constellation" that maintains that the two "mutually dependent terms" are an organizing force behind "the modern episteme."[148] Inspired by Black feminists, Weinbaum proposes that a "surrogacy/slavery nexus" continues to affect contemporary social and economic relations.[149] This nexus, and her argument that "biocapitalism relies on *reproduction as a racializing process*,"[150] builds on the work of Spillers and other Black feminist scholars. Saidiya Hartman, for example, has stressed reproductive labor as "central to thinking about the gendered afterlife of slavery and global capitalism," while Sarah Clarke Kaplan has argued that "Black reproductive acts, capacities, and labor" are "a condition of possibility for U.S. racial capitalism."[151] The site of unresolvable contradictions inherent in the U.S. state, material acts of Black reproduction have facilitated "the maintenance of white possessive individualism . . . and the necessary conditions for white life," even as they disrupt "ideals of racial purity."[152] Thinking with these Black feminist scholars to understand reproductive labor in simultaneously raced and gendered terms, the "gestational language"[153] of surrogation and surrogacy helps us appreciate dance-ins in midcentury Hollywood as the condition of possibility for the "body proper" of dancing white stars while leading us back to the Black reproductive acts that give the lie to notions of white corporeal purity.

Archival Sleuthing and Research at the Margins

At the risk of stating the obvious, the challenges of researching dance-ins are manifold. Uncredited by design, marginalized in relation to both stars and choreographers, dance-ins are what Anthony Slide calls "Hollywood unknowns," a status they share with "extras, bit players, and stand-ins" who are indispensable to the making of films and "linked by a common thread of anonymity."[154] As a quick Google search establishes, "dance-in" is a terrible search term. Even that nomenclature lacks fixity: industry players and researchers alike have alternately referred to dance-ins as "doubles," "stand-ins," "understudies," and even "ghosts."[155] Because there is no systematic way to research them, the history of dance-ins this book provides is unavoidably partial. Yet that partiality is consistent with the lessons dance-ins offer: they compel us to wrestle with omissions in archival sources as much as in filmic images of stars' dancing bodies. Accounting for the labor of the dance-in requires reading archives, filmic texts, and corporealities differently: a combination of healthy skepticism that what is there on the page and who is there on the screen can be taken at face value and an abiding belief that lack of visibility does not mean lack of presence.

Dance-ins, it is worth emphasizing, are not absent from film archives. Rather, reflecting their status in Hollywood's labor hierarchy,[156] they reside in archival margins: the incidental spaces of sources designed to capture more central players and events. Befitting their capitalist function, dance-ins show up in assistant director (AD) reports, part of the "detailed record keeping of the studio system," and in studios' payroll accounts, budget ledgers, and labor contracts.[157] These sources are hardly complete, however. Movie studios did not have uniform methods of record keeping, and the thoroughness, organization, and accessibility of different studios' archives, which are dispersed across institutions, vary widely. The University of Southern California's Cinematic Arts Library, for example, houses the archives for MGM's Arthur Freed unit, which specialized in producing big-budget musicals, as well as for Warner Brothers films. The AD reports for MGM musicals were a particularly rich font of information about day-to-day (and even minute-to-minute) activities on set. But such reports don't exist for every MGM film musical. The archives for Twentieth Century-Fox, once housed at the University of California, Los Angeles, are now controlled by Fox. Thanks to their Clip and Still Licensing Department on the thirteenth floor of Fox Plaza in Century City, I was able to scroll through microfiche of production files for specific films and "deal files" for some choreographers. The archives of Universal Studios films, by contrast, are reserved for "internal business units of NBCUniversal" and not open to external researchers.[158] The Margaret Herrick Library's vast collection of film archives yielded many useful tidbits about the production of Hollywood films. Yet their "general subject files," which include files for stand-ins and body doubles, contain no designated file for dance-ins.

Stitching together the stories of dance-ins therefore required knowing what to look for—or, more precisely, who to look for. As a result, there is a degree of serendipity to which dance-ins I focus on in the following pages. For instance, I came across the name of Angie Blue, the first dance-in about whom I write at length, only by chance, in the course of reading John Franceschina's study of choreographer Hermes Pan.[159] This quickly became a key component of my method: searching for and sometimes finding references to dance-ins in published accounts of or by the more famous choreographers and stars whom they assisted. Accordingly, *Hollywood Dance-ins* benefited enormously from the numerous biographies, autobiographies, oral histories, popular press monographs, and blogs that are devoted to the history of Golden Age Hollywood musicals.[160] Larry Billman's *Film Choreographers and Dance Directors: An Illustrated Biographical Encyclopedia* was an invaluable source,[161] and I made other discoveries thanks to Debra Levine's *arts meme* blog.[162] Levine also introduced me to Barrie Chase, one of the few living dancers who was active during the period my book covers and whose lucid memory and generous insights about dance-ins and the making of Hollywood film musicals were extremely helpful.

Even so, my research was filled with starts and stops, and many of my initial leads about specific dance-ins led nowhere. Compounding the difficulties, in yet another example of their instability, was the fact that dance-ins, and background dancers at large, are prone to being misidentified. Though they

26 HOLLYWOOD DANCE-INS

mostly suffer from a lack of credit, supporting dancers are sometimes credited in places they shouldn't be. IMDb, for all its convenience, is far from error-proof, as I discovered when production records failed to corroborate its claim that Carol Haney appeared in the 1945 film *Ziegfeld Follies*.[163] Jeanne Coyne is erroneously credited in multiple places as one of the on-screen dancers in the "A Day in New York" ballet in *On the Town* (1949).[164] The misspelling of dancers' names, meanwhile, created obstacles even when I knew who I was looking for. Marie Bryant appears in one written document as Julie Bryant and Marie Bruant in another.[165] Alex Romero's name is misprinted as Romera and Romaro,[166] and Becky Varno, who danced in for Nancy Kwan in *Flower Drum Song*, sometimes appears as Becky Vorno.[167] In addition, while most of the dancers about whom I write have sadly passed away and most of my attempts to contact their descendants were fruitless, when I did succeed in tracking down and securing an interview with a dancer, they were not necessarily able to recall details about long-ago rehearsals.[168]

And yet enough times, one breadcrumb about a dance-in led to another and then another, in a process that often felt like archival sleuthing. As is standard for dance historians, newspapers and magazines proved to be essential primary sources in my detective work; they provided scraps of information about dance-ins, usually indirectly, via news items and gossip about movies in production, interviews with stars and choreographers, and reports of studio set visits. Searchable collections like newspapers.com and Charlene Regester's extraordinary two-volume annotated bibliography *Black Entertainers in African American Newspaper Articles* made finding such sources significantly easier.[169] Movie reviews were also occasionally useful. Yet because my focus is more on off-screen practices and relations between dancers than on spectatorship, I approached these reviews mostly for what they could reveal about how a star's dancing body was perceived relative to whatever I could discern about its conditions of production.

One of the joys of interdisciplinary research is discovering unanticipated points of intersection. As I learned, there is overlap between the emerging subfield of feminist production studies in film and media studies and historical work in dance and performance studies, both of which share a commitment to "ma[king] hidden labor visible."[170] Although dance studies is a relatively young field, dance historians are well practiced at assembling the "disparate residual traces" that bodies leave behind and at confronting gaps in documented records.[171] Dance scholars have argued for the need to tend to "invisibilized" presences and to combat the "institutionalized silencing"

INTRODUCTION 27

that threatens to erase minoritized subjects from history.[172] And they have demonstrated how our understanding of dance history can change when we treat "marginally appearing dancing bodies as laborers."[173] An even younger field, feminist production studies, as Miranda Banks explains, resists "top-down hierarchies" and "highlights production at the margins."[174] This involves centering so-called noncreative labor that is often labeled "women's work"—female-dominated jobs like costume designers, script clerks, and secretaries.[175] Because (as dance historians also know) feminized labor is devalued labor, researching below-the-line "women's work" requires scouring "the footnotes and margins of other people's histories."[176] This was certainly true of women dance-ins, who were subordinates of male choreographers and female stars, and whose labor was regarded as derivative rather than creative.

Black performance scholars, as Nadine George-Graves points out, have been at the forefront of developing methods designed to unearth materials that "fill in the gaps and tell the stories of those forgotten."[177] She cites a 1981 article by VéVé Clark, which calls for an archaeological approach to Black theater that "looks for and at the process of creation," including what transpires backstage, rather than focusing primarily on finished cultural products.[178] Across the humanities more broadly, scholars of queer, subaltern, and racially minoritized histories are accustomed to archival evidence that is "thin and scattered,"[179] and they too offer models for learning to read for that which "lie[s] in the space between full presence and total absence"[180] by giving weight to the "traces, glimmers, residues, and specks of things."[181] Black feminist scholars have additionally demonstrated the value of what Saidiya Hartman calls "critical fabulation" and Tavia Nyong'o calls "afro-fabulation": resisting "the demand that a representation be either true or false" and instead "imagin[ing] what . . . might have been said or might have been done."[182] Fabulation serves as a check against the "impulse to repair the injured historical subject" by "restoring" her to a place of transparency and knowability.[183]

In the case of the dance-in, the limits of the archives did at times require conjecture and educated guesses about what took place behind the camera. I assert repeatedly that dance-ins shaped film stars' corporeality via their roles as surrogates, but the details of the exchanges between choreographers, dance-ins, and stars are often if not always opaque. The persistence of such gaps forces us to dwell in what Nyong'o calls "zones of indistinction,"[184] which here could describe the spaces between the live and the filmic, between one

28 HOLLYWOOD DANCE-INS

dancer and another, and between speculation and verifiable fact. Those gaps have their own rewards, for they prevent an overemphasis on "setting the record straight" or restoring "proper" credit.[185] The piecemeal traces that dance-ins left behind allow us to glimpse the contours of a widely used labor practice that was codified by the movie industry even as they hold at arm's length the micro-negotiations of power and the give-and-takes that were surely as dynamic and contingent as they were unquantifiable.

Photographs of dance-ins rehearsing with choreographers and stars, while not consistently or abundantly available, do provide us some access to these indistinct zones of transmission, and I turn to them whenever I can for hints about the relations of reproduction. Yet rehearsal photographs raise an epistemological conundrum that lies at the heart of this book: if, as I argue, we cannot assume that filmic representations of stars' dancing bodies are indexically stable, what kind of "indexical certainty" should we ascribe to behind-the-scenes photographs, and what kind of "proof" do they provide?[186] If filmic images of dancing bodies are capable of concealing their conditions of production, are not photographs, which capture only a fraction of time, as well? Addressing the irony surrounding the "lure of *historiographic knowability*" in film history, Jane Gaines notes that "while an entire field has already critiqued a cinematic illusionism that produces the tug of 'realism' on the spectator, we have stopped short of applying this critique to our own scholarly research methods." "One could . . . argue," she adds, "that moving image historians want to have it both ways, that is, to critique cinematic 'realism' as well as 'objectivity' but still undertake archival research undeterred."[187] The circumstances in which most of the behind-the-scenes photographs contained in this book were taken, including whether they were staged for publicity purposes, as rehearsal photographs often were, are indeed unknown. There is thus a certain parallel between the tension in my claims about bodies—that they are dogged by ideological fictions *and* that we must take their materiality seriously—and my approach to images, which I rely on methodologically *and* maintain are indexically fraught. These tensions need not cancel each other out, though. With Gaines, I believe it is possible to advocate for archival research while remaining interested in the "historical conditions of 'unknowability,'" just as I believe it is possible to hold on to the opacity and indeterminacy of images (and of bodies) while insisting on their importance as "anecdotal" evidence.[188] Taking a cue from Tina Campt, who urges attention to the "unspoken relations" and "fissures, gaps, and interstices" of photographs, I regard rehearsal images as evidence of relations that underwrite but are obscured by film, and as themselves structured by fissures and gaps that we can only guess at.[189]

I have been emphasizing the limits and rewards of archival sources in recovering dance-ins' largely unseen reproductive labor, but the results of this labor can be found within film musicals themselves, which are available for repeat viewing. These films, too, are important sources and allow me to make use of the dominant methods in dance and film studies: analyzing the choreographed moves, bodily comportment, camera angles, shot sequences, and editing choices that are more directly visible on screen. In keeping with a production studies approach, however, I proceed from the premise "that knowledge of the cultural and industrial modes of production will not just inform, but alter one's reading not only of the media text, but of the media."[190] With respect to dance-ins, this altered reading means being alert to the twin "tugs" of realism and of absent presences. It means believing the dancing we are seeing is loaded with material significance. But it also means being attuned to the intercorporeal exchanges and displaced bodies that are masked by but not completely erased from seemingly unified images. The analytical lens I adopt shares something with the interpretive strategy that media studies scholar Hye Jean Chung, drawing on Foucault's notion of heterotopias, calls "compositing": "challeng[ing] the notion of cinematic space as a seamless unity" by tending to the "spectral effects" of "forms of creative labor that leave legible or perceptible traces of residual materiality onscreen." Like Chung, my interest is in teasing out the contradictions between "the *rhetoric* of a fluid, effortless mobility idealized in a film's narrative" or, in my case, in idealized perceptions of stars' dancing bodies, and "the *reality* of local circumstances," which include the distribution of reproductive labor across multiple bodies in a racially and gender-stratified ecosystem.[191]

Because it was not uncommon for dance-ins to appear as chorus dancers in the films on which they worked, part of this critical reading practice entailed learning to train my eye on the dancers who occupy the background of film musicals, dancing alongside and behind (and occasionally in place of, as is the case in a number I examine in *Flower Drum Song* in Chapter 5) the star. I say "train" since this kind of viewing requires looking against the grain of the star system's "promotion of the individual," against beliefs that the star is the "film musical's primary, unifying element," and against the cinematography itself, for camera angles and editing often make it literally difficult to focus on chorus dancers rather than on the star.[192] Sometimes I watched with the single-minded goal of trying to identify a dancer about whom I was

30 HOLLYWOOD DANCE-INS

writing. At other times, I studied how a chorus member's dancing compared to the star's, looking for traces of what might have been transmitted, however unevenly, across their bodies. And at still other times, I watched with a sense of awe and mystery: Who were all these dancers?[193] What behind-the-scenes roles might they have played? Like the stories of dance-ins that fill this book, this mode of viewing may raise as many questions as it answers. But that is merely the cost of recognizing how many more stories lay tucked away in the margins, waiting to be told. It is the cost, too, of treating filmic images, behind-the-scenes photographs, and bodies themselves as never fully self-evident.

Coming Attractions

In each of the five chapters that follow, I focus on a different set of corporeal relationships between dance-ins (or related figures) and film stars of mid-twentieth-century Hollywood musicals and probe some of the conceptual issues brought to light by those relationships. Although arranged chronologically, the chapters need not be read in that order, for each offers a stand-alone argument about the reproductive practices out of which star dancing bodies were forged. Readers of the book in its entirety will notice that I circle back to certain issues: Chapters 1 and 5 both raise explicit questions about indexicality, while Chapters 1 and 3 engage most directly with questions of surrogation. As I indicated above, there is some arbitrariness, given the methodological challenges, to whose stories *Hollywood Dance-ins* tells. It is also true that I was drawn to examples in which the raced and gendered dynamics of the relations of reproduction between stars and their dancing intermediaries were particularly salient. It should come as no surprise to those who have read the work of scholars like Brenda Dixon Gottschild, Carol Clover, Thomas DeFrantz, Brynn Shiovitz, and Pamela Krayenbuhl that, even when Black dancers were on neither the payroll nor the movie set, they had a massive influence on film musical dancing.[194] My book emphasizes and honors Black dance and Black dancers' centrality to Hollywood's corporeal ecosystem, even as I remain committed to racializing white bodies and to representing the multiracial nature of Hollywood's dance landscape.

Chapter 1, "'Doing Angie': Betty Grable, Surrogation, and the (Non) Indexicality of Whiteness," inaugurates the book's efforts to interrogate the racialized and gendered reproduction of stars' corporeality. The chapter opens by considering the earliest documented example of a dance-in—by the white child star Shirley Temple in 1935—and the implications of Temple's embodiment of white innocence for our understanding of dance-ins' functions. It then turns to its main subject, the relationship between Betty Grable, who came to personify white femininity in the 1940s, and two women whose reproductive labor left an imprint on her filmic body: the white Angie Blue, Grable's dance-in throughout the 1940s, and the African American Marie Bryant, whose coaching of Grable in 1950 shared certain qualities with the labor of a dance-in. Looking at their respective relationships through the conceptual lenses of surrogation and indexicality, I show how Grable's emulation of these women's physicalities blurs the lines between original and copy and between image and referent and exposes the ideology of white bodily autonomy as a conceit. A genealogical approach to Grable's corporeality also reveals the overlaps between intra- and interracial forms of surrogation and highlights the racially stratified ways in which Grable's films both remember and forget her surrogates.

Chapter 2, "Marie Bryant, Black Reproductive Labor, and White Parasitism," delves more deeply into the relationships between Bryant and the striking number of Hollywood stars she coached. Though not officially employed as a dance-in, Bryant was reportedly the first African American to earn the title of assistant dance director, a designation that was celebrated in the Black press for cracking the white monopoly on such positions in Hollywood. Devoting a full chapter to Bryant's off-screen interactions with stars throws into relief the simultaneity of Hollywood's institutionalized racism and its parasitical dependence on Black reproductive labor. It also provides insight into how such a talented and well-connected dancer could be both so ubiquitous and so susceptible to erasure. Rather than attempting to "restore" Bryant to wholeness, the chapter tracks her flickering appearances in the archives, paying special attention to a series of photographs that ran in a 1950 feature on her in *Ebony* magazine pairing her with white stars. I also examine her private coaching of the white dancer Vera-Ellen, who partnered Gene Kelly in *Words and Music* (1948) and *On the Town* (1949) and whose ascendance as a star can be directly traced to Bryant's training. The chapter concludes by considering evidence that Bryant "polished" the act of her friend Lena Horne, one of the very few Black performers to become a star in midcentury Hollywood, and reflects on the implications that our primary access to Bryant's reproductive labor is via the traces she left on other surfaces.

32 HOLLYWOOD DANCE-INS

Chapter 3, "Female Reproductive Labor and White Corporeal Debt in *Singin' in the Rain*," revisits questions of credit and debt in the celebrated 1952 film musical to argue that white women's dancing bodies are important participants in the talent "relocations"[195] that the movie both foregrounds and conceals. Here I concentrate on the relationship between Debbie Reynolds, who was a novice dancer when she was cast in the film, and assistant choreographer Carol Haney and dance-in Jeanne Coyne, the two white women dancers who helped shape Reynolds's filmic body. Uniting often disconnected gendered and racial analyses of the film, the chapter returns to the concept of surrogation to emphasize the gendered forms of labor and the multiracial genealogies through which the musical's dancing was reproduced. It also shows how the guise of white credibility enabled Reynolds to mask her intercorporeal and multiracial debts. Taking stock of the parallels between my own disclosure of Reynolds's debts and the film's diegetic disclosure of Lina Lamont's, meanwhile, leads to a discussion of both the politics of exposure and the shifts in whiteness as a racial formation at midcentury. Finally, the chapter addresses the appearance of dancers of color in the film, most notably the Puerto Rican–born Rita Moreno. In contrast to her bigger and better-known role as Anita in *West Side Story* (1961), Moreno's racial identity as Zelda Zanders in *Singin' in the Rain* is much less determinate. Her presence in the film, which is narratively tied to the "outing" of white doubles, reminds us that nonwhite dancers haunt the chains of white corporeal debt that bind Reynolds to Haney and Coyne.

Chapter 4, " 'Cool It, Alex': Queering the Dance-in," examines the relationship between the white Gene Kelly and his Mexican American dance-in Alex Romero, who assisted Kelly on films such as *Words and Music* (1948), *On the Town* (1949), and *An American in Paris* (1951). Bearing in mind Kelly's project of asserting dance as a masculine activity, the chapter asks whether there is something queer about the homosocial and arguably closeted relations that the dance-in ushers into existence. First charting the ways Romero functioned as Kelly's off-screen mirror and double, I then analyze the "erotic triangles" that structured a significant amount of the choreography the men co-created, both in rehearsal and, in the case of *On the Town*, on screen. I also consider the implications of Kelly's being "caught" in the act of reproduction and the gendered threat that Romero's blurring of the original/copy binary posed to Kelly's masculine reputation. Lastly, I address how Romero's racial positionality—he was light enough to pass as white but darker than Kelly and

INTRODUCTION 33

not immune to anti-Mexican racism—shifts our sense of Kelly's corporeality and demonstrates the existence of a "brown commons"[196] in Hollywood.

Chapter 5, "Racial Dis/Orientations and the Ambivalence of Nancy Kwan's Dancing Body," turns to the performance of the Hong Kong–born, biracial, ballet-trained star Kwan in *Flower Drum Song*, the 1961 film with a predominantly Asian/American cast and a predominantly white production team. While the film tends to get eclipsed in histories of Hollywood's Golden Age musicals by *West Side Story*, released the same year, it has been well attended to by scholars in Asian/American studies.[197] Drawing on that scholarship, the chapter juxtaposes a newspaper reporter's disorienting encounter with Kwan's white dance-in, Becky Varno, with contemporary criticism that grapples with the ambiguous racial status of Kwan's filmic image. Kwan, the chapter proposes, exemplifies how the fiction of bodily integrity has been withheld from nonwhite stars. Through an examination of her indexical instability and competing racial orientations across three of *Flower Drum Song*'s numbers, I situate Kwan in relation to her white interlocutors and her fractured filmic image as well as to her pan-Asian castmates, including the Filipino-born Patrick Adiarte, whose embodiment of Africanist jazz dance points us toward a triangulated approach to Asian/American corporeality. Ultimately, the tensions that characterize Kwan's racial status make visible the layering of corporeal histories, the distributed acts of transmission, and the multiple racial formations and imaginaries out of which Hollywood star dancing bodies are forged.

The book's coda analyzes a televised duet between the African American star Lena Horne (who worked closely with Marie Bryant) and the white dancer/dance-in/choreographer Carol Haney (who assisted Gene Kelly and trained Debbie Reynolds) on a 1962 episode of *The Perry Como Show*. Though perhaps an unlikely final scene to a history of film musical dancing, the performance is suggestive of the trajectory of a number of the book's key figures, who found work in television when big-budget movie musicals entered a period of decline. Despite and because of the absence of information about the conditions of production of the number, the duet is an opportunity to contemplate what dance-ins can teach us about how to read for the traces of off-screen histories in moving images of dancing bodies. In the (almost) synchronized dancing of two differently racialized women occupying different positions in Hollywood's corporeal ecosystem, we can detect echoes of the racialized and gendered relations of reproduction that have structured popular forms of U.S. screen dance.

1

"Doing Angie"

Betty Grable, Surrogation, and the (Non)Indexicality of Whiteness

In 1935, the *Los Angeles Times* ran a seventy-word article under the headline "Dance Stand-In," explaining a new phenomenon in Hollywood: "'Stand-ins,' persons who take the places of stars while the cameras are being properly focused, have become an accepted fact around the studio sets. Now comes Shirley Temple, youngest star of them all, with a new kind of stand-in—a dance stand-in. Marilyn Harper, one of the Meglin Kiddies, is Shirley's dance stand-in. Marilyn goes through all the terpsichorean motions for Shirley until she is ready to take her place."[1] The use of "dance stand-ins," eventually condensed to "dance-ins," coincided with the rise of the film musical in the early 1930s. Ushered in by the 1927 advent of sound in Hollywood, film musicals created a demand for dance numbers and for stars contracted by the newly integrated studios to dance on screen.[2] So it was that Marilyn Harper joined the ranks of other "Hollywood unknowns"—extras, stand-ins, stunt doubles—who were key to the operation of moviemaking but seldom heralded and, with the rare exception of notices like the *Times* jotting, almost never credited.[3]

In a compelling 2000 article titled "Missing Persons and Bodies of Evidence," Ann Chisholm traces the roots of body doubling, which became commonplace in Hollywood after the repeal of the Motion Picture Production Code in the late 1960s, to the precedent of stand-ins. First emerging in the 1920s as the film industry, like the nation as a whole, moved "toward efficiency and replication," stand-ins became useful as technological advances in filming heightened the need for rehearsals. Initially played by an inanimate dummy and required to do nothing more than fill "the space left absent by the star prior to filming," stand-ins were increasingly required to resemble the stars they stood in for and became labor-saving devices for "replicating the appearance of stars during distinct moments of the production process," particularly lighting checks. As such, stand-ins were "perfect

Hollywood Dance-ins and the Reproduction of Bodies. Anthea Kraut, Oxford University Press.
© Oxford University Press 2025. DOI: 10.1093/oso/9780197789667.003.0002

"DOING ANGIE" 35

candidates for doubling," often served as photo doubles for stars in long shots, and often worked with the same star across a number of years.[4]

However much the "ostensibly secondary and supplementary bodies" of stand-ins and body doubles functioned "to guarantee the economies undergirding filmic discourse," they were repeatedly disavowed or disparaged as "second-rate physical cop[ies]." Chisholm cites the example of Geraldine de Vorak, who doubled for the white film star Greta Garbo in the 1920s. De Vorak was described as "an exact replica of Garbo in every respect"—save for "'the mysterious ingredient that made Greta Garbo.'" "How is it," Chisholm asks, "that body doubling can be a historical effect that has been devalued within the US film industry and yet at the same time yields effects that are vital to the industry and to the texts it produces?" Dwelling on this contradiction, Chisholm highlights the ambiguities and slippages generated by the supplementary bodies that form part of the cinematic apparatus, bodies that are both marginal and essential, both omnipresent and perpetually "missing."[5]

Unlike a stand-in, the body (or body parts) of a double appears on screen, masquerading as that of the star. The use of doubles therefore necessitates some sleight-of-hand film editing, designed to trick spectators.[6] In the case of dance doubles, which predated dance stand-ins,[7] this deception can become controversial, as was evident in the 2011 scandal over the doubling American Ballet Theater's Sarah Lane did for Oscar-winning actress Natalie Portman in the 2010 film *Black Swan*.[8] Because the double creates questions about whose body we are seeing on screen, it destabilizes the assumed correspondence between a star's on-screen image and her off-screen corporeality. In film studies, this destabilization is part of a larger issue that has been described as the "politics of indexicality," which I will return to below.

While stand-ins' and dance-ins' lack of on-screen visibility[9] means they have not required the same kind of cinematic subterfuge, they are no less capable of producing slippages. This is evident in the very language of the *Los Angeles Times*' announcement of the dance stand-in's emergence. Take the last sentence of the article: "Marilyn goes through all the terpsichorean motions for Shirley until she is ready to take her place." The "she" here is clearly Temple, but whose place is Temple taking? That of Harper, her dance-in? Or her own "rightful" place as star?[10] This imprecision invites us to read "her" in a double sense: when the star takes her place before the camera, she is taking both her own and her dance-in's place. To belabor this even further, recall that the first sentence in the article defines stand-ins as those who take the place of stars. Both stars and stand-ins, then, perform the action of taking an/other's place, a two-way place-taking that, where dance-ins are concerned, precedes any dancing we ultimately see on screen.

Even if coincidental, the uncertain referentiality of pronouns in the *Times* piece might be seen as symptomatic of the dance-in's ability to muddy the discreteness of bodies more broadly. Dance-ins remind us that behind the image of a star's seemingly singular dancing body are bodies plural and that others carried out the on-screen choreography prior to the star herself. They also remind us that multiple kinds of reproduction, including "live," flesh-and-bone exchanges and substitutions, are required to produce filmic images of dancing bodies. Because they occupy a position of simultaneous marginality and centrality in the movie industry, dance-ins expose the operations of power by which some corporealities come to be perceived as autonomous.

This chapter inaugurates this book's interrogation of Hollywood's reproduction of bodies by focusing on the relationship between the white film star Betty Grable and two women who danced in her place. Perhaps best known for her pin-up image that circulated among American GIs stationed around the globe during World War II (see Figure 1.1), Grable was an icon of white womanhood who acted, danced, and sang in over forty movies in the middle of the twentieth century. Across many of these films, the "terpsichorean motions" she performed were imitations of Angie Blue's, the white woman who was a longtime assistant to choreographer Hermes Pan and regularly served as Grable's dance-in. Blue was not the only model for Grable's dancing, though. Around 1950, the star also received coaching from the African American dancer Marie Bryant. While not an official dance-in, Bryant, like Blue, demonstrated moves for Grable and then stood aside once cameras were rolling (and literally stood aside on film, as I will show). Grable's dependence on these women provides a window onto two different if related kinds of substitution on which idealized white corporeality has rested: on a codified system of white women contracted by the movie studio system to resemble and replace one another, and on a less official but no less entrenched system of Hollywood stars' emulating and displacing of dancers of color.

While Grable's intercorporeal relationships with Blue and Bryant might seem an arbitrary starting point for this book's excavation of dance-ins, there are several reasons—methodological, historical, and theoretical—that these specific "she's" are a productive place to begin. Research-wise, Blue was the first dance-in I learned about in the course of reading John Franceschina's

"DOING ANGIE" 37

Figure 1.1 Betty Grable in her famous 1943 pin-up pose. Courtesy of Photofest.

carefully researched biography of Hermes Pan.[11] Franceschina's account makes clear that, in her work with Grable in particular, Blue played an active role in shaping the star's physicality, even more so than an emphasis on the labor-saving function of a "stand-in" would suggest. Franceschina's extensive documentation of Blue, although still limited by gaps in the archives, made it possible to begin recovering traces of Hollywood dance-ins, Blue and others.

38 HOLLYWOOD DANCE-INS

From a historical and theoretical perspective, the 1940s are a useful decade through which to investigate how the conjunction of what film scholar Daniel Bernardi has called "classic Hollywood, classic whiteness" played out at the level of the body. As discussed in the introduction, the classical period of Hollywood, generally thought to extend from the late 1920s to the early 1960s, was defined not only by the ascendancy of "continuity filmmaking" and the efficiency of the studio system but also by the reign of whiteness in everything from "white characters to white lighting techniques to stories of white superiority."[12] As I explore below, with her blonde hair and "peaches and cream" complexion,[13] Grable epitomized "classic" whiteness. She was also very much a product of the studio system. While she accordingly helps expose the co-constitutive nature of "whiteness" and "film star" during the classical period, Grable's whiteness is instructive for reasons that extend beyond her visual appearance.[14] In her reliance on a dance-in, Grable offers insight into whiteness as a set of material, corporeal, and reproductive relations. In what follows, after briefly reviewing relevant theorizations of whiteness in critical race studies, performance studies, and film studies, I unpack how Grable's filmic image was forged out of relationships with Blue and Bryant. Taken together, these relationships point to the reproductions and substitutions that must be forgotten in order for the white female star's body to maintain its alleged singularity and integrity.

Whiteness, Surrogation, and Privileged Embodiment

Here it is worth doubling back to the fact that the *L.A. Times* article cited above names Shirley Temple as the first to benefit from a dancing stand-in. The most popular child star of the 1930s, Temple personified innocent white femininity.[15] That the dance-in emerged in service of Temple encourages us to ask some preliminary questions about how this supplemental body functioned as a technology of gendered whiteness.[16]

It is by now widely accepted that whiteness is constructed and that, in the United States, film has played an outsized role in framing whiteness as a universal norm and aesthetic ideal.[17] Film scholars, correspondingly, have been active in theorizing whiteness. For example, Michael Rogin has pointed to the donning and removing of blackface as a major mode of producing whiteness on screen. Richard Dyer has argued that movie lighting creates "a look that assumes, privileges and constructs an image of white people," and that

"DOING ANGIE" 39

idealized images of white women in film are fashioned through lighting techniques that make them appear to glow.[18] It is significant in this regard that one of a stand-in's primary functions was to allow cinematographers to determine the proper lighting for the star and that stand-ins were thus required to approximate the star's "height, weight, and coloring."[19] Although little is known about Marilyn Harper, Temple's dance stand-in,[20] both she and Temple got their start with Meglin's Kiddies, a Los Angeles–based dance studio (actually a collection of studios) that groomed white children for show business. An online clip of a 1933 vaudeville act featuring "Meglin's Famous Kiddies" shows a sea of white children tap dancing and performing acrobatic tricks.[21] An entire industry stood ready to supply dancers who could visually match Temple on film.[22]

But the white stand-in who dances in place of a white star does more than resemble that star and so offers insight into how whiteness is reproduced in ways that exceed white physical appearance or the performance of blackface. One of those ways is through the outsourcing of labor: like stand-ins, dance-ins were first and foremost labor-saving devices for stars. Given Temple's youth, it's certainly possible that child labor laws played a role in dance-ins' emergence. Although it was not until 1938 that the Fair Labor Standards Act placed limitations on child labor, in her autobiography Temple writes that stand-ins "made good business sense" for the studios because California state law "limited [her] to four hours work each day, plus the three hours of school."[23] Yet there are also indications that Temple felt entitled to be spared from any "excess" labor. Describing the creation of the four-minute "At the Codfish Ball" number for the 1936 film *Captain January*, historian Larry Billman relays how the white choreographer Jack Donohue and white dancer Buddy Ebsen "worked for three days with a dance-in," at which point, "Shirley arrived in a limousine to see the number. They performed it for her, asked if she liked it, and then suggested that she learn the routine. 'Is it set?' the seven-year old asked without batting an eye. When Ebsen admitted there might be some changes, she said, 'Let me know when it's set and I'll learn it.' Her waiting limousine whisked her away. Once the routine was set, the talented star learned it in two half-hour sessions."[24] Apocryphal or not, this tale of Temple's insistence that her unnamed dance-in take her place until the choreography was finalized—reducing Temple's rehearsal time to sixty minutes—signals the privilege the young white star enjoyed. More than just a filmic projection, the white innocence that Temple embodied on screen was preserved by the labor of her surrogate.[25]

In referring to Temple's dance-in as a "surrogate," I invoke performance studies scholar Joseph Roach's influential theorization of performance as "the process of trying out various candidates in different situations—the doomed search for originals by continuously auditioning stand-ins." For Roach, surrogation describes the reproduction of the social fabric, including the social fabric of whiteness, in a broad sense: "the enactment of cultural memory by substitution" as "survivors attempt to fit satisfactory alternates" into "the cavities created by loss through death or other forms of departure." Applied to the figure of the dance-in, surrogation becomes both literal and mundane, for the "vacancies" that stars and their proxies fill are part of the quotidian practices of film production. By a similar token, as I will address in more detail toward the end of this chapter, white film stars like Temple and Grable deployed what Roach terms the "opportunistic tactic" of forgetting that inevitably accompanies the process of surrogation. It is this forgetting that allows whiteness to conceal its impure composition of "mixtures, blends, and provisional antitypes."[26] Absent (or nearly absent) from the filmic record and thus easy to erase from memory, dance-ins enable white stars to assume their privileged embodied form as seemingly pure and seemingly original.

As discussed in this book's introduction, my approach to white embodiment is indebted to the insights of critical race scholars and Black feminists in particular. Perhaps most fundamentally, I draw on Hortense Spillers's 1987 essay "Mama's Baby, Papa's Maybe: An American Grammar Book," in which she asserts that the distinction between "body" and "flesh" is "the central one between captive and liberated subject-positions." For Spillers, the "socio-political order of the New World" entails not only "a scene of *actual* mutilation, dismemberment, and exile" for African and Indigenous peoples, but also the masking of the "severe disjunctures" of flesh underneath "the cultural seeing by skin color."[27] Building on Spillers's incisive analysis, Rizvana Bradley argues that "the aesthetic form that is 'the body' turn[s] upon a racial division of corporeality, for which blackness is the absent center. The corporeal order at once conscripts and expels the black, who becomes the negative vestibule for the spacetime of the (proper) body and its others."[28] There is no proper white body, in other words, without the violent racialization and exclusion of Blackness.

Also building on Black feminists like Spillers, as well as on legal scholar Cheryl Harris's theorization of whiteness as property,[29] American studies scholars Eva Cherniavsky has proposed that one of the key privileges of whiteness is "incorporated embodiment," the "*articulation of bodily form for the subject at risk of dispersal.*"[30] The fiction of bodily integrity, that is, upholds white supremacy by establishing the ideological grounds on which whites are protected from the incursions of capital that defined stolen Africans' entry into the United States as violable flesh.[31] Cherniavsky sees film as playing a prominent role in managing the contradictions on which the myth of white incorporation is premised. If, as she suggests, "cinema marks the inaugural appearance of the white body in the inorganic, depthless form of the commodity-image," it poses a crisis to whites' privileged incorporation. This is especially true for the white female body, which "constitutes the primary commodity-image of Hollywood cinema." Asking how "the mechanically reproduced body [can] remain 'white,'" Cherniavksy points to the "visual grammar" of film; she argues, after Dyer, that the "soft style of cinematography" produces a "white feminine 'glow'" that sets white skin in motion, thus "protect[ing] the white body from appropriation by others." The body of the star, she concludes, must be "hyperbolically white because never sufficiently white."[32]

Like Cherniavsky, I'm interested in what white female film stars can tell us about how the contradictions of white corporeal privilege are managed so as to maintain its fictive coherence and autonomy. In contrast to Cherniavsky, however, I'm interested in the contradictions that precede and predetermine the mechanically reproduced filmic image. The multiple surrogations between dance-in and star expose the white female body as *already* dispersed prior to her appearance on the screen, and dispersed across both other white bodies and expelled bodies of color.

The Ambivalence of the Index

As suggested above, the uncertainty that surrogates, especially in the case of body doubles, can create around whose body is depicted on film intersects with a recurrent concern of visual art and media theorists: the slippage between on-screen image and off-screen referent. Often arising in debates about the relationship between art and "reality," this slippage tends to be framed in terms of American semiotician Charles Sanders Peirce's concept of the "index." As art theorist Margaret Iverson has outlined, Peirce "understood the sign as a tripartite entity binding together the sign, the thing signified, and the cognition or feeling produced in the mind of the interpreter." For Peirce, the index was "the most 'forceful' type of sign: it signifies by

42 HOLLYWOOD DANCE-INS

establishing an existential or causal link to its referent, either by drawing our attention to something or by being physically impressed or affected by it."[33]

Significantly, as both Iverson and film scholar Mary Ann Doane have emphasized, there is an inherent ambivalence or contradiction within the index. Frequently thought of in a direct sense as an "imprint or trace," the index can also operate in a more figurative manner. A footprint, insofar as it implies "a material connection between sign and object," embodies the index in its more direct sense. A "pointing finger," in contrast, exemplifies the figurative dimensions of the index; here there is "always a gap between sign and object."[34] I'll return to this tension below, for it helps elucidate a corollary tension inherent in the white filmic dancing body, which bears the material traces of dance-ins' labor but capitalizes on the gap between sign and object to obscure those traces.

For now, it's worth noting that the shift in the late twentieth century from the celluloid (or "analog" or "photochemical") era of film to the dominance of digital media occasioned a certain anxiety, or "identity crisis," around the question of indexicality. In film scholar Kara Keeling's succinct explanation of the crisis, "[t]he filmic regime of the image claims to be an index of that reality, thereby encouraging identification between the image and its presumed referent, while the digital complicates that schema of identification by calling into question the very notion of a 'prefilmic reality' to which the digital image might lay claim." Yet, crucially, as Keeling goes on to say, even a glancing familiarity with representations of Blackness in cinema gives the lie to the idea of film as an index of reality. "Where images of blacks are concerned," she argues, "cinema's indexical identity has always been in crisis or, at least, it has always been interrogated and undermined."[35]

Keeling's observation helps cast this study of Hollywood dance-ins in the middle of the twentieth century as a return to a historical moment in which white bodies on film were still presumed to have stable referents. My contention is that, even in a predigital era, even in the absence of actual dance doubles, the relationship between on-screen image and off-screen materialities was far more slippery than it appeared. It is relevant here that Keeling's analysis centers Black spectators' recognition of screen images of Black bodies as fallacies.[36] Conversely, in dominant accounts of Hollywood musicals, images of white dancing stars continue to be regarded as "truthful" representations of their putatively unique physicalities.[37] Erin Brannigan, to cite one example, has argued that the dance star served as the "primary, unifying element" of film musicals and that what unified the star was her "corporeal specificity" or "gestural idiogest."[38] In other words, the Hollywood musical star's dancing body is seen as so specific and coherent that it not only "provide[d] the link between the various elements of filmic performance" but also created "a fluidity between 'life' and 'performance.'"[39] I have argued elsewhere for the concept of corporeal signature[40] and certainly don't refute the idea that dancers have distinctive ways of moving. Rather, I'm interested in investigating what and whom the notion of idiogest—the idea that the filmic image of a dancing star is a unified and direct reflection of their corporeality—might obscure. Using the example of the construction of Betty Grable's white dancing body, and building on the work of the above theorists, I probe who else Grable's iconically white and seemingly self-referential body was indexing.

"Doing Angie"

Actress, singer, and dancer Betty Grable's (1916–1973) career spanned three decades, over the course of which she appeared in eighty-three shorts and feature films.[41] The height of her fame came between 1940 and 1950, when she starred in twenty-seven films for Twentieth Century-Fox, becoming the highest-paid female star (and therefore the highest paid woman in the United States).[42] All but four of her films for Fox were shot in Technicolor, the film coloring process that produced bright, saturated colors and seemed designed "to take advantage of" Grable's whiteness, described by historian Larry Billman as "sunflower yellow blonde hair . . . sky blue eyes . . . ruby red lips and . . . peaches and cream complexion."[43] Indeed, Grable was so associated with Technicolor that Fox's publicity department had to apologize to fans each time she made a black-and-white film, and she eventually had Technicolor written into her contract.[44] Her legs reportedly insured for over a million dollars with Lloyds of London, Grable came to represent white womanhood and "all things American."[45] She also became the reigning "pin-up girl" when her photographic image was distributed to 5 million servicemen during World War II. Historian Robert Westbrook, reminding us that "the war in the Pacific was a race war," cites a *Time* magazine report that "soldiers preferred Grable to other [less blonde] pin-ups 'in direct ratio to their remoteness from civilization.'" Grable's "obvious whiteness," Westbrook argues, made her the "superior image of American womanhood."[46] In 1950, the *Saturday Evening Post* anointed her the "world's most popular blonde."[47]

Grable's popularity coincided with the peak of the Hollywood studio system, a "star machine" whose efficiency resembled a "factory system."[48] Typically, the manufacturing of stars involved finding the right "type" to insert into a "star vehicle" and then fashioning them "out of the raw material of the person,"[49] a process that required the labor of numerous personnel. It also led to a sense of stars, and women stars specifically, as fungible and interchangeable.[50] This was certainly the case for Grable, part of a succession of "Fox blondes" who followed on the heels of the 1930s "blonde bombshell" Jean Harlow at MGM.[51] Accounts of Grable's ascent typically describe her break as an "accident of history" that arose during the shooting of the 1940 musical *Down Argentine Way*. When that film's initial star, Alice Faye, Fox's leading blonde in the 1930s, was incapacitated by appendicitis, Grable was tapped to take her place.[52] Scholar Jane Gaines notes that the "theme of one blonde replacing another, slipping in when the established star falls off, was used [again] when [Marilyn] Monroe superseded Grable" as Fox's reigning blonde star.[53] As much as the star machine employed "above-the-line" forms of substitution—one marquee star being replaced by another—closer attention to Grable's dancing directs us to "below-the-line" structures of surrogation that were equally integral to the reproduction of whiteness.[54]

Throughout the 1940s, a white woman named Angela (Angie) Blue (1914–?) served as Grable's dance-in. Blue's career "ran the gamut of film dance,"[55] but she got her start performing in vaudeville with her sister Theodora (Figure 1.2). Born in Duluth, Minnesota, and billed as the "Blue Sisters—Angy and Teddy, The Dancing Cutie Kids," they toured Florida, Georgia, and the Keith Circuit in California.[56] Angie's film break came when she was cast as a chorus dancer in the 1933 film *Footlight Parade*, and she went on to appear as an uncredited dancer in a number of 1930s films. Her first interaction with Grable occurred on the set of RKO's 1934 Fred Astaire–Ginger Rogers film *The Gay Divorcee*, in which Blue had a small chorus part and Grable was featured in a number called "Let's Knock Knees." Describing the impression the future star made on her during rehearsals on set, Blue later wrote that Grable was "quick at taking direction" and "vibrant and alive in projecting the stuff she had just learned."[57] Before long, Blue would be providing some of that direction.

The Gay Divorcee was also the occasion for Blue's first encounter with Hermes Pan, the prolific white Hollywood choreographer best known for his work with Astaire. Just as Grable made an impression on Blue, so Blue made one on Pan. In an unpublished autobiography, he wrote, "The first

Figure 1.2 Undated image of "The Blue Sisters," from the personal collection of Tracy Kadlec. Angela and Theodora were first cousins of Kadlec's grandmother. The sister on the left bears a decided resemblance to Betty Grable.

time I saw Angie Blue was in the early 1930s in a chorus audition lineup. She was wearing a bikini bathing suit and a live marmoset on her shoulder. Her appearance was so outrageous, I hired her just because I thought she'd be fun. And she was. Her devil-may-care attitude brought a lot of laughter and good spirits to years of rehearsal and film work."[58] Pan considered Blue a

46 HOLLYWOOD DANCE-INS

"marvelous dancer" with a "quirky gaminesque quality," and by 1937 he hired her as his assistant.[59] The two continued to collaborate until 1957, making some eighteen films together for RKO, Fox, and MGM.[60] Particularly useful to Pan, Blue was, in his words, "pliable." He recalled, "I could grab her by the hand and throw her into position and she'd just do it.... I could turn her around and whip her like a piece of clay and she would fall into things. She was like putty."[61]

According to Billman, 1937 also marked the first time Pan used Blue as a dance-in, initially in support of the white star Joan Fontaine for the RKO film *A Damsel in Distress*.[62] When Pan began creating choreography for Grable for the Fox film *Moon over Miami* (1941), the blonde Blue was a natural choice to serve as Grable's dance-in. The two women subsequently developed a close friendship that lasted for years.[63] Reflecting on their relationship in a 1949 *Photoplay* article, Blue wrote, "For almost eight years I have lived with Betty Grable in all her working hours." Blue counted herself among Grable's closest confidantes on and off the film set, a confidence that once entailed keeping Grable's pregnancy a secret from the rest of the studio.[64]

While records of Blue's work for RKO and MGM are spotty or no longer extant, contracts and memorandums between Twentieth Century-Fox's studio executives, housed in Fox's archives, show an escalation in Blue's duties over time. A legal document dated June 28, 1944, for example, explains, "Between 1937 and 1941 Miss Blue was hired from time to time to work in various pictures as a skater and dancer along with other skaters and dancers at the regular union scale rates for such work." On March 2, 1942, Fox put Blue on the payroll as an assistant dance director, ushering in a period of more steady employment for her. Her starting salary in that role was $75 a week, an amount that was increased to $100 a week in early 1943, "based on the fact that she had meritoriously performed her duties as Assistant Dance Director." The document goes on to request approval to pay Blue an additional $16.67 a day for "four days of extra services" for appearing on screen as a dancer in the 1944 film *Irish Eyes Are Smiling* (in the number titled "Bessie in a Bustle").[65] Blue remained under contract at Fox as an assistant dance director until 1954, in which capacity she supported Pan and other male choreographers, including Seymour Felix and Billy Daniels.[66] While Blue's salary gradually increased with time (a June 23, 1948, memorandum from Fox's executive manager puts her weekly salary at $150),[67] male dance directors were paid seven to eight times that amount.[68]

The Fox archives contain only one reference to Blue's work as a dance-in, though the role is described as a stand-in. An interoffice correspondence memo dated June 2, 1944, requests a $25 per week pay raise for Blue (subject to approval by the War Labor Board) to account for the fact that she "will be required to stand-in for Betty Grable in all of the musical numbers involved in our production 'Diamond Horseshoe' besides continuing her regular duties as Assistant Dance Director."[69] According to the studio, in Blue's initial days, those "regular duties" began as "the drilling of chorus ensembles" but expanded to include the "creating and evolving [of] new dance routines and the teaching of the same to chorus ensembles," an expansion that involved "creative work" and "demand[ed] initiative and imagination."[70] From Fox's legal and administrative standpoint, then, the work of an assistant dance director was distinct from that of a dance-in or stand-in, the former consisting of conceiving and transmitting choreography and the latter taking a star's place in advance of filming musical numbers. In practice, however, the nature of Blue's work was amorphous and wide-ranging. Blue, for her part, listed her duties as Pan's assistant as "working out, with my boss, all of Betty's dance routines, rehearsing her in them and checking the final performance when it goes on film."[71] Her account is notably more extensive than Fox's, encompassing the work of generating choreography for the star (not just the chorus) and vetting Grable's final performance for the cameras.

In a 1983 interview about his process of creating film numbers for Astaire and Rogers, film scholar Dan Georgakas asked Pan how much "input" the "women dancers" had in devising dance sequences. "Very little," Pan replied, explaining that "most of the time they weren't around." "It seemed easier," he elaborated, "to work things out ahead of time and then call them in later. Even when they were available, we would often work with a dance-in. I would work with Angie Blue and then Fred would work with her and then the star would come in and Angie would show her what to do."[72] The contradiction in Pan's remarks here is striking. First noting that women dancers "weren't around," he immediately describes how critical his work with Blue was. Such was the paradox of the dance-in's simultaneous ubiquity and marginalization. Notwithstanding Pan's elision, both he and Blue confirm how blurry the lines between dance-in and choreographic assistant were.

Where Grable was concerned, Blue's labor was even more essential, for, like Shirley Temple before her, Grable preferred to learn choreography as late as possible. "Betty Grable hated to rehearse and admitted it," Pan told biographer Franceschina. "She'd say, 'Oh, just show it to me and I'll do it.'"

48 HOLLYWOOD DANCE-INS

Consequently, "working with Betty Grable involved Pan and Angie Blue creating complete routines ahead of time and teaching them to her, much in the same way they might work with a dancing chorus."[73] Though Grable trained in dance from an early age and danced in nearly all of her films, assessments of her dancing were decidedly mixed. To my eye, her tapping in the "Let's Knock Knees" in *The Gay Divorcee* looks proficient, but Pan once claimed that she "really was not a great tap dancer and she couldn't do great ballet." "But she could move," he elaborated, "and she had very beautiful legs, and . . . [h]er color was beautiful."[74] Never one to inflate her abilities, Grable maintained that she was only an average dancer, and she was content to just do "what she was told."[75]

For Grable and for Blue, creating, learning, and performing choreography was therefore a process of dual impersonation.[76] When Blue and Pan worked out routines for Grable, Blue would "be Grable," assuming the role of the star. Once the choreography was set, "Betty Grable was . . . instructed by Pan to 'do Angie.'" In fact, a 1991 article about Pan reported that "the famous Grable itty-bitty walk as well as the bathing suit, hands on hips, over the shoulder pin-up of the 1940s was simply her 'doing Angie.'"[77] This is a rather remarkable revelation in its inversion of the presumed relationship between star/original and stand-in/copy. Among the unofficial "rules" for stand-ins listed in a 1938 article about Bette Davis's stand-in, Sally Sage, was the following: "Study your star. Be able to copy her walk and her stance."[78] In Grable's case, by contrast, the star's job was to study and imitate her surrogate.[79] Though this is the sole reference to the "famous Grable itty-bitty walk" that I have come across, the moniker implies it was considered, at least by some, to be one of her most distinctive moves.[80] The contention that Grable's signature step was just Grable "doing Angie" recasts a gesture of self-referentiality as a gesture of emulation.

As indicated, there was a multidirectionality to this emulation. An anecdote relayed by Blue in the article she penned for *Photoplay* makes this patently clear. Describing her first job with Grable on the 1941 film *Moon over Miami*, Blue recalls how "Betty came in, in the morning, to learn a routine Hermes Pan and I had spent weeks working out." "In an hour," Blue reports, "she knew it as well as I did." She continues:

> At noon, word came down that the producer would come on the set in the afternoon to look at the number. "Angie had better show it," Hermes decided. After all, Betty had barely learned the steps. At two o'clock, the

producer came in, followed by a retinue of all the most important people on the lot. "Angie!" the assistant director bellowed. I was sitting next to Betty, muttering not so much to her as to myself, "I can't, I just can't, I'm too scared."

"I'll do it, kid," Betty put in at this point and whirled onto the set. She did the whole routine with great style, feeling no pain.[81]

In this narration, Grable saves the day by filling in for Blue when Blue's nerves get the better of her. This is, minimally, a double act of surrogation: Blue fills the vacancy left by Grable in rehearsals; Grable fills the vacancy left by Blue for studio executives. Even prior to this moment, there is both an exactness and a muddiness to performance-as-surrogation: Grable inserts her body into the choreographic score Blue helped establish, even as Blue rehearses that score as if she were Grable.

The *Photoplay* article ran with a rare photo of the two rehearsing together for an unknown number (Figure 1.3). Grable, on the viewer's left, appears to be in costume, with a large boa draped over her extended arms, while Blue wears trousers and a blouse. Both angle their bodies away from their extended right leg as they look at each other and smile. The accompanying caption reads, "For Betty and Angie, rehearsing a dance routine, friendship is set to sweet music." On the whole, the article reinforces the women's closeness,

Figure 1.3 Betty Grable (left) and Angie Blue (right) from a 1949 issue of *Photoplay*.

50   HOLLYWOOD DANCE-INS

though at times Blue reminds us of the power differential between them. At the end of the piece, Blue credits Grable with saving her from receiving a pink slip "when the axe began swinging" at Fox in the late 1940s. Grable, she surmises, must have gone directly "to the front office and sewed [Blue's] job up tight."[82] Blue highlights the incident as an example of the star's munificence, but we can just as easily read it as an acknowledgment of how vital Blue was to Grable.

The claim that Grable's iconic over-the-shoulder pose was an impression of Blue only amplifies Blue's value to Grable, for this was the shot of Grable that was distributed as a pin-up poster to American servicemen across the globe (Figure 1.1). There is, it should be noted, no shortage of origin stories for this photo. As Grable biographer Doug Warren relays, Grable herself told various untrue versions, including that she faced away from the camera to conceal a pregnancy. Fox's official still photographer Frank Polowney, who took the photo, maintained that the idea for the shot came to him when he happened to catch Grable glancing back over her shoulder as she was walking away.[83] Scholar Jane Gaines, who determined that the photo was taken during the shooting of *Sweet Rosie O'Grady* (1943) and first used in publicity for *Coney Island* (also 1943), points out that the over-the-shoulder pose "was, in fact, one of the positions in the popular 'language' of pin-up art" throughout the 1940s, used to "accentuat[e] the back side and . . . produc[e] a physical expression of coyness."[84] According to *The Telegraph* and Rob Easterlea, the former director of Twentieth Century-Fox's photo archives, the pin-up photograph of Grable was also the product of airbrushing. Easterlea is quoted as saying, "They airbrushed out a garter she was wearing on her left leg, to make her look less slutty, and enhanced the shadows under her left butt, to make it really pop. So you're left with healthy-as-apple-pie sexuality, which GIs went crazy for when the United States entered the war."[85] Whatever the circumstances of the shot's creation, because Blue assisted Pan and Grable on both *Sweet Rosie O'Grady* and *Coney Island*, Grable was surely in the habit of imitating Blue at the time the photo was taken. If there is even a chance that Grable was "doing Angie" when she looked back at the camera over her raised right shoulder, hands on hips, weight shifted slightly over her right leg, then it's equally possible that Grable's most Grable-like image was a reproduction of the corporeality of her largely uncredited dance-in.

This prospect not only underscores the mediated, composite nature of whiteness but also calls to mind film scholar Sean Redmond's proposal that whiteness, in its simultaneous ordinariness and ability to evade detection as a racial signifier, operates as an "invisible presence that only ever really leaves a trace, an imprint or an echo of itself on the power structures and symbols of the world." "*Whiteness is a photograph of itself*," he asserts.[86] The pin-up image of Grable would seem to directly support this assertion. But Grable's dependence on Blue invites us to press further on what Redmond, drawing on the work of John Ellis and Roland Barthes, terms the "photo-effect of whiteness." As Ellis explains, Barthes's concept of the "photo-effect" names "the specific and poignant way in which photographs create their sense of reality" by making images that "occurred in another time and place" appear "astoundingly . . . present" despite their absence.[87] Extending the photo-effect to Grable, her pin-up image appears to reference a prior moment in which her live body struck an over-the-shoulder pose. But it may well reference a moment (or moments) prior still, in which Blue struck an over-the-shoulder pose, observed and then imitated by Grable. To the extent that the pin-up image bears any traces of Blue, it highlights the indexical ambiguity that inheres in whiteness-as-photograph. There is no single or singular "her" in the photograph, no single or singular absence or presence, and no single or singular prior moment. Grable's photographic and filmic whiteness index Grable's insured flesh as well as Blue's corporeal shape, Grable's imitation of Blue as well as Blue's imitation of Grable, not to mention a more generalized lexicon of pin-up poses. And lest we are tempted to locate the traces of Blue's presence in the silhouettes that also appear in the photo—a literalization of the stand-in's role as the "star's shadows"[88]—those shadows, as we shall see, index additional unseen bodies. Modifying Redmond, we might say that whiteness is a photograph of multiple corporealities that must be concealed in order to cohere as the singularity of "itself."

"Bogus Brunettes"

As much as Blue's undercompensated and barely credited labor propped up Grable's iconic whiteness, it would be a mistake to gloss over the privileges her own whiteness afforded her. In addition to benefiting from her physical resemblance to Grable, which helped her secure employment as Grable's dance-in, Blue profited from Hollywood's racist preference for casting white dancers in ethnic drag over dancers of color. This is well captured in an episode described in a 1940 article in the *Coshocton Tribune* and repeated in Franceschina's biography of Pan. Titled "Greeks' Dancing Wins War, Claim," the article reports that Pan, who shortened his name from Panagiotopolos for the "convenience of 20th Century-Fox bookkeepers," attributed Italy's recent failed invasion of Greece to the superiority of Greeks' dancing. Tongue in cheek, the article notes that Pan himself had recently lost a more personal fight, "instituted and won by a couple of blondes, the Misses Angela Blue and Pearlie May Norton." The piece continues:

> Angela and Pearlie May are movie dancers, who haven't had work for six long months because they were blondes. It seems all the big musical movies lately have had Latin American motifs. Either that, or South Sea island settings.
>
> Pearlie May and Angela, upon hearing that Pan was casting a chorus for another South American picture, "The Road to Rio," burst into his office, pinned him against the wall, and made him listen.
>
> Upshot was that they got jobs. So did numerous other blondes. They'll all wear black wigs as a concession to the movies' ideas of how Latin dancers ought to look.
>
> For six weeks now Pan and his chorus of bogus brunettes have been working eight hours a day on their three big dance numbers. These will total exactly five minutes on screen.[89]

As the piece suggests, the late 1930s and early 1940s saw an uptick in film musicals set in Latin America and the Pacific Islands, a response to shifting U.S. geopolitical interests. On one hand, the "Good Neighbor" policy and Hollywood efforts to court Latin American audiences when World War II cut off access to European markets led to the "flooding" of U.S. screens with "films utilizing Latin stars, locales, and historical heroes."[90] Meanwhile, scholar Delia Malia Caparoso Konzett has shown, Hollywood's fascination with the South Pacific, dating back to the late nineteenth century and coinciding with and justifying U.S. expansionism, produced an "endless series of films" that took Hawai'i and the South Seas as a backdrop. Spanning a range of genres, these cinematic representations included a spate of fantasy films and musicals in the lead-up to World War II that featured an "exotic, primitive, and mythical Hawaii." Some of these films did cast Latinx, Asian

American, and Pacific Islander talent in featured roles and as chorus dancers and extras. But in the vast majority of cases, "Hollywood rewarded its white performers handsomely for impersonating and performing the cultural Other."[91] The "concession" of black wigs, that is to say, was standard practice in an industry where blackface had not entirely disappeared and brownface, yellowface, and redface were still accepted conventions.

There is no small degree of irony, then, in Blue's and Norton's claim of blondeness as a disadvantage, a claim that has the familiar ring of white replacement conspiracy theory. The irony is compounded by the fact that, as the *Coshocton* article affirms, the women's bid to land jobs for themselves in the "South America picture" was successful. Released in 1941 as *That Night in Rio*, the film stars Grable's blonde predecessor Alice Faye and features Brazilian samba singer Carmen Miranda. Blue assisted Pan on the film, including on the opening number, "Chica Chica Boom Chic,"[92] an example par excellence of the kind of stylized, fantastical "Latin number" that theater scholar Brian Herrera has identified as the product of the Good Neighbor Era.[93] The number opens on Miranda, wearing her trademark *baiana* costume complete with fruit-adorned turban, singing in Portuguese on a stage set designed to look like Rio de Janeiro.[94] She's joined by Don Ameche, who arrives by car and sings of sending "felicitations to our South American relations." An editing cut transitions us to a close-up of a drum, and when the camera pulls out, we are transported to the floor show of a casino. Another cut shifts our focus from the men percussionists to a pair of dancers dressed in "tropical" attire, circling their torsos with one arm raised above their heads (see Figure 1.4). The woman in the pair appears to be Blue, a bit of brown hair peeking out of her headpiece. The camera continues to pull back to reveal a full ensemble of sixteen light-skinned, dark-haired couples who shimmy, shake their hips, and do a version of the samba before being rejoined by Miranda and Ameche.[95]

For stars and supporting players alike, whiteness was thus maintained via several overlapping modes of surrogation. Just as Grable's filmography is full of minstrelized roles—including in *Song of the Islands* (1942), in which she performed a "hula-inspired" dance, and in *Coney Island* (1943) and *The Dolly Sisters* (1945), in which she appeared in blackface[96]—so too did white chorus dancers "stand in" for and take the place of dancers of color.[97] The fact that Blue served as assistant dance director and dance-in for Grable when she engaged in these racial impersonations multiplies the acts of substitution

Figure 1.4 Screen capture of Angie Blue and unknown dancer in "Chica Chica Boom Chic" from *That Night in Rio* (1941).

and the referents of Grable's filmic body even further. Accounts of how the film industry engineered the reproduction of whiteness must therefore include practices like "doing Angie" without forgetting who else Hollywood's white dancers were "doing."

The Other Betty

Considering how much the dancing that filled Hollywood screens at midcentury owed to African diasporic dance styles,[98] it is perhaps inevitable that attending to Grable's connections to Blue also leads us to the "Black presence in [the] white family tree."[99] As this book argues, the dance-in was key to a racialized and gendered corporeal ecosystem that fueled the production and reproduction of white film stars' images. Though my focus is on these largely forgotten assistants, surrogates, and intermediaries, Pan's comparison of Blue to "putty" is a reminder of how much power choreographers had within this system. And the corporealities of the white men choreographers who dominated Hollywood's "Golden" Age were no less products of reproductions, including cross-racial ones, than were those of stars and dance-ins.[100] A 1991 profile of Pan in the *Dancing Times* opens with the following:

> In 1915, when Hermes Pan was six years old, the family mammy, a big black woman who was called Aunt Betty, took the boy home with her one night to her apartment in the black ghetto of Nashville known, as it was in many cities in the American South, as Black Bottom. It was there that the child was first exposed to what was called "gut-bucket" jazz and the shuffles and foot-slapping dancing of the local black Americans. His reaction was an exhilaration which he recalled seventy years later, his eyes still lighting up with joy at the memory, as nothing short of "sensual." That was Pan's first exposure to what he knew as "dance."[101]

This is by now a familiar story in American dance, proving once again Brenda Dixon Gottschild's argument about the Africanist influences on the development of all manner of U.S. dance genres.[102] The presence of a "mammy" in the narrative of Pan's dance origins adds yet another layer to the story.

A photograph of an infant Pan seated on the lap of his "Aunt" Betty, likely taken around 1910, appears in Franceschina's biography of Pan (Figure 1.5).[103] The image, along with Pan's recollections, force us to confront the centrality of another kind of surrogation to U.S. racial formations: the long history of Black women serving as surrogate mothers to white children. They also return us to Spillers, whose essay "Mama's Baby, Papa's Maybe" opens by citing the litany of ways Black women in the United States have been marked, including as "Aunty." Such "confounded identities," Spillers argues, construct bodily tropes out of Black flesh and deprive Black women of individualized personhood.[104]

In her critical analysis of shifting depictions of the mammy figure in U.S. culture, Kimberly Wallace-Sanders writes that the "mammy's body serves as a tendon between the races, connecting the muscle of African American slave labor with the skeletal power structure of white southern aristocracy."[105] In like manner, Aunt Betty serves as the connective tissue between Black surrogate motherhood and the structures that enabled white reproductions of African American dance. For, as the anecdote about Pan's exposure to jazz dance goes on to note, Pan's first dance lesson entailed "imitating the steps" he and his sister "learned from the family's black

Figure 1.5 "Aunt" Betty and an infant Hermes Pan, circa 1910. From the Collection of Vasso Pan Meade.

houseboy," who, according to some reports, was Betty's biological son, Sam Clark (Figure 1.6).[106] Elsewhere, Pan described Clark as "a black kid who was our houseboy and drove for us.... He was a little older than I was and he used to teach me all kinds of shuffles, the Black Bottom and the Charleston. From these beginnings, I got my show business start." Pan thus quite directly traced his show business career back to Clark. As he reported in an interview, on his first day working with Astaire, when asked if he had any ideas to fill out a solo tap dance, "something clicked in my mind and I remembered a break

Figure 1.6 Sam Clark, Hermes Pan's first dance instructor. From the Collection of Vasso Pan Meade.

58   HOLLYWOOD DANCE-INS

that Sam Clark had taught me back in Tennessee. I showed it to Fred and he loved it. After that he always called for me."[107]

Pan's case thus makes it possible to draw a line between the two Bettys: the Greek American Pan family's Black domestic employee (not afforded a last name) and the white film star. It also underscores the cross-racial antecedents of the surrogation that characterized the star/dance-in relationship. In "doing Angie," Grable was imitating a white dance-in whose corporeality was shaped in part by a white choreographer whose corporeality was shaped in part by Black dancers. Reproduction and surrogation all the way down. Looked at through this lens, Grable's famous pin-up posture—arms akimbo, leaning into one hip, shoulders twisted—becomes not only a coy, come-hither pose but an asymmetrical, Africanist one.[108] Awareness of Pan's Aunt Betty, in turn, encourages us to train our eyes on still other Black surrogates who were lurking in the shadows, simultaneously indexed and masked by filmic images of white star dancing bodies.

Marie Bryant and Betty's Buns

As Grable's career continued, the influence of Black dancers on her corporeality became increasingly direct. A three-part 1950 article in *Ebony* magazine discloses the pivotal behind-the-scenes role that the African American artist Marie Bryant (1919–1978) played in Grable's later dance performances.[109] A supremely talented dancer, as well as a singer, Bryant toured with Duke Ellington; danced in the chorus of films with Lena Horne, one of Hollywood's only midcentury Black stars; assisted some of Hollywood's most influential choreographers; and taught at dance schools run by Katherine Dunham and Eugene Loring.[110] Ellington, Gene Kelly, and Hollywood dance director Nick Castle separately described her as one of the best dancers they had ever seen.[111] Evidence of her skill survives on screen, including in an uncredited role with Harold Nicholas in the 1944 film *Carolina Blues*.[112] While the next chapter offers a fuller account of Bryant's place in Hollywood's corporeal ecosystem and a more thorough analysis of *Ebony*'s feature on her, a brief discussion of her work with Grable is useful here for expanding our understanding of the reproductions that shaped Grable's filmic image.

According to *Ebony*, Grable and her husband Harry James first became aware of Bryant when Bryant was headlining at the Los Angeles Cotton Club. Grable subsequently asked her to help stage dances for the 1950 film

Wabash Avenue, whose choreography is credited to the white dance director Billy Daniels. Grable and Bryant continued to work together on the 1951 film *Meet Me after the Show*, on which Daniels and white jazz choreographer Jack Cole served as dance directors, both of whom Bryant assisted.[113] The third part of the feature in *Ebony* explains the nature of Bryant's work as assistant to Daniels: "Marie, Daniels and his other assistant, Frances Grant, report on a picture, create the choreography for the stars. Then the three of them block out the steps, acting in place of the stars, who stand by, watching, then learning the dance routines."[114] As described here, Bryant and Daniels's white assistant Grant collaborated with Daniels on creating choreography and demonstrating it for its intended stars. Dance directors and their assistants, in other words, generated and transmitted choreography by "acting in place of the stars," a process of surrogation in keeping with that of a dance-in.

This operation is made especially clear when we compare one of the photos that appeared in the *Ebony* feature with a screen capture of a scene from the film (see Figures 1.7 and 1.8). The photograph shows Bryant and Daniels dancing in profile, butt cheek to butt cheek, facing away from but looking back toward one another, in the "My Honey Man" number in *Wabash Avenue* (misidentified as "Buns Away" in the caption). Both dancers stand on their backstage leg with their downstage knee and hip raised and their arms out in front of them. In the film version, the moment occurs just as the tempo of the number speeds up and the two dancers transition from facing downstage to facing stage left.[115] Comparing photograph to film confirms that, just as Blue danced Grable's role in rehearsals with Pan, so too did Bryant dance Grable's role in rehearsal with Daniels. Once the choreography was set, Grable inserted herself into the choreography mapped out and modeled by Bryant.

According to Daniels, Bryant's training efforts left their mark on one of Grable's body parts in particular. "During work at 20th," he told *Ebony*, "Marie was teaching Betty Grable a hard routine. After a couple of tries, Betty started to do such a fine dance that Marie suddenly yelled at her, 'That's it, Betty! Those buns are great! Oh those buns!'"[116] At a time when the Arthur Murray Dance School warned (white) ballroom dancers not to emphasize the backside, and amid a legacy of white objectification of Black female bottoms, Bryant reverses the white gaze as she works to cultivate an explicitly Africanist aesthetic in Grable.[117] To be sure, Grable's dancing looks notably different in several numbers in *Wabash Avenue* than it does in *Coney Island*, of which the former was a remake. Whereas Grable is mostly flinging limbs

Billy Daniels, top Hollywood dance director, hired Marie for his team teaching movie stars dance routines for pictures. They go through "Buns Away" number taught Betty Grable for the film *On Wabash Avenue*.

Figure 1.7 Marie Bryant and Billy Daniels from the April 1950 issue of *Ebony Magazine*. Photo by Larry Barbier. Published by permission of the Barbier Estate.

Figure 1.8 Screen capture of Betty Grable and Billy Daniels in *Wabash Avenue* (1950).

in "Put Your Arms around Me, Honey," the opening number of *Coney Island*, her movements in both "I Wish I Could Shimmy Like My Sister Kate" and "My Honey Man" in *Wabash Avenue* are more contained and finely articulated, allowing her to isolate different body parts with more precision. If Grable's legs comprised her most Grable-like (and therefore her most valuable) feature, the way she used them was hardly self-indexical.

Notably, Blue was also employed as an assistant on *Wabash Avenue* and *Meet Me after the Show*.[118] The extent to which Blue and Bryant interacted on these films is unknown. It was commonplace for different choreographers and coaches to work with stars on different numbers on a given film, and film musicals were typically shot over the course of several months. As I address in the next chapter, moreover, segregation limited Bryant's access to Hollywood studio sets. Still, it seems highly likely that Blue and Bryant knew of one another and distinctly possible that they crossed paths at some point as assistant dance directors and Grable's coaches. The difficulty of proving or disproving that crossing is a reminder of the archive's silence about the relations among and between historical figures who occupy the margins. Yet even archival silences can speak: the fact that the Fox archives contain an individual file for Blue but "no individual deal file" for Bryant[119] attests to the unevenness of power within the margins.

The filmic record itself contains moments in which the unequal status of the women who shaped Grable's corporeality is made fleetingly if glaringly evident. As I've indicated, as significant as their off-screen roles were, Blue and Bryant also had small roles in front of the camera, Blue in particular appearing in the choruses of a number of Grable films. There are two notable instances, in two different films, in which Grable briefly but conspicuously, if you know to look for them, shares screen time with each of them.

For Blue, this moment occurs in the 1944 film *Pin-Up Girl*, in which she had a featured though uncredited role dancing with choreographer Pan. In what has been described as an "apache blues number"[120] (though they are not technically dancing an apache dance), Blue, wearing a brunette wig—presumably to distinguish her from Grable—saunters on the stage-within-the-film and begins a seductive dance with Pan, before Grable begins to sing from a balcony, sending Blue off stage left (see Figure 1.9).[121] The exchange calls to mind Roach's observation that surrogation often produces anxiety that can materialize in the form of a "momentary self-consciousness" in

Figure 1.9 Screen capture of Angie Blue and Hermes Pan in *Pin-Up Girl* (1944).

performance in which an "alien double ... appear[s] in memory only to disappear." We might then say that the footage momentarily remembers Blue as Grable's surrogate so that we can forget that Grable was "doing Angie." That Grable's dancing is somewhat stiffer than Blue's only highlights the way the surrogate's fit can never "be exact."[122]

Bryant's on-screen performance with Grable, meanwhile, demonstrates that not all moments of self-consciousness about surrogates play out identically. In addition to helping choreograph *Wabash Avenue*, Bryant shares the screen with Grable in a credited but nondancing role, as Elsa, the personal maid to Grable's character, Ruby. The star and dancer/coach appear together in three scenes in the middle of the film: one in Grable's dressing room as Grable is preparing to perform (Figure 1.10), one backstage just before Grable takes her place on stage, and one backstage just after Grable's performance has ended.[123] In the latter, Bryant greets Grable's character with a fawning "Oh, Miss Ruby" as Grable thrusts her bouquet of flowers at Bryant and walks off stage right past her. Bryant's presence here is so brief that it's

Figure 1.10 Screen capture of Marie Bryant, Betty Grable, and Victor Mature in *Wabash Avenue* (1950). Bryant plays Grable's character's maid, Elsa.

64   HOLLYWOOD DANCE-INS

easily missed. Grable doesn't even make eye contact with her. There is a near violence to this one-sided transmission—the hand-off of flowers from Grable to Bryant, Bryant's unreturned gaze—that intimates an urgency to forgetting that Bryant once danced in Grable's place and helped mold Grable's body on this very film.[124]

In addition to highlighting the divergent ways surrogates could be remembered and forgotten, this pair of scenes returns us to the ambivalence of indexicality. Recalling Keeling's insight about the falsity of film images of Blackness in the predigital era, the misremembering of Bryant as maid rather than dance coach confirms the failure of film to index the off-screen relationship between Bryant and Grable. At the same time, recalling the simultaneous figurative and material registers of indexicality emphasized by Iverson and Doane, we might see these flickers of shared screen time between Grable and Blue and Bryant as revealing something fundamental about how whiteness maintains its fictive corporeal autonomy. Appearing alongside her off-screen double, Grable's on-screen image metaphorically "points a finger" toward another woman, a symbolic nod to the star–dance-in exchanges that preceded and mediated the white star's filmic dancing body. Yet that same nod may also divert our attention away from the footprint-like indexicality of Grable's filmic body: away from the ways her screen image bears the direct, material traces ("doing Angie"; "Oh those buns!") of the corporeal instruction she received from these women. Put another way, what the camera briefly establishes as a relationship between Grable and Blue and Grable and Bryant also records the women as corporeally separate and distinct. And this is perhaps in part what enables Grable's image to *seem to be* a faithful representation of her own physicality, to appear to be a photograph of only itself. Gesturing briefly to her surrogates, Grable conceals the extent to which her bodily image is a reproduction of their corporealities, thereby preserving the semblance of self-referentiality.

Under this light, the white incorporation that Cherniavsky theorizes as the privileged form of embodiment is clearly a myth, one that the technology of the dance-in both explodes and preserves. The body of the white female dancing film star is not just at risk of dispersal; it is already dispersed, already an assemblage of others' terpsichorean motions and teachings. Seen through the lens of Hollywood at midcentury, the privilege of white corporeality lies simultaneously in the right to reproduce others' motions and the right to conceal those reproductions. It lies simultaneously in the right to occupy the position that others have saved for you and to displace those who have stood and danced in your place. It lies in the right to choose when to return your surrogate's gaze and when to refuse to see. It lies in the right to appear autonomous and original when the flesh that your own body indexes is staring you in the face.

2

Marie Bryant, Black Reproductive Labor, and White Parasitism

It's November 2018, and I'm at the University of Southern California's Cinematic Arts Library, paging through production records for the MGM musical *On the Town* (1949). Among the script, production memos, and interoffice communications are the assistant director's (AD) daily progress reports, which detail who was on set and for how long on each day of production. The names of the white stars and their assistants dominate, but also listed are some of the white chorus dancers who appear in numbers like "Miss Turnstiles" and "A Day in New York." And then I stumble upon this tidbit: on August 10, 1949, on a day in which production was dedicated to "loops only," two performers appeared on set between 2:45 and 4:00 p.m. to post-dub their vocals: Florence Bates, who played the Russian ballet instructor of the film's female lead, and "Marie Bruant."[1]

"Bruant," of course, is a typo, an accidental or careless misspelling of "Bryant." As discussed in the previous chapter, Marie Bryant (1917–1978) was a dancer and singer, as well as an assistant dance director and coach to Hollywood stars like Betty Grable in the 1940s and 1950s.[2] Although she appears briefly in a number of other films, including in the background with Lena Horne in *Broadway Rhythm* (1944) and *Ziegfeld Follies* (1945), and in bit parts in *They Live by Night* (1948) and *Wabash Avenue* (1950), to my knowledge no other source has documented her performance in *On the Town*.[3] The finding of her (misspelled) name in the archives sends me running back to the film. And now that I am looking for her, there she is—unmistakably—at the 1:05:00 mark, dancing as part of the chorus line in the film's Club Dixieland scene (Figure 2.1). Her performance lasts all of thirteen seconds. She smiles radiantly as she swings her hips, makes a vocal whoop, does a spin in front of Gene Kelly, Vera-Ellen, and the movie's other white stars, and then vanishes from the screen. I rewind and rewatch, rewind and rewatch. In light of what I have learned about Bryant's shaping of star bodies, her fleeting, smiling appearance in *On the Town* takes on an uncanny aura.[4]

Hollywood Dance-ins and the Reproduction of Bodies. Anthea Kraut, Oxford University Press.
© Oxford University Press 2025. DOI: 10.1093/oso/9780197789667.003.0003

Figure 2.1 Screen capture of Marie Bryant, far left, in the "Club Dixieland" scene in *On the Town* (1949).

Bryant is present in the archives for *On the Town* only because her vocal whoop required her to return to the MGM studio to record her sound—the "looping" referenced in the AD report. This chapter performs its own kind of looping, doubling back to Bryant to provide a fuller account of her intercorporeal relationships with Hollywood stars. Though I have found no evidence that she was ever employed as a dance-in per se, she was a seemingly ubiquitous presence behind the scenes of midcentury Hollywood musicals, working alongside dance directors and stars alike. As a former neighbor of hers put it, "[A]lmost every dancer from [Fred] Astair [sic] through Cyd Charisse was coached by Marie."[5] While a complete list of the recipients of Bryant's coaching is not recoverable, Vera-Ellen, Bob Hope, Paulette Goddard, Ava Gardner, Lena Horne, Debbie Reynolds, Mitzi Gaynor, Marge and Gower Champion, Maria Cole, and Pearl Bailey, in addition to Grable, Astaire, and Charisse, would all be on it.

Dedicating an entire chapter of this book to a Black woman who was not technically a dance-in may not be an obvious move, but it is a deliberate one. Conceptually, it enables a more expansive consideration of the unseen

68   HOLLYWOOD DANCE-INS

reproductive labor that facilitated the construction of star bodies. If dance-ins exemplify this reproductive labor especially vividly, they also broaden our awareness of how commonplace acts of doubling and substitution were in the making of Hollywood dancing bodies. Methodologically, devoting a chapter to Bryant helps counterbalance the hierarchies of both Hollywood and the archives, two systems that have been and continue to be skewed toward the white and the powerful. Though white dancers served as dance-ins for stars of color (as was the case with Becky Varno for Nancy Kwan, to be discussed in Chapter 5), and light-skinned dancers of color served as dance-ins for white stars (as was the case with Alex Romero for Gene Kelly, to be discussed in Chapter 4), darker-skinned dancers were not, to my knowledge, ever employed as dance-ins for white stars. There were, to be sure, Black stars who danced on screen in midcentury Hollywood, as the scholarship of Donald Bogle, Charlene Regester, Constance Valis Hill, Miriam Petty, Susie Trenka, Brynn Shiovitz, and Pamela Krayenbuhl has documented.[6] They too were supported by dance-ins, at least occasionally.[7] Nevertheless, as I address in this chapter, Hollywood's institutionalized racism meant fewer opportunities for Black stars and below-the-line Black dancers alike. From a historical perspective, then, the fraught nature of Bryant's position in Hollywood—her proximity to and influence on so many stars combined with her exclusion and marginalization—makes her an indispensable figure for elucidating the racial structures that governed Hollywood's corporeal ecosystem at midcentury. Given what I argue was her centrality to that system, it is only fitting that she serve as the subject of her own chapter rather than be confined to a supporting role for Betty Grable.

Remembering Bryant

Even as I call attention to Bryant's marginalization, I want to be careful to avoid creating the impression that she was ever "lost." Credited or not, her appearances in the films listed above, in addition to many others, make her a part of the film historical record. Film and dance historians like Donald Bogle, Jeanine Basinger, Debra Levine, Brenda Dixon Gottschild, Susie Trenka, and Robert Jackson have all written about her, and she has an entry in *Notable Black American Women, Book II*.[8] In 1975, three years before her death, choreographer Alvin Ailey paid homage to Bryant in *The Mooche*, his tribute to four Black women jazz artists, set to Duke Ellington's music.[9]

Though never lost to history, Bryant has been susceptible to partial, missing, and mis-attribution.[10] As mentioned in the previous chapter, while several sources cite Bryant as an assistant to jazz dance choreographer Jack Cole, I have located no archival documentation of her work with him—a reminder of the archive's racialized silences.[11] As recently as 2014, in an echo of the typo in *On the Town*'s production records, a comprehensive volume titled "Hollywood Films Featuring Broadcast Personalities and Programs" misidentifies her as "Julie Bryant."[12] Even in her own time, some raised concern about the public's failure to recognize her achievements. Writing in the *Chicago Defender* following a press screening of *Wabash Avenue* (1950) (discussed at greater length in the previous chapter), critic Dolores Calvin lamented that Bryant "lost her credit without any reason that we can see or understand." Calvin worried that "the average layman, not knowing of her great talent" will mistake her for "just another maid," overlooking her contributions to the film's dancing. "Maybe that's just Hollywood," Calvin concluded.[13] Bryant's death from cancer in 1978 only magnified the stakes of film's inadequacy as a record of her creative labor.[14] In the wake of her passing, Dale Wasserman, a playwright and friend of Bryant's, wrote a letter to the *Los Angeles Times* warning about the precarity of her place in history. "Marie was one of those rare people who link lives together, who become important without becoming famous, who leave indelible imprints on everyone they touch," he explained. "It is urgent," he added, "that such people be remembered."[15] Following the lead of Black dance scholars who have taken up "the challenge to write forgotten women of color back into history," this chapter heeds the call to remember Bryant as a linker of lives and shaper of flesh.[16] It also seeks to better understand the conditions that allowed Bryant to leave indelible imprints on other bodies as well as on the filmic record *even while* being at such risk of erasure.

As much as I share Calvin's concern about the misrecognition of Bryant and Wasserman's sense of urgency around remembering her, I am also alert to the pitfalls of historical recovery projects. Black feminist scholars and queer theorists such as Tavia Nyong'o and Heather Love have cautioned against "emotional rescue" projects and against trusting that archives can ever "establish what 'really' happened."[17] Rather than aiming to "liberate" Bryant from an obscurity that never actually existed, I want to center her labor in a way that reflects its importance to the reproduction of Hollywood star bodies at midcentury. This is not the same as trying to restore Bryant to three-dimensional wholeness. Certainly, what Calvin refers to as the "meniality"

70 HOLLYWOOD DANCE-INS

of Bryant's screen image in films like *Wabash Avenue* fails to index her "great necessity" to so many Hollywood stars. But it is possible to demonstrate that failure without reimposing a binary between mediated (and hence "false") images and unmediated (and therefore "true") materiality. Any effort to "recuperate" Bryant's corporeal integrity from its cinematic distortions, moreover, would fly in the face of this book's goal of placing pressure on the very idea of bodies as organic sites of unvarnished truth.

To chart a path that emphasizes Bryant's historical significance while hopefully sidestepping some of the traps of recovery, I turn to media scholar Kara Keeling's concept of "the witch's flight." Riffing on Deleuze and Guattari's assertion that "to think is always to follow the witch's flight," Keeling envisions the figure of the witch as a Black femme who "exists on . . . the shoreline between the visible and the invisible, the thought and the unthought." "Because she is often invisible, (but nonetheless present)," Keeling continues, "when she becomes visible, her appearance stops us, offers us time in which we can work to perceive something different, or differently."[18] Like Keeling's Black femme, Bryant must be understood as present even when she does not appear in the visual frame. Like the Black femme, too, Bryant's moments of visibility provide an occasion to stop and perceive differently. Looking for Bryant hones our ability to look for corporeal imprints within spaces of opacity.[19] It helps us glimpse the Black reproductive labor that lurks within filmic images of white star bodies. And it can force us to contend with the symbiotic but never symmetrical power relations that uphold the seeming autonomy of white bodies. Indeed, one of the most urgent reasons to remember Bryant is that she illustrates how the corporeal coherence of white stars' dancing bodies "require[d] parasitism in order to survive."[20]

In the remainder of this chapter, I trace Bryant's "flight" across the surfaces of films, photographs, press accounts, and the biographies of her more famous students. First sketching the contours of Bryant's pre-Hollywood career and the racism that structured the Hollywood landscape, I then revisit the 1950 feature on Bryant in *Ebony* magazine, briefly discussed in the previous chapter. In its wealth of accompanying photographs pairing Bryant with both white men and white women, *Ebony* exposes the racial and gendered logic that governed her respective relationships with each. Next, I zoom in on Bryant's coaching of the white star Vera-Ellen. Conducted in Bryant's home, their training sessions transformed Vera-Ellen's mobility, both literally and figuratively. Though primarily focused on Bryant's relationships with white stars, in the latter part of the chapter I briefly consider the work she did "polishing" the acts of Black stars, which returns us to questions about what surface images can and can't make visible. I close by reflecting on my own complicity in a racially stratified ecosystem that capitalizes on Black reproductive labor.

Bryant's Early Flights

Bryant's early life and career intersected with two early twentieth-century phenomena: the mass migration of African Americans northward and westward to escape threats of racial terror in the South and the burgeoning of African American jazz dance and music. Born in Meridian, Mississippi, in 1917 and raised in New Orleans, Bryant "grew up surrounded by the sights and sounds of jazz" and "learned to sing and dance at a very early age," Janette Prescod writes in her *Notable Women* biography.[21] According to a remembrance from Bryant's friend Alan Marston, her first public performance came at the age of ten at a church social, where she did an impersonation of Josephine Baker, Bryant's idol. "I copied everything she did," Bryant told Marston. Later, Baker reportedly became "Marie's good friend, confidante and mentor," one of a seemingly countless number of Bryant's celebrity friends.[22]

Bryant was still a child when she experienced the threat of white terror firsthand. As relayed in the 1950 *Ebony* feature and by film historian Donald Bogle in *Bright Boulevards*, the family's decision to leave Mississippi was hastily made after white neighbors discovered that Marie's light-complexioned mother had been passing as white to shop at a white grocery market. When "a little white boy—aware of their ruse—taunted Marie by calling her [the N-word] . . . [s]he pounced on the boy and punched him." Her parents, "[f]earing some type of retaliation from their neighbors," left Meridian for New Orleans two days later.[23]

By 1929, Bryant had moved to Chicago, where she became a student of Mary Bruce.[24] Bruce trained generations of Black dancers, first in Chicago and then in Harlem, where she relocated in the late 1930s after her sister Sadie opened a rival studio in the Windy City.[25] From Mary Bruce, Bryant received a "basic education" in dance,[26] which likely included tap and ballet. Bryant also performed in Bruce's annual shows at Chicago's Eighth Street Theater.[27] Bruce, Bryant maintained, taught racial pride alongside dance, reportedly giving her pupils white and chocolate milk with the instruction to remember which tasted "nicer" if they ever "felt bad about being colored."[28] Bryant named Bruce as one of the major influences on her dance style.[29]

Bryant's professional debut came in 1934, when she was hired as a chorus dancer at the Grand Terrace nightclub, Chicago's version of the Cotton Club. Dance vocalist Cholly Atkins recalled her as "another fabulous dancer in the line" who "laid into whatever she did" and "had enormous physical projection."[30] By 1936, she was working as a nightclub performer in Los Angeles at venues like the Paradise Club and later Club Alabam.[31] While Los Angeles became her home base, she toured frequently, including with Duke Ellington, and had extended stints in New York in the mid-1940s and in Europe in the early 1950s.[32]

Either in Chicago or New York, Bryant met the visionary modern dance artist Katherine Dunham, who fused Afro-diasporic dance and ballet and whom Bryant named as her other primary dance influence. Bryant reportedly "studied the Dunham method" before working in nightclubs, and she later served as a faculty member at Dunham's New York dance school on West 43rd Street, in what would be the first of myriad teaching gigs.[33] At the Dunham School of Dance and Theater, Bryant taught tap dance, Lindy Hop, swing dance, and "Boogie," and was one of the school's primary disseminators of jazz dance.[34] Actor Marlon Brando and jazz dance choreographer Peter Gennaro were among her pupils.[35] Bryant also performed with the Dunham Company at times. A photo that appears on dance critic Wendy Perron's blog, on a page devoted to the career of Dunham dancer Syvilla Fort, shows Bryant posing with fellow performers, dressed in costume for one of Dunham's stage revues (perhaps *Bal Nègre*).[36] Bryant replaced Dunham herself on at least one occasion. Dale Wasserman, who served as the Dunham Company manager in the 1940s, fondly recounted an incident during a 1942 San Francisco La Fiesta nightclub engagement, when an "emergency call for Marie to fill in for Katherine . . . brought her promptly to the scene—eight months pregnant." "Just find me some full-cut costumes, baby," Marie reportedly said. "I'll knock 'em dead."[37] The image of a pregnant Bryant cheerfully dancing in Dunham's stead foreshadows the reproductive labor that would come to define Bryant's career in Hollywood.

In 1941, Duke Ellington cast Bryant in a prominent singing and dancing role in his musical revue *Jump for Joy*, which opened in Los Angeles and ran for three months, when the war led to its closure (see Figure 2.2). Wasserman described being "awed at the explosive vitality that [Bryant] unleashed on stage" in the musical, and Marston remembered her "singing and dancing up

Figure 2.2 Marie Bryant, center, flanked by Louise Franklin, Alice Key, Hyacinth Cotten, and an unnamed dancer in a publicity still for *Jump for Joy*, July 8, 1941. *Los Angeles Herald Examiner* Collection, Los Angeles Public Library.

a storm in the show stopping 'Bli-Blip' number," which featured Bryant along with singer-dancer Paul White.[38] In another *Jump for Joy* number, Bryant played Katharine Hepburn. On its opening night, the show "generated more buzz than any other black theater production on the West Coast."[39]

Trying to Crash the Movies

The proximity of Hollywood to the Los Angeles nightclub and theater scene brought Black performers, many of whom migrated west hoping to launch movie careers, to the attention of film producers.[40] For some, including Bryant, this led to screen opportunities. Her first film appearance may have been as a "sepia extra" in a Louis Armstrong Harlem sequence in the 1937 film *Artists and Models*. The following year she appeared in the all-Black musical film *The Duke Is Tops*, performing a two-minute solo in a specialty "exotic" dance number. (The film was Lena Horne's earliest screen appearance; she played a young, aspiring singer.) Footage of this same dance number was recycled for the 1940 film *Gang War*.[41] In 1944, Bryant danced in a pair of Black "soundie" film shorts—*Big Fat Butterfly* and *Juke Box Boogie*[42]—as well as with Lennie Bluett in the film *When Strangers Marry*[43] and alongside Harold Nicholas in the "Mr. Beebe" specialty dance number in the musical film *Carolina Blues*, which starred white actors Kay Kyser, Ann Miller, and Victor Moore. Bryant's appearance in the latter lasts little more than ten seconds, but her looseness, articulation, and mobility make her body practically jump off the screen (see Figure 2.3). In 1945, Bryant shot *Jammin' the Blues*, another film short, this one directed by the white *Life* photographer Gjon Mili, which depicted a jazz jam session featuring Lester Young. Bryant sang "Sunny Side of the Street" and danced with Archie Savage, one of the principal dancers in the Dunham Company.[44]

Figure 2.3 Screen capture of Marie Bryant and Harold Nicholas in the "Mr. Beebe" number in *Carolina Blues* (1944).

This string of small but featured film roles created a sense of momentum for Bryant's film career. In 1947, the *Chicago Defender* reported that Bryant had been hired to sing "Your Red Wagon" in the RKO film *They Live by Night* and was "finally . . . getting the break she long deserved." Describing her as "one of the most unusual girls in stage and screen," columnist Harry Levette noted that "all watching her in action predict that both she and the picture will be a terrific hit."[45] Despite these predictions, Bryant's star turn never came. She later told Marston, "I never became a superstar and it's probably just as well. I wouldn't know how to handle it. My head was in too many places. But I had a ball trying and I made some wonderful friends along the way."[46]

Notwithstanding her seeming resignation, there is no question that what media scholar Maryann Erigha terms "the Hollywood Jim Crow" stood between Bryant and stardom.[47] The experiences of two of her contemporaries, Jeni LeGon and Avanelle Harris, illustrate how devastating the movie industry's institutionalized racism was for Black talent. LeGon, one of the first Black women to be signed by a major Hollywood studio, received a five-year contract from MGM in 1935 and was slated to appear with white tap dancer Eleanor Powell in the film *Broadway Melody of 1936*. But when LeGon outperformed Powell at a promotional gala for the film, MGM pulled the former from the film and bought out her contract, claiming "they couldn't have two tap dancers on the show."[48] "[B]ecause I was the brown one," LeGon recounted, "they just let me go." The studio executives' flimsy excuse, as dance scholar Nadine George-Graves has written, was no doubt a cover for Powell's refusal "to be further upstaged by LeGon's superior dancing."[49] That LeGon was perceived as a threat to Powell demonstrates how directly white film stardom was contingent on suppressing Black artistry.

Aspiring film star Avanelle Harris never even got a chance at a contract. After appearing in uncredited film dance roles for years, she penned a cover story for a 1946 issue of *Ebony* magazine titled "I Tried to Crash the Movies."[50] In it, she relays how she "shouted for joy" when Lena Horne signed her seven-year contract with MGM in 1942, for rumor had it that "Metro was going to ink about ten of us to studio deals to back Lena's singing." "You see," she explained, "every major studio has some white cuties on contract. So . . . we were excited, on edge."[51] Although Harris "got the call" for the all-Black film musical *Cabin in the Sky* (1943), served for a time as Horne's stand-in, and appeared in the background of many of Horne's films, no contract ever materialized. Alternately deemed too light-skinned and too dark-skinned, losing roles to white women who were artificially darkened to play nonwhite parts, Harris and her colleagues made the "bitter" discovery that "all Lena was ever going to do was sing, do spot numbers" with nothing but "classy drapes as background."[52] After struggling to make it in Hollywood for two decades, Harris concluded, "Sure, there's Lena Horne—but only one Lena Horne." Both the near monopoly white performers held on starring roles and the withholding of contracts from Black supporting players had ripple effects throughout Hollywood's ecosystem. One of these effects was that Bryant, denied her own stardom, was available to remake the bodies of white stars.

"He Still Calls Her Pocahontas"

Blocked from starring roles on camera, Bryant found success behind it, becoming, in *Ebony*'s words, "the first Negro to crack the technical side of Hollywood with the official title of assistant dance director." While the full extent of Bryant's work as an assistant choreographer is not recoverable,[53] *Ebony*'s multipage 1950 feature on her is by far the most thorough contemporaneous account of her "technical" labor. I return to it here for the insight it provides into Bryant's simultaneous centrality and marginalization within Hollywood's corporeal ecosystem.

Running across five pages under the title "Movie Dance Director," the article contains two subsections: "Marie Teaches Stripteasers More Art and Less Come On" and "Stars Usually Ask for Her Help in Staging Routines." Sixteen photos, either taken by freelance photographer Larry Barbier or provided by the movie studios, are spread across the five pages. In only one of them is Bryant pictured alone (see Figure 2.4). In it, she holds the back of a chair (acting as a makeshift barre) and demonstrates what the caption describes as the "'controlled release' warmups based on Dunham techniques" that Bryant used to "loosen up stomach and back muscles": elbows bent, legs straight, torso arching forward, and buttocks extending behind her, she appears to be mid-hip-isolation.[54] Three of the other photos feature white women stars with whom Bryant worked: Betty Grable, Paulette Goddard, and Cyd Charisse, each in costume and rehearsing or performing on a movie set (Figure 2.5). Bryant herself is absent from these. (These images without Bryant are most likely

Figure 2.4 Bryant demonstrates her "controlled release" technique in an April 1950 issue of *Ebony*. Photo by Larry Barbier. Published by permission of the Barbier Estate.

the only photos not shot by Barbier.) In all of the remaining photos, Bryant is paired with a white body. While a series of six photos show her teaching a new routine to the white-appearing "strip teaser" Genii Young (Figures 2.6 and 2.7), the others show her with Vera-Ellen, Ava Garner, Gene Kelly,

78 HOLLYWOOD DANCE-INS

Figure 2.5 From top, Betty Grable (with Billy Daniels and chorus dancers), Paulette Goddard (with John Ireland), and Cyd Charisse (with background dancers), from the April 1950 feature on Marie Bryant in *Ebony*. Bryant coached all of the white women stars pictured.

Bob Hope, Nick Castle (Figures 2.8–2.12) and, as discussed in the previous chapter, Billy Daniels (Figure 1.7).

As a whole, these images are remarkable not just for the glimpses they offer into Bryant's behind-the-scenes role in Hollywood but also for their displays of shared physicality and corporeal transmission in the midst of uneven power relations. In the photo of Bryant and Kelly, for example (Figure 2.10), both are shown in profile looking directly at one another with wide smiles. Kelly's left hand grips Bryant's right upper arm while she rests her right hand under his left elbow, as if they are about to or have just embraced. The caption reads, "Gene Kelly thanks Marie Bryant for help in staging dance sequence in *Words and Music*. They met while she was performing

Figures 2.6 and 2.7 "Bryant Teaches New Routine to Burlesque Strip Teaser." Photos by Larry Barbier. Published by permission of the Barbier Estate.

Vera Ellen, MGM star, goes through steps for "Slaughter On Tenth Avenue" number in *Words And Music*. Marie also did dances for Miss Ellen in Marx Brothers film, *Love Happy*. She currently has personal dancing and singing role in RKO's *They Live By Night*.

Figure 2.8 Bryant and Vera-Ellen in *Ebony*. Photo by Larry Barbier. Published by permission of the Barbier Estate.

at Billy Berg's night club and he hired her to help in setting up his dances."[55] Similarly, in the photo with Nick Castle (Figure 2.12), Bryant and Castle stand facing one another, appearing to be in midconversation. Both of their bodies are in three-quarter view and their faces in profile, and they both have their hands in their pockets. The caption reads, "Nick Castle, famed dancer, has included Marie on his list of ten best dancers."[56] There is no

Ava Gardner is regular pupil of Marie's, picked up unusual ease and agility in costume clothes for her part in *Carriage Entrance*. Marie teaches class of Hollywood wives including Mrs. John Garfield and Mrs. Richard Conte. She charges stars $15 an hour.

Figure 2.9 Bryant and Ava Gardner. Photo by Larry Barbier. Published by permission of the Barbier Estate.

mention of them working together. In the photo of Bryant with Bob Hope (Figure 2.11), both are sitting with their hands clasped in front of them, looking directly at one another. Bryant is smiling, and Hope looks as if he has just finished speaking. The caption informs readers, "Bob Hope was assisted by Marie in staging Indian-Chinaman sequence in *Fancy Pants*. He still calls her Pocahontas. She started as a dancer in Los Angeles Club making $17 a week in 1935, worked with the then unknown [jazz musician] Lionel Hampton."[57]

Gene Kelly thanks Marie Bryant for help in staging dance sequence in *Words And Music*. They met while she was performing at Billy Berg's night club and he hired her to help in setting up his dances.

Figure 2.10 Bryant and Gene Kelly. Photo by Larry Barbier. Published by permission of the Barbier Estate.

Bob Hope was assisted by Marie in staging Indian-Chinaman sequence in *Fancy Pants*. He still calls her Pocahontas. She started as dancer in Los Angeles club making $17 a week in 1935, worked with then unknown Lionel Hampton.

Figure 2.11 Bryant and Bob Hope. Photo by Larry Barbier. Published by permission of the Barbier Estate.

On the most basic level, the photos that pair Bryant with a more famous white man offer visual evidence of her prominence in Hollywood's ecosystem. Here she is, they say, side by side with some of Hollywood's leading directors, actors, and choreographers. In the mirroring of body language they depict, and insofar as it's impossible to determine who is echoing whom, the photos might even present Bryant's relationship with these men as symbiotic—interdependent and mutually beneficial. Yet the captions disrupt this equilibrium, confirming Zakkiyah Iman Jackson's reminder that symbiosis is neither "incompatible with asymmetry and hierarchy" nor does it imply "the absence of incommensurability."[58] In the Bryant-Kelly example, the asymmetries still seem mutually advantageous: Bryant finds

Nick Castle, famed dancer, has included Marie on his list of ten best dancers. Marie appeared in two Broadway shows, *Are You With It* and *Beggar's Holiday*. She also sang in pioneer jazz movie short, *Jammin' The Blues*.

Figure 2.12 Bryant and Nick Castle. Photo by Larry Barbier. Published by permission of the Barbier Estate.

employment thanks to Kelly, and Kelly is the beneficiary of Bryant's help.[59] Hope's reference to Bryant as Pocahontas, however, announces the "perils" of intercorporeality "under conditions of unequal power."[60]

Details about how Bryant ended up helping stage the "Indian-Chinaman sequence" in *Fancy Pants*, the 1950 film starring Hope and Lucille Ball, are scant. The movie, a romantic comedy about an American actor impersonating a British butler (Hope) and the nouveau-riche family (Ball plays the daughter) who recruits him to pass as a nobleman in their New Mexico town, contains a "specialty number" called "Home Cooking," which takes place just past the hour mark in the movie. Set in a kitchen, the number involves Hope and Ball, plus Jack Kirkwood playing Ball's father and two kitchen workers: "Wampum," played by the white actor Joseph Vitale in redface (he also "played Indian" in the 1948 film *The Paleface*),[61] and "Wong," played by the Filipino actor Joe Wong (born José Ocampo Cobarrubias).[62] It is chock-full of racist lyrics, Orientalist musical tropes, and offensive gestures, including faux Native American war cries and "chopstick" fingers. It also contains some simple jazz-tap steps and a torso-swinging chorus-line-like exit. The number's official choreographer was Billy Daniels, who hired Bryant and Frances Grant, his other regular assistant (also mentioned in the *Ebony* feature), to help with the staging.[63] Production records list Grant as "assistant dance director" and Bryant as "2nd team dancer," suggesting that Bryant had not yet "cracked" that Hollywood ceiling when *Fancy Pants* was filmed in the summer of 1949. Her lower status also gave her significantly less pay: Daniels's weekly salary was $800, Grant's was $175, and Bryant's only $135.[64]

Digital media and performance studies scholar Anna Watkins Fisher's theory of artistic parasitism helps parse Bryant's involvement in a number like "Home Cooking." Writing about artists' ambivalent relation to power under neoliberalism, Fisher explains that parasitism originally referred to "a performance of complicity with subversive potential in ancient religious practice." Contemporary artists, she argues, deploy parasitism as a "tactic of complicit resistance" in contexts in which their own power is constrained.[65] Certainly Bryant's attempt to "crash the movies" was an attempt to gain a foothold in a white supremacist institution. Her description of the terms of her entry into a Hollywood film lot is instructive: "They're pretty shocked when I first check in a studio lot," *Ebony* reports her saying. "Much looking, double takes, eyebrow raising and all that. Still when they see what I teach and the results I get, they accept me quickly."[66] So unusual was a Black woman's arrival on the film lot that her presence is literally disorienting to studio gatekeepers.[67] In this scenario, to adapt Fisher, Hollywood is the host that only reluctantly admits Bryant, and her survival in the system is contingent on her ability to produce "results." Assisting on a racist specialty number that was standard Hollywood fare was part of the bargain of Bryant's hard-won and only ever provisional acceptance in this system.[68] But the fact that Hope reportedly "*still* calls her Pocahontas" suggests that Bryant's role extended beyond the two-and-a-half-minute "Home Cooking" number in which she doesn't even appear. Because it blurs the boundaries between filmic representation and conditions of production, the nickname demands that we attend not only to the racist "comedy" taking place in front of the camera but also to the racial drama that shaped relations behind it.

86 HOLLYWOOD DANCE-INS

Hope's name for Bryant betrays how comfortably her position in Hollywood sat within a preexisting white racial imaginary that cast non-white women as helpmates to the formation of whiteness. As numerous scholars have shown, Pocahontas (Powhatan) has functioned "as a controlling metaphor in the American experience."[69] While her marriage to settler John Rolfe constitutes what historian Clara Sue Kidwell deems "the most famous interracial marriage in American history,"[70] her alleged romance with and rescue of Captain John Smith casts her as the "savior" of the white man. Both narratives reinforce the white settler myth of Native women's sexual availability and serve to authorize and "consolidate America" by "imagining and asserting a program of European absorption of Native cultures and lands."[71] Accordingly, Bryant-as-Pocahontas marks her as the female savior of the white man (she helps Hope look good dancing on film) and positions her as an upholder of white supremacy (she helps stage a racist number that "consent[s] to mainstream American modes of imperialism").[72] At the same time, insofar as the figure of Pocahontas "signals a national identity crisis regarding the composition [and supposed purity] of the American national body,"[73] so too does Bryant-as-Pocahontas mark the reproduction of the white star's dancing body as a racially mixed affair.

Finally (although this surely does not exhaust the range of implications), the allegorical casting of a Black woman in the role of Pocahontas demonstrates the interchangeability and interarticulation of racial categories in mid-twentieth-century Hollywood. On-screen, stock racist figures of the Indian and the Chinaman lend their domestic support to the white lead characters. Off-screen, a white settler myth is invoked to frame a Black woman's reproductive labor in service of a white star. As such, Hope's term of putative endearment for Bryant reminds us of the colonial legacies and larger structures of gendered racism in which Hollywood's corporeal system was situated.[74]

White Women and the Black Reproductive

While the images that accompany *Ebony*'s feature on Bryant show her with white men and white women alike, white women appear in eleven of the sixteen photos. Among those eleven, three different types of scenes are pictured: Bryant actively instructing a white woman, Bryant and white women doubling one another, and white women on movie sets with Bryant nowhere in sight. Collectively, these scenes serve a pedagogical function, prodding us to recognize a Black woman's material labor in discursive images of white women's seemingly autonomous star bodies.

In two triptychs (Figures 2.6 and 2.7), Bryant is shown teaching a "new routine to burlesque strip teaser" Genii Young, which the caption clarifies is "designed to give more grace to dance." In the first triptych Bryant and Young run through the routine side by side. Its first image shows Young looking to Bryant as Bryant demonstrates how to hold a scarf angled across her body. The next two show Bryant and Young facing upstage, going into a backbend movement and turning their heads to look back at the audience. Bryant's backbend is noticeably deeper than Young's. The second triptych includes one photo of Young seated on the edge of the stage looking up at Bryant as Bryant models how to position Young's scarf just so, one photo of Young and Bryant apparently testing out what the caption describes as "foolplay with net bra . . . designed to make audience believe there is nothing under top bra," and a final photo, which is captioned "Stripper goes through routine by herself for Marie's okay." In this last image, we see Bryant from behind, seated on a chair and smoking a cigarette, her legs crossed and propped up on the stage, where Young poses with arms raised. Together, the sequence of photos depicts Bryant's alternation between dancing for, dancing with, and observing her white pupil.[75]

In the two photos of Bryant with white women stars, by contrast, we see only the moment when they are dancing alongside one another. Just next to the photo of Bryant and Gene Kelly mid-embrace is an image of Bryant and Vera-Ellen "go[ing] through steps for 'Slaughter on Tenth Avenue' number in *Words and Music*," as the caption tells us (Figure 2.8). The women, both dressed in crop tops and short shorts, are in an unmarked space.[76] They lean into their left hip and extend their arms in a bent second position, their left arm raised slightly higher than their right. Bryant is positioned several feet diagonally behind and to the viewer's left of Vera-Ellen, whom she watches out of the corner of her eyes. Vera-Ellen looks off to her right (the viewer's left) but likely cannot see Bryant. The composition of the photo of Bryant with Ava Gardner (Figure 2.9) is nearly identical, and Bryant is shown performing a nearly identical move. Here, though, Bryant and Gardner look directly at one another. Gardner is in costume—a full-length white dress with giant puffed-sleeve shoulders—for *My Forbidden Past* (1951) (which the caption identifies by its early title, *Carriage Entrance*), while Bryant wears

88 HOLLYWOOD DANCE-INS

a white collared shirt, a vest, and an untied bowtie. The caption here reads, "Ava Gardner is regular pupil of Marie's, picked up unusual ease and agility in costume clothes for her part in Carriage Entrance. Marie teaches class of Hollywood wives including Mrs. John Garfield and Mrs. Richard Conte. She charges stars $15 an hour."[77]

These images of Vera-Ellen and Gardner attempting to match Bryant's physicality are supplemented by three images of white women stars (Figure 2.5). In the first, Betty Grable stands in costume on the film set of *Wabash Avenue* (1950), choreographer Billy Daniels just to her left (viewer's right) and several white chorus girls behind her. The caption identifies neither Daniels nor the chorus girls but reads, "Betty Grable had her dances in new film On Wabash Avenue [*sic*] staged by Marie. Movie star was so pleased with Marie's work that she presented her with leather handbag after completion of picture. Marie has taught at Katherine Dunham school."[78] Below the photo of Grable is an image of actors John Ireland and Paulette Goddard, the latter who snaps her fingers with her arms raised above her head, on the set of *Anna Lucasta* (1949). The caption makes no mention of Ireland, instead offering, "Paulette Goddard was instructed on shimmy dance in Anna Lucasta by Marie. For three years Marie worked with Duke Ellington band and appeared in his West Coast musical, *Jump For Joy*. She has made two song recordings for Keynote." Another photograph captures Cyd Charisse mid-chaîné turn in a number from *Words and Music* (1948) with white-appearing supporting players in the background. Although there is no evidence that Bryant worked with Charisse on the balletic number pictured, the caption tells us that "Cyd Charisse, dancing star of *Words And Music*, is another Marie Bryant student. Martha Raye has also taken lessons from Marie. She is one of most versatile in show business—singing and acting besides dancing everything from boogie to ballet."[79]

In describing this series of photos and quoting verbatim from their captions, I mean to call attention to the seeming nonalignment between image and explanatory text. Against convention, the captions direct our attention away from the women pictured and toward various facets of Bryant's career: her work behind the camera, her dancing, singing, and teaching credentials, the forms of compensation she received. When we see these white stars dancing on screen, *Ebony* implies, we are seeing the effects of Bryant's labor, her imprints on their bodies. To put an even finer point on it, we might say that the images of white women stars without Bryant deconstruct the taken-for-granted privilege of whiteness to function, following

Sean Redmond, as "a photograph of itself," as discussed in the previous chapter. Instead, *Ebony* teaches us to see images of whiteness as indexical of Black reproductive labor, anticipating Sara Clarke Kaplan's argument that "Black reproductivity [is] a historical *trace* immanent to" white womanhood, embodied here by midcentury white women film stars.[80]

That this lesson in reading images of white women comes from the Black press is neither surprising nor inconsequential. It was the *Defender's* Dolores Calvin, recall, who rang the alarm over *Wabash Avenue's* misrepresentation of Bryant as "just another maid." For Black Hollywood, the exploitation of Black talent behind the scenes was hardly news. Writing about the 1942 film *Pardon My Sarong*, starring the white actress Virginia Bruce, for example, a reporter for the *Afro-American* explained that Universal Studios hired Katherine Dunham to "tutor" Bruce for "a dancing role leaning on the native side" but "turned Katherine down for a part in the movie." As a result, the article declares, "we'll see Virginia Bruce on the screen but Katherine Dunham dancing."[81] Revisiting Kara Keeling's incisive assertion (discussed in the previous chapter) that "the relationship between the projected black image and 'prefilmic blackness' problematizes cinema's claims to function as an index of a prefilmic reality," we might press even further. As Bryant and *Ebony* demonstrate, it is not only "the case of the black image" in mainstream cinema that "contains the seeds of the crisis in cinema's identity as an indexical medium" but also the case of the white image in midcentury film musicals.[82]

Helping Vera-Ellen Fall Up

Among its many other offerings, *Ebony's* feature on Bryant gives us an origin story for her employment as a coach to white stars. The very first line reads, "Movie star Gene Kelly started it." Kelly, it goes on, "needed 'just a little something' for his 'Slaughter on Tenth Avenue' sequence in MGM's *Words and Music*. He telephoned one 'of the finest dancers I've ever seen in my life,' asked her to come to Metro and help his dancing partner Vera Ellen work on the number. The newcomer provided that dash of 'just a little something' so brilliantly that Kelly's friend, Paulette Goddard asked her to stage the shimmy dance for *Anna Lucasta*." The "dash" that Bryant provided proved transformative for Vera-Ellen's career. To the extent that it's traceable, the relationship between Bryant and Vera-Ellen is one of the most illuminating

90 HOLLYWOOD DANCE-INS

examples of how Black reproductive labor could reshape white corporeality and drive white stardom.

Despite *Ebony*'s claim that Bryant and Kelly met at Billie Berg's Trouville Club in Los Angeles, where Bryant was performing in the early 1940s, in a 1978 interview Bryant maintained that she met Kelly before she relocated to Los Angeles, back when she was performing with Ellington in New York.[83] In this regard, we might see the Club Dixieland scene in *On the Town*, in which Bryant performs for Kelly, Vera-Ellen, and friends, as a reenactment of an earlier encounter between Kelly and Bryant, perhaps at New York's Cotton Club, which was surely a model for the fictional Club Dixieland.[84] By the time that scene was filmed, which production records indicate took place in April 1949,[85] Bryant had already worked with Vera-Ellen on two prior films. It is possible, in fact, to draw a straight line from Bryant's coaching of Vera-Ellen for *Words and Music* to Vera-Ellen's starring role in *On the Town*.

Released in December 1948, MGM's *Words and Music*, a musical biopic about composers Richard Rodgers and Lorenz Hart, was in production from April through July 1948.[86] The "Slaughter on Tenth Avenue" number, composed by Rodgers, originally appeared in Rodgers and Hart's 1936 Broadway production *On Your Toes*, where it was choreographed by George Balanchine. Both the Broadway and film versions center on a tragic love story between a man and a woman prostitute who is ultimately shot and killed. In the film version, in which Kelly falls for Vera-Ellen as the prostitute, the two dance together in and around a nightclub before a gangster shoots her, sending her tumbling down a flight of stairs. Kelly was hired to both choreograph and star in the number.[87] While reviews of the film were mixed, the almost seven-and-a-half-minute-long "Slaughter" received (and continues to receive) wide acclaim.[88]

In a 1952 interview with Charles Samuels for *Motion Picture and Television Magazine*, Vera-Ellen cited her performance in "Slaughter" as a turning point in her career. Before that role, she explains, she had done "only light taps and other frothy kinds of dancing," leaving her nervous about her ability to pull off the sensual dancing the choreography required.[89] She conveyed her doubts to Kelly, who originally sought her out for the role, despite the fact that, as he later told an interviewer, she was "bright and perky and vivacious" and therefore less "suited to voluptuous dancing." By way of clarification, he added that Vera-Ellen, like many other "trained dancers" at the time, lacked "what Katherine Dunham's group had."[90] To translate Kelly's barely coded assessment, Vera-Ellen had no training in Africanist aesthetics. Enter Bryant.

Bryant may have initially come to the MGM lot to work with Vera-Ellen, but the bulk of their lessons took place "every day for a month" at Bryant's home. Although Vera-Ellen told Samuels that Bryant lived "in the heart of the Negro district section, on Central Avenue,"[91] extant communication from a former neighbor places her on West 36th Place.[92] This would have been a few miles west but still part of the Eastside, as the Black business district on Central Avenue and surrounding neighborhood were known. Due to Los Angeles's racially restrictive covenants, it was one of the few areas African Americans were permitted to live.[93] This was not a trivial distance for Vera-Ellen to travel. Lena Horne pegged it as "more than an hour's cab ride" from Hollywood to Central Avenue.[94] The fact that their training sessions occurred in Bryant's private home rather than on a studio lot casts some doubt on how much access Bryant had to Hollywood spaces. It also positions Bryant as host to Vera-Ellen. Whereas Fisher helps us see parasitism as a tactic deployed by minoritarian artists in relation to majoritarian hosts, that is, Bryant reveals the converse: parasitism as a strategy[95] deployed by white stars in relation to Black artists who, despite their marginality, could and did serve as hosts, both literally and figuratively.

In 2000, a former neighbor described Bryant's home's interior: "Her front room or living room was very long and the interior wall was cover[ed] from floor to ceiling with mirrors. I can't remember if there was a [barre] there but I think that was the case. This is where Marie the master teacher, finisher or act polisher would hold forth during the workday." Where Jack Cole had his famed Studio 10 on the Columbia Pictures lot, Bryant had her living room.[96] Born in part or whole of the exigencies of segregation, Bryant's home studio made guests out of the stars who came to her for instruction; it also invited them into her domestic space. The location of this training thus evokes certain parallels between Bryant's dance labor and the domestic labor that was historically one of the only sources of employment available to Black women in the United States.[97] Bryant's work may have taken place inside her own home rather than in a white home, but the fact that she labored in service of white bodies in a site of domesticity aligns her with other Black women who "were conscripted to a role that required them to care for and replenish the needs of the white household."[98]

The only firsthand account of what transpired between Bryant and Vera-Ellen in Bryant's living room comes from Vera-Ellen. She told Charles Samuels that when she showed up in a puffed-sleeves rehearsal outfit, Bryant "shook her head." " 'Honey,' [Bryant] said, 'you can't wear that dress

92 HOLLYWOOD DANCE-INS

if you're gonna do that kinda dance. Mr. Gene Kelly told me to teach you. I can't see your body in such an outfit. I gotta see it, 'cause you talk with your body in this dance. I gotta see it to know what you're saying with your body as you move around.'" Once Bryant swapped out Vera-Ellen's dress for "a couple of kerchiefs," the training began. At the end of a hard day's work, Bryant reportedly said, "'You're dancing fine, honey, but what are you thinking about?' I told her I was just thinking about the steps. She said that was no good, not enough. I had to think of what that sexy dance tried to say. 'If you don't think of men and sex while you're dancing,' she told me, 'your body won't say anything about those things to the folks watching you.'"[99] While Vera-Ellen's telling hints at Bryant's emphasis on bodily articulation over and above the execution of steps, her reduction of Bryant's pedagogy to a directive to think about sex and men reinforces primitivist tropes about Black women's sexuality. Bryant, for her part, adamantly rejected such characterizations. "My dancing is described by some as the kind of dancing 'only Negroes can do because it's sexy and kind of lowdown,'" the *Ebony* article quotes her as saying. "But that isn't so. My work is controlled and artfully routined."[100]

A write-up about a class Bryant taught just a couple of years later at Eugene Loring's American School of Dance in Los Angeles offers another perspective on her pedagogy. In a feature titled "Marie Bryant: Boogie at the Barre" (though in it, Bryant "hastens to add that her technique involves more than boogie"), the school's newsletter describes a "blend of primitive, Afro-Cuban, and jazz elements," the "resulting product . . . distinctively her own." The newsletter also relays how Bryant's class moved from "strenuous and exacting" barre work, where students performed "exercises derived from Dunham technique and used for warming up the body," to center work, where the focus was on performing the "more relaxed" movements of syncopation and isolation (see Figure 2.13).[101]

Whether or not Bryant incorporated any of these exercises into her private training sessions with Vera-Ellen, the outcome of those sessions was appreciable. Calling her dancing in "Slaughter" "sensational," the article by Samuels describes a complete transformation in Vera-Ellen's way of moving: she walked with a new slinkiness, performed a "more wicked rumba," and was finally considered "sexy."[102] Elsewhere, Vera-Ellen referred to her lessons with Bryant as her "introduction not only to [her] best role but to a completely new screen personality."[103] The effects on Vera-Ellen's career were especially pronounced. Kelly and choreographer-director Robert Alton were

Figure 2.13 A photo taken by Barbara Plunk captures Bryant in action at Eugene Loring's school, demonstrating the "controlled release," "systematic relaxation," and isolation that her technique sought to cultivate. Her students look somewhat stiff and awkward, perhaps unintentionally illustrating the "rigid torso idea" that the American School of Dance Newsletter identifies as the very reason ballet-trained dancers would benefit from studying "boogie." Eugene Loring Papers, Langson Library, Special Collections & Archives, University of California, Irvine.

so impressed with her dancing that they extended her role in "Slaughter," and her performance in that number paved the way for her being cast as Ivy Smith in *On the Town*, a role that "cemented Vera's status as a movie star" and led MGM to offer her a long-term contract.[104] Bryant felt the returns on Vera-Ellen's altered corporeality as well. She later told a reporter, "I changed Vera Allen's style of dancing, and she was such a success[,] other famous people came to me for tuition."[105]

Yet if Bryant's coaching sessions with Vera-Ellen were mutually beneficial, they were scarcely equally so. Bryant's work with the white star may have helped launched Bryant's career as a dance coach and eventually assistant dance director, but she never received the kind of roles or screen time that Vera-Ellen did. Comparing the snippets of Bryant's dancing that

94 HOLLYWOOD DANCE-INS

survive to Vera-Ellen's "Slaughter" performance, moreover, it's hard not to be struck by what Jasmine Johnson has described as kinetic "casualties."[106] Vera-Ellen's motion, however transformed, is visibly constrained compared to Bryant's distinctive looseness and fluidity. This is especially on display, to my eye, during Vera-Ellen's solo jazz walk in the opening thirty seconds of "Slaughter," when her somewhat stilted hip movements seem to require the focus of her entire body. I see evidence of control here but little evidence of release.[107]

My purpose, to be clear, is not to suggest that Vera-Ellen lacked talent nor that Bryant's coaching was unsuccessful.[108] Vera-Ellen was certainly a capable dancer, and her crash course in Bryant's Dunham-inspired Africanist technique surely helped her pull off choreography that stretched her corporeal range. But there is also no question that her ability as a jazz dancer pales in comparison to Bryant's.[109] In this sense, the fact that the magazine story in which the white star most fully recounts her work with Bryant is titled "Vera-Ellen Took a Tumble, yet Her Fall Sent Her Up!"—a reference, on the surface, to her fall down a set of stairs after her character gets shot six minutes into the "Slaughter" number—could also unwittingly denote the "unjust magic of whiteness"[110] that propels so much white upward mobility.

Returning to Bryant's thirteen seconds in *On the Town* and the even briefer on-screen encounter between Bryant, Kelly, and Vera-Ellen at Club Dixieland, which was filmed the year after "Slaughter,"[111] we can now recognize the extradiegetic precursors that the scene both remembers and forgets. If the film's depiction of Bryant performing for white spectators reenacts an earlier meeting between Kelly and Bryant, the diegetic relationship between white spectators and Black performers fails to index the simultaneously symbiotic and parasitical relationship between Bryant and Vera-Ellen, in which Bryant played host to Vera-Ellen and labored in service of Vera-Ellen's corporeality. Within *On the Town*'s narrative frame, Madame Dilyovska, played by the white actress Florence Bates, is Vera-Ellen's only dance teacher, while Bryant is reduced to the flickering object of the white gaze.[112]

Yet despite, and possibly even because of, such moments of forgetting, Bryant's presence remains. At times, this presence takes the form, almost literally, of what scholar Tiffany Lethabo King terms the "Black phantasmic."[113] In Vera-Ellen's final reflection about "Slaughter on Tenth Avenue" in the *Motion Picture and Television Magazine* write-up, just after she remarks "I'll never stop being grateful to Gene Kelly for having given me my chance at doing it with him," she adds, "They play the music of Slaughter a lot over the air even now. If I hear it while driving I have to stop the car, pull over on the side of the road—and listen to it. Hearing that music makes me shiver and quake. I get goose-flesh at the memory. Though we rehearsed it for six weeks, it lasted exactly seven minutes on the screen, the greatest seven minutes of my professional life."[114] Even as her words bypass Bryant to credit Kelly, we might see Vera-Ellen's corporeal response—pulling over, shivering and quaking, getting goosebumps—as one more trace of the witch's flight, the haunting of Vera-Ellen's flesh by Bryant.

Polishing Black Acts

However pivotal Bryant's reproductive labor was to the (re)making of white stars' filmic images, she worked behind the scenes in support of Black stars as well, before, during, and after the peak of her support of white stars. One of her last roles, in fact, was as understudy—yet another kind of unseen doubling—to Pearl Bailey in the all-Black production of *Hello, Dolly!*, which ran on Broadway in the late 1960s.[115] For all her friendships with white stars, moreover, one of her closest and longest friendships was with Lena Horne.[116] Horne dances remarkably little in her films compared to white contemporaries like Betty Grable,[117] but there is good reason to believe that, as was the case with Grable, Bryant was not only Horne's friend but also her dance coach.

In the 1950s, frustrated with Hollywood's racism and blacklisted as a communist sympathizer,[118] Horne embarked on a successful nightclub career, with performance runs in Los Angeles, Las Vegas, and New York. In a recollection after her death, Bryant's neighbor wrote that, without being sure, they "suspect[ed] that [Bryant] is the person who finished Lena Horne's act as the stunning production that it was."[119] Though the neighbor did not specify which act, Horne's 1956 performance at the Empire Room in New York's Waldorf-Astoria Hotel is a viable possibility. It was that performance, according to Horne biographer James Gavin, at which singer-dancer-actor Sammy Davis Jr. "sat ringside with a pad and pencil, noting everything Horne did," and modern dance choreographer Martha Graham "watched in fascination" and commented, "There is not one spontaneous gesture. . . . It's as calculated as Kabuki or a Hindu dance."[120] However couched in Graham's Orientalist terms, the precision and economy of Horne's act may well be markers of Bryant's touch.[121]

96 HOLLYWOOD DANCE-INS

What exactly Bryant's "finishing" of Horne's nightclub act might have entailed is uncertain. Perhaps it was some combination of choreographing and coaching, both of which Bryant had honed in her official and unofficial roles as assistant dance director and private coach. Surely it involved some kind of intercorporeal exchange. While no visual evidence of that exchange survives, a photograph of Bryant coaching Maria Cole, the widow of Nat King Cole, for whose television show Bryant served as resident choreographer, captures her in a similar role.[122] The image (Figure 2.14), which accompanies a 1966 *Ebony* article about Cole's return to a singing career, shows Bryant before a microphone occupying the position of performer.[123] She stands with feet hip-width apart, her head tilted upward, her mouth open as if mid-note, her eyes slightly squinting and focused up and out into the distance, while her arms are bent and raised, with what looks like a cigarette in her left hand. Cole is standing behind her and to her right and appears to be carefully studying Bryant's physicality. The caption reads, "Pointers on stage delivery are offered by Marie Bryant, veteran coach, who is assisting Mrs. Cole in the staging of her act."[124] (A review of Cole's show at the Flamingo Hotel in the *Los Angeles Sentinel* lists Bryant as the show's choreographer and reports that Bryant's "talented guidance" was "evident throughout.")[125] Below the image of Bryant and Cole are three photographs of Cole in front of the same microphone "display[ing] her technique as a polished songstress" (Figure 2.15). Though these images are cropped, preventing us from seeing who else is in the room with Cole, it's possible that Bryant was standing behind and to the viewer's left of her. What these images reveal, and perhaps partially conceal, then, is the same kind of mirroring, mimesis, and swapping of positions that characterized much of Bryant's off-camera work in Hollywood.[126]

The terms "polishing" and "finishing," both used at times to describe Bryant's labor as a coach or a choreographer, imply the training of bodies to achieve a smooth and practiced look.[127] "Finishing" might also constitute what scholar Amber Musser, writing about fleshiness and racialized femininity, terms a "surface technology." In contrast to metaphors of depth and interiority, "surface thinking" traffics in imitability and reproducibility. It invites us to recognize "citation" and "dual embodiment" as strategic modes of selfhood for Black femmes.[128] And it moves us away from trying to determine what might be original or singular to a body. If Bryant's "finishing" lay somewhere between choreographing and illustrating more "polished," economical ways of moving, it has the value of reminding us of the murky space

Pointers on stage delivery are offered by Marie Bryant, veteran coach, who is assist-

Figures 2.14 and 2.15 Bryant demonstrating for singer Maria Cole, who then takes her place. Photos by Bill Gillohm. Johnson Publishing Company Archive. Courtesy of J. Paul Getty Trust and Smithsonian National Museum of African American History and Culture. Made possible by the Ford Foundation, J. Paul Getty Trust, John D. and Catherine T. MacArthur Foundation, The Andrew W. Mellon Foundation, and Smithsonian Institution.

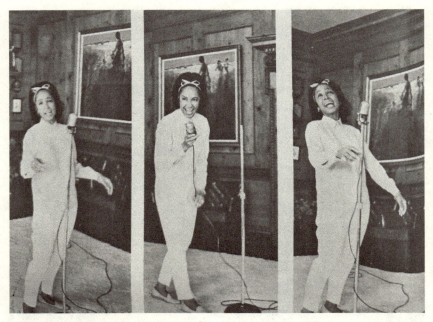

Figures 2.14 and 2.15 Continued

between creating and reproducing, a space that is also filled by relations of exchange between bodies.

"Finishing" seems an apt term to describe the nature of Bryant's work, too, given how much our knowledge of her reproductive labor relies on photographic surfaces. There is no direct access to Bryant's interiority or subjectivity, nor to the "truth" of her flesh. By the same token, there is so much that surfaces cannot divulge about the exact nature of the intercorporeal exchanges that took place between Bryant and the stars she trained. Yet and still, surfaces, whether isolated moments captured in photographs, fleeting images of Bryant moving across the screen, or the recollections of those who witnessed her kinetic gifts, allow us to catch glimpses of those exchanges and their corporeal effects. They offer us a window, however limited, onto a larger corporeal ecosystem in which stars relied on a particularly talented Black woman to reshape their bodies and thereby fuel their careers and in which a particularly talented Black woman leveraged her corporeal skill to teach, coach, and polish—to imprint the flesh of, to stand in for, and then stand aside for—her more famous friends and colleagues.

* * *

It's February 2019, and I'm at the Jerome Robbins Division of the New York Public Library, paging through an entire folder of clippings and notes devoted to Marie Bryant. The folder is part of the research files of D'Lana Lockett, who, according to the archive catalog, "was a tap dancer, dance instructor, and dance researcher who began research on a book on African American female tap dancers." Lockett, a Black woman, died in 2006 at age forty-four; these files are what remain of the book that she never got to write. Thanks to Lockett, Bryant's presence in the archives here, in contrast to the USC film records, is substantive and purposeful. Learning about Lockett through Bryant, and learning about Bryant through Lockett, it is clear that Bryant was never a lost subject waiting to be recovered. It is clear, too, that my own output, like that of the white women stars I've been analyzing, exists in a symbiotic but asymmetrical relationship with the labor of a Black woman whose shortened life surely cannot be disentangled from structural racism and racialized health disparities.[129] In tracing Bryant's flight, I too retrace the steps and stand in the place of a Black woman before me, and I too participate in a loop that is always in part indexing and in part obscuring its sources and debts.

3

Female Reproductive Labor and White Corporeal Debt in *Singin' in the Rain*

In the mid-1990s, Carol Clover wrote compellingly about the extent to which the much-loved 1952 film musical *Singin' in the Rain* is riven by a racialized anxiety about doubling and unpaid debts. In her reading, the film narrative's worry over restoring credit to the character of Kathy Selden, played by Debbie Reynolds, for the voice dubbing she provides for the character of Lina Lamont, played by Jean Hagen, masks how much Gene Kelly's and Donald O'Connor's virtuosic tap dancing owes to African American dancers, who are entirely absent from the film. Noting the irony that the film "enacts the kind of talent 'relocations' it claims to deplore and correct," she presents the musical as haunted by the influences of Black dance artists like Bill "Bojangles" Robinson and the Nicholas Brothers. Given that "the real art of the film musical is dance" rather than singing, and given that white artists like Kelly were aware of their indebtedness to Black dance traditions, Clover concludes that the movie's underlying concern "is not white women's singing voices but black men's dancing bodies."[1]

But Reynolds, too, was an active participant in the film's "real art" of dancing. As Selden, she works as a chorus dancer before she becomes Lamont's voice double, and she dances alongside Kelly and O'Connor in the well-known "Good Morning" number and with Kelly in "You Were Meant for Me." Clover and others have noted that Reynolds was not actually doing her own singing in the film (an uncredited white woman named Betty Noyes dubbed several of her songs) and that her tap sounds were post-dubbed by others.[2] Reynolds's execution of the film's choreography, by contrast, seems to align with the film's attempt to achieve "cinematic authenticity" in its visual representation of dancing. As film scholar Peter Wollen writes, because dancing was "Kelly's own province," all of the film's dancing, including Reynolds's, had to "be shown as unfaked, through the use of long takes and wide frames."[3] This mandate for "unfaked" dancing required Reynolds, who

---

Hollywood Dance-ins and the Reproduction of Bodies. Anthea Kraut, Oxford University Press.
© Oxford University Press 2025. DOI: 10.1093/oso/9780197789667.003.0004

had no professional dance experience when she was cast as Selden, to undergo rigorous training prior to filming.

Though it is indeed Reynolds we see dancing in the film, her body is arguably no less mediated than her singing voice or her tap sounds, and it is no less haunted than Kelly's and O'Connor's by the influence of other dancers. Most immediately, the physicality she displays on screen is indebted to the labor of two "below-the-line" white women dancers with whom she worked intensively in the period leading up to the film shoot: Carol Haney (1924–1964), who served as Kelly's assistant on the film, and Jeanne Coyne (1923–1973), who served as the movie's designated dance-in and went on to become Kelly's assistant, despite being better known for having first been married to the film's co-director Stanley Donen and later marrying Kelly (Figure 3.1).[4] As intermediaries between choreographer and star, and as coaches and surrogates for Reynolds, Haney's and Coyne's contributions to

Figure 3.1 From viewer's left to right, Jeanne Coyne, Stanley Donen, Gene Kelly, Carol Haney, and Donald O'Connor on the set of *Singin' in the Rain* (1952). Courtesy of Photofest.

the construction of Reynolds's dancing body were as vital as they were invisible. Notwithstanding the amount of critical attention *Singin' in the Rain* has received, the relationship between Haney, Coyne, and Reynolds has yet to be thoroughly investigated.[5]

Clover's jump from white women's singing voices to Black men's dancing bodies thus misses a chance to interrogate how white women's dancing bodies participate in the "talent 'relocations'" that *Singin' in the Rain* simultaneously thematizes and suppresses. Without diminishing the irrefutable importance of African American men to the film's kinesthetic genealogy, I'm interested in what more we can learn about the interplay of credit and debt, on-screen and off-, if we foreground the conditions of production of Reynolds's "unfaked" white dancing body.[6] A closer examination of the ways Haney and Coyne shaped Reynolds's filmic body unites often disconnected gendered and racial analyses of the film by exposing how white women's reproductive labor simultaneously transmits and conceals debts to dancers of color.

To be clear, the goal of this chapter is pointedly *not* to return credit to Haney and Coyne. Neither film studies nor dance studies, it should go without saying, suffers from a lack of focus on white women. As Stefano Harney and Fred Moten have asserted, moreover, "[r]estored credit . . . is always the renewed reign of credit . . . a hail of obligations to be met, measured, meted, endured."[7] To assign authorship of Reynolds's dancing body to Haney and Coyne would shift but not disrupt notions of corporeal originality that this book seeks to push against. Instead, my aim is to advance understandings of credit and debt as racialized and gendered relations that play out at the level of the body while furthering this book's investigation of how those relations structured Hollywood's corporeal ecosystem at midcentury. An analysis of one of the most popular film musicals that probes rather than glosses over the dancing of its white female star makes it possible to tease apart the intercorporeal debts that bind subjects to one another and the corporeal claims of credit that cover over and suppress those ties. At the same time, it provides reminders of the uncertainties that hover over projects of disclosing debts.

In what follows, I first address how recent theorizations of credit and debt apply to the embodied realm of dance. I then situate Haney and Coyne within extant accounts of Reynolds's kinesthetic makeover for *Singin' in the Rain* and examine the gendered labor that Haney and Coyne carried out in training Reynolds to dance alongside Kelly and O'Connor. Approaching

Haney's and Coyne's labor as reproductive in nature returns us to the ways women functioned as surrogates for stars and choreographers alike and foregrounds white women's role in transmitting multiracial genealogies of jazz dance. Reynolds's ability to conceal this gendered reproductive labor behind a cloak of white credibility enabled her emergence as a star in what I argue amounted to a kind of "passing." Yet as the chapter goes about the business of "outing" Reynolds, it becomes impossible to ignore the parallels between my own exposure of Reynolds's debts and the film's outing and shaming of Lina Lamont, the musical's diegetic debtor. Acknowledging those parallels leads not only to a discussion of the politics of revelation, both within and about the film, but also to a consideration of the historical shifts within formations of whiteness in the mid-twentieth-century United States. *Singin' in the Rain*, however, was not an all-white film, and the chapter closes by demonstrating how the presence of dancers of color in the film, most notably the Puerto Rican Rita Moreno, haunts the chains of white corporeal debt that tether Reynolds to Haney and Coyne.

Corporealizing Credit and Debt

With the rise of neoliberalism and in the aftermath of the 2008 global financial crisis, scholars have increasingly highlighted debt as a defining feature of contemporary life. Debt has been deemed "the central issue of international politics" and "*the* determining economic and thus social relation, superseding relations of production or consumption as the socially formative economic dynamic."[8] But debt is hardly new, as the title of David Graeber's book, *Debt, the First 5,000 Years*, indicates. Nor is it newly imbricated with the structuring forces of race and gender. In their introduction to a September 2012 special issue of *American Quarterly* on "race, empire, and the crisis of the subprime," Paula Chakravartty and Denise Ferreira da Silva emphasize the "racial and colonial logic of global capitalism" that undergirds and predates the recent financial crisis.[9] In a U.S. context, the blaming of Black and Latina/o "subprime debtors" for the financial crisis[10] is a contemporary manifestation of constructions of the fugitive slave as an indebted person or the burdening of the emancipated slave with the condition of indebtedness.[11] Correspondingly and conversely, one of the chief unearned privileges of whiteness is the presupposition of creditworthiness. As scholar Amaryah Shaye has argued, "to be white" is "to be included within relations that traffic in credibility."[12] Writer Eula Biss has likewise proposed that "the condition of white life" is that "[w]e are moral debtors who act as material creditors."[13] Building on the insights of these scholars, this chapter takes a closer look at how white debt gets converted into credibility, how gender intersects with race in that conversion, and how that conversion materializes within and between bodies.

Part of what makes dance such a productive site of inquiry into relations of credit and debt is its encapsulation of the tensions between the two. Harney and Moten's distinction between credit as "a means of privatization and debt [as] a means of socialisation" is useful here.[14] With its dependence on transmission between bodies, dance "brings people into relation," Susan Foster writes.[15] At the same time, as a kinesthetic form, at least in hegemonic Western contexts, dance can play "a crucial function in establishing . . . the individual's body schema (a sense of the body as bounded and discrete)," as Carrie Noland writes.[16] We might say, then, that dancing bodies exist at the intersection of, or oscillate between, the individuation of credit and the relationality of debt. By a similar token, it is simultaneously true that dance, like popular culture more generally, "*is* because it borrows" and that there are implicit "rules of thumb" about when attributions are warranted.[17] It is also true that dance history is rife with examples of the racialization and gendering of credit and debt; for centuries, white artists have reaped the rewards of dance innovations that are directly and indirectly indebted to dancers of color, while male artists have risen to fame on the backs of the labor of women dancers.[18]

Equally important, dance draws attention to the literal incorporation of debts: their ability to infuse a body's very way of moving, to shape muscle memory, and to lodge within flesh and bone. Carried physically, lurking in plain sight, corporealized debts are nonetheless easily concealed by white bodies granted the privilege of assumed credibility. Thinking credit and debt through the body is thus another way to make evident how our very conceptions of corporeality are racialized. What an analysis of the relations of credit and debt in *Singin' in the Rain* offers, then, are additional examples of how intercorporealities—the intersubjective acts of reproduction and transmission out of which physicalities are forged—come to masquerade as seemingly coherent and discrete white star bodies.[19] As "two-dimensional, technologically produced representations"[20] that are so incontrovertibly mediated, the filmic bodies in *Singin' in the Rain* prove all the more instructive a site for unpacking the material and ideological operations that prop up white dancing bodies.

Modes of Accounting

The fact that Debbie Reynolds (1932–2016) was "not a dancer" when she was cast at the age of nineteen in *Singin' in the Rain* alongside Gene Kelly (1912–1996), who was thirty-nine at the time, is repeated in virtually every account of the making of the film. Earl Hess and Pratibha Dabholkar tell us this verbatim twice in the space of three pages in their behind-the-scenes history of the musical.[21] Reynolds's "dancing experience was almost nil," writes film historian Rudy Behlmer, who goes so far as to describe her as "the antithesis of Kelly and O'Connor in song-and-dance experience."[22] Reynolds herself readily admitted that she was "totally untrained." A 1978 article quotes her as saying that when she signed up for the 1948 Miss Burbank contest that eventually led to her discovery by talent scouts for the movie studios, all she knew "was time step and soft shoe. No ballet, no jazz, no real tap."[23]

Explanations of why the inexperienced Reynolds was cast in the role of Selden vary, but there are two leading, and competing, narratives: Kelly claimed he insisted that Reynolds be cast after being charmed by her performance singing "Abba Dabba Honeymoon" (and performing some basic dance steps) in the 1950 film *Two Weeks with Love*; Reynolds maintained that MGM head Louis B. Mayer cast her without Kelly's knowledge and to his dismay.[24] Regardless of who made the casting decision, Reynolds's youth and inexperience were central to her appeal. As "the wholesome girl next door,"[25] Reynolds personified white innocence, and narratives that reinforce her status as an ingénue reinforce her similarities to the character of Selden, who, like Reynolds, is transformed into a star in the course of the film.

Off-screen, that transformation began with three months of dance training. From early April through mid-June 1951, when filming got underway, Reynolds rehearsed every day on the MGM lot. She was assigned three instructors: Ernie Flatt, Carol Haney, and Jeanne Coyne. All three appeared as background dancers in a number of films and were well-versed in jazz and ballet. In her autobiography, Reynolds describes her daily dance instruction as consisting of a two-hour tap class with Flatt and a two-hour class with Haney, with Coyne following up on Haney's teaching.[26] Archival records, in the form of the AD's report housed in the University of Southern California Cinematic Arts Library, paint a slightly different picture: from April 2 to April 18, Reynolds worked with Flatt and Haney; on April 22, Coyne joined Haney and Reynolds in rehearsal, and Flatt's name drops out, although he later worked as a "weekly" background dancer during film

106 HOLLYWOOD DANCE-INS

production; on April 23, Kelly joined the three women, and the next day O'Connor did as well. The five of them were on set together, rehearsing daily, with occasional wardrobe fittings and prerecording sessions, through mid-June.[27] It appears, then, that Flatt gave Reynolds basic instruction in tap and that Haney and Coyne worked more extensively with her to help her master all of the film's choreography. Both women were present continuously during all of Reynolds's rehearsals with Kelly and O'Connor. Hess and Dabholkar reach the same conclusion, writing that "Kelly relied on Flatt to demonstrate the basic steps to Reynolds, and trusted Haney and Coyne to take her further along in her dance education."[28]

Despite the significant roles played by Haney and Coyne, most narratives of how Reynolds was made screen-ready for *Singin' in the Rain* focus on how demanding Kelly was and how physically taxing the work was for Reynolds. Likening Reynolds to other untrained dancers with whom Kelly worked, critics and scholars underscore his perfectionism and praise his ability to "extract" talent from novices.[29] Other tellings reinforce Reynolds's indebtedness to Kelly even as they highlight her work ethic and perseverance, often citing the physical exhaustion she endured.[30] In other words, in what Miranda Joseph might call the "modes of accounting" for the construction of Reynolds as star, credit flows readily and abundantly to Kelly, figured as the "genius" choreographer and master teacher, with a smaller share apportioned to the hard-working female star.[31] Haney and Coyne, meanwhile, barely warrant a nod.[32] As I explore below, this gendered allocation of credit is made possible by a gendered division of labor, with Haney and Coyne performing reproductive work that had to be forgotten for the white female star to emerge. Crucially, this reproductive labor entailed the transmission of debts to dancers of color, which were rendered doubly invisible by their passage through the bodies of white women dance-ins and assistants.

Reproductive Labor

In both her 1988 and 2013 autobiographies, Reynolds draws an analogy between making *Singin' in the Rain* and giving birth: "Singin' in the Rain and childbirth were the hardest things I ever had to do in my life."[33] Her insistence on linking the labor of motherhood with the labor of cultural production, meant to accentuate the effort and pain of preparing for her screen performance, calls to mind performance studies scholar Joshua

Chambers-Letson's discussion of the "resemblance between biological re-production and the reproduction of performance." Noting that the "dis-course of maternal reproduction" is largely absent from both Marxist and performance theory, Chambers-Letson proposes that, notwithstanding this neglect, "performance's mode of reproduction takes a form that is more akin to the process of biological, rather than mechanical, reproduction" in its si-multaneous reproduction of sameness and difference.[34]

If the mother is "missing" from "the scene of reproduction in both Marxist theory and performance theory,"[35] mothers are hard to miss in conventional models of dance history, where the creation of "family trees" was long the prevailing mode of historical analysis.[36] In the racially divided historiog-raphy of U.S. dance, Loïe Fuller, Isadora Duncan, Ruth St. Denis, and Martha Graham have all been figured as "mothers" of white modern dance, while Katherine Dunham and Pearl Primus have been celebrated (and segregated) as "mothers" of a Black concert dance tradition.[37] Family-tree models per-vade histories of ballet as well, though, in contrast to modern dance histories, the focus in ballet is on male choreographers and paternal lines of descent, with George Balanchine tagged as the "father of American ballet." Dance scholar Carrie Gaiser Casey's feminist response to this model is to "re-center" ballet history in the acts of transmission that take place inside the ballet studio and in the interpersonal, intercorporeal relationships between female teachers and their female students.[38] Given that the gendered divi-sion of labor and allocation of credit in Hollywood bear some pronounced similarities to the ballet world, Casey's approach is useful for shifting to a "mode of accounting" that can properly register the behind-the-scenes labor of Haney and Coyne.[39]

Returning to and riffing on Reynolds's childbirth analogy, my contention is that Haney and Coyne facilitated the "birth" of Reynolds as star and that their reproductive labor included the interrelated functions of serving as surrogates for choreographer and stars and reproducing genealogies of jazz dance. As discussed in this book's introduction and first chapter, my invo-cation of the term "surrogation" expands on the influential work of perfor-mance theorist Joseph Roach, for whom historical transmission takes place via a process of cultural substitution in which communities rely on alterna-tive figures to fill vacancies created by death or departure. Roach also de-veloped the concept of "genealogies of performance" as a means to describe "the historical transmission and dissemination of cultural practices through collective representations."[40] Framing Haney's and Coyne's labor in terms of surrogation and genealogy gives weight to the acts of transmission and substitution that played out on the MGM lot and on which Reynolds's on-screen appearance depended.

Even so, in casting their work in reproductive terms, I am cognizant of the perils of consigning women to maternal roles "in order [for them] to be recognizable as subjects."[41] I am also mindful that genealogical inquiries are as capable of reifying origins—especially racial origins—as of deconstructing them.[42] If approaching Haney's and Coyne's labor as reproductive runs the risk of reinforcing equations between women and mothers, or of repositioning women as vessels for racial inheritances, it is worthwhile precisely because, insofar as "women's work" is so easily overlooked,[43] it abets the forgetting of nonwhite antecedents, which is fundamental to the reproduction of whiteness. The gendered politics that allowed Haney's and Coyne's work to fly beneath the radar, that is, helped occlude white stars' racial debts to nonwhite dancers and thereby helped perpetuate the myth of white autonomy.

Regarding Haney and Coyne as surrogates has two additional advantages. First, it calls attention to gendered reproductive practices that are not identical with conventionally dominant (heterosexual, biological) forms of mothering; it thus actually loosens the equation between women's work and idealized (heteronormative) views of maternity.[44] Second, surrogation's cognate form, "surrogacy," is what Alys Weinbaum has termed a useful "heuristic device" for discerning the connections between contractual forms of reproductive labor and the legacies of slavery. Following the lead of Black feminists, Weinbaum argues that surrogacy's "epistemic proximity" to the commodification of human biological life "makes visible relationships between the slave past and the biocapitalist present" and brings the race-making functions of reproduction to the fore. To the extent that "slave breeding [was] a conceptual antecedent" for contemporary practices of surrogacy, we should be equally alert to how the outsourcing of reproductive labor in dance studios and on film sets that I am calling surrogation also participates in the "reproduction of white racial hegemony."[45]

As indicated above, Haney and Coyne officially held different roles in the making of *Singin' in the Rain*, with Haney listed as the assistant dance director and Coyne as dance-in. The differentiation of their roles is reflected in their disparate compensations: a budget estimate on June 30, 1951, puts Haney's pay at $175 per week for a total of twenty-one weeks of work and Coyne's at $137.50 per week for a total of fifteen weeks.[46] Though contracted in different capacities, the near-constant pairing of their names in production records suggests that Haney and Coyne functioned as a team and that, in practice, their roles overlapped considerably.[47]

A 1952 report in the *New York Times* by Stephen Watts on how Kelly "arranged terpischore for the camera eye" identifies Haney as his assistant, refers to Coyne as Haney's assistant, and explains their importance to the filming process:

> It is when the time comes to bring his conceptions to life in front of the camera that the full scope of the task Kelly has undertaken becomes apparent. The basic difficulty—being in two places at the same time—he has solved very simply, if surprisingly. When he wants to be at the camera end to see how a scene, in which he will be the central figure, looks as a whole, his place is taken by Carol Haney, a 27-year-old dancer from New Bedford, Mass. Miss Haney, a slight figure in blue jeans and a sweater, looking oddly pale among the made-up company, not only dances all the routines, but acts as Kelly's assistant dance director. He picked her when she was dancing in one of the ballets from "On the Town" and she has been with him ever since.
>
> Miss Haney has in turn an assistant, even younger, even slighter and more girlish, Jeanne Coyne (like Kelly, a Pittsburgher), who also has a telepathic-seeming knowledge of what Kelly wants.[48]

Watts's explication offers a cogent picture of the acts of surrogation required to, in another reproductive metaphor, "bring [choreographic] conceptions to life" on the screen. Here surrogates are needed to fill vacancies created by a body's inability to be in multiple places at once. The account of Haney taking Kelly's place in front of the camera is as clear a characterization as any of the substitutive work of a dance-in. And even as Watts unmistakably feminizes Haney and Coyne by emphasizing their youth, slightness, and "girlishness," he highlights the simultaneous mental and physical nature of their labor: they had to be able to replicate all of the film's choreography as well as inhabit Kelly's directorial sensibility. Other accounts bolster this view of Haney and Coyne as Kelly's double-bodied proxy. A 1954 newspaper article quotes Kelly calling them "his right and left hand, respectively," and editorializes that "they better might be described as his extra pair of feet."[49]

As the film's dance-in, Coyne also performed this surrogate labor for Reynolds, taking the place of the female star as cameras were being focused or when Reynolds was needed elsewhere on set. The AD's report indicates

110 HOLLYWOOD DANCE-INS

that there was only one day during the mid-June to mid-August shooting of Reynolds's scenes when Reynolds was present but Coyne and Haney were not, and the production log is peppered with annotations like "rehearse with dance in to playback for camera." During the shooting of the "Good Morning" number on June 26, for example, records note that from 8:48 to 8:53 a.m. the director was rehearsing "boom moves with standin and danceins."[50] And on June 30, the log indicates that from 1:26 to 1:53 p.m. "Miss Reynolds and dance-in and Mr. Kelly rehearse for camera moves." While it is not clear which dance was being rehearsed here, the presence of Coyne alongside both stars, plus the use of the plural "danceins" in the June 26 entry, suggest a fluid interchange and frequent swapping of places between Haney, Coyne, and the film's on-screen stars.

Given their role as assistants and off-screen doubles, *Singin' in the Rain*'s choreography necessarily passed through Haney's and Coyne's bodies on its way to Reynolds's. To gauge the effects of this "passing through," we must return to the crash course in dancing that Haney and Coyne gave Reynolds prior to filming. Recalling Jasmine Johnson's observation that the "guiding philosophy of any dance class is to reproduce . . . an instructor's choreography" as well as "a social order,"[51] it behooves us to ask what choreography and what order were being reproduced in the exchanges between these white women.

Without question, training Reynolds to dance on screen alongside the skilled Kelly and O'Connor involved drilling her in the choreographic proclivities of these men. In her 1988 autobiography, Reynolds explains, "Gene had certain steps he liked to do. Donald . . . had certain steps *he* always did; and so Carol assembled everything for Gene to approve."[52] Reynolds's 2013 follow-up contains the similar explanation that "Jeanne and Ernie taught me Donald's and Gene's signature steps," and elsewhere she reported that she "worked like crazy trying to match Gene's style."[53] While much attention has been paid to the synchronization of voices and bodies in *Singin' in the Rain*,[54] the work of kinesthetically synching Reynolds's body to those of her co-stars was arguably even more time- and labor-intensive. This synching, too, required mediation, as Reynolds's nod to Haney's "assembl[ing]" and Coyne's and Flatt's teaching acknowledges. And it is within this space of mediation that the kinesthetic predilections of Haney and Coyne also entered the transmission process.

Significantly, both women trained with Jack Cole, who, in the white patriarchal genealogy of the genre, is often figured as the "father" of jazz dance.[55]

SINGIN' IN THE RAIN 111

His theatrical jazz style was actually an amalgam of multiracial dance sources: the Orientalist mining of "ethnic dances" he inherited from white modern dancers Ruth St. Denis and Ted Shawn; the classical Indian dance he studied with the white La Meri; the Spanish dance he learned from Paco Cansino (the film star Rita Hayworth's uncle); and the African American and Afro-Latin social dances that he witnessed in New York nightclubs.[56] Coyne's exposure to Cole came when she worked with him in a Broadway production of *Something for the Boys* (1943). Haney was a core member of his ensemble, is generally considered an "exemplar" of his technique, and even served as "a model on whom he created much of his choreography."[57]

Genealogically speaking, then, Kelly is not the exclusive source of Reynolds's on-screen corporeality in *Singin' in the Rain*. Nor are Haney and Coyne, who, in transmitting Kelly's choreography to Reynolds via their bodies, also reproduced some of Cole's aesthetic. But neither is Cole. Instead, we might think of Haney and Coyne as the connective tissue between Cole's multiracial debts and the dancing in the film musical. Again, this is not to undermine how much *Singin' in the Rain* owes to African American tap dancers like the Nicholas Brothers, John Bubbles, and Bill Robinson, whose styles and steps were undeniable influences on Kelly and O'Connor. It is, however, to recognize that the labor of Haney and Coyne as assistants, coaches, and dance-ins matters to a genealogy of the film's dancing and to the choreographic order they reproduced in their rehearsals with Reynolds. And just as Clover points to the film's "sideways glances to dancing and blacks" that tug against its surface attention "to singing and whites,"[58] so too can we find evidence within the film of the multiple and disparate racial sources that infused the dancing of the women who worked in front of and behind the camera.

One of the "sideways glances" that Clover documents is O'Connor's performance of the Charleston, a dance with decidedly African American roots. But the Charleston actually surfaces multiple times in *Singin' in the Rain*, including in the "Good Morning" trio. This is not surprising, given that the film is set in the 1920s, when the dance was at its peak of popularity.[59] Although chiefly a tap dance number, "Good Morning" contains an interlude in which O'Connor, Kelly, and Reynolds grab each other's raincoats and hats and take turns performing sixteen-count solos.[60] With Kelly's raincoat wrapped around her waist to resemble a skirt, Reynolds performs an approximation of a Hawaiian hula dance, swaying her hips and undulating one hand as Kelly and O'Connor strum imaginary ukuleles (Figure 3.2). Kelly follows with a Spanish dance.[61] With O'Connor's hat pushed down

Figure 3.2 Screen capture of Debbie Reynolds performing an approximation of a Hawaiian hula dance as O'Connor and Kelly (from viewer's left to right) look on, part of the eruption of a multiracial genealogy of jazz dance in the "Good Morning" number of *Singin' in the Rain*.

over one eye, he swings his raincoat like a matador's cape, flicks one heel, and circles around himself. To conclude the section, O'Connor performs the Charleston with a raincoat as an imaginary partner, after which the three resume their high-spirited tap dancing. Arising in the middle of a tap dance, these citations of Indigenous Hawaiian, Spanish, and African American social dance are eruptions of jazz dance's multiracial sources.[62] Before these diegetic "racialized gestural vocabularies"[63] were recorded on film, they circulated between the off-screen bodies of Haney, Coyne, and Cole and the on-screen star bodies of Reynolds, O'Connor, and Kelly.

Other iterations of the Charleston are more closely tied to Haney and Coyne and thus serve as more conspicuous reminders of the role white women played in the reproduction of Africanist source material. The first time we see the Charleston in the film, it is performed by Reynolds and eight other white women during "All I Do Is Dream of You," the number in which Reynolds as Selden pops out of a cake only to discover that Kelly as

Lockwood is one of the guests at the party where she has been hired to dance as a chorus girl. It is here that we can most directly glimpse the transmission of Coyne's choreographic order to Reynolds. In Donald Knox's book *The Magic Factory*, which collects oral histories from players involved in the making of Kelly's 1951 vehicle *An American in Paris*, the female star Leslie Caron recalls learning the Charleston from Coyne, who served as the official dance-in on that film as well. (Haney served as assistant dance director.) "I'd never done anything like that," Caron remarks. "Jeanne Coyne was best at that; she was very jazzy."[64]

Proof of Coyne's skill at the Charleston can be found to Reynolds's immediate right (screen left for the spectator) during "All I Do," since, in addition to her off-screen duties, Coyne appeared on screen as a chorus dancer.[65] Although she comes in and out of view throughout the dance, the shot is wide enough during the Charleston section to see her fully (Figure 3.3). The choreography has all of the chorus dancers performing in unison, but

Figure 3.3 Screen capture of Coyne (front row, viewer's far left), Reynolds (front row, second from the left), and fellow chorus dancers mid-Charleston in "All I Do Is Dream of You" in *Singin' in the Rain*. Coyne is visibly lower to the ground than Reynolds.

114 HOLLYWOOD DANCE-INS

Coyne is more bent over, her torso a bit closer to the ground than Reynolds's as they perform the distinctive forward-and-backward-moving, foot-swiveling, arm-swinging steps of the Charleston. Put another way, Coyne's Charleston is ever so detectably more Africanist than Reynolds's. Before our eyes in this moment, then, we have a representation of the same dance performed with a difference by teacher and student, surrogate and star. It is an illustration of how an Africanist approach to movement, as Brenda Dixon Gottschild has shown, gets transmitted and modified as it passes between bodies, with Coyne's more get-down stance giving way to Reynolds's more upright, bouncy version of the Black social dance.[66] It is an illustration, too, of how jazz dance's multiracial debts are simultaneously reproduced and obscured—or, more precisely, how they are obscured *via* their reproduction by white women surrogates.

Passing and White Credibility

Assessments of Reynolds's Charleston aside, a consensus holds that her crash course in dancing paid off. On the commentary that accompanies the DVD of *Singin' in the Rain*, film historian Behlmer notes that "when you look at her on film . . . she looks good."[67] Kelly biographer Clive Hirschhorn concluded that "for all Debbie Reynolds' misgivings about her abilities, she . . . has never worked as well" as in the 1952 musical.[68] Reynolds was similarly pleased—and not a little surprised—by her performance in the film. Her 1988 autobiography describes her experience at the movie's premiere:

> Then suddenly the screen lit up with this amazing movie. And there she was, popping out of that cake, dancing up and down those stairs, singing and smiling and holding her own with those two dancing geniuses. If there was ever a single moment when Mary Frances [Reynolds's birth name] was transformed into Debbie, it might have been then. I thought, hey, I'm good! All that pain and the kid is good! I was amazed. To this day I am amazed at what I accomplished in so short a time. I knew then and there where I belonged. Gene had pushed and the girl was good.[69]

Coming face to face with her on-screen image, Reynolds is startled to find herself "holding her own" with Kelly and O'Connor. In a sign of that aston-ishment, she repeats the assessment "she was good" not twice but three times, alternating between past and present tenses and between the third person ("the kid is good" and "the girl was good") and the first person ("hey, I'm good"). In this telling, Reynolds's successful transformation from nondancer to dancer, attributed to the "pain" she bore and to Kelly's pushing, enabled the emergence of Debbie Reynolds as star. Differently put, Reynolds becomes a credible star when she successfully "passes" as a convincing dancer.

In invoking the discourse of "passing," I am suggesting a correlation between the crossing of identity categories that the term typically references and Reynolds's crossing over from novice to dancing film star. Where, as literary scholar Elaine Ginsberg has written, "passing" allows an individual to shed one identity and access "the privilege and status" of another,[70] so too have scholars in the field of star studies pointed to the "process of fabrication" that has underwritten Hollywood's construction of female stars, including the erasure of "a star's previous identity" and all kinds of modifications to her physical appearance.[71] Reynolds's singling out of her performance alongside Kelly and O'Connor as the precise moment of her emergence as Debbie Reynolds the star makes clear how central dance—and its occluded gendered and multiracial debts—was to this transformation. And just as "passing" connotes some level of fraudulence,[72] Reynolds's amazement at the image of herself dancing on screen hints that she has gotten away with something.

Like all acts of passing, Reynolds's depended on "silencing and suppression."[73] Yet she was anything but silent about her lack of prior dance training; she seemed to trumpet it every chance she got. Instead, what is silenced and suppressed in the moment of her materialization as star is her indebtedness to the off-screen dance teachers—Flatt, Haney, and Coyne—who, as she describes no fewer than ten pages earlier in her autobiography, spent eight hours a day in a rehearsal studio with her for three months and who were at least as responsible for shaping her on-screen corporeality as was Kelly. That Haney and Coyne, who trained, danced alongside, and exchanged places with Reynolds before and during production, are elided the moment Reynolds sees herself dancing on film, and that they are missing from so many accounts of her performance, confirms the "selective forgetting" and "failures of memory" that subtend the reproduction of gender hierarchies and white privilege.[74] What Reynolds has gotten away with is credibility as a dancer that, Shaye reminds us, hinges on the "misrecognition" of the "flesh and blood" that is "being used to pay for the credit of others."[75]

Acknowledging the conversion of indebtedness into credibility in *Singin' in the Rain*, Clover notes that the singing voice of the white woman who dubbed the song "Would You?" for Reynolds—the uncredited Betty Noyes (sometimes referred to as Royce)—is left "on permanent deposit in the account of Debbie Reynolds."[76] Attention to the roles of Coyne and Haney in the making of the film not only reveals that the debts in Reynolds's account (like those in Kelly's and O'Connor's) were multiple, involving dancing as well as singing; it also broadens our understanding of what it means to make a permanent deposit in the account of another. The fact that it is impossible to parse exactly where Haney's and Coyne's influence on Reynolds's dancing body begins and ends, in contrast to our ability to delineate Noyes's voice from Reynolds's body, suggests that deposits made kinesthetically are perhaps as permanent as they come. Reynolds's "account" in this case was her very corporeality, including her ability to move her body in certain ways. Once incorporated (internalized corporeally) by Reynolds, Haney's and Coyne's deposits, never isolatable, could hardly be returned. That Reynolds's dancing in the film musical was neither "faked" nor "dubbed" does not mean that it was any less indebted to the bodies of others. But its very authenticity—its achievement of credibility—enabled and rested upon amnesia about the reproductive labor of other white women, whose own incorporations in turn masked the multiracial deposits and erasures of debts to dancers of color in the account of American jazz dance at large.

Disclosing White Debts and Ethnicizing Whiteness

The irony of *Singin' in the Rain*, of course, is that Reynolds serves diegetically not as the debtor but as the lender, and much of the musical's plot pivots around the question of when and to whom the "truth" of Kathy Selden's role as surrogate to Lina Lamont will be revealed. The climactic unveiling occurs at the 1:40 mark of the film, when the trio of Kelly as Lockwood, O'Connor as Cosmo, and Millard Mitchard as movie producer R. F. Simpson raises the curtain separating Lamont, lip-synching the film's title song, from Selden, singing the song behind Lamont's left shoulder.[77] The diegetic audience breaks into raucous laughter, and when Cosmo runs on stage, nudges Selden away from the microphone, and begins singing in her place, the "outing" of Lamont is complete.[78] Reading this "iconic curtain scene" through the lens of Eve Sedgwick's critique of the "epistemology of the closet," Bonnie Honig has recently proposed that the curtain, like the closet, "cultivates forensic curiosity." As such, the curtain is not only capable of yielding "epistemic satisfactions" but can also be wielded as a weapon to produce "injurious knowingness about revealable truth."[79] Given my own figurative raising of the curtain on Reynolds's surrogates in this chapter, the politics of exposure merit further reflection.

One image in particular throws into relief the parallels between this chapter's revelation of debts and the film's (see Figure 3.4). Taken by Maurice Terrell for *Look* magazine, the photograph depicts Coyne, Kelly, Reynolds, and Haney in rehearsal on what appears to be an empty sound stage. In the foreground, Coyne and Kelly clasp hands with arms outstretched and legs crossed over in a deep lunge toward stage left (viewer's right). Behind them, Reynolds and Haney echo their pose, with Haney just barely visible behind Kelly's body. A comparison with a screen capture from *Singin' in the Rain*'s

Figure 3.4 From viewer's left to right, Coyne, Reynolds, Kelly, and Haney in rehearsal for *Singin' in the Rain*. Photograph by Maurice Terrell. Courtesy of the Library of Congress *Look* magazine collection.

curtain scene (Figure 3.5) shows that compositionally, Reynolds occupies the same position in both images, either singing or dancing behind the left shoulder of her counterpart. The images diverge in terms of what they reveal. Where the diegetic image fractures the deceptive coherence of Lamont's voice and body, the rehearsal image fractures the sense of Reynolds's dancing body as unmediated, or mediated only by Kelly. Still, in both cases, visual evidence of "backstage" operations "lifts the curtain" on a white star's uncredited double. What, then, separates *Singin' in the Rain*'s treatment of Lamont from my treatment of Reynolds?

This is especially worth asking given what critics have pointed to as Lamont's "vilification" and "abjection" within the film.[80] "Poor Lina carries a heavy burden," Clover writes. "She is the scapegoat not only for all the actors, male and female alike, whose voices flunked the shift to sound, but for all the white performers who danced the art of unseen others which is to say for the film musical itself. No wonder her exposure must be so brutal and

Figure 3.5 Screen capture of Jean Hagen (left) and Debbie Reynolds (right) in *Singin' in the Rain*'s "iconic curtain scene," in which Kathy Selden is revealed as Lina Lamont's vocal double.

SINGIN' IN THE RAIN   119

her humiliation so complete; she is the repository of a guilt so much greater than her own."[81] In insisting that we shift our focus to Reynolds's debts, does this chapter transfer the burden of the film musical onto her? Addressing this question requires clarifying the conceptual and historical stakes of "outing" Reynolds's debts to other white women.

On a conceptual level, comparing the film's politics of unmasking to this chapter's reinforces the point I have been making that, when it comes to corporealized credit and debt, there is no single or "original" body to whom credit can or should be restored. Across the film, the voice of Selden indexes Reynolds's, the unseen Noyes's, and in one place, in the most ironic of twists (to which I return below), Jean Hagen's.[82] Reynolds's diegetic tap sounds were post-dubbed by both Kelly and Haney.[83] Even within the film, Cosmo must displace Selden to make "knowable" Lamont's debt to Selden. There are no direct reveals here. Correspondingly, an archival exposé cannot establish a one-to-one substitution of Reynolds's dancing body for Coyne's. In fact, the choreography that Coyne, Kelly, Reynolds, and Haney are performing in the *Look* rehearsal photograph has no exact match in the film. Its closet diegetic equivalent, at least to my eye, is a moment around the 44:24 mark of the film, during "You Were Meant for Me," the "gentle love duet"[84] in which Kelly/Lockwood expresses his love for Reynolds/Selden against the artificial backdrop of a movie lot (see Figure 3.6). "You Were Meant for Me" is the sole *pas de deux* between Kelly and Reynolds, and the clasped hands and lunge on the diagonal resemble no other choreography that I've discovered in the film. Because the only date that's attached to Terrell's photograph, however, is the date that it was added to *Look*'s collection, February 7, 1952, it's possible that the photograph was not even shot during film production (the previous summer), and more than possible that it was staged for the sake of publicity.[85] If the foursome in the photograph was restaging choreography from "You Were Meant for Me" when Terrell visited the film set, then the "revealable truth" of this figurative curtain scene is twofold: first, dance-ins were as much a part of the cinematic apparatus as the wind machine and movie lighting that the film number presents as "fake";[86] second, corporeal reproduction produces copies that may have no original. The visual evidence of the rehearsal photograph may rupture the illusion of the "artlessness" of Reynolds's body,[87] but its own indexical instability highlights the impossibility of tracing her filmic corporeality back to a single extradiegetic moment or single prior source.[88] There are no epistemic certainties here.

Figure 3.6 Screen capture of Kelly and Reynolds in "You Were Meant for Me," in which Kelly's Lockwood expresses his love for Reynolds's Selden against the artificial backdrop of a movie set.

From a historical standpoint, meanwhile, unmasking Reynolds's debts enables us to contextualize and particularize her whiteness. Instead of shifting the debt burden from one white woman to another, that is, situating Reynolds alongside Hagen on one side and Coyne and Haney on the other, invites us to consider the variegations within whiteness as a racial formation in the mid-twentieth century. As Michael Rogin, Steven Cohan, and Pamela Caughie have demonstrated, the figure of Lina Lamont not only represents an older generation of white female star—the "obsolete silent-screen star"—in contrast to the ingénue Selden; her shrill, "uncultured" voice, which is the barrier to her transition to the sound era and the reason she needs to be dubbed, also marks her as "distinctly lower class" and distinctly ethnic.[89] As it turns out, there is a case to be made that Hagen's Lamont is coded, however subtly, as Jewish. Rogin, for example, reading *Singin' in the Rain* alongside the 1927 film *The Jazz Singer*, remarks, "Hagen plays Lina Lamont as a self-worshipping Cantor Rabinowitz; both older figures block the younger generation's access to show business success and romantic love."[90] According to Cohan, *Singin' in the Rain*'s Jewish screen writers, Betty Comden and Adolph Green, originally wrote the part of Lamont for their friend Judy Holliday, born Judith Tuvim, a comedienne known for the "dumb blonde" persona she developed. Though Holliday was unavailable for the role, her "shrill voice, uneducated diction, and insubordinate attitude," described elsewhere as a "New York yawp peppered with Yiddish," were a model for Hagen's Lamont.[91]

Notably, the post–World War II period was a pivotal time in the transformation of whiteness as a racial category in the United States, ushering in both the "whitening" of European immigrants, including Jewish Americans, and the hardening of racial distinctions between whites and those not of European descent.[92] Pitted against Reynolds's "wholesome girl next door" whiteness,[93] Hagen/Lamont's inability to transcend or permanently conceal her "vulgar ethnic voice"[94] is also a failure to ascend to full whiteness. Significantly, in an early version of the screenplay, Lamont's humiliation extends beyond her exposure as Selden's debtor. A final scene that was ultimately cut from the film, Karen McNally explains, "has Lina suffering an even worse fate": introduced at the premiere of Selden and Lockwood's new movie "as Cosmo's new wife and 'the former Lina Lamont,'" a columnist announces, "She is now appearing in 'The Jungle Princess,' in which she doesn't say a word—she just grunts!"[95] This is a rather pronounced reversal of the trajectory of "white ethnic mobility" that Rogin charts for Jewish Americans in Hollywood, from blackface to white assimilation.[96] Seen in this light, Reynolds/Selden's credibility emerges as a historically specific mode of youthful, postwar white femininity in part by distinguishing itself from an older form of ethnicized, gendered whiteness that cannot completely shake its genealogical roots in blackface.

Yet when we position Reynolds's whiteness in relation not only to her above-the-line co-star Hagen but also to the below-the-line dance coaches who helped shape her corporeality and filmic image, this intraracial division becomes less tidy. Haney and Coyne were, to the best of my knowledge, Anglo-American.[97] But as we've already seen, their whiteness was inflected and reinforced by the African American, Latin, and Asian influences that were lodged in their bodies by virtue of their jazz dance training. In other words, an *"inferential ethnic presence,"* to use scholar Ella Shohat's terms for "the various ways in which ethnic cultures penetrate the screen without

122 HOLLYWOOD DANCE-INS

always literally being represented by ethnic and racial themes or even characters,"[98] operates in *Singin' in the Rain*'s all-white dance scenes, its all-white rehearsal studios, and in the corporealities of its "purely" white dancing stars. The postwar "innocent" whiteness that the film valorizes and that Reynolds appears to embody, therefore, does not so much expel ethnic whiteness as incorporate it differently—by passing off its multiracial debts as "artless" dancing.

Rita Moreno and Sidelined Labor

Singin' in the Rain's curtain scene is not the only instance of exposure in which questions of passing, ethnic status, and knowability converge.[99] Roughly ten minutes prior to the scene of her public "outing," Lamont first learns of the movie studio's plan to replace her voice with that of Selden (see Figure 3.7). The scene unfolds when Lamont's friend Zelda Zanders ushers the former into a recording studio, where Selden has just dubbed Lamont's dialogue (though it is actually Hagen's regular speaking voice that we are hearing here, not Reynolds's).[100] Discovering Lockwood and Selden mid-kiss, Lamont screams and then proclaims, "Thanks, Zelda, you're a real pal. I want that girl off the lot at once. She ain't going to be *my* voice. Zelda told me everything."

> Don (sarcastically): "Thanks, Zelda, you're a real pal."
> Zelda (equally sarcastically, before exiting): "Oh, anytime, Don."

Described in the film as "that famous Zip Girl of the screen, the darling of the flapper set," Zelda Zanders is played by Puerto Rican singer-actor-dancer Rita Moreno, who went on to win an Academy Award as Anita in the 1961 film version of *West Side Story*. Unlike Reynolds, Moreno trained and performed as a dancer from an early age. Her first instructor was Paco Cansino, who also taught Spanish dance to Cole and Kelly. By the age of nine, Moreno (born Rosa Dolores Alverio) was touring nightclubs with Cansino, in addition to taking lessons in modern dance, ballet, and tap, though she maintained she "was a Spanish dancer, period" during her earliest movie roles.[101] In 1949, she signed a seven-year contract with MGM.[102]

As originally conceived by script writers Comden and Green, the role of Zanders was much more prominent and was involved in much more

Figure 3.7 Screen capture of, from left to right, Reynolds as Kathy Selden, Kelly as Don Lockwood, Jean Hagen as Lina Lamont, and the Puerto Rican singer-actor-dancer Rita Moreno as the flapper Zelda Zanders, telling Lockwood "Oh, anytime, Don" after he sarcastically thanks her for revealing Selden as Lamont's voice double.

dancing. Listed as "Zelda Zonk" in the earliest screenplay drafts, the character functions as a competitor and foil to Reynolds's Selden. A script dated August 10, 1950, has Zelda dancing a Charleston at one point, and other scripts indicate that she was to appear in a big chorus number, initially to a song called "We'll Make Hay While the Sun Shines," later changed to "I've Got a Feeling You're Fooling." A script with a date of October 20, 1950, describes Zelda as "tearing herself to pieces in the number."[103] During a panel celebrating *Singin' in the Rain*'s fiftieth anniversary, Moreno recalled being taught "a little tango ... step" by Kelly, apparently to be included in a party scene near the beginning of the film.[104] This suggests that the tango dance scene at least made it to the rehearsal phase, though Zelda's other dance numbers didn't survive script revisions.

However reduced, Moreno's on-screen presence in *Singin' in the Rain* complicates the seemingly all-encompassing whiteness of the film. In

124   HOLLYWOOD DANCE-INS

point of fact, Moreno was not the only person of color to appear on screen. Production records list Robert Ossorio, a Filipino dancer who later became a ballet patron in New York City, as one of the film's "weekly dancers," along with three dancers with Spanish surnames: Rudy del Campo (who went on to play a member of the Puerto Rican Sharks gang in *West Side Story*), Rudy de Silva, and Shirley Lopez.[105] While information about these dancers is hard to come by, Lopez, who appeared as an uncredited chorus dancer in several other films and later taught ballet and modern dance in Westport, Connecticut, received her dance training with Carmelita Maracci, for whom she also performed.[106] Maracci, who was partly of Spanish descent, was a well-known teacher and performer of a fusion between ballet and Spanish dance.[107] Lopez, like Moreno, is thus a material, bodily link to the submerged Spanish dance influences on *Singin' in the Rain*.[108]

Although the U.S. Census at midcentury considered those of Latin descent white, theater scholar Brian Herrera has argued that Latinas/os increasingly came into legibility on screen during the 1950s and were frequently cast in roles that exploited their "uncertain or mixed raciality."[109] Noting that Moreno played characters of Asian descent in *The King and I* (1956) and on the television show *Father Knows Best* in 1958 before she played Puerto Rican in *West Side Story*, Herrera cites these as examples of "stealth Latino" performance—"instances in which an actor's known or perceived Latina/o identity haunts his or her portrayal of a particular role in ways that . . . contribute to the performance's effectiveness in its contemporary moment."[110]

What, then, should we make of Moreno's performance as Zanders in *Singin' in the Rain*? On the one hand, donning a red wig, she's playing an icon of white American femininity: her "Zip girl" starlet was a nod to the 1920s white "It" girl Clara Bow (Figure 3.8). Moreno has talked about being typecast as the "house ethnic" in Hollywood and has described the *Singin' in the Rain* role as a "sweet prize," since she "would not be playing a coy little ethnic maid with [her] own pidgin accent."[111] She credited Kelly with the "foresight" to cast her in a "nonethnic role," though film scholar Priscilla Ovalle notes that "her actual performance was deemed too ethnic without the temporary modification of her hair."[112] Is Moreno passing for white in the not-actually-all-white *Singin' in the Rain*? Yes, according to scholar Patricia Mellencamp, who states explicitly that Moreno was "passing for Anglo" in her role as Lamont's friend.[113] Mary Beltrán's characterization of Moreno's role as the "(non-Latina) tattletale Zelda Zanders" suggests the same, as does the fact that MGM changed Moreno's first name from Rosita to Rita.[114] On

Figure 3.8 Screen capture of Moreno being introduced as "that famous Zip Girl of the screen ... Zelda Zanders" with Stuart Holmes as J. Cumberland Sandrill III, "that well-known, eligible bachelor."

the other hand, John Mariani's 1978 account of the making of *Singin' in the Rain* claims that Moreno was brought in specifically "to play Latin spitfire Zelda Zanders."[115]

If Moreno's Latina identity does subtly haunt her role as Zelders in the manner that Herrera suggests, her diegetic outing of one white female body as a stand-in for another becomes more complicated and more significant. Even as Moreno's performance as Zanders suggests the possibility of a brown woman (almost but not quite) passing for white, her actions in *Singin' in the Rain* lay bare the female reproductive labor on which Lamont's star status rests, and those same actions set in motion Lamont's decision to take credit for that labor by continuing to "pass" as a singing and dancing film star. Narratively, Zanders thus interrupts and facilitates the conversion of white debt into white credit, at least before that credit is stripped from Lamont and returned to Selden. As a would-be competitor to Selden and ally to Lamont, Zanders is an on-screen reminder of the stratifications within whiteness, even as both she and Lamont serve as the (ever so subtly ethnically coded)

126 HOLLYWOOD DANCE-INS

backdrop against which Selden ascends. Given that Selden's ascent was also Reynolds's, it is arguably a cruel twist that the role that Moreno celebrated as nonethnicized indirectly helped usher in what she later described as the "Debbie Reynolds world" of postwar Hollywood.[116] This was a world that, as Beltrán writes, elevated "unambiguously white stars such as Reynolds" in the 1950s and 1960s while pigeonholing Moreno into roles that consistently racialized her as nonwhite.[117]

No matter how small her on-screen role in *Singin' in the Rain*, and no matter how that role contributed to Reynolds's rise, Moreno was reportedly a constant presence off-screen. "I was always there watching," she writes. "I never left the sets, even when I was not in a scene."[118] This off-screen presence aligns her in certain ways with Haney and Coyne, much as her on-screen presence is aligned with Lamont. Extradiegetically, Moreno is a ghost counterpart to Haney and Coyne, reminding us that alongside and behind the white women who surrounded, mediated, and propped up the dancing of idealized white female stars were still other women, some of them brown.

Ultimately, attending to the conditions of white women's dancing in *Singin' in the Rain* reveals parallels between the diegetic female reproductive labor that enabled the credibility of the fictional white star Lamont and the extradiegetic female reproductive labor that enabled the credibility of Reynolds. It also reveals the technology of the moving body itself—and not just the technological contrivances of moving pictures—as a potent site for the conversion of intercorporeal debts into, and their concealment as, corporeal credit. And when we learn to look a bit more closely at on-screen bodies that appear to be all white, we discover that the chains of corporeal debt that exist between white women are haunted narratively and genealogically by "inferential ethnic presences" that include women dancers of color, sitting just off camera.

4

"Cool It, Alex"

Queering the Dance-in

In July 1953, on the eve of the premiere of the MGM film musical *The Band Wagon* (1953), a *Newsweek* reporter published a feature on the rising star Cyd Charisse. In *Band Wagon*, she dances opposite tap dance star Fred Astaire, but her break came when she partnered Gene Kelly in "The Broadway Melody" dream ballet in the previous year's *Singin' in the Rain*. The feature emphasizes "the literally exhausting work [that] goes into the shaping of a dance production," citing Charisse's twelve-hour days. It also points to the group effort required to convert choreographer Michael Kidd's ideas into concrete dance steps, including the "well nigh indispensable help" that both Astaire and Charisse received from their dance-ins.[1] These supporting figures, the article explains, "are the dancers' counterpart to the movie actor's 'stand-ins'—people who accommodate the director, cameraman, costume and scenic designers, etc., when the actors themselves are not on the set." Actually, the article goes on to say, the "inside help" provided by dance-ins makes them "much more useful": "For while the stand-ins are not expected to act, but merely to correspond to the physical presence of those they represent, the dance-ins are supposed to help the dance director formulate his ideas. While the stars are off the set, the dance-ins work out parts of routines which they will later demonstrate to the leading dancers, thus saving the latter a good deal of time and energy." In a rare exception to their typical anonymity, *Newsweek* names the dance-ins in question. Supporting Charisse was Patricia (Pat) Denise, "a girl who ordinarily practices with [Charisse] at the *barre*." Supporting Astaire was "Alex Romera" [*sic*].[2]

Denise (1922–2018) was a white, Canadian-born dancer who performed with the Ballet Russes, appeared in the choruses of a number of Hollywood films, and assisted choreographers Hermes Pan, Jack Cole, Eugene Loring, and Jack Baker.[3] "Romera" is a misspelling or misprinting of "Romero." Born Alejandro Bernardo Quiroga, Alex Romero (1913–2007) was a Mexican American dancer who was proficient in Spanish dance, ballet, tap, and jazz,

Hollywood Dance-ins and the Reproduction of Bodies. Anthea Kraut, Oxford University Press.
© Oxford University Press 2025. DOI: 10.1093/oso/9780197789667.003.0005

128 HOLLYWOOD DANCE-INS

trained with Cole, and served first as a contract dancer, then as assistant choreographer, and eventually as staff choreographer for MGM. He is perhaps best known as Elvis Presley's choreographer or, as the title of Mark Knowles's biography of him submits, "the man who made the jailhouse rock."[4]

Separately and together, Denise and Romero crossed paths with the dancers who have figured in this book's foregoing chapters. Prior to *The Band Wagon*, Romero worked with Astaire on the 1949 film *The Barkleys of Broadway*, on which Pan, assisted by Angie Blue, was also employed as choreographer for a time.[5] Pan employed Romero as an assistant on the 1953 film *Kiss Me Kate* and Denise on the 1955 film *Jupiter's Darling*, where she worked as a dance-in alongside Blue.[6] Like Marie Bryant, Romero appears as an uncredited dancer in *On the Town* (1949), though with much more screen time, as I will discuss below. Romero and Carol Haney were Cole dancers together in the 1940s, and it was reportedly Romero who first suggested Haney to Kelly when the latter was looking for female assistants for *On the Town*.[7] Denise appears as an uncredited chorus dancer in *Singin' in the Rain* (1952); she is the dancer to Debbie Reynolds's left (the viewer's right) in the "All I Do" number (see Figure 3.3 in Chapter 3). Although not officially involved in *Singin' in the Rain*, Romero was working on an adjacent MGM lot during its production and may have helped Kelly and Charisse (along with Haney) work out the scarf dance in the "Broadway Melody" dream ballet.[8] Romero met Rita Moreno when he assisted with the choreography for the 1950 film *Pagan Love Song* (in which Moreno, in brownface, played a Tahitian native), and the two became close friends.[9] In 1959, Romero choreographed two dances for Reynolds in *Say One for Me*, and the two developed a "close working relationship as well as a deep friendship."[10] Such was the nature of Hollywood's corporeal ecosystem at midcentury: a crisscrossing of a steady group of dancers who were predominantly but not exclusively white, who played small on-screen and large off-screen roles, and who supported predominantly white men and women stars and predominantly white men choreographers.

Thus far, this book has focused on the reproductive labor of women dance-ins (and women coaches and assistant dance directors who functioned as dance-ins) within this ecosystem. This should not, however, be taken as an indication that women were overrepresented among dance-ins or choreographers' assistants. Men unequivocally dominated the rank of official choreographer in Hollywood, and centering women dancers behind the camera offsets this dominance. But choreographers regularly employed both men and women assistants on any given film. While Denise is no less deserving of study, this chapter turns its attention to Romero. As the sole male dance-in this book examines, he offers insight into additional kinds of gender relations that existed between choreographer, star, and dance-in, whose labor, as the *Newsweek* article reminds us, involved both physically representing the star and assisting in the creation and transmission of choreography.

Romero differs from the other dance-ins featured in this book, too, by virtue of the fact that he is already the subject of his own biography. Based on extensive interviews with Romero and many of his collaborators, Knowles's book is an invaluable source on Romero's life and career, and I rely heavily on it, as well as on other published interviews and various archival and photographic sources. Unlike the biography, my emphasis is not on Romero's trajectory from dancer to choreographer but on his role as dance-in and assistant,[11] and specifically his working relationship with Kelly. The two first met in 1944, first worked together in 1948 on *Words and Music* (whose "Slaughter on Tenth Avenue" number was discussed in Chapter 2 and to which I return below), and went on to collaborate on *On the Town* and *An American in Paris* (1951), both of which appear on the American Film Institute's list of the twenty-five "Greatest Movie Musicals of All-Time."[12] On their own and jointly, Kelly and Romero contributed to the popularization of a distinctive but eclectic style of jazz dance on film, one that borrowed from and combined the Africanist rhythms of tap dance, the Latin-, Africanist-, and South Asian–inflected technique developed by Cole, and the European aesthetics of ballet.

As other scholars have convincingly argued, Kelly made it his mission to combat perceptions of dancing as a "feminine undertaking" by projecting a "virile star image" and vigorously promoting dancing as a masculine activity.[13] Kelly's union with Romero presents an opportunity to approach the construction of the star's masculine image from another angle, by asking how its conditions of production may have paradoxically "put . . . pressure on masculinity."[14] Often working behind the scenes in tandem with a single woman dancer, Romero and Kelly lend themselves to analysis in terms of Eve Kosofsky Sedgwick's influential theorization of triangulated homosocial desire.[15] At the same time, the nature of their collaboration muddied questions of authorship and generated anxiety about choreographic paternity. As such, Romero and Kelly's working methods open up a space for

130 HOLLYWOOD DANCE-INS

considering whether there was something queer about the relations of re-production between the male star and his male dance-in. This, of course, is not the same as suggesting that either Kelly or Romero was queer. (Both were married to women, although that precludes nothing.) It is, rather, to ask how Clare Croft's understanding of queer as a force that disrupts the gender binary and José Muñoz's understanding of "queerness as a restructuring of relationality" apply to the reproductive relations engendered by the dance-in.[16] Building on these understandings, as well as on queer readings of stage and film musicals,[17] this chapter proposes that the intercorporeal exchanges that take place in rehearsal rooms may be queerly charged, even when the filmic images they produce are heteronormative.

Romero's collaboration with Kelly is also the most sustained cross-ethnic relationship between star and dance-in that this book considers. As a Mexican American working in white Hollywood, Romero enables us to extend the previous chapter's discussion of the racialization of Latinas/os in the middle of the twentieth century. He also provides another vantage point on how dance-ins mediated the reproduction of whiteness. As will become clear, Romero and Kelly shared certain physical characteristics but not others, and they copied, traded places with, and assisted one another within an intimate but uneven field of power. Their creative partnership thus involved a mode of transmission that was not the same as Kelly's appropriation of African American dance styles, as documented by scholars like Carol Clover and Pam Krayenbuhl. Ultimately, Kelly and Romero expand and nuance our view of the off-screen interactions that supported but also complicated the reproduction of white masculinity in the mid-twentieth century U.S. film musical.

In what follows, I take four different looks at the Romero-Kelly relationship and its various undercurrents. In the first, I establish the ways Romero functioned as Kelly's off-screen double and begin to probe the presence of desire in their relations of looking and reciprocal embodiment. In the second, I examine the "erotic triangles" that frequently structured the men's corporeal configurations, not only in the rehearsal studio but also, in the case of "A Day in New York" in *On the Town*, on screen. I then assess the implications of being "caught" in the act of reproduction and the gendered threat that Romero's blurring of the original/copy binary posed to Kelly's masculine reputation. Finally, I ask how Romero's racial status bears on the "relational schema"[18] that existed between white choreographer-star and brown dance-in.

Romero as Double and Mirror

In a 2017 online post on Facebook, Gene Kelly's widow, Patricia Ward Kelly, framed his use of a dance-in in labor-saving terms that echo those of the *Newsweek* article cited above. "You always have a dance-in," she recalls Kelly saying. "For instance, if you want to set it up for the camera you have a dance-in go in and hit the marks and dance for you while they're lighting. Otherwise you were pooped out before you went in and did the take. Then you rehearse a couple times. But they rehearse it for you. They hit the marks." The memory accompanies a photo of Kelly rehearsing for the 1976 retrospective compilation film *That's Entertainment Part II*, flanked by Alex Romero and Robin Hoctor, a white woman.[19] The dance-in depicted here is a figure of efficiency who helps the cinematographer anticipate the choreographic marks they need to hit to create projectable images, thus sparing the star from "pooping out" too soon.

But in a 1975 interview with Marilyn Hunt, housed at the New York Public Library for the Performing Arts, Gene Kelly made clear that, at least earlier in his career, Romero's "indispensable help" also included helping Kelly "formulate his ideas," to again cite the *Newsweek* feature. Recounting the rehearsal process for the ten-minute "Slaughter on Tenth Avenue," the slinky, jazz-ballet number featuring Kelly and Vera-Ellen in *Words and Music* (1948)—and the same dance that necessitated Vera-Ellen's training with Marie Bryant (see Chapter 2)—Kelly shared, "I had an assistant at that time who later choreographed at MGM. His name was Alex Romero and he now teaches dancing in a suburb of L.A. He was very strong and my size. And we both had enough muscles to lift the girl all day and to try these various things." Acknowledging his frequent reliance on Carol Haney and Jeanne Coyne (see Chapter 3), Kelly maintained that, because he "couldn't have girls doing lifts and things like that," and because his otherwise collaborator Stanley Donen "wasn't that complete of a dancer," Romero became vital to him. Kelly elaborates on their choreographic process: "We'd stand, we'd look at each other and try these different lifts. . . . At times like that, you want to see how a lift will look. If he does something whether accidentally or tries something, or I'll say, 'Try another twist. We know we have her up there.' And he does something, I'll see it. Even if he doesn't quite know what he did because so much of that, as you know, is trial and error, when you get a variation on a lift."[20] Here, Romero does much more than hit Kelly's predetermined marks and much more than save the star from fatigue. Engaging in a back-and-forth

132   HOLLYWOOD DANCE-INS

exchange with Kelly, who juggles his roles as dancer and choreographer, he helps Kelly determine what and where those marks should be. And as Kelly's masculine counterpart, Romero helps him uphold the heteronormativity of the choreography, enforcing the maxim that only men "lift the girl."

Knowles's biography of Romero includes an anecdote about the making of *Words and Music* that casts Romero's involvement in still another light. One day Romero, newly placed on contract at MGM as a choreographic assistant to dance director Robert Alton, was standing alongside Alton in one of MGM's rehearsal halls when in walked Kelly. "Gene, come on over here," Romero recalled Alton saying. "I want you to meet Alex Romero. He's one of Jack Cole's dancers." "God, you guys are great," responded Kelly. He then asked Alton if he could "borrow [Romero] for a few minutes" to show him the "Slaughter" set. Knowles's account continues: "Kelly and Alex walked to another hall where the number was being rehearsed. The set was a rough, unpainted mock-up of the one that would eventually be used in the movie. Kelly asked Alex, 'You see that bar over there? First off, I want you to choreograph my number and part of Vera-Ellen's. She does part of the dance with me, and I do part of it alone. Get me up on that bar and give me nothing but Jack Cole stuff.'"[21] Left alone with a recording of the music, Romero proceeded to "play around" until he had devised some choreography, including a Cole-style slide and knee drop. When Kelly returned ninety minutes later, Romero showed Kelly what he had come up with. Kelly loved it, and the two "collaborated on finessing the routine" over the next six weeks.[22]

Placed side by side, Kelly's and Romero's accounts of their work on "Slaughter" offer conflicting narratives about their choreographic roles. I juxtapose them not to pit their claims to authorship against each other (though I will return to those claims as they bear on the men's gendered relations) but to explore what they reveal about the multiple facets of the men's partnership. In Kelly's telling, Romero is an ideal assistant because he is a "complete" dancer and because his strength and size match Kelly's. In Romero's telling, his value lies in what he possesses that Kelly does not: Jack Cole training. One of the original twelve members of Cole's Columbia Pictures troupe, Romero studied with and danced for Cole for three and a half years between 1944 and 1947, appearing in Cole's nightclub acts and his ensemble in a number of films.[23] He left the troupe just three weeks before he met Kelly. However similar in stature and musculature, Romero and Kelly did not have identical movement backgrounds.

"COOL IT, ALEX" 133

With this in mind, there is even more to Kelly's description of the men's collaborative process than first meets the eye. In Kelly's account, creating the "Slaughter" duet depended on carefully observing one another as he and Romero tried out different movement possibilities: "We'd stand, we'd look at each other" and "he does something, I'll see it." Unlike a stand-in, Romero is not dancing for the camera in Kelly's absence here. Rather, he is dancing both *as* Kelly and *for* Kelly. Projecting his physicality back to Kelly, Romero is Kelly's double and mirror. Yet because Romero's physicality also bore the immediate traces of his training with Cole, it was not an exact replica of Kelly's; as a mirror, Romero did more than just reflect. Given that Romero had the "Jack Cole stuff" that Kelly wanted, might there have been an element of desire in what Kelly saw in Romero's image? And when Kelly took his place in the choreography, which "he" was he inhabiting?

In some respects, these questions could be asked of all acts of transmission between dancers, including those that accompany the acquisition of "technique." In a foundational 1997 essay, Susan Leigh Foster theorizes dancing bodies as constructed via the training processes that instruct them. Western systems of dance training, Foster argues, depend upon and create two bodies: a "perceived and tangible body" derived from the "sensory information" a dancer takes in—"visual, aural, haptic, olfactory, and perhaps most important, kinaesthetic"—and an "aesthetically ideal" body that combines aspects of the dancer's perceived body with "fantasized visual or kinesthetic images of a body, images of other dancers' bodies, and cinematic or video images of dancing bodies." These bodies operate together in dance classes, where the emphasis is typically on "seeing a movement and then performing it." For Foster, this operation is strictly desexualized. The kinesthetic empathy that arises from watching how another body moves, she maintains, "rarely includes erotic feelings." Yet when Foster delineates a "third kind of body," the possibility of desire slips in. Supplementing the perceived and ideal body is the "demonstrative body," a figure who "mediates the acquisition of ... skills by exemplifying correct or incorrect movement." Explaining that the demonstrative body "displays itself in the body of the teacher, and sometimes in one's own image in the mirror and in the bodies of other students in the class and their mirror images," Foster notes, "[W]hen I look at another student in class, I see her or his body not as that of a friend or an acquaintance, but as the bodily instantiation of desired or undesired, correct or incorrect, values."[24] Though couched in the language of movement values, here is an

134   HOLLYWOOD DANCE-INS

acknowledgment, slight as it is, that relations of desire may be activated when a dancer hones their corporeality in the image of another.

Applying Foster's framework to Kelly and Romero's choreographic process, we might say that, for Kelly, Romero alternates between the perceived body, the ideal body, and the demonstrative body, or perhaps embodies all three at once. To the extent that he provides data back to Kelly of what the latter's similarly sized and similarly shaped body might look like in certain positions with a female partner, Romero is the perceived body. To the extent that his movement proclivities are informed by the sought-after "Jack Cole stuff," Romero is the aesthetically ideal body. And to the extent that he serves as the "bodily instantiation" of "desired or undesired" choreographic moves, Romero is the demonstrative body. Kelly, recall, was not only creating choreography for "Slaughter" in these rehearsals but also fashioning his own filmic image. That Romero played such a pivotal role in that process, and that his body served, for Kelly, as a projection of Cole, of Kelly, and of himself, would seem to exemplify what queer theorists have called the "slippery relation . . . between desire and identification."[25] In all the looking, all the testing out of movements, all the imagining of one's body in the space of the other, all the swapping of positions, all the replication, how can one disentangle identification from desire, and how can one rule out the potential for an erotic charge?[26]

Romero and Erotic Triangles

In June 1949, *Life* magazine hired freelance photographer Jon Brenneis to document the collaboration between Kelly and composer Leonard Bernstein on the MGM set in Hollywood, where the film version of *On the Town*, co-directed by Kelly and Stanley Donen, was in production. The same musical in which Bryant makes a thirteen-second appearance (see Chapter 2), *On the Town* tells the story of three white sailors, played by Kelly, Frank Sinatra, and Jules Munshin, on shore leave in New York City for twenty-four hours. Kelly's character, Gabey, falls in love with Ivy Smith, played by Vera-Ellen, whose image he encounters on a "Miss Turnstiles" poster on the subway. The sailors spend the rest of the film searching for Ivy at various locations around the city. Bernstein composed the score for the 1944 Broadway version of the musical, but much of that score was jettisoned for the film.[27] The exception was the seven-and-a-half-minute "A Day in New York" number, a dream ballet in which Kelly's Gabey relives his day pining after Vera-Ellen's Ivy, for which Bernstein rearranged and revised pieces of his original score.[28] Over four hundred negatives of Brenneis's shots survive in his photographic archive at the University of California, Berkeley's Bancroft Library.[29] In addition to capturing Kelly with Bernstein, Brenneis took numerous photographs of Kelly, Vera-Ellen, and an ensemble of dancers rehearsing "A Day in New York." Appearing in approximately 150 of these is Romero.

Romero's ubiquity in these shots reflects his dual role as Kelly's assistant dance director on the film and a featured dancer in "A Day in New York." Doubling on-screen for the non-dance-trained actors Sinatra and Munshin, he and dancer Lee Scott,[30] together with Kelly, form the sailor trio in the dream ballet. While I address Romero's film performance below, I turn first to Brenneis's rehearsal photographs for the visual evidence they offer of Kelly and Romero's partnership. In the place-switching and triangulated relationships they depict, the photos direct us to the existence of potentially queer circuits undergirding filmic images of heterosexual duets, circuits that created an opening for desire to flow in multiple directions.

More than a dozen of the photos shows Romero, Kelly, and Vera-Ellen working out the choreography for the middle section of "A Day in New York," in which Kelly and Vera-Ellen perform a duet that unfolds on, underneath, and around a ballet barre, where Vera-Ellen as Ivy has been practicing ballet exercises. Shot almost exactly a year after the same trio rehearsed *Words and Music*'s "Slaughter on Tenth Avenue," the photos seem practically designed to illustrate the choreographic process described by Kelly above ("We'd stand, we'd look at each other and try these different lifts"). Figure 4.1, for example, shows Romero and Kelly both helping Vera-Ellen position her body on top of the ballet barre. In Figure 4.2, Romero is positioned below the barre and Vera-Ellen above it, while Kelly stands back to observe them—an instance of Romero rehearsing both for and as Kelly. In Figure 4.3, a screen capture from that same segment of "A Day in New York," Kelly has taken Romero's place underneath the barre.

In addition to exemplifying how Kelly and Romero doubled for one another, these photos make conspicuous what I have glossed over to this point: Vera-Ellen's presence during the men's exchanges. I have already addressed Vera-Ellen's corporeality in the context of her parasitical relationship to Bryant, whose training helped Vera-Ellen land the starring role in *On the Town* (see Chapter 2). Here it is the white female star's corporeality with respect to Romero and Kelly that must be accounted for. In the interview with

Figure 4.1 From left to right, Alex Romero, Vera-Ellen, and Gene Kelly rehearsing "A Day in New York" from *On the Town* (1949) on the MGM lot. Jon Brenneis Photograph Archive, BANC PIC 2002.171, Bancroft Library, University of California, Berkeley. Brenneis took the photograph while employed by *Life* magazine in July 1949. Jon Brenneis/The LIFE Images Collection via Getty Images.

Hunt cited above, Kelly credited Vera-Ellen with working hard as a dancer on "Slaughter on Tenth Avenue," but also stated that he "only had Alex on that show." Regarding her role in working out the number's lifts, he told Hunt, "She was literally black and blue all over. She could have cared less."[31] The depiction in Figure 4.1 of Romero and Kelly manipulating her on the ballet barre reinforces this sense of Vera-Ellen as a docile body, willingly participating in her own manhandling.[32] Yet however objectified, her materiality means the relations we need to grapple with are those of a trio rather than a duo.

The composition of that trio seems tailor-made for analysis through the lens of Sedgwick's theorization of "erotic triangles." As scholar Robyn Wiegman explains in a 2015 essay reflecting on Sedgwick's influence, Sedgwick's "key focus" in her 1985 book *Between Men: English Literature and Male Homosocial Desire* "was the 'erotic triangle'—a figure she drew from René Girard's well-regarded study *Deceit, Desire, and the Novel*, which

"COOL IT, ALEX" 137

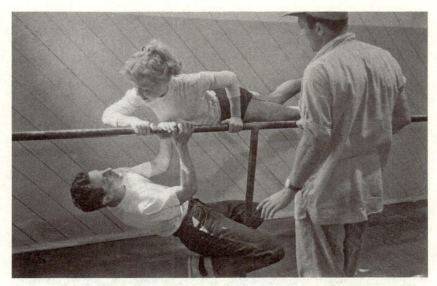

Figure 4.2 Gene Kelly observes Alex Romero and Vera-Ellen rehearsing "A Day in New York." Jon Brenneis Photograph Archive, BANC PIC 2002.171, Bancroft Library, University of California, Berkeley. Jon Brenneis/The LIFE Images Collection via Getty Images.

explored the plot lines of major European texts in which two men enter into a rivalrous relationship with one another for the attention/love/devotion of the same woman."[33] Drawing on Girard and on Gayle Rubin's framework of "male traffic in women," Sedgwick argued that the "homosocial bonds" that existed between rivalrous men produced "homosocial desire," which they displaced by routing it through the bodies of women.[34] What Sedgwick's analysis made visible, Wiegman writes, is "that the structuring prohibition that barred ... men from choosing one another as sexual objects existed in dramatic tension with the priority afforded masculine bonds in Western modernity—and further that this tension was routinely defined by, if not organized through, relationships to women, whether real or imagined, rejected or pursued."[35] The triangle has thus served as a mechanism for "maintaining and transmitting patriarchal power" in a "male-dominated society," and the homosocial desire it facilitates is at least "on par with, if not at times more socially valuable than, the heterosexual bond that was otherwise taken to found the triangle's erotic life."[36]

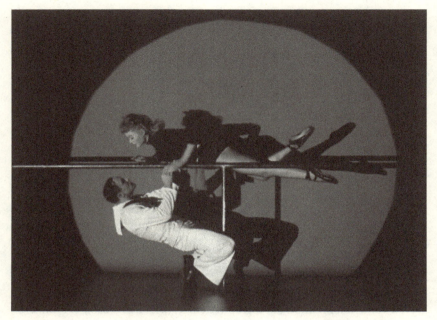

Figure 4.3 Screen capture of Gene Kelly and Vera-Ellen in "A Day in New York" from *On the Town* (1949). Kelly has assumed the position tested out in rehearsal by Romero in Figure 4.2.

In Sedgwickian terms, Vera-Ellen's presence simultaneously reinforces Kelly and Romero's patriarchal power and increases the possibility of erotic affect between them. In Figure 4.1, both men are touching Vera-Ellen, whose body bisects theirs. She appears to need both their efforts to hoist her up on the barre, and all three focus their gaze on their intersecting point of contact. In Figure 4.2, their bodies form the literal shape of a triangle. They may not touch each other directly, but Vera-Ellen serves as a vector between them. After Sedgwick, the fact that the choreography they are co-creating is a heterosexual duet (as seen in Figure 4.3) hardly nullifies homosocial desire; to the contrary, it provides a sanctioned channel for desire to circulate between Romero and Kelly. To be sure, whereas in Figure 4.2, Kelly looks on as Romero and Vera-Ellen gaze directly at one another, in a photo of the trio rehearsing a different moment from "A Day in New York" (Figure 4.4), it is Romero who looks on, smiling, as Kelly and Vera-Ellen lean in toward one another for a kiss. In still another photo (Figure 4.5) the men have swapped positions yet again: Romero and Vera-Ellen are crouched down in

Figure 4.4 Romero, standing at the piano, looks on as Vera-Ellen and Kelly rehearse the lead-up to a kiss from "A Day in New York." Jon Brenneis Photograph Archive, BANC PIC 2002.171, Bancroft Library, University of California, Berkeley. Jon Brenneis/The LIFE Images Collection via Getty Images.

an embrace, while Kelly watches from a nearby chair, seemingly unable to keep his body from enacting the choreography. (Bernstein and another man watch in the background.) Yes, Kelly, Romero, and Vera-Ellen are rehearsing and acting in all of these photos, and no, I'm not suggesting that any of them desired each other sexually. But neither should we dismiss the prospect that the repeated staging of heterosexual desire via the structure of a triangle, combined with Kelly and Romero's constant exchanging of places, made the relations between desire and identification all the more slippery.

It is notable in this regard that contemporary scholars have called the duet in the middle of "A Day in New York" "tender and erotic" and "deliberately sensual."[37] Kelly biographers Earl Hess and Pratibha Dabholkar confirm that he intentionally sought to infuse the duet with erotic energy:

> Kelly was captivated by the application of color to this sequence, believing it was "rather dull" when he saw it in black and white rushes. Once the Technicolor people finished bathing the sequence in rich colors, especially

Figure 4.5 Kelly watches as Romero and Vera-Ellen rehearse another moment of romantic longing. Leonard Bernstein is seated at the piano. Jon Brenneis Photograph Archive, BANC PIC 2002.171, Bancroft Library, University of California, Berkeley. Jon Brenneis/The LIFE Images Collection via Getty Images.

"COOL IT, ALEX" 141

red, everything jelled. "It heightened the fact that these two people were yearning for each other," he recalled. But Gene's choreography also highlighted that yearning. He developed some of the most sensual moves of his career as the two slide together over and around the barre assembly to Bernstein's bittersweet music. "Yet I never laid a glove on her. There was nothing the censors could say."[38]

The two-minute duet in question both opens and closes with Kelly and Vera-Ellen looking longingly at one another across a stage, where the ballet barre is located. In between are a series of moves in which they lunge toward and away from each other, often separated by just the barre (including the moment depicted in Figure 4.3). The sensuality is amplified by the projection of their silhouettes on the wall behind them, forming a shadow couple. The duet culminates with Kelly lifting, spinning, and finally kissing Vera-Ellen. Kelly's insistence that he "never laid a glove" on her takes on a certain irony given the rehearsal shots of him placing both hands on her, though his point was that he succeeded in evading censorship under the Motion Picture Production Code's prohibition of dances "suggesting or representing sexual actions."[39] The restriction of more explicitly sexual moves in a dance about longing arguably only increased the duet's erotic tension.

In his examination of the seeming contradictions between the mass popularity of MGM's mid-twentieth-century film musicals and the camp sensibility they enacted, Steven Cohan argues that "what Kelly signified as a male dancer during his years at MGM was more complicated, less stable and coherent" than a straightforward "recuperation of a confident heterosexual masculinity."[40] By way of example, he cites the tensions within Kelly's "elaborately produced and expensive ballet[s]" (such as *Words and Music*'s "Slaughter," *On the Town*'s "A Day in New York," and *Singin' in the Rain*'s "Broadway Melody"), which simultaneously worked to "openly heterosexualize . . . his dancing by pairing him with an equally expert female dancer trained in classical ballet" and, at the same time, "repeatedly depict . . . heterosexual loss, recounting an inner narrative of Kelly's losing the woman with whom he dances."[41] Cohan also notes the prevalence of homosocial relations in Kelly's films—he quotes film historian Gerald Mast's line that "dancing is something Kelly does with his buddies"—and the triangulation of these relations with a female figure.[42] Writing about *Singin' in the Rain*, Cohan observes that the union between Kelly as Don Lockwood and Reynolds as Kathy Selden "is not achieved by heterosexually combining

142   HOLLYWOOD DANCE-INS

man and woman but by subtracting the extra male [Donald O'Connor as Cosmo] from the initial equation."[43] This, as we have seen, is precisely the operation that played out during the creation of "Slaughter" and "A Day in New York": same-sex buddy pairing, triangulation with a female figure, subtraction of the buddy. The difference is that Romero's subtraction took place prior to filming rather than within the diegesis.

Actually, Romero and Kelly performed this same sequence on-screen in "A Day in New York," in which, as indicated above, Romero doubles for Sinatra or Munshin.[44] Dressed in white sailor uniforms, the trio of Romero, Scott, and Kelly dances in unison in front of a cutout of the New York City skyline in an exuberant reenactment of the film's opening "New York, New York" number. The choreography, dance scholar Beth Genné writes, "combines stylized vernacular movements—running, walking, skipping, and jumping steps—with influences from a variety of dance sources, ranging from ballet to social dance ... to sports, jazz, and modern dance."[45] About forty seconds into the trio, two women dancers, Marie Groscup and Carol Haney, doubling for Ann Miller and Betty Garrett, appear behind them, the former dressed all in yellow and holding a red scarf, the latter dressed all in green and holding a yellow scarf.[46] Looking serious and seductive, the women pose with a hand on their hip and one heel popped. Once they catch the men's attention, Groscup and Haney break into a jazzy, Cole-inspired set of movements, including hip swivels and slinky walks. The men are immediately smitten, and when the women drop their scarves, Romero and Scott rush to pick them up and then pursue the women. Scott, paired with Groscup, and Romero, paired with Haney, begin to dance cheek to cheek, leaving Kelly the odd man out. The camera pans to the right to follow Kelly as he trails the now traveling Romero and Haney. Tapping Romero on the shoulder, Kelly "steals" Haney by taking Romero's place, making Romero the odd man out. But when Haney temptingly dangles her scarf in front of Kelly's face, Romero seizes the opportunity: giving Kelly a kick in the torso, he sends Kelly sliding backward across the floor, where he bumps into the "Miss Turnstiles" poster that features Vera-Ellen's image. This sets in motion Kelly's fantasizing about her, which in turn leads to the duet at the barre described above. A condensed version of the romantic equation that Cohan identifies as characteristic of Kelly's MGM films, this short choreographic sequence is also a filmic rendering of the place-swapping, triangulation, and subtraction that typified Kelly and Romero's off-screen collaborations.

A number of the Brenneis photos capture rehearsals for this sequence. Figure 4.6 shows Romero, Kelly, and Haney in one such image. Haney taunts Kelly with her scarf; Kelly closes his eyes, opens his mouth, and extends his hands as if in the throes of desire; and Romero looks on jealously. (A third man watches the action in the background. This could have been Scott or Eugene Freedley, who was also part of the "rehearsal unit" for the ballet number and who, other Brenneis photographs suggest, may have danced in for Kelly when Kelly and Romero were in a scene together.)[47] Put in Sedgwickian terms, Haney, flanked by Kelly and Romero, seduces the former while mediating a rivalry between the two. Desire is centered here, and it is routed through Haney's body. That it is Haney rather than Vera-Ellen who mediates the homosocial relationship in this instance underscores the regularity with which erotic triangles could arise in front of and behind the camera, between stars and supporting players alike.[48] In this single photograph, a rare document of two dance-in/assistants rehearsing their own filmic performance, we catch sight of just how far from straight(forward)— how multiplicitous the pairings, triangulations, and substitutions, how potentially queer—the relations that structured choreographic representations of heterosexual unions could be.

Romero as Queer Mode of Reproduction

However much these on- and off-screen erotic triangles facilitated the circulation of homosocial desire, a third look at the transmission of movement across Romero's and Kelly's bodies reveals still other "disturbance[s] to heteronormality" within their relationship.[49] In this book's previous chapters, I analyzed the reproductive labor of women dance-ins through the lens of surrogation (see especially Chapters 1 and 3). The Romero-Kelly pairing invites comparison to other technologies of reproduction that, like surrogacy, disrupt biological models rooted in a heterosexual gender binary.

In a 2001 interview with Romero, titled "The Assistant," photographer and author Rose Eichenbaum asked him to clarify "what exactly . . . a choreographer's assistant do[es]?" He began as follows: "The way it normally works is you stand behind the choreographer, and every time he makes a move, you learn it. You have to be plenty sharp at picking things up because he doesn't know what he's going to leave in or take out. He throws out so much stuff that he doesn't always remember what he's done. He'll come back

Figure 4.6 From left to right, Romero, Carol Haney, and Kelly rehearsing "A Day in New York" on the set of *On the Town*. Jon Brenneis Photograph Archive, BANC PIC 2002.171, Bancroft Library, University of California, Berkeley. The photo appeared in the December 26, 1949, issue of *Life*. Jon Brenneis/The LIFE Images Collection via Getty.

to you and say, 'What did I just do?' And you have to repeat whatever he demonstrated."[50] In this account, Romero is neither left alone to generate choreography nor engaged in a back-and-forth trading of ideas with the choreographer. Instead, he acts as the choreographer's shadow, duplicating each of his moves. But here Romero shadows not so he can serve as instantaneous mirror but to document what the choreographer has done—akin to the cinematic apparatus itself. This is precisely how Eichenbaum responds to Romero's description. "You're like a human video recorder," she remarks. Romero replies with a simple "Yes." Standing behind the choreographer's body and standing in for the choreographer's bodily memory, Romero "records" movement so it can be "rewound" and viewed on command.

The analogizing of Romero to a video recorder not only adds to the list of the kind of doubling the dance-in/choreographic assistant performs; it also renders his dancing a "machinic practice."[51] Insofar as he functions like a camera and a playback device, Romero illustrates dance scholar Harmony Bench's claim that "bodies are not antithetical to machines, but . . . are themselves already machines and come into relationships with technologies as machines."[52] Yet Romero's "likeness" rather than equivalence to a video recorder acknowledges a gap between technological and body-to-body modes of reproduction. Indeed, the slight divergences in Romero's and Kelly's comportment in Figures 4.2 and 4.3—note their different hand positions and the different angles of their heads—are evidence of the inexact nature of human mimesis. And, as should by now be clear, the dance-in/assistant does not just replicate movement (if never identically) but also helps materialize new choreography through "trial-and-error" embodiment. This raises the question: What kind of reproduction produces both originals and copies?

Elsewhere in their interview, Eichenbaum asks Romero if "choreographers ever pick[ed] your brain for dance moves," to which Romero responds, "Oh, yes." Explaining that he "would make suggestions, but only when . . . asked to," he offers the following story:

> One day I'm in a rehearsal room with Gene Kelly, and he's doing this number, you see, when suddenly he gets stuck. "Alex," he says, "what can I do next?" I think to myself, "Well, he never went in that direction and maybe we could add a turn over here," and suddenly this thing is coming together. He says, "That's great. Do a little more." So I choreograph at least a quarter of the number, and he's applauding me, when suddenly the door

146 HOLLYWOOD DANCE-INS

opens and in walks the producer, Arthur Freed. Gene pushes me aside and says, "Cool it, Alex."

Seeking clarification, Eichenbaum asks if Romero means "that Gene Kelly didn't want anyone to see that you were helping him." Romero confirms with a slight variation: "He didn't want anyone to know that he might need help."[53] Romero's assertion that he was responsible for "at least a quarter" of the choreography for an unnamed movie number that was attributed to Kelly is noteworthy. But I am not interested here in ascertaining which number, nor in reassigning credit for it. Instead, I want to focus on Kelly's actions when producer Freed enters the rehearsal space. Much as the movie industry has historically "shrouded" its use of body doubles, Kelly's pushing aside Romero and his instructions to "cool it" betray a nervousness about his dependence on a "supplementary" body.[54]

Performance studies scholar Rebecca Schneider's discussion of Western fears about copies helps unpack this nervousness. In her 2001 article "Hello Dolly Well Hello Dolly: The Double and Its Theatre," Schneider relates the anxiety around the 1997 cloning of Dolly the sheep to "a rather ancient Western cultural distrust of mimesis." This distrust, she explains, is connected to "a fear of indiscreet origins. . . . The fear is that the copy will not only tamper with the original, but will author the original—or, perhaps most fearful, that the copy (the rib, the second) will come to be acknowledged as author, father, First."[55] As Schneider's rhetoric (indebted to the insights of Freudian psychoanalysis and Derridean deconstruction) implies, threats to originality have a distinctly gendered subtext—or, rather, gendered subtexts, plural. On one level, the inversion of the original/copy hierarchy unsettles the patriarchal order and the "proper" lines of heteronormative, genealogical transmission: rather than the father begetting the son, the son produces the father. On another level, cloning and mimesis are reproductive practices with differently gendered significations. While "'cloning' has long been synonymous with high tech, and high tech has been associated with masculinity," the "no tech" practice of mimesis has been figured as "primitivized, feminized, and debased."[56]

Kelly's attempt to conceal his reliance on Romero also seems driven by gender-inflected fears. Disclosing Romero, Kelly's assistant and dance-in, as the creator of a chunk of film choreography would have compromised Kelly's status as "author, father, First." "You have to understand," Romero tells Eischenbaum, "that [Kelly] had a huge reputation to maintain."[57]

Correspondingly, Kelly's nudge and "Cool it" directive can be seen as gestures that trigger "relations of the closet." "Closetedness," Sedgwick writes in her follow-up to *Between Men*, is "a performance initiated as such by the speech act of a silence." Silencing Romero, Kelly casts the "true" nature of their relationship as in need of closeting and thus, retroactively, as transgressive. Once ushered into being, moreover, the closet enacts its own set of relations, described by Sedgwick as "the relations of the known and the unknown, the explicit and the implicit."[58] That is to say, the very existence of a closet creates a "distinction between inner and outer (where only the latter is assumed to be knowable, and the former is a 'secret' perhaps even to the self)," as well as an accompanying "skepticism" about the distinction between the two.[59] In Romero and Kelly's case, the "secret" is that Kelly's film choreography was partially generated by his assistant—that, behind closed doors, the star's shadow is directing the movements of the star. In a disturbance to the patriarchal order of things, the masculine original has swapped places with the feminized derivative. But the treatment of this *as* a secret "cultivates . . . curiosity" about that which is not spoken in Romero's account but is its logical implication: how can we ever know the extent to which Kelly's dancing and his corollary filmic image are "singularly and unwaveringly his"?[60]

If Romero, at least in certain circumstances, posed a threat to Kelly's masculine "huge reputation" and presumed originality, the gendering of Romero's reproductive function is itself anything but stable. Machine-like (he records and can "play back" Kelly's movements) and mimetic (every time Kelly makes a move, he repeats it), Romero blurs the lines between masculinized technology and feminized "no tech," just as his alternation between replicating and generating choreography blurs the lines between the masculinized author and the feminized copy. The dance-in/assistant, like the clone, thus disrupts "the heteronormative tenet that femininity and masculinity are fully distinct from each other."[61] This disruption was arguably literalized at times for Romero, who was occasionally called upon to help craft, rehearse, and teach both men's and women's dance parts, and therefore to inhabit the choreography of both men and women stars. Romero attributed his skill at performing and transmitting across genders to Cole, who reportedly told his company members, "'I want you boys to dance like girls and I want you girls to dance like men'" so that they could "teach either sex when assigned on a movie."[62] Performing gender fluidity and enacting reproductive relations that destabilized the norms of patrilineal genealogy,

148 HOLLYWOOD DANCE-INS

Romero embodied "an ambiguity that play[ed] across the binary of sexual difference."[63]

Romero as Dark Copy

In a 2005 essay that picks up on her earlier examination of originality, doubling, and repetition, Schneider quotes artist Antoinette LaFarge's assertion that, with the primacy of the copy, art has become "virtually identical with its dark twin, forgery."[64] In response, Schneider asks, "[W]hy is the twin marked as dark? Why is it color that draws a line between one twin and its criminalized other?" Her questions highlight the tendency in Western dichotomies between the original and the copy to not only feminize but also racialize the copy.[65] In the case of the Mexican American Romero and the Irish American Kelly, the matter of the copy's racial charge must be considered in more than metaphorical terms. In this fourth and final look at the pair, I weigh how the men's nonidentical racial positionalities structured the field of power in which their intercorporeal exchanges played out.

As we saw in the previous chapter's discussion of Rita Moreno, the racial status of Latinas/os in the United States at midcentury was neither fixed nor certain. While the 1930 U.S. Census included "Mexican" as a separate racial classification, that category disappeared in subsequent years. Sociologist Clara E. Rodríguez reports, "From 1940 to 1980, Puerto Ricans, Mexicans, and all other Latinos were classified as 'white' unless the census interviewer determined (or the respondent indicated to the interviewer) that they were of some other race category, such as black or Asian. Prior to 1980, the U.S. Census Bureau had, at various times, also counted samples of Latinos using cultural indicators, such as whether the person's mother tongue was Spanish (1940) and whether he or she had a Spanish surname (1950) or was of 'Spanish origin'" (1970).[66] Latinas/os at midcentury were also caught up in the contradictions of a wartime mobilization that relied on nonwhite participation but perpetuated practices of segregation and discrimination that led to increasing racial tensions.[67] In Los Angeles, these tensions culminated in the so-called Zoot Suit Riots of 1943, "ten days of violent clashes between Mexican American youth and Anglo servicemen, joined quickly by civilians."[68] In Hollywood, while the Good Neighbor Policy's bid to court Latin American markets launched a string of Latin-themed films, a vogue for Latin-themed numbers, and attempts to disseminate more positive depictions of Latinas/os during the 1930s and 1940s, the end of the war led to a return to "tried-and-true formulas" of racial stereotyping, even as Latina/o actors became useful for their racial "interchangeability" and their ability to "portray . . . a diverse array of nonwhite characters."[69]

Knowles's biography of Romero does not directly address the significance of race to Romero's career, but it does tell us that "Alex was . . . proud to be Mexican, and his Latino heritage defined a large part of who he was."[70] It also provides details that help situate Romero in the U.S. racial landscape in the 1940s and 1950s. Romero was born in 1913 to a theatrical and politically elite family from Monterrey, Mexico.[71] That same year, armed forces in the Mexican Revolution killed Romero's father and a number of his brothers, prompting his mother, possibly pregnant with Alex, to flee to Texas along with his remaining siblings. In the 1920s, the family settled in a "poor Mexican neighborhood" in Los Angeles, where his older brother Carlos had come to pursue film work.[72] As a teenager, Alex accompanied his surviving brothers as they toured vaudeville in a Spanish dance act that took them around the United States and to Europe. Having changed their name to Romero to avoid mispronunciations of Quiroga, the troupe was a competitor to the Cansino family, the famous Spanish dance ensemble headed by Rita Hayworth's uncle.[73] When the act disbanded at the start of World War II, Romero turned to film work and earned a spot in Cole's dance ensemble.[74]

Across these years, Romero appears to have lived a number of the contradictions that Anthony Macías describes in his book *Mexican American Mojo: Popular Music, Dance, and Urban Culture in Los Angeles, 1935–1968*. This period, Macías tells us, was "one of emerging middle-class formations and burgeoning civil rights expectations" that was nonetheless "beset by police brutality, vigilante violence, racial discrimination, underfunded schools, Anglo stereotyping," and other forces of urban racism.[75] In school, where "[t]he American kids hated the Mexicans. I mean, *hated* them," Romero's teacher Anglicized his name from Alejandro to Alex. This did not prevent him from being teased by his white peers, although his darker-skinned brother Mario, who "looked the most Mexican," bore the "brunt of prejudice." As Romero recounted to Knowles, for example, Mario was once turned away from a public pool while Alex was allowed in. Relative to Mario, Alex "looked 'like an Anglo,'" and his light skin no doubt aided his ability to break into Hollywood. Still, he continued to face ethnic bias, including from the father of his eventual wife, Faun Driscoll, who was white.[76]

Like the Mexican American musicians about whom Macías writes, Romero absorbed Euro-American as well as African American cultural influences, even while preserving elements of his Mexican heritage. As Romero told Eichenbaum, while touring vaudeville, he was so taken by the hoofing of the African American trio King, King, and King that he taught himself tap dance. He also gave lessons to his brothers so they could incorporate it into their act.[77] When the act broke up, Romero took jobs teaching Spanish and tap dance while trying to break into the film business.[78] Once he joined Cole's ensemble of predominantly white studio dancers on contract at Columbia Pictures, he absorbed all kinds of racial influences: African American, Afro-Cuban, South Asian, European. In general, Romero's dance fluency and light skin allowed him to fully integrate into white Hollywood, so much so that it could be a source of friction for him. In a footnote, biographer Knowles alludes to a conflict between Romero and the Mexican comedian Cantinflas that arose when both worked on the 1960 film *Pepe*, produced by Columbia Pictures. Knowles writes, "Alex found out that Cantinflas was shunning him because he considered Alex a *pochos*, a Spanish word meaning a native-born Mexican who denies his heritage," adding that "Cantinflas's behavior was hurtful to Alex, who always maintained a fierce pride about his Mexican heritage."[79]

If he moved with relative ease (especially compared to Black artists like Marie Bryant) within Hollywood's dance milieu, Romero was not guaranteed the privileges of whiteness outside that milieu. While on a break from rehearsals for the 1957 film *Les Girls*, choreographed by Cole and featuring Kelly in his last starring role for MGM, Romero left the studio lot to deposit a paycheck when, he told Knowles, two officers in a cop car stopped him, asked him if he was drinking, requested identification, and questioned the legitimacy of his paycheck. Admittedly, he was practicing "a Cole jazz move" as he waited at a stoplight, so it is possible that the police read his dancing body as sexually "deviant."[80] Whatever the motive, the incident suggests that, rather than enjoy unfettered mobility as he moved through Los Angeles, Romero was susceptible to the Los Angeles Police Department's notorious surveillance and harassment of Mexican Americans and African Americans.[81] Especially in the wake of the "Bloody Christmas" of 1951, in which members of the LAPD severely beat a group of young Mexican American men being held at a police station, Romero's run-in may well have carried the threat of violence.[82]

In his history of Latina/o performers on stage and screen in the twentieth century, Brian Herrera shows that their "ethnic or racial legibility . . . varied

"COOL IT, ALEX"   151

widely depending on the audience, the role, or both."[83] The same was evidently true of Romero. When he performed on screen in uniform, as in *On the Town*'s "A Day in New York" or as one of four American servicemen who danced with Kelly in the seventeen-minute ballet in *An American in Paris* (1951), Romero appears to be racially "unmarked."[84] But things get a little murkier in some of his other filmic roles. As part of Cole's ensemble, Romero performed in an Afro-Brazilian "big voodoo dance" with Ann Miller in *The Thrill of Brazil* (1946) and as a Greek god in the Rita Hayworth vehicle *Down to Earth* (1947).[85] Along with all of Cole's dancers, Romero thus assumed a kind of racial "interchangeability." Did such performances "whiten" Romero by aligning him with the dual representational conventions of white modern dance that Susan Manning argues were operational on both sides of World War II: "metaphorical minstrelsy," in which "white dancers' bodies made reference to nonwhite subjects," and "mythic abstraction," in which white dancers "eschewed references to subjects of color"?[86] The recollection of dancer Barrie Chase, who also assisted Cole, implies as much. She remarked that she never thought about Romero's race or ethnicity at the time, although "he was Latin-looking."[87] At other times, Romero's "stealth Latino" identity may have informed how he was cast.[88] After he left Cole's group and between his appearances in *On the Town* and *An American in Paris*, Romero assisted choreographer Robert Alton on the making of MGM's *Annie Get Your Gun* (1950). In a version of the blatantly racist "I'm an Indian Too" number that was ultimately cut from the film when Judy Garland, its original star, was fired, Romero performs as the "White Indian chief" alongside Garland. The omitted number, which appears in the 1994 documentary *That's Entertainment III*, shows Romero in white full-body paint, a white buckskin loin cloth, and a giant white feather headdress, getting thrown into the air off a trampoline, leaping around Garland, who is also dressed in faux-Native garb, and performing stereotypically "Indian" dance moves.[89] Given this range of racially marked and unmarked roles, it is equally plausible that Romero's on-screen performances mobilized his Latino "nonwhiteness" as that they facilitated his "passing" as white.[90]

But we should not automatically assume that Romero's ethnicity had the same bearing on his off-screen collaborations with Kelly as it did on film. Here it is worth revisiting Kelly's description of Romero as matching him in size and strength. While the two men did share a similar build, in photographs of them together, like Figure 4.4, Romero's skin appears slightly darker than the Irish American's. Might the men's different ethnic backgrounds have hovered

152 HOLLYWOOD DANCE-INS

over or even infused their exchanges? When Romero rehearsed with, for, and as Kelly, was he embodying whiteness? Alternatively, when Kelly watched Romero performing choreography they co-developed, did the white star see brownness reflected back at him?

Scholars like Clover and Krayenbuhl have written persuasively about how Kelly's staging of masculinity was mediated by Blackness, typically absented on screen but invoked via his dance vocabulary and movement style. Krayenbuhl coins the term "blackbodying" to describe Kelly's "post-blackface" mode of adopting an Africanist bodily comportment, which injected his dances with a "racial indeterminacy" that served to "hedge against [their] gender ambiguity."[91] His work with Romero suggests that Kelly was also engaged in "brownbodying," refracting his filmic image through the body of the "not quite/not white" Romero.[92] Or perhaps it is more accurate to say that Kelly's blackbodying was at times mediated by the multiracial-bodying Romero, who was first trained in Spanish dancing, who had physically assimilated Black, Middle Eastern, South Asian, and European dance styles, and whose ethnic legibility was contingent on context. Romero's encounter with police officers while dancing in the streets of Los Angeles, it should be noted, is uncannily similar to Kelly's run-in with a policeman during his iconic "Singin' in the Rain" performance, which Clover maintains "hints at some other story behind this one, some other dancer and some other policeman." However coincidental the parallels between Romero's off-screen and Kelly's on-screen confrontations, the "racial resonances" that haunt Kelly's dancing must include brownness as well as Blackness.[93]

We should nevertheless take care not to collapse the distinctions between Kelly's appropriation of Blackness and his intercorporeal exchanges with Romero. The labor-saving nature of Romero's work as a dance-in and Kelly's reliance on Romero to help create choreography while preserving credit for himself do partially reproduce patterns of white exploitation, "love and theft," and invisibilization.[94] But the complexity of the doubling and mirroring Romero and Kelly performed for one another, the circulation of desire and identification between them, and the "racial fluidity"[95] of Romero's position make "appropriation" an insufficient term for characterizing their relationship. If the power imbalances between the celebrated white choreographer/director/star and the lesser-known Mexican American dance-in/assistant are too undeniable to constitute the mutuality and intersubjectivity of a "utopian performative,"[96] we might think of the site of their exchange as a "rich, complicated, and sometimes troubling collaborative scene," to borrow

José Muñoz's depiction of the literary relationship between the white Eve Sedgwick and the African American Gary Fisher. For Muñoz, the concept of "the communism of the incommensurate" is a useful alternative to relations of either equivalence or "pure submission and domination." As a "relational schema," the communism of the incommensurate allows for the "experience of being-in-common-in-difference" and of thinking of subjecthood as "imbricated in a larger circuit of belonging."[97]

Romero himself certainly grasped the incommensurability that structured his relationship with Kelly. "I understood what was at stake," he told Eichenbaum after sharing the anecdote about Kelly pushing him aside when Freed entered their rehearsal space, "[a]nd I didn't care about getting any credit." "I always felt that Gene Kelly respected me and appreciated what I did for him," he insisted, adding, "I loved the man."[98] Aware of the uneven field of power and accepting of private expressions of respect and indebtedness over public acknowledgments of credit, Romero pronounces his love for Kelly. This love—an articulation of affection for and closeness to the man whose reliance on him helped him carve a space for himself in the overwhelmingly white Hollywood, whose filmic image Romero replicated and helped shape, whose body he stood in for and stood aside for—speaks to the intimacy of their queer working relationship, a relationship of homosocial, intercorporeal interdependence in which power was never equalized.[99] Romero's pronouncement, to lean again on Sedgwick and Muñoz, might also be seen as evidence of a "reparative impulse" on Romero's part, one that contrasts the more defensive, "paranoid" impulse behind Kelly's "Cool it" utterance.[100]

And yet it should not go unnoticed that once Romero found employment as a lead choreographer and dance director, he "rarely used assistants, preferring to work alone,"[101] with one major exception: after casting a dancer named Alex Ruiz in the 1957 Presley film *Jailhouse Rock*, Romero hired Ruiz as an assistant, and the two worked closely together for the next decade or so. According to Knowles, Ruiz was a "powerful, athletic dancer who understood Romero's style immediately." To avoid confusion on film sets, Ruiz was known as "Little Alex" to Romero's "Big Alex."[102] Larry Billman's *Film Choreographers and Dance Directors*, which contains a short entry on Ruiz, reports that he was born in Arizona and raised in San Francisco, trained in tap and ballet, and danced in both Hollywood films and the San Francisco Ballet.[103] A series of photographs in a January 1962 *Dance Magazine* article on Romero show Romero and Ruiz rehearsing for MGM's *The Wonderful*

World of the Brothers Grimm (1962) with the actress Yvette Mimieux (see Figures 4.7 and 4.8).[104] Although the *Dance Magazine* article does not address the ethnic/racial identity of Ruiz, it does discuss Romero's and Mimieux's: "Alex Romero is of Spanish extraction, Yvette Mimieux's mother is Mexican. A mutual interest in bull-fighting is inevitable. The subject is discussed, with gestures, as Yvette and her much-respected choreographer stroll across the studio lot."[105] As with Kelly and Romero, Romero and Ruiz appear to be similar in stature and muscularity, the latter's skin tone ever so slightly darker than the former's. Where once Kelly and Romero took turns developing choreography with Vera-Ellen, here Romero and Ruiz do the same with Mimieux. Repetition—but with a difference. Now in a position to select his own double and mirror and to orchestrate his own "communism of the incommensurate," Romero does so by generating what Deborah Paredez might call a "circuit of Latinidad."[106]

The co-presence of "Little" and "Big" Alex on the film set is another example of the literal doubling and swapping, supplementing and subtracting

One of the challenging tasks of a Hollywood choreographer is to make non-da resemble trained dancers. Romero and his assistant, Alex Ruiz, enjoy the ent astic response of supple starlet Yvette Mimieux.

Figure 4.7 From left to right, Alex Ruiz, Yvette Mimieux, and Alex Romero in rehearsal for *The Wonderful World of the Brothers Grimm* (1962). Photographs by Seymour Linden for *Dance Magazine* (January 1962).

Figure 4.8 Ruiz, Mimieux, and Romero in rehearsal for *The Wonderful World of the Brothers Grimm* (1962). Photographs by Seymour Linden for *Dance Magazine* (January 1962).

of bodies on which the creation of dance for film rested. It also points again toward the queer latencies particular to the dance-in's reproductive relations: the blurring of gendered distinctions between original/author and copy/derivative; the spawning of erotically charged heterosexual representations through homosocial pairings and Sedgwickian triangles that facilitate the multidirectional circulation of desire; the construction of a corporeal filmic image through the embodiment of movement *for* another and *as* that other, with all the attendant slipperiness between desire and identification. And in the midst of that slipperiness, Romero's subtle act of centering brownness in the white-dominated studio spaces of Hollywood is a reminder that bodily materialities always matter to the relations of reproduction, even when those materialities are concealed behind and help underwrite projections of white masculinity.

5

Racial Dis/Orientations and the Ambivalence of Nancy Kwan's Dancing Body

In April 1961, *New York Times* reporter Larry Glenn visited the Hollywood set of *Flower Drum Song* (1961), the first big-budget Hollywood film with a majority Asian/American cast.[1] Directed by the German-born Henry Koster, the film was an adaptation of the third of Rodgers and Hammerstein's "Oriental" musicals, which ran on Broadway from late 1958 to May 1960 under the direction of Gene Kelly.[2] Based on the 1957 novel of the same name by Chinese/American author C. Y. Lee, the musical tells the story of an arranged marriage and the tensions it creates between first- and second-generation Chinese immigrants in San Francisco. As the *Times* reporter toured the $310,000 film set, which re-created a section of San Francisco's Chinatown on a Hollywood sound stage, he came across Hermes Pan, the film's choreographer, rehearsing his dancers in what Glenn characterized as "a delightful bit of inspired nonsense." Amid this "nonsense," he noted this: "A Caucasian dancer was standing in—dancing in?—for Miss [Nancy] Kwan, and, while she lacked the latter's sullen loveliness, she was pert and expert in her movements."[3]

While the question mark in Glenn's description suggests his lack of familiarity with the by-then common practice of using dance-ins to rehearse a film's choreography in place of the star, his identification of the unnamed dancer as Caucasian hints at what he may have found equally curious.[4] In an article that refers to the "Asian and Eurasian principals of the picture" but not to the whiteness of producer Ross Hunter, composers Rodgers and Hammerstein, or choreographer Pan, each of whom is mentioned by name, Glenn's racialization of the white dance-in stands out. To riff on Sara Ahmed's insights about the disorientation that tends to arise from the "presence of bodies of color in white spaces," here it is the presence of a white woman in an ostensibly "Asian space" that unsettles the reporter, or at least

Hollywood Dance-ins and the Reproduction of Bodies. Anthea Kraut, Oxford University Press.
© Oxford University Press 2025. DOI: 10.1093/oso/9780197789667.003.0006

his rhetoric.[5] Perhaps in response, no sooner does Glenn classify the dance-in as white than he situates surrogate and star in a racial binary, pitting the former's "pert and expert" dancing body against the "sullen loveliness" of Kwan's absent body. (Kwan was on a nearby sound stage, shooting a retake of a minor scene.) In the space of a single sentence, Glenn reinscribes an equation between energy, enterprise, and whiteness on the one hand, and aloofness, hypersexuality, and the Orient on the other.[6]

Fast-forward in time, and we find that, for twenty-first-century critics, it is Kwan's on-screen performance that is racially unsettling. Pointing especially to the number "I Enjoy Being a Girl," in which Kwan as the showgirl Linda Low sings and dances about the pleasures she takes in the trappings of heteronormative femininity, multiple scholars have commented on the ways Kwan's performance threatens to dissolve the "ontological gap between Asian and American."[7] Chang-Hee Kim, for example, has written, "It is uncanny for the white spectator to watch [Kwan's] 'Westernized' body, which always already confuses them with the stereotyped hypersexuality of Asian women."[8] Anne Cheng likewise depicts Kwan as embodying a "fantasmatic promise of *substitutive* whiteness and exoticism" that disturbs "the security of that binarism even as it offers the complacent pleasure of having it both ways."[9] Christina Klein describes "I Enjoy Being a Girl" as "a visual representation of Chinese American whiteness" and asserts that the "problem with Linda Low is that she is too assimilated, she is too 'white,' she has lost any significant ties to China."[10] For Jennifer Chan, Kwan's performance renders her "a kind of cyborg: in appearance, she is clearly white *and* Chinese."[11] *Flower Drum Song*'s narrative ultimately reconciles this contradiction by exposing Low's identity as an exotic dancer and sentencing her to a life of "heterosexual monogamy."[12] At the film's end, the Chinese immigrant Mei Li frees herself from a marriage contract binding her to the nightclub owner Sammy Fong, making it possible for him to marry Low, and Low's one-time romantic interest Wang Ta to marry Mei Li. Still, the ambivalence surrounding Kwan's performance, whether measured in narrative terms or by the amount of critical attention devoted to it, suggests that there is something disorienting about the racial connotations of her filmic body.

Rewinding again to the film set, we can identify the unnamed white dance-in in Glenn's report as (most likely) Becky Varno, a "longtime associate" of Pan and one of his assistants on *Flower Drum Song*.[13] Information about Varno, like most dance-ins, is sparse at best, and she too appears to have been plagued by multiple or misspellings of her name. Calling her the

158   HOLLYWOOD DANCE-INS

"most loquacious interview subject I encountered," Fred Astaire's biographer Peter Levinson refers to her as "the late Becky Vorno [*sic*]" and explains, "She would often dance with Fred in rehearsal once Fred and Hermes had devised a dance routine."[14] In 1959, she appeared as one of the Hermes Pan Dancers in the televised special *Another Evening with Fred Astaire*. She continued to assist Pan when, two years after *Flower Drum Song*, he served as choreographer on Warner Brothers' *My Fair Lady* (1963). Visiting that film's Hollywood set, a reporter for a Memphis newspaper also came across Varno dancing in place of the female star, in this case the white Audrey Hepburn. Describing the rehearsal he encountered, he wrote, "Becky Vorno [*sic*], a tiny blond dancer who works with Choreographer Hermes Pan, then teaches her steps to Miss Hepburn, was standing in for Eliza."[15]

Insofar as dance-ins were typically expected to resemble their star counterparts in "height, weight, and coloring,"[16] Varno and Kwan came close on the first two. In a 2019 interview, Astaire dancer Barrie Chase, for whom Varno also served as a dance-in,[17] recalled Varno as "kind of short-ish and slight" and therefore a good match for Kwan.[18] The similar statures and disparate racial positionalities of Kwan and Varno bring to mind aspects of the Gene Kelly–Alex Romero partnership, the subject of the previous chapter. Here I continue to interrogate the cross-racial exchanges out of which stars' corporeal images were forged in midcentury Hollywood. As the only non-white star to whom this book devotes a full chapter, however, Kwan raises a different set of questions about the racial dynamics that structured those exchanges and their resulting images. Taking Glenn's startled response to Kwan's off-screen proxy and contemporary critics' uneasy response to her on-screen image as points of departure, this chapter approaches Kwan as the site of a racialized breakdown in the indexical logic that assumes a correspondence between filmic image and material referent.[19]

As I have discussed in earlier chapters, the historic (and ongoing) correlation between Hollywood stardom and idealized images of whiteness meant that only a handful of performers of color attained star status in the mid-twentieth century.[20] The Hong Kong–born Kwan (1939–), whose mother was English Scottish and whose father was Chinese, was among the few who, at least for a short time, did (see Figure 5.1). She shot to fame following her appearance in the 1960 box-office hit *The World of Suzie Wong*, a fame on which *Flower Drum Song* capitalized. Kwan's later films never matched the success of her first two, though, and her occasional nickname, the "Chinese

Figure 5.1 Uncredited, undated publicity photo of Nancy Kwan. Billy Rose Theatre Division, New York Public Library.

Bardot," signals how thoroughly her celebrity was determined by and measured in relation to whiteness. Yet as the critics cited above establish, Kwan's relationship to whiteness—her status as an "uncanny double of white female sexuality"[21]—is complicated. The biracial star of a film musical with a predominantly Asian/American cast and a predominantly white production

160   HOLLYWOOD DANCE-INS

team, Kwan is an important figure to include in this study of dance-ins precisely because her screen image failed to smooth over the interracial and "panethnic" acts of corporeal reproduction that shaped it.[22] The indexical instability that marks Kwan's filmic body in *Flower Drum Song*, that is, is a powerful illustration of how unevenly the fiction of bodily coherence has been allocated across racial lines.

In what follows, I investigate the cracks in Kwan's coherence and the overlapping and competing racial orientations of her dancing body in three of *Flower Drum Song*'s numbers: "I Enjoy Being a Girl," a ten-second dance she shares with the Filipino/American Patrick Adiarte, and "Grant Avenue," in which Kwan and an ensemble of dancers perform on the streets of a diegetic Chinatown. While the first positions Kwan between whiteness and Asianness and demonstrates the filmic and extrafilmic conditions that contributed to her racially refracted image, the latter two help situate Kwan within a broader multiracial and multiethnic corporeal landscape and shift attention from Kwan's off-screen white interlocutors to her on-screen Asian/American dance partners.

Cold War Orientalism and the Paradoxes of Integration and Assimilation

As the "first musical and one of the first films about Asian Americans, starring Asian Americans,"[23] *Flower Drum Song* has not suffered from a lack of attention, and the insights of a number of scholars make clear the political and historical stakes of its representation of Asian/American corporeality. Coming on the heels of Rodgers and Hammerstein's *The King and I* (Broadway premiere, 1951; film, 1956) and *South Pacific* (Broadway premiere, 1949; film 1958), *Flower Drum Song* was part of a spike in Asian-themed productions during the Cold War.[24] Unlike these other musicals, however, it was "specifically preoccupied with the Asian presence in the United States."[25] Scholars attribute U.S. fascination with Asian/America in the years following World War II to shifts in both international foreign policy and domestic immigration law. Christina Klein's term "Cold War Orientalism," an extension of Edward Said's still relevant formulation,[26] describes the simultaneous "proliferation of popular American representations of Asia" and the "unprecedented"

U.S. expansion of its "political, military, and economic power" in Asia between 1945 and 1961.[27] More pointedly, Bruce McConachie asserts that Rodgers and Hammerstein's trilogy "helped to establish a legitimate basis for the American war against the people of Southeast Asia in the 1960s" by depicting the "Americanization" of Asian cultures.[28]

The years between the 1940s and early 1950s also saw a number of legislative reforms to immigration law. These reforms "reopened the door to Asian immigration and allowed Asians within the U.S. to become naturalized citizens" for the first time since the 1882 Chinese Exclusion Act, which prohibited the immigration of Chinese laborers and denied them naturalization.[29] The result, as Josephine Lee notes, was a gradual rise in the number of Asian immigrants living in the United States in the years leading up to the 1965 Immigration and Nationality Act, which abolished national quotas and led to more significant demographic changes.[30]

These international and domestic policy changes produced a "uniquely American paradox" between the need for the United States to project itself as a democracy-promoting global superpower that could halt the spread of communism and its "deep-seated practice of domestic racism."[31] As Chang-Hee Kim writes, "In the early Cold War era, with memories of Pearl Harbor, Nagasaki, and Hiroshima still very fresh in the collective mind, one of the most complicated aspects of this dilemma was resolving how the nation could assimilate Asians into its antiracial endeavors."[32] Questions of integration and assimilation took on a spatial dimension during this era as well, as Chinatown ethnic enclaves, which dated back to the first wave of Chinese immigration in the late nineteenth century, expanded in the wake of relaxed restrictive covenants, and Asian Americans began "moving in unprecedented numbers into previously all-white neighborhoods."[33] This was the period when racist stereotypes that cast Asians as a threatening "yellow peril" began to give way to (or rather, were joined by) the myth of Asian/Americans as "model minorities," an antiblack construction that pathologized African Americans.[34]

Flower Drum Song thematizes the issue of how to incorporate Asian immigrants into the U.S. body politic as their status shifted from "unknowable exotic to assimilable ally."[35] In the musical, the dilemma plays out in generational and gendered terms: through the tensions between the character Wang Ta's parents, who uphold more "traditional" Chinese norms, and a younger generation, exemplified by Wang Ta's baseball-loving younger

162　HOLLYWOOD DANCE-INS

brother Wang San, and between the "oppositional doubles" who compete as Wang Ta's love interests: the "fresh off the boat" Mei Li (played by Japanese actress Miyoshi Umeki), who arrives as an undocumented immigrant," and the assimilated Linda Low (the Eurasian Kwan).[36]

In many ways, the film thus highlights the tensions embodied by the very term "Asian/American." As Lisa Lowe, Karen Shimakawa, Yutian Wong, Ju Yon Kim, and other scholars have shown, the variegated but overlapping racialization of Asian ethnic groups is a fundamentally contradictory formation that positions Asian/Americans as the "foreigner-within": "the Chinese as alien noncitizen, the American citizen of Japanese descent as racial enemy, and the American citizen of Filipino descent as simultaneously immigrant and colonized national," Lowe writes.[37] Conceptualizing this vexed status through the framework of abjection, Shimakawa has shown how U.S. culture positions Asian/Americans as simultaneously "constituent element and radical other."[38] In Wong's formulation, "belonging for Asian American subjects" has had to be "proven rather than presumed," and in Kim's, "the model minority can never *be* American, but can only mimic Americanness."[39] Following the lead of David Palumbo-Liu, some scholars use a slash between "Asian" and "American" as a way of marking this dynamic of exclusion and inclusion.[40] For Sean Metzger, the slash designates an "interface" and "a membrane of connection and disjunction . . . that is both permeable and malleable."[41] In her study of racialized aesthetics and the consumption of Chinese film stars, Mila Zuo finds the slash "particularly useful when discussing transnational and immigrant stars who frequently travel to live and work in multiple countries (including the United States), and whose identities suggest the split, sliding, and flexible nature of their global citizenship."[42]

Taking my cue from these scholars, I too adopt the slash between "Asian" and "American" and, like Zuo, find it an apt way to limn Nancy Kwan's complicated racial orientations in *Flower Drum Song*. A mixed-race international subject, Kwan epitomizes the "racial ambiguity" of nonwhite transnational artists,[43] a point driven home by the white producer Ray Stark's description of her as "many girls of many nations, packaged on one body."[44] A closer look at the conditions of production of Kwan's dancing body in *Flower Drum Song* brings this ambiguity into sharper focus (paradox intended), showing how it manifested in the film's own self-consciousness about her indexical instability.

The (False) Indexicality of the Mirror

As was commonplace for dance-ins, there were times when Varno filled in for Kwan during *Flower Drum Song* production and times when the two worked alongside one another. A photograph of Kwan rehearsing "I Enjoy Being a Girl" next to a woman I believe to be Varno captures an instance of the latter (see Figure 5.2).[45] Camera equipment and the silhouette of a cameraman occupy the foreground of the viewer's left, framing the shot and partially obscuring the body of Pan, who stands in the background observing an exchange between Varno and Kwan. The two women are positioned in front of a three-way mirror, creating multiple images of them from different

Figure 5.2 Hermes Pan (left) observes as Becky Varno adjusts Nancy Kwan's stole for "I Enjoy Being a Girl" on the *Flower Drum Song* (1961) set. Courtesy Photofest NYC.

164 HOLLYWOOD DANCE-INS

angles. Kwan wears a white strapless negligée, a white headband, and heels, while Varno is dressed, like Pan, in dark pants and a light-colored collared shirt. Kwan's right knee is popped and she gazes down at her right shoulder, where Varno is adjusting a white fur stole around her arms. A rehearsal photograph of a number that is explicitly about the performance of femininity, the image is a useful place to begin probing Kwan's corporeality, both because the number has been the locus of assessments of her unsettling racial ambiguity and because, as the photo shows, the number makes literal the reproduction of her filmic body.

In the commentary track included on the DVD of *Flower Drum Song*, Kwan discusses how difficult "I Enjoy Being a Girl" was to film.[46] This was largely because, at one point, as I explore more fully below, three different images of Kwan dressed in three different ensembles appear on screen simultaneously. To get a clean shot of each image, Kwan's dancing had to remain within the narrow space dictated by a single mirror panel. If she moved too much to the right or left, she explains, her hand would move into the next frame or go out of frame. Seen in this light, Varno's adjustment may have been an attempt to ensure that the image of Kwan with her stole adhered to these conditions. What the photograph captures, then, is Varno literally orienting Kwan's body on set to ensure its proper orientation on film. In her role as intermediary between choreographer and star, Varno helps mold Kwan's on-screen corporeal shape. This is not to lessen the role Pan played in directing Kwan's dancing in *Flower Drum Song*. It is to insist, rather, that we not dismiss how instrumental women like Varno were to the off-screen transmissions that gave rise to stars' filmic dancing bodies.

"I Enjoy Being a Girl" begins when Kwan as Low hangs up the phone, having just agreed to meet Wang Ta, played by the Japanese/American James Shigeta, for a date. Sauntering from her bed to the three-way mirror in her dressing room as the camera follows her, she plants herself in front of the center panel. With knees slightly bent and feet turned out, she tilts her torso away from the mirror, extends her arms downward, opens her palms to the mirror, and begins to sing to her reflection:

> I'm a girl and by me that's only great,
> I am proud that my silhouette is curvy,
> That I walk with a sweet and girlish gait,
> With my hips kind of swivelly and swervy.

As she sings, she pops a shoulder and subtly swivels her hips while approaching and then retreating from her reflection in the mirror. During the remainder of the roughly four-minute number, she continues to perform largely gestural choreography, including arm and hand flourishes that often mime the lyrics (indicating her "eyelashes all in curls" or applying "a pound and a half of cream upon [her] face"), sometimes interlaced with light balletic steps. Filmed from a mostly immobile camera (whose position we can see in Figure 5.2), the number alternates between medium shots that depict four images of Kwan (one of her body in front of the mirror and three reflections in each of the mirror panels), closer shots that show two images of her (her body plus one reflection), and shots when she moves away from the mirror entirely and we see only one image of her body.

Halfway through the number, however, after Kwan has returned to the three-way mirror and is observing her reflection while seated on an ottoman, daintily crossing and recrossing her legs, a break occurs: the Kwan in the mirror panel on the viewer's right stands up and exits the screen, only to return with a large white muff and fancy white hat. After a cut to a close-up of this adorned Kwan, we return to a shot of all four Kwans, three of whom (those sans muff and hat) dance together. The Kwan in the left-most mirror then grabs a stole (the same one we see in the rehearsal photo with Varno). The camera zooms in so we see only the three differently accessorized Kwans in the mirror panels, who briefly dance in unison until the Kwans on both the right and left sides spin out of the frame. When they spin back in, they are wearing dresses, one white and ruffled, the other orange and high-fashion. For a brief moment, we see the "original" Kwan seated on the ottoman watching this pair of reflections in the outer mirror panels, yet strangely creating no reflection of her own: the middle mirror panel remains empty— until a Kwan dressed in a yellow bikini hops into it (see Figure 5.3). Finally, the Kwan before the mirror and her three nonidentical reflections, now all seated on the ottoman, sing in harmony:

> I'm strictly a female female,
> And my future I hope will be,
> In the home of a brave and free male,
> Who'll enjoy being a guy, having a girl like me.

During this last line, all four Kwans rise and turn to their right. As they turn, they all revert back to their initial costume, the negligée. The number

Figure 5.3 Screen capture of Kwan and her three nonidentical reflections in "I Enjoy Being a Girl."

concludes as it began, with Kwan posing before her three matching reflections, singing in one voice.

As I hope this description has begun to illustrate, "I Enjoy Being a Girl" is remarkable for the way its cinematography both highlights and muddies issues of indexicality. As discussed in Chapter 1, film scholars have drawn on semiotician Charles Peirce's notion of the index to emphasize celluloid film's "privileged relation" to reality. In its photochemical era, film, like photography, was regarded as bearing "a material connection" to its referent, with the image serving as "imprint or trace" of its represented object.[47] A mirror, too, is an "indexical medium" insofar as it "contains a causal connection between its referent and what it displays"; the mirror has accordingly been considered "a privileged filmic object."[48] For the first half of "I Enjoy Being a Girl," mirrors are indeed strictly indexical; what we see in triplicate in the three-way mirror bears a direct, referential relationship to Kwan's singing, dancing body. This indexicality is ruptured midway through, though, when the image of Kwan in the right-hand mirror exits the frame, unprompted by the Kwan who remains seated on the ottoman. For most of the rest of the number, the mirrors become at least partially "nonreflective" or create a "false reflection" in that they "reflect... something other than the person who looks at it."[49] It is still Kwan/Low whom we see reflected, but the versions of her in the mirror no longer correspond to the Kwan who we would expect to produce the reflection. Shot at different times and spliced together in postproduction,[50] the nonidentical Kwans "unsettle" and "disorient" the spectator, as film scholar Julian Hanich puts it, by foregrounding viewing as a mediated act.[51]

Yet "I Enjoy Being a Girl" does more than foreground the mediation of Kwan's filmic body: it both underscores *and* disrupts a one-to-one relationship between Kwan and her mirror images. It's as if the film can't decide whether Kwan as Low is hyperreflective (as when she produces multiple identical reflections), a false reflection (when she produces nonidentical reflections), nonreflective (when she produces no reflection at all), or some combination of all three. As one would expect, the labor required to produce this vacillation was not trivial.[52] While the rehearsal photograph of Kwan, Pan, and Varno gives us a peek of what some of this labor entailed, on the *Flower Drum Song* DVD commentary Kwan discloses that, not only did it take two days to shoot the mirror scenes but they had to be reshot when "they discovered some fly or some speck on the camera lens."[53] These efforts leave little doubt as to the film's fascination with Kwan's simultaneous reproducibility and uncertain indexicality. As I argue below, this fascination is part of a more general uncertainty about the relationship between Kwan's filmic image(s), her extradiegetic corporeality, and, crucially, the racial coordinates of each.[54]

White Voice/Yellow Face?

The production of Kwan's image in "I Enjoy Being a Girl" involved other kinds of mediation as well, for like most Hollywood musical stars in the mid-twentieth century, Kwan's singing vocals were dubbed in the film, including in this number. On the film's DVD commentary track, Kwan explains that it was considered "cleaner" for the dancing and singing to be recorded separately and for someone else to record the singing. In Kwan's case, that other singer was the white B. J. Baker, a prolific backup singer during the 1950s and 1960s, who Kwan recalled as "a very nice lady" who was tall and blonde.[55] Like the diegetic mirrors that reflect and refract, the fact that a white woman generated the sound that appears to emanate from Kwan's body throws questions of indexicality into sharp relief.

In conversation with film historian Nick Redman on the commentary track, Kwan describes what the synching of voice to image required. Baker, she explains, "came on the set and . . . I guess she studied the moves and everything else . . . of the numbers, dance numbers, the singing numbers,

168　HOLLYWOOD DANCE-INS

and then I was given a tape, and I used to listen to it at home and mouth it so that it would match the mouthing when . . . we shot it." This two-way process—Baker studying Kwan's moves, Kwan studying Baker's mouthing—accords with that described by the white singer Marni Nixon, who dubbed the singing of white female stars Natalie Wood, Deborah Kerr, and Audrey Hepburn in the mid-twentieth century. Recounting her work with Kerr on the film version of *The King and I* (1956), Nixon explains how the two "mirrored each other's actions":

> I would follow her around like a shadow, mimicking each of her movements and copying her stance down to the angle of her head. After a while we started to look like twins. As we would both sing "Hello, Young Lovers," for example, I would picture the inside of her vocal chords and stretch my own neck and throat into that shape as we formed the words and sang together. I actually imagined myself inside her body in order to sound like her. . . . The goal was to become one Anna.
>
> Conversely, Deborah would watch me as I sang so that she might absorb my way of singing. . . . She was learning how my body looked when I sang the songs so that she could incorporate the same body language, stance, and breathing techniques into her performance. All of these would visually contribute to the illusion that she was really singing in the finished film.[56]

While Kwan and Baker's collaboration may have been less intensive, Nixon's account illuminates the multidirectional and intercorporeal mimicry required to create the "fiction of fidelity": to unite two bodies into a single filmic image "without the seams showing."[57] Much more than a technical alignment of image to playback recording, vocal dubbing was an intricate, embodied process of scrutinizing, copying, and projecting oneself inside the body of another.

In the context of "I Enjoy Being a Girl," the separation between visible body and unseen voice, combined with the labor (corporeal and technological) required to bring them into alignment, compounds Kwan's indexical ambivalence. As described above, the moment in which the indexicality of Kwan as Low is the most conspicuously fractured—when the diegetic mirror fails to produce reflective images of Kwan/Low—is also a moment when we hear not one voice but four, singing in harmony. In other words, when we see four disparate images of Kwan, we are also hearing four different recordings of Baker, harmonizing with herself through the magic of postproduction mixing.[58] From one perspective, the fact that the multiplication of Baker's voice matches the multiplication of Kwan's image helps maintain the fiction that image and sound are moored, that there is no slippage between "the real" and the "postproduced," and that Kwan as Low is hyperreflective.[59] As such, the supplementary voices would seem to lend support to Kaja Silverman's argument that synchronization "performs a supervisory role with respect to sexual difference, enforcing the general dictum that female voices should proceed from female bodies." The lyrics sung by the voices that appear to emanate from Kwan's bodies at this moment ("I'm strictly a female female") even, if unwittingly, nod to the gendered dimensions of this "rule of synchronization."[60] Yet from another perspective, the multiplicity of that synchronization—not just a female, but a female female; not just one body with one voice but four bodies with four voices—threatens the singular-ness of Kwan as Low. She may be synched, but she is eminently, even frenetically reproducible. The proliferation of voices and bodies in "I Enjoy Being a Girl" both doubles down on and cracks open the seeming coherence of its star.

As far as Kwan and Redman were concerned, the stitching together of singing voices and dancing bodies resulted in the creation of a seamless Linda Low. "I thought she did a great job," Kwan remarks of Baker, Redman adding that it feels as if "that voice could come out of you."[61] Contemporaneous reviewers seem to have concurred. While James Powers of the *Hollywood Reporter* considered Kwan "a perfect choice" for the part of Low and noted that "her singing (dubbed by B. J. Baker) is adroitly handled,"[62] most reviewers didn't even mention the dubbing.[63] More recent critics, though, have taken issue with the film's crossing of the "sonic color line."[64] Scholar David Lewis, for example, writes that the use of "unseen vocalist B. J. Baker" for the "lip-synching non-singer" Kwan deprives "I Enjoy Being a Girl" of "visceral authenticity" and makes it "just another synthetic prop of feminine self-indulgence."[65] For musicologist William Everett, the vocal dubbing "whitens the overall production in unseen and indeed hidden ways."[66] In these appraisals, the gap between Baker's white singing body and Kwan's nonwhite, nonsinging body cannot be sutured; the "acousmatic whiteness"[67] of "I Enjoy Being a Girl" simply cannot index the Asianness of Kwan's off-screen corporeality, no matter the mimesis between the women. Lewis, in fact, sees transmission in only one direction. "The way that Kwan was directed to imitate a typically jaded '50s sex kitten," he asserts, "she hardly looked Asian at all."[68]

170 HOLLYWOOD DANCE-INS

Any clear-cut division between Kwan's "irreducible, extradiegetic Asian presence"[69] on one side and the whiteness of her diegetic sound and image on the other, however, begins to unravel when we factor in other aspects of her filmic construction. In a 1962 interview, producer Stark claimed that Kwan "certainly doesn't look Chinese" and that "[a] make-up man had to make her eyes look Oriental for both [*The World of Suzie Wong*] and *Flower Drum Song*."[70] Gossip columnist Hedda Hopper likewise reported that Kwan's "brown eyes have to be slanted with make-up when she plays an Oriental."[71] Given celebrations of the film's "insistent display of the Asian body" and its general eschewing of yellowface (in contrast to the Broadway musical's casting of a white actor in the part of Sammy Fong), there is no small irony in the fact that the same technology used to create fictional Asians was applied to Kwan.[72] In this regard, the Kwan we see on screen is not, or not only, Kwan imitating her white interlocutors, but Kwan in Asian drag.[73]

Taking these assessments together, Kwan's two-dimensional screen image, whether viewed as whitened or "Orientalized," is in constant tension with her three-dimensional corporeal presence, which was either irreducibly Asian or not Asian enough. Indexical instability, as I have tried to show throughout this book, was no less inherent in the filmic images of white stars' dancing bodies, which also bore the traces of the doublings and surrogations, synchronizations and subtractions that shaped them. Yet in Kwan's case, unlike those of white stars, the tensions between filmic image and material referent keep announcing themselves on-screen and off- and keep producing uncertainty about her body's racial signifiers. Kwan thus crystallizes how impossible it is to disentangle questions of indexicality from racialized ideologies about corporeality.

Inscriptions of the Flesh

While some aspects of Kwan's racially ambivalent status in *Flower Drum Song* are specific to or heightened by the film, confusion about how to map her racial positionality onto her corporeality exemplifies what a number of scholars have argued is a condition of Asian/American embodiment more generally.[74] Anne Cheng's theory of "ornamentalism" as the defining condition of the "yellow woman" is particularly relevant here. Diagnosing and critiquing a centuries-long practice of "tying . . . ornamental artifice to Asiatic femininity in Euro-American visual and literary cultures," Cheng sees in it the basis for an alternative mode of theorizing racial embodiment, apart from Frantz Fanon's "epidermal racial schema," which shows how the white colonial gaze shatters the possibility of "natural" corporeality for Black subjects, and Hortense Spillers's distinction between flesh and body.[75] "Orientalism, by contrast," Cheng asserts, "relies on a decorative grammar, a fantasmatic corporeal syntax that is artificial and layered."[76] "Ornament becomes—is— flesh for Asian American female personhood," she maintains. For Cheng, Kwan's famous "porcelain skin" typifies this construction of Asian women's embodiment as ornamental, inorganic, and synthetic.[77]

Comparisons of Kwan to a "China doll," as a 1962 issue of *McCall's* magazine titled a feature on her, lend support to Cheng's theory.[78] Yet accounting for Kwan's dancing body complicates matters. As much as this book seeks to problematize the assignment of coherence and corporeal integrity to (white) dancing bodies, it also insists that no dancing body is empty of history and that corporeal genealogies tug at the surface of filmic images. In keeping with Ahmed's reminder that "one's racial dwelling is shaped by the conditions of one's arrival," the fact that Kwan arrived on the *Flower Drum Set* as a classically trained ballet dancer must factor into our understanding of her filmic image, her extradiegetic corporeality, and their often competing racial significations.[79]

Alongside their struggles to place Kwan's "curiously Oriental-Occidental face," narratives about Kwan's rise repeatedly cite her ballet training as part of her backstory.[80] As reported in these accounts, Kwan took her first ballet classes in Hong Kong at the age of six and, after moving to England to attend boarding school around age twelve, studied at Sadler's Wells Ballet School. She eventually performed for two years with the Royal Academy of Ballet in London, taking small parts in Romantic ballets such as *Sleeping Beauty* and *Swan Lake*. Before being "discovered" by Hollywood producer Stark, Kwan was planning to open a ballet school in Hong Kong.[81] Multiple sources, including Kwan herself, hailed her casting in *Flower Drum Song* as a chance for her to put her dance training to use. A 1961 article in *Dance Magazine* even attributed "much of [Kwan's] sudden stardom to years of training at Sadler's Wells Ballet School."[82]

When we talk about Kwan's corporeality, then, we are talking about a body that was physically inscribed by ballet technique. As dance scholar Sally Ann Ness has argued, the rigorous, repetitive physical training required by classical forms like ballet leaves its mark in and on a dancer's body—not only on the outer layers of her flesh but also in the interior spaces of her muscle fibers,

172 HOLLYWOOD DANCE-INS

ligaments, and even bones.[83] These marks were apparent to a *Cosmopolitan* magazine reporter, who commented after a lunch date with Kwan that her "carriage shows her ballet training; she walks with her back arched and her toes pointed out."[84]

Understanding the inscriptions of ballet as constitutive of Kwan's corporeality does several things. For one, it prompts us to consider how she moves as much as what she looks like, to attend to her body's habitus[85] as much as her body's surfaces. Correspondingly, it demands a more nuanced reading of her relationship to her off-screen surrogates, as well as to whiteness. The fact that Kwan's body was already oriented toward ballet when she began filming *Flower Drum Song* affected the direction she received from Pan and Varno as well as how she received it.[86] Looking at Kwan through the lens of this corporeal history makes it possible to discern its imprint on the filmic image. Although the movements of "I Enjoy Being a Girl" are, as indicated, largely gestural and restricted by the spatial constraints of the three-paneled mirror, Kwan's ballet training is evident in her pulled-up torso, her turn-out, and the curvilinearity of her arms. This was the comportment that Baker studied in preparing to dub Kwan's voice.

How this ballet training affected Kwan's racialization is less easy to discern. If whiteness "is an orientation that puts certain things within reach,"[87] is the Eurocentric technique of ballet an orientation that put the whiteness of movie stardom within Kwan's reach? Certainly, her ballet training (along with her private school education in England) was a marker of her class status.[88] But what role might Kwan's balleticized body have played and continue to play in perceptions of her "substitutive" and "uncanny" whiteness? Is her ballet training a sign of her body's colonization, a corporeal counterpart to the colonization of Hong Kong by England? Or an index of her "mixed genealogy"?[89] (Kwan asked a *Cosmopolitan* magazine reporter, "Why should I look Chinese, for goodness' sake? Everybody know [*sic*] I am one-half English.")[90] As numerous dance scholars have shown, ballet's aesthetics cannot be divorced from Western imperialism.[91] But neither is ballet only and always a whitening agent.[92] The presence of ballet technique in the interior spaces of Kwan's body may align her with whiteness even as it destabilizes the whiteness of ballet. At the very least, it is a reminder that the production of Kwan's filmic body in "I Enjoy Being a Girl" was more than a matter of multiplying and refracting her image, more than a matter of ventriloquizing her white surrogates, and more than a matter of ornamenting her with the accouterments of white femininity. A complicated corporeal history lodged within and beneath her flesh exerted its own complicated sway on the film's surface.

Triangulated Orientations

At this point, it is necessary to pause, rewind, and unsettle the binary between Asianness and whiteness that I have been both parsing and reproducing thus far. While Kwan's parentage and transnational upbringing position her between whiteness and Chineseness, England and Hong Kong, biological inheritance "does not always hold things in place but instead keeps open the space for new arrivals, for new objects, which have their own horizons."[93] Indeed, however much Kwan's corporeality prior to *Flower Drum Song* was oriented around ballet, her dancing across the film extended her corporeal horizon well beyond what "I Enjoy Being a Girl" required of her. In keeping with the stylistic norms of U.S. musicals at midcentury, Pan's choreography for the film included a combination of ballet, jazz, and social dance forms. So too did Kwan's affiliation with this range of styles crop up in discussions of her stardom. The *Saturday Evening Post*'s Pete Martin, for example, reported that "the Hollywood star . . . hot-rods around in a white British sports car, chews gum, dances to Latin rhythms, reads Chinese history against a musical background of Johnny Mathis records," while *McCall's* proclaimed in a photograph caption that Kwan "blends the wisdom of the East with the wiggle of the West."[94] Even as these remarks impose a racialized mind/body binary onto Kwan, their emphasis on her familiarity with Latin rhythms, an African American singer's records, and a Western "wiggle" aligns her with an Africanist rather than a strictly Europeanist corporeal aesthetic. Kwan's racial orientations must therefore be "triangulated," to use scholar Claire Jean Kim's term for the ways Asian/Americans have been "located in the field of racial positions with reference" to both Blackness and whiteness.[95]

Kwan's embodiment of this triangulated racial schema places her within a genealogy of other Asian/American dancers whose "Orientalization" was simultaneous with their performance of European, Africanist, and Latinx movement repertoires. As SanSan Kwan has documented, during the 1930s and 1940s, Asian/American dancers toured the U.S. "Chop Suey" circuit in nightclub acts that presented "the spectacle of Asian American bodies dancing 'American' dances that themselves have fraught histories of ethnic appropriation."[96] These same acts were also the source material for *Flower*

Drum Song, in more ways than one: the Celestial Gardens nightclub where Kwan's Low is a featured dancer is modeled on San Francisco's Forbidden City, the "most popular and longest surviving" of the Chinese/American nightclubs;[97] and the directors, choreographers, and producers for both the Broadway and film versions visited Chinatown nightclubs as part of their casting process (more about which below).

Attending to Kwan's dancing apart from "I Enjoy Being a Girl" lays bare these genealogical connections and the multiracial histories behind her "wiggle." Because she does not dance solo (or only with refracted versions of herself) in other *Flower Drum Song* numbers, they help situate her corporeality in relation to the film's other Asian/American dancers. Rather than understanding her body's orientations primarily through the lens of her prior ballet training or the lens of the film's white production team, that is, we can approach her corporeality horizontally: through her interactions with the multiethnic, pan-Asian cast of dancers she appears alongside, some of whose names are known and others not. While Kwan dances in a pair of "exotic" nightclub acts that directly parallel the chorus lines of Forbidden City ("Fan Tan Fannie" and "Gliding through My Memories"), I focus here on two dance numbers in which her triangulated orientations are most visibly part of the filmic record.

Panethnicity and Patrick Adiarte's Rock 'n' Roll Aesthetic

One number that emphatically displays the gamut of dance styles Pan employed in *Flower Drum Song* is the large ensemble "Chop Suey," a "Chinese square dance"[98] that actually features social dances of European origin, like the quadrille and waltz, and African American and Afro-Latin origin, like the Charleston and cha-cha.[99] Kwan does not appear in "Chop Suey," but she does perform a short burst of dancing just after it has concluded. (This was likely the "delightful bit of inspired nonsense" in which *Times* reporter Glenn observed Varno dancing in for Kwan.)[100] Accompanied by the song "You Be the Rock," the approximately ten-second dance is a duet between Kwan/Low and the Filipino/American dancer Patrick Adiarte, who plays Wang San, the Americanized younger brother of Low's love interest, Wang Ta. It takes place when Kwan as Low, dressed, uncharacteristically, in a traditional chi-pao in an attempt to perform authentic Chineseness, crashes Wang Ta's college graduation party.[101] Approached by Wang San and asked if she sings rock 'n' roll, she responds, "I dig that the most." When he asks if she knows "You Be the Rock," she replies, "Sure!" Handing off her clutch, she and Adiarte break into a basic swing dance step (Figure 5.4). The danced eruption, which *Cosmopolitan* reporter Jon Whitcomb identified as the 1950s rock 'n' roll dance "The Slop,"[102] betrays the "truth" of Low's irrepressible Westernized corporeal orientation, that is, her "wiggle." Anne Cheng describes the moment as an example of how "the 'real' Linda keeps resurfacing."[103]

For scholar Palumbo-Liu, the short dance scene "signals a unidimensional assimilative movement" that "dispens[es] with 'Asia' and rehears[es] a completely contemporaneous, ahistorical enactment of 'America.'"[104] If, diegetically, the dance exchange with Wang San exposes the Americanness that lurks just beneath Low's surface Chineseness, extradiegetically that "Americanness" is oriented as much around Blackness as around whiteness. Although, to my knowledge, Juanita Hall, playing Madame Liang in

Figure 5.4 Kwan as Linda Low and Patrick Adiarte as Wang San in "You Be the Rock." In their brief shared screen time, Adiarte's body is visibly more angular than Kwan's. Courtesy of Photofest NYC.

176 HOLLYWOOD DANCE-INS

yellowface, was the only African American who worked directly on *Flower Drum Song*, Adiarte's dancing body throughout the film is a visible index of what Brenda Dixon Gottschild calls the Africanist influences on American dance.[105] In the brief snippet of movement he shares with Kwan, Adiarte's body is perceptibly more angular and more grounded than hers. Within the film, this makes him the exemplar of the rock 'n' roll aesthetic that marks the younger generation's assimilation. What may appear unidimensional and ahistorical is thus achieved only through Adiarte's skilled incorporation of both European and African diasporic aesthetics, a product of his training in ballet, tap, and jazz dance and his prior experience working with choreographers Jerome Robbins, Gene Kelly, and Carol Haney.[106] His stylistic versatility is even more apparent in his two featured solos in the film: one during "The Other Generation," in which Adiarte, dressed in a baseball uniform, tap dances in sneakers before doing a series of double *pirouettes*, a split jump, and impressively high *temps levées* with one knee completely bent and both arms extended; the other during "Chop Suey," in which, after performing *tours en l'air*, knee switches that skim the ground, and hip swivels, he relaxes into an asymmetrical pose—shoulders shrugged, torso contracted, arms hanging loose, one leg bent and the other out to the side—embodying the looseness, "get-down" stance, and "aesthetic of the cool" that are hallmarks of the Africanist aesthetic.[107]

Though Kwan and Adiarte's shared screen time lasts merely seconds, Kwan told Whitcomb during his visit to the film set that her feet hurt from doing the "'rock'n'roll' song and dance number" with Adiarte "all morning."[108] On the *Flower Drum Song* DVD commentary track, she tells Redman that she took jazz and tap dance lessons from Adiarte and that they spent time with each other socially during the musical's filming.[109] The exchange between Kwan and Adiarte that's captured on film, then, is only an isolated moment in an intercorporeal relationship that extended both backward and forward in time. Their duet is also what we might think of as a "panethnic moment," to borrow scholar Anthony Ocampo's term for instances in which Filipinos, with their history of Spanish colonialism and U.S. imperialism, might feel a sense of "collective identity with either Latinos or other Asians."[110] In the case of Adiarte and Kwan, panethnicity describes not only the coming together of his Spanish-Filipino and her English-Scottish-Chinese background; it also applies to the transnational and multiethnic genealogies that shaped their respective corporeal orientations. While these orientations converged around their shared training in ballet, they were hardly identical, given Adiarte's tap and jazz dance training and his experience with a Broadway tradition of American jazz dance that was indebted to European, African American, Asian, Spanish, and Latinx sources.[111]

At the same time, approaching Adiarte and Kwan's intercorporeal meeting as panethnic highlights the seams that *Flower Drum Song*'s casting practices—and the term "Asian/American"—cover over. While Adiarte and Kwan each play an assimilated Chinese/American, their racialization was not equivalent. As discussed above, Kwan's stardom was measured by her distance from or proximity to the racial and gender norms of both idealized white femininity and exoticized Chineseness. Adiarte's character Wang San, by contrast, may be the exemplar of assimilation, but Adiarte's darker skin color and Filipino ethnicity situate him within a differently raced and gendered matrix, one shaped by the ongoing legacy of the U.S. colonization of the Philippines.[112] Described in *Dance Magazine* as "dark and slight," Adiarte himself once joked, "When I make an appointment for Patrick Adiarte, people always expect to see a tall, read-headed Irishman. Then I come in— little and brown."[113] Wittingly or not, Adiarte's joke rehearses a colonialist rhetoric that positions Filipinos as "America's 'little brown brothers.'"[114] His mastery of American dance styles, meanwhile, aligns him with tropes of exceptionalism, mimicry, and naturalized dance ability that are particular to Filipino colonialism.[115] Contemporaneous observers of Adiarte's dancing reinforced these tropes when they cited his "standout" ability to "whip-lash . . . his head and swivel . . . [his] hips and kick . . . with abandon" while remarking on "his distinctive face and lithe frame."[116]

"You Be the Rock" is thus the site of overlapping orientations that operate on both filmic and extrafilmic registers and that work in tandem with and at cross-purposes from one another. Within the film, the duet serves to telegraph Kwan's "true" Westernized corporeality. In preproduction, however, the same duet disoriented a white reporter surprised by the sight of a white woman dancing in Kwan's place. Simultaneously, in its literal linking of Kwan/Low with Adiarte/Wang San—they physically touch hands as they share a dance step—"You Be the Rock" is a panethnic exchange that reorients Kwan away from a white/Asian binary and away from her off-screen white interlocutors. And because the "rock'n'roll" step Kwan and Adiarte engage in is an African American one, the exchange orients Asian panethnicity around Black aesthetics. Yet that orientation is not uniform, for the different material histories that Kwan and Adiarte carry in and on their bodies—in terms of both their dance training and the transnational and colonial legacies that shaped

178 HOLLYWOOD DANCE-INS

their arrivals—inflect their corporealities differently. Contained in the pair's ten seconds of dancing are the variegated racial and gender formations that constitute and are (nearly) concealed behind filmic "Chineseness."

Anonymous Chorus Dancers and the Asian Space of "Grant Avenue"

By far the number that best showcases Kwan's dancing ability and orients her most unequivocally in relation to *Flower Drum Song*'s large Asian/American cast is "Grant Avenue," the three-and-a-half-minute dance number that made use of the film's expensive "facsimile of a three-block portion of San Francisco's Grant Avenue situated in the heart of Chinatown."[117] Following on the heels of "You Be the Rock" by roughly ten minutes, "Grant Avenue" picks up on the jazz dance thread of that much shorter number. To the extent that it situates Kwan in a mixed-gender group of chorus dancers in which men and women are differently attired but perform the exact same choreography, it also serves as a counterweight to the performances of sexualized femininity in "I Enjoy Being a Girl" and "Fan Tan Fannie" elsewhere in the film.[118] For scholar Julianna Chang, the "outright claiming of public space" by a "critical mass of acculturated Chinese Americans" in "Grant Avenue," a full four years before the abolition of national immigration quotas, is an "exhilarating" sight to behold.[119] The number does not ignore Kwan's star status: her costume is slightly different from those of the ensemble, and she occupies a position front and center (see Figure 5.5). But in contrast to Adiarte's virtuoso dancing in "The Other Generation" and "Chop Suey," the skill, style, and energy of Kwan's dancing here are wholly commensurate with those of the chorus dancers.

Let me be upfront about how little I know about what went on behind the scenes of "Grant Avenue." While the archive establishes that Baker again dubbed Kwan's vocals,[120] I have no documented proof of dance-in Varno's involvement, though it's safe to assume that, as Pan's assistant, she played a role in the creation, teaching, and rehearsing of the number.[121] On the commentary track that plays over the number on the *Flower Drum Song* DVD, Kwan tells us that "Grant Avenue" required being very "aware of [her] space" and that its many turns took a toll on her knee. Asked about working with Pan, Kwan describes demonstrating what she was capable of, being shown steps by him, learning them through a process of emulation, and then

Figure 5.5 Kwan and ensemble dancers in a photo still from "Grant Avenue." Courtesy of Photofest NYC.

adding her own "layer" or "personality" to them.[122] There is some discrepancy about the choreography's derivation: Jerome Delameter's *Dance in the Hollywood Musical* asserts that the film number "is quite clearly adapted from Gene Kelly's choreography for the stage version," though this statement completely elides that it was Haney, not Kelly, who choreographed the Broadway musical.[123] To my knowledge, no extant footage of Haney's version of "Grant Avenue" exists.[124] But in his memoir *Ballet for Life*, Finis Jhung, who appeared in both the Broadway production of *Flower Drum Song* and in the film version's dream ballet (but not in Pan's "Grant Avenue"), calls the Broadway choreography "the perfect fit for Jack [Cole]'s brand of theatrical jazz dance movements," in keeping with assessments of Haney as a major propagator of Cole's style.[125] Despite the paucity of evidence about its conditions of (re)production or its degree of indebtedness to Haney's Cole-inspired choreography, the dancing in "Grant Avenue" is itself a record of substitutions and intercorporealities both overt and tacit.

Its lyrics proclaiming it "a western street with eastern manners," "Grant Avenue" is set in the middle of a Chinatown New Year parade, with Kwan as Low performing on a float advertising the Celestial Garden nightclub that employs her. The number opens with "Orientalist banalities"[126]: appearing from behind a large gong, Kwan kneels with her head bowed, her hands pressed together in prayer. After delicately gesturing toward the elders seated on either side of her, a display of "obeisance to ancestors,"[127] she abruptly strips off her pink silk wrap, jumps to her feet, and strikes an angular, asymmetrical, and grounded (read: Africanist) pose. Joined first by six men dancers and then eight women dancers, she enthusiastically sings of the "most exciting thoroughfare I know" and of being simultaneously in Hong Kong and "California, U.S.A." Kwan then exits behind the float, as the chorus dancers jump down and begin what *Variety* termed a "flashy street strut,"[128] dancing toward and away from the camera, punctuating their traveling movements with syncopated halts, kicks, turns, and slides to the ground, all while a large Asian/American crowd observes from the surrounding sidewalks. About a minute later, thanks to an editing cut, Kwan suddenly reappears in the middle of the ensemble just as the song breaks into a stereotypical Eastern-sounding instrumental riff. As the riff plays, Kwan and the other dancers perform an almost comical dance move that has them placing the first and second fingers of their right hand in front of their right eye as they shake their left hand in front of them while their lower body performs a hip-swinging cha-cha-esque step.[129] In unison, Kwan and the ensemble then resume the jazzier, ground-covering choreography from the dance's first half, consistently tracked by the camera and framed head to toe. The number culminates as all of the dancers perform a double turn and hit an open-armed pose, prompting the diegetic crowd to break into applause.

In many ways, "Grant Avenue" replicates the racial triangulation of "You Be the Rock": the choreography juxtaposes what Cheng would likely identify as ornamental gestures meant to signify Chineseness—hands in prayer, fingers framing eyes—with the space-eating, full-bodied movements of American musical theater jazz. Differently put, the choreography here layers Orientalized gestures on top of bodily comportments and propulsive steps that combine an Africanist and Europeanist aesthetic and that may, by way of Haney, also bear traces of Cole's "Orientalist" approach to jazz dance.[130] To put it yet another way, "Grant Avenue" mobilizes a layered history of cross-racial influences, appropriations, impersonations, and erasures. Taking into account the dancing's heterogeneous sources, Kwan's racially triangulated body in "Grant Avenue" is arguably an index of an entire genealogy of American jazz dance that includes white men like Pan, Kelly, and Cole, who dominated the field; the overlooked or forgotten white women, like Haney and Varno, on whom those men relied; the many dancers of color whose practices were woven into the fabric of jazz dance; and the Asian/American dancers who performed "Chinese"-branded versions of popular African American and Afro-Latin social dances across the United States in the 1930s and 1940s, including in Chinatowns like the one represented in *Flower Drum Song*.

While this complicated corporeal history may not be immediately visible behind the screen of Kwan's ambiguously racialized body, right in front of our faces the filmic image does document certain kinds of substitution. As indicated, for about a third of the "Grant Avenue" number, Kwan is absent, while fourteen uncredited chorus dancers fill the space. The fact that she temporarily goes missing recalls that earlier scene of absence: Varno dancing in for Kwan. Insofar as they hold the star's place while she is elsewhere, the chorus dancers in "Grant Avenue" might be said to perform a function analogous to Varno's. In that sense, they are on-screen proxies for the dance-in; they represent the danced, place-holding labor that was part of the off-screen apparatus of filmmaking.

As Chang writes, the presence of so many background Asian/American actors and dancers in *Flower Drum Song* is "quite extraordinary in the history of Hollywood racial images." Given how little is known about their identities or what became of them after their appearance in the musical, she also describes these anonymous players as "filmic apparitions"—"uncanny, strange, and spectral."[131] As such, the ensemble dancers in "Grant Avenue" are yet another example of the indexical instabilities that envelop the film. Diegetically, their bodies comprise the all-Asian space of "Grant Avenue"; extradiegetically, they are fleeting occupants of white Hollywood. They fill the screen, but then disappear from the movies. They embody the material labor that goes into the production of film images, but they never come fully into focus.

In fact, a kind of elusiveness characterized the musical's chorus from the outset. Repeatedly, accounts of the making of both the Broadway and film versions of *Flower Drum Song* emphasize how hard it was to cast Asian/American actors and dancers. Writing in the *Los Angeles Times*, composer Richard Rodgers remarked, "We hadn't realized how few Chinese actors were available as singers and dancers."[132] *Dance Magazine* likewise reported that Pan "had enormous difficulty rounding up a dance chorus."[133] Yet there is reason to wonder whether some of these accounts were protesting too much. As David Lewis writes, "It is puzzling that they did not find more bodies at

182 HOLLYWOOD DANCE-INS

San Francisco's still-vibrant 'Chinese' nightclub, Forbidden City—or, for that matter, at any of the other night spots in the pagoda district."[134] The dancer Ivy Tam, who was married for a time to Forbidden City's owner Charlie Low, remembered "Gene Kelly and other Hollywood stars coming and going all the time, sitting down to enjoy the floor shows," as well as the casting director and producer of Hollywood's *Flower Drum Song* speaking with her and tapping some of Forbidden City's dancers for the film's chorus.[135] But she could not recall "any formal *Drum* auditions anywhere in Chinatown, Forbidden City included. Neither [did] anybody else."[136] It is possible, Lewis speculates, that dancers like Dorothy Toy and Paul Wing, who were billed as the "Chinese Fred Astaire and Ginger Rogers" and were still performing in the early 1960s, "would have taken too much focus off the principals."[137]

Intentionally or not, the narrative of scarcity with respect to the chorus justified assembling what Rodgers called "a cast with a hodge-podge of backgrounds—Chinese, Japanese, Hawaiian, Filipino, Puerto Rican, Negro, American Indian, East Indian and Caucasian."[138] Though the film version, as I have indicated, relied less on yellowface than the Broadway version, closer scrutiny of the chorus dancers in "Grant Avenue," cross-referenced with the admittedly partial and undocumented listings on IMDb,[139] reveals that, of the six men dancers, one is the Mexican American Rudy del Campo (who also appeared as a chorus dancer in *Singin' in the Rain* and as a Shark in *West Side Story*; he is the dancer on the viewer's far right in Figure 5.5); one is the Filipino Colombian José de Vega, who played Chino in *West Side Story* (see the dancer just behind and to the viewer's right of Kwan in Figure 5.5);[140] and two appear to be white—likely Frank Radcliffe, Pan's assistant, and Jack Tygett, one of Pan's regular dancers (see the white-appearing dancer on the viewer's far left in Figure 5.5).[141] The women dancers, by contrast, appear to all be Asian/American, though they were almost certainly not all Chinese/American.[142] That it has gone unnoticed, including initially by me, that a few of these dancers are not Asian at all is perhaps attributable to the prevalence of yellowface. Or perhaps it is a product of the obscuring effect of anonymous chorus dancers. In any case, what Chang calls the "dancing Chinese American crowd" and what I called the "all-Asian space of 'Grant Avenue'" is actually a space of panethnic and cross-ethnic encounters and substitutions: nonindividuated chorus members dancing in unison with and standing in for the film's biracial star; pan-Asian, Latinx, and white dancers standing in for Chinese/Americans; multiracial jazz dance standing in for assimilated "Americanness."[143]

It is out of this series of encounters and substitutions that Kwan's filmic image was forged. As the only star of color to figure so prominently in this book, Kwan demonstrates how the presumed coherence and indexical stability of star bodies was withheld from nonwhite stars. For Kwan, whose mixed-race Asianness "foreclosed her full incorporation into white female privilege,"[144] the seams and fissures of her filmic body's constructedness (seams and fissures that are inherent in all filmic images and arguably all corporealities) played out in equivocations about her racial status, about whether she was superficially white or superficially Asian, overdetermined by whiteness or irreducibly Asian.

As much as the incoherence of Kwan's filmic body was wrought by the vexed racial logic dictating the terms of Asian/American embodiment, it also points us toward alternate understandings of corporeality. Kwan, that is, presents an opportunity to take seriously Anne Cheng's suggestion that we set aside "the fantasy of the organic flesh [that] has remained the single most cherished site of feminist and racial redemption" and Rachel Lee's proposal that we think "embodiment more in terms of distributed parts and patterns of circulation."[145] Instead of attempting to restore Kwan to wholeness or determine what was organic to her, we can learn from what she makes visible about corporeality as layered, distributed, and imperfectly sutured. Perhaps, in fact, Kwan's dancing body in *Flower Drum Song* is not indexically unstable at all. Perhaps, whether she is producing refracted versions of herself in a three-way mirror or dancing in front of, disappearing from, and blending in with a collective of dancers, her filmic image is indexing her flesh, her interlocutors, and the colonial legacies and mixed-race genealogies that shaped American film musical dancing at large.

* * *

And yet we should not be too quick to hold up corporealities whose detectable seams lead us to histories of substitution and panethnic encounters as the answer to questions about bodily indexicality. In a photo that ran in the tabloid newspaper the *Los Angeles Mirror* just as filming for *Flower Drum Song* was getting underway, Kwan appears alongside the actor Iron Eyes Cody, dressed in full Native American garb, as he fastens a headdress on her (Figure 5.6).[146] The caption reads, "Nancy Kwan, known to movie-goers as 'Suzie Wong,' has new world [*sic*] today. Nancy, half Chinese, half Scotch-English, has become a Cherokee Indian and has been named 'Little Deer.' She was inducted into tribe [*sic*] by Iron Eyes Cody, full-blooded Cherokee and long-time adviser

Figure 5.6 Iron Eyes Cody fastens a headdress onto Nancy Kwan, March 1961. Photograph by Bettman, Getty Images.

on Indian films."[147] Viewed in relation to *Flower Drum Song* and to the other examples in this book, the image and caption point us in several directions simultaneously: backward to Bob Hope's nicknaming Marie Bryant Pocahontas (see Chapter 2); forward to a musical number that appears late in *Flower Drum Song*, a "humorous pantomime ballet" called "Sunday," in which Kwan as Low fantasizes about a life of domesticity, only to be interrupted by a cowboy/Indian pair who break out of a television set;[148] and recursively toward the ongoingness of racial surrogation in U.S. film and culture.

On one level, the photograph and caption instructively encapsulate the heterogeneity and mutability of Kwan's racialization.[149] In practically the same breath, the caption aligns Kwan with the sexualized, Orientalized role that launched her stardom, establishes her biraciality, and sanctions the bestowal of Native American identity upon her. She is decisively other but also racially fluid, thoroughly foreign and yet assimilable into the U.S. nation-state via tribal adoption. This latter move is a reminder of the overlapping racial formations that structured Hollywood and its corporeal ecosystem. As with the framing of Bryant as Pocahontas, Kwan's position in Hollywood's racial schema is figured through a Native American imaginary, another measure of how close to Hollywood's surface the specter of the nation's genocidal founding lurked.[150] Indeed, the seemingly out-of-nowhere announcement of Kwan as Little Deer has a filmic counterpart in the "strange" surfacing of the cowboy and Indian who intrude on Low's daydream in *Flower Drum Song*'s "Sunday" number, staged by Pan. Commenting on this number, Chang writes, "Even a film like *Flower Drum Song*, in which the formerly Wild West city of San Francisco presumably has been long settled and urbanized, finds itself unable to avoid the primal scene of attachment and antagonism between settler and native."[151]

Among its other racializing moves, the behind-the-scenes moment of panethnic exchange between foreign and domestic racialized others is also not what it seems. As Michelle Raheja has written, though Iron Eyes Cody was for much of the late twentieth century the "quintessential symbol of the American Indian" through his role as the "crying Indian" in a 1971 Keep America Beautiful television campaign, he was "most likely not an Indian at all," but Italian American, as members of Native American communities had long suspected.[152] Cody, like Joseph Vitale (discussed for his role in *Fancy Pants* [1950] in Chapter 2), appeared in redface in *The Paleface* (1948). Unlike Vitale, Cody "played Indian" both on- and off-screen. What we are seeing, then, is the Euro-American Cody in "buckskin drag"[153] conferring Cherokee membership on the racially amorphous Kwan, whose *Flower Drum Song* performance, depending on who you ask, required her to enact substitutive whiteness or Asian drag.

Attending to these layers of racial masquerade returns us to the epistemological uncertainty that cuts across filmic bodies, photographic bodies, and live bodies alike. As much as Cody's "passing" as Native "force[s] us to confront the dominant culture's desire for discrete, bounded, essential categories of identification,"[154] the photograph thwarts our ability to treat "backstage" images as truth-telling documents. Paired with Iron Eyes Cody, Kwan alerts us to the pitfalls of treating either on-screen or off-screen bodies as sites of knowable identity. Even behind the scenes, even when viewed relationally and intercorporeally, bodies evade transparency.

Coda

There's a clip online of Lena Horne and Carol Haney dancing together to an instrumental version of the jazz standard "Deed I Do" on an October 17, 1962 episode of *Perry Como's Kraft Music Hall* variety show, which aired on NBC-TV (Figure C.1).[1] I can't recall what I was looking for when the clip popped up in my search results. I spent time researching Horne and Haney separately—Horne in the initial phases of this project, as I hunted for evidence of dance-ins supporting Black stars, and Haney as I tracked her work as a dance-in and assistant to Gene Kelly. And here they were dancing together, in what one newspaper report identified as "Lena's first dance number directed by choreographer Carol Haney."[2] The duet begins as if Haney is teaching Horne the dance in real time: Haney holds up her index finger, says "First," and shows Horne a step, which Horne then repeats, prompting Haney to respond, "Very good." But very quickly they are dancing in unison and engaging in some light banter about their dancing. Despite accounts that Horne was not a great dancer, she more than holds her own with Haney, whose dance talent has been more widely celebrated. The dance steps are not complicated, and their movements are relatively contained, sometimes even minute. And yet the duet is utterly riveting to me.

This television clip is perhaps an unlikely focus for the coda to a book about Hollywood dance-ins. Most of the foregoing chapters were launched by some scrap of behind-the-scenes evidence that opened up a query about the relations between on-screen and off-screen bodies in the making of a film musical. By contrast, I know virtually nothing about the conditions of production for this episode of Como's show, and nothing about what Haney and Horne's relationship was like. I don't even know whether a dance-in was used in rehearsals for their duet, although dance-ins were not unusual in preproduction for television variety shows like Como's.

Yet precisely because I know so little about how Horne and Haney's number came to be, their televised dance presents an opportunity to consider how we might glimpse the "spectral effects" of Hollywood's corporeal ecosystem, even in the absence of information about a number's specific

Hollywood Dance-ins and the Reproduction of Bodies. Anthea Kraut, Oxford University Press.
© Oxford University Press 2025. DOI: 10.1093/oso/9780197789667.003.0007

CODA 187

Figure C.1 Screen capture of Carol Haney (left) and Lena Horne in "Deed I Do" on an October 17, 1962, episode of *Perry Como's Kraft Music Hall* variety show.

material conditions of production.[3] Framed as a scene of instruction and collaboration between an established choreographer and an established star, the dance may be more transparently about transmission and exchange than most, but the tensions between what we can and cannot directly perceive on-screen make it all the more compelling.[4] What echoes of the racialized and gendered relations of reproduction that fueled the production of Hollywood film musicals can we detect in Horne and Haney's televised dance? In broader terms, how might this book's account of dance-ins shape our approach to screen images of dancing bodies when all we have are the images—which, after all, are the most common way we interact with screen bodies? In the remainder of this coda, I offer a reading of Horne and Haney's duet informed by the preceding analysis of dance-ins in midcentury film musicals. Featuring a Black woman and a white woman who occupied different positions in Hollywood's ecosystem and who dance together but not entirely in synch, the duet elucidates how off-screen histories of reproduction can leave their imprint within the textured details of screen performances.

* * *

188 HOLLYWOOD DANCE-INS

At the start of the clip, Como, Haney, and five of Como's regulars[5] are gathered together when Horne emerges behind Haney, taps her on the shoulder, and says, "Hey, Carol, I think I'm ready for the dance." Haney responds, "Great," before Como announces to the regulars, "I'm very sorry, kids, Lena's gonna dance this thing with Carol," then asks, "Is that all right?" An off-camera piano breaks into a few chords, and the regulars respond in song, "Yes, it's all right . . . yes, it's all right . . . it's allll right with me," a call-back to the Cole Porter song "It's All Right with Me," which Como, Horne, and Haney sang as a trio at the top of the show.[6] The ensemble members begin snapping on the off-beat as they repeat "me . . . me . . . me."

Haney grabs Horne by the hand and leads her stage left (viewer's right). The camera pans to follow them, framing them in a medium shot that displays their full bodies. They let go of hands, make eye contact, and gesture at one another, and, just as we hear the opening bars of "Deed I Do," played by the unseen Ayres Orchestra, Haney shows Horne the first step: a simple touch of the foot to the right and left, accompanied by a subtle hip tilt. Haney pauses while Horne echoes the move. Haney then calls out "Time step" while executing it (stomp, hop, step, fa-lap step). Horne again echoes the step, uttering "Yeah" and looking to Haney as she does so. Haney then says something I can't make out, at which point both women lift their left leg slightly and balance on their right, as Horne half-sings in time with the music, "Ahhh, don't hold that too long." Haney continues to call out the steps, though the women now dance in unison. "Shim Sham," Haney says, as they perform the shuffle steps of the routine generally regarded as tap dance's national anthem, and Horne again vocalizes "Ahhh."[7] They continue to converse as they dance. "Why is this so much fun?" asks Haney. "I don't know," Horne responds, "'cuz you can sit down and do it." "Yeah, in a chair," Haney answers, before announcing "Break" (another part of the Shim Sham). From there, the two continue the breezy jazz number full of simple weight changes, low kicks, and small hip articulations.

After about a minute, seven other dancers, presumably members of the Peter Gennaro Dancers,[8] join in behind them. We cut to an overhead shot of the entire group dancing in unison before returning to the medium shot focused on Haney and Horne. The dance ends as they all repeat a side-to-side, weight-transferring, hip-switching step, with Haney and Horne picking up their conversation. "Later!" Horne shouts. "Don't go away anybody," Haney adds. "I think we're full," Haney observes (likely referring to the studio audience, whom we can hear but not see), and then, "Who are all those people?"

"I don't know," Horne replies. They hit the final step as the orchestra hits the final note, and the audience breaks into applause. Haney reaches out to Horne and the two shake hands and soak in the applause. After a beat, Como enters downstage right (viewer's left) and asks, "Anybody gonna dance with me? Lena? Carol?" They each swiftly depart stage left (viewer's right). "Frank? John?" Como continues, as the rest of the dancers exit, until the show's announcer, Frank Gallop, dressed in the same white cardigan sweater and white hat that Horne, Haney, and the ensemble members are all wearing, enters and snaps his fingers in Como's face. The audience roars in laughter as he asks, "Shall we take it from the top, Mr. C?" The clip ends there.

Hollywood's Corporeal Ecosystem in the Age of Television

Among other facets of the duet's usefulness as a final scene to this book, the coming together of Haney and Horne is another sign of how few degrees of separation existed between dancers in Hollywood's corporeal ecosystem. While the televised number may have been the first time the women came into close contact, they both had prior experience working with jazz choreographer Jack Cole: Haney when she was a core member of his dance troupe and a principal disseminator of his technique, and Horne when she starred in the 1957 Broadway production *Jamaica*, which he choreographed.[9] Separately, Horne and Haney are each linked to the other dancers featured in this book. As discussed in Chapter 2, Horne was best friends with Marie Bryant, who reportedly assisted both Cole and Hermes Pan[10] and became the suspected "polisher" of Horne's nightclub act. According to her obituary, Bryant, like Haney, also did "choreo stints" for Perry Como at one time.[11] As mentioned in Chapter 4, Haney danced with Alex Romero in Cole's company and in *On the Town* (1949), and both served as long-term assistants to Gene Kelly (see Chapters 3 and 4). Kelly is credited with first hiring Bryant as a coach for Vera-Ellen, for whom Haney evidently danced "miles" as a stand-in.[12] Haney also choreographed the 1958 Broadway production of *Flower Drum Song*, directed by Kelly and featuring a young Patrick Adiarte, who would later dance with Nancy Kwan in the Pan-choreographed 1961 film version (see Chapter 5). And these are just the most readily discernible connections.[13] The extent to which these performers interacted on film lots or television sets, at nightclubs, or in social gatherings like those hosted by Bryant (see Chapter 2) remains unknowable. Nevertheless, the weblike

190   HOLLYWOOD DANCE-INS

nature of these affiliations and proximities highlights the constant traffic between dancers in Hollywood—and the complicated network of corporeal influences—that took place beyond the reach of the camera.

That Horne and Haney encountered one another in a television studio rather than on a Hollywood lot is also significant, for it indicates shifts to the entire ecosystem of dance on-screen at midcentury. Although the "death" of film musicals in the late 1950s is overstated, the dismantling of the studio system set in motion by studios' court-ordered divestiture of movie theater holdings contributed to their decline.[14] By 1960, when "about 90% of all American homes had TV,"[15] dancers in Hollywood increasingly turned to the television industry for work, many splitting their time between television and the movies. Save for two exceptions, this was also true of the dance-ins who appear in this book. Angie Blue, Pan's long-time assistant and Betty Grable's long-time dance-in, ran the dance department of Twentieth Century-Fox's contract talent school and choreographed "'small things' for films 'when they didn't want to bring in a choreographer'" until 1962, at which point she entered the Carmelite Monastery in Carmel, California.[16] Jeanne Coyne, Kelly's assistant and Debbie Reynolds's dance-in in *Singin' in the Rain* (1952), married Kelly in 1960, became a mother shortly after, and appears to have stopped working in entertainment. But Marie Bryant, Alex Romero, and Becky Varno, in addition to Haney, all found at least occasional employment in television in the late 1950s and early 1960s: Bryant as the resident choreographer for the *Nat King Cole Television Show*,[17] Romero as the dance director for NBC-TV's *The Eddie Fisher Show*,[18] and Varno as a dancer in the 1959 television special *Another Evening with Fred Astaire* and, as documented in the previous chapter, as Nancy Kwan's dance-in for a 1961 Bob Hope holiday special.[19] Far from an aberration, the appearance of Horne and Haney on the Como show in 1962 typifies the trajectories of stars and behind-the-scenes players alike.[20]

Female Pairings and Homosociality

Returning to Horne and Haney's duet, the joke that closes the number—Como's solicitation of Horne and Haney, their rejection of him, and Gallop's attempt to dance with Como, played for laughs—calls attention to its gender dynamics. What we just witnessed was a duet between two women, Como's reappearance reminds us. In turn, the duet calls attention to the fact that, however obscured they were by what a 1967 *Dance Magazine* article called "Hollywood's choreographic fraternity,"[21] women transmitting movement to each other and dancing together in their capacities as assistants, coaches, dance-ins, and stars was a fixture of Hollywood's corporeal ecosystem. Whether or not a dance-in was used in preparation for Horne and Haney's duet, the gender configuration it makes visible indexes an arrangement that was completely routine in rehearsal rooms. Think of all the female pairs that appear in this book: Angie Blue and Betty Grable, Marie Bryant and a multitude of white women stars, Becky Varno and Nancy Kwan, not to mention the female trio of Haney, Coyne, and Reynolds. Some of these collaborations led to long-term friendships. Others may have been more strictly transactional. Some were no doubt a combination of both. Regardless, Horne and Haney help make plain that women working above- and below-the-line regularly danced together in ways that challenge or at least complicate the heterosexualized pairings that dominate film musicals, as well as the patriarchal structures that elevated male choreographers while (and by) assigning women dancers to reproductive roles.

As I argued in Chapter 4, the intimate working relationship between Kelly and Romero—their constant swapping of places and mirroring of one another, the "erotic triangle" they formed with a female dancer, Kelly's anxiety about the disclosure of Romero's choreographic influence—raises the possibility that there was something queer about their relations of reproduction. The specter of queer desire within those relations, it warrants stating, cannot be disentangled from the homophobia that has attended the figure of the male dancer under Western modernity.[22] While this same homophobic stigma is the basis for the "joke" that Como may be forced to repeat Horne and Haney's duet with his male announcer, the image of two women dancing together does not invite the same laughter or uneasiness. Still, it is worth observing the discrepancy between the slacks and sweaters Horne and Haney wear during their danced duet and the conventionally feminine evening gowns they don during the show's opening and closing sung numbers.[23] Performing in gender-neutral clothing in a gender-neutral dance framed by the departure and then return of the show's male star, Horne and Haney prod us to ask what this book has largely ignored: might there also have been something queer about the relations between women stars and their female dance-ins/coaches?[24]

Theater scholar Stacy Wolf has argued that, even as "[h]eterosexuality structures and ideologically underpins the plots of musicals of the 1940s and

192 HOLLYWOOD DANCE-INS

1950s," the frequency of female duets in these musicals undermines their "heterosexual closure." Wolf identifies two types of female duets: "queer collaborative duet[s]," in which "two women collude on a plan or support each other emotionally," and "queer pedagogical duet[s]," in which one woman teaches another a lesson. Wolf's argument is premised on the fact that female duets in musicals "are not queer in isolation" but occur within the musical's heteronormative narrative context. Horne and Haney's duet, by contrast, occurs outside any surrounding narrative. But Wolf's categories hardly seem irrelevant to the pair's dance number, which clearly contains elements of pedagogy (Haney teaching Horne the steps) and collaboration (the two dancing in unison while engaging in verbal patter). The sense of closeness created by their shared movement and dialogue, moreover, arguably creates what Wolf describes as the "intimate [kinetic] relationship on which the female duet capitalizes."[25] As a dance pairing that deviates from at least two norms— the heterosexual duet and male choreographic instruction—Horne and Haney's number underscores the utter regularity of female homosociality in Hollywood's corporeal ecosystem, while leaving open questions about what kinds of desire and gender fluidity such homosociality may have facilitated.

Cross-racial Pairings and Not-Quite-Synched Unison

In an analysis of a sung duet between Lena Horne and Judy Garland that aired on the short-lived *Judy Garland Show* almost exactly a year after the Horne-Haney duet on Como's show, Deborah Paredez argues that "Horne resists the racial liberalist framing of their staged act and queers its constructions of racialized femininity" by "refus[ing] to submit to the . . . interracial sisterhood that Garland attempts to enact." Reading Horne's gestural, postural, and sonic choices, Paredez shows how Horne's "legible restraint in the face of Garland's advances" and her failure to orient her body in "a relational position" indicate "an incipient nationalist desire for a radical break from 'harmonious' relational possibilities in which racial harmony comes at the direction of white authority."[26] Horne later described the spring and summer of 1963 as turning points in her public involvement with the intensifying civil rights movement. In May of that year, at the invitation of James Baldwin, Horne attended a meeting with Attorney General Robert Kennedy; in June, at the invitation of Medgar Evers, she sang at a civil rights rally, just days before Evers was murdered.[27] If 1963 brought about a "marked departure" for Horne, away from her "previously maintained persona of withholding and distance" and against "white liberal desires for interracial unity,"[28] what kind of interracial relations did Horne and Haney enact in 1962? How does their dance collaboration compare not only to Horne's later sung duet with Garland but also to the off-screen pairings examined in Chapter 2, between Bryant and white women stars?

It is important not to gloss over the differences between these cross-racial couplings. At the time of taping their duet, Horne was fed up with Garland, whose absence from run-throughs required Horne to rehearse with a stand-in prior to filming.[29] Conversely, she reportedly thought highly of Como and made numerous appearances on his show in the 1960s, both before and after her duet with Haney.[30] That Horne's duet with Haney is danced rather than sung also matters. Horne's film career did include some dance numbers, such as "The Spring" in the 1942 film *Panama Hattie* (choreographed by Jeni LeGon, who also served as Horne's dance-in for the number, and whose contract, as discussed in Chapter 2, MGM rescinded) and "Brazilian Boogie Woogie" (in which Bryant dances alongside Horne) in the 1944 film *Broadway Rhythm*. For the most part, though, Horne stood still in her films, "pinned to a column singing away in Movieland," as she later lamented.[31] When Horne and Haney came together in 1962, Horne was famous as an actress and singer, and Haney, having garnered acclaim for her dancing in *The Pajama Game* on Broadway in 1954 and on film in 1957, was in demand as a choreographer but less publicly known than Horne. The power dynamics of Horne and Haney's duet, then, are necessarily different from those between Bryant and white women stars and those between Horne and Garland.

Dancing together, Horne and Haney look loose and relaxed and appear to be enjoying themselves immensely. On the surface, this is exactly the kind of "racial liberalist staging" that Paredez argues Horne resists in her duet with Garland. Closer attention to the dancing, however, reveals something more than uncomplicated harmony. When two differently racialized women dance "various forms of unanimity—taking turns, echo, unison,"[32] the duet suggests, they can enact female camaraderie while simultaneously reiterating and subverting white authority. Recognizing that paradox requires engaging with what is and is not on display in the act of performance.

Given Haney's status as a working choreographer, there is nothing particularly notable about the fact that the instruction in the duet comes from her. Neither is it surprising that the jazzy choreography includes tap dance staples like the time step and Shim Sham, both of which Horne and Haney

194 HOLLYWOOD DANCE-INS

were surely familiar with long before they set foot on the stage of Manhattan's Ziegfeld Theatre, where Como's show was shot. Nor is it extraordinary, given U.S. dance history's patterns of appropriation, to see a white choreographer dictating steps whose African American origins must be consistently asserted because they are so frequently contested or erased.[33] And yet there is something striking about the conspicuousness of a white choreographer "giving" Black dance steps to a Black star, even as it echoes other chains of transmission we've seen in this book. It was Haney, recall, who created and taught choreography influenced by Jack Cole's Asian/Afro-Latin/Afro-Caribbean/African American–influenced style of jazz dance to a largely Asian/American cast in the 1958 Broadway production of *Flower Drum Song*. Put another way, what plays out before our eyes in Horne and Haney's danced exchange reproduces other, less visible cross-racial exchanges. The scene of instruction that their duet stages, like any scene of instruction, is haunted by a longer string of multiracial genealogies and racialized displacements that are part of star dancing bodies' conditions of possibility.

If these conditions are only implicitly present, the duet more explicitly captures the inexactness of dance exchanges—the "casualties"[34] and surpluses that inevitably accompany acts of reproduction. Part of what first captivated me about the number, no doubt, is how often Horne's body fails to synch precisely with Haney's. There are times, for instance, when Horne keeps her shoulders raised just a fraction of a second longer than Haney (Figure C.1), when she articulates her hips with just a fraction more precision, and when her head reverberates in a wobble after stepping her foot down. In fact, in the very moment she is saying "Ahhh, don't hold that too long," Horne holds her leg up a beat longer than Haney. (Is Horne's comment a cue to herself? Or a repetition of a note from Haney that she fails to take?) This happens again in the final seconds of the dance, when Horne takes some extra shoulder rolls and lifts her hands up to her head just before letting her left foot hit the floor on the song's final note. Actually, she lands a half-beat after Haney and adds another slight head bobble.

Horne's ability to both sit back in the choreography and add that "something 'extra'" infuses her dancing with an "authoritative panache" and an "aesthetic of the cool" that signal her Africanist approach to movement (an aesthetic that was especially pronounced in the dancing of LeGon and Bryant).[35] These moments of delay and stylistic flairs might also be taken as refusals on Horne's part to bring her body perfectly in line with Haney's.[36] In dancing *with* Haney and *like* Haney but *not identically to* Haney, Horne demonstrates that acts of transmission can shape but cannot dictate exactly how a dancing body will perform and that Black aesthetics are not performed equivalently across bodies. She reminds us that the work of synching bodies can never be wholly successful, not only because every dancing body is oriented by their prior training and preexisting corporeal dispositions, but also because stars may be granted wiggle room that contract dancers are not, and because the labor of the choreographer, as well as the labor of the dance-in, can always be resisted. And if we choose to regard her gestures of nonalignment as micro-refusals of interracial harmony, Horne shows us that the structuring logic of a corporeal ecosystem designed to uphold idealized images of whiteness can be contradicted, even if not overturned, by the choices dancers make when they move.

From a certain perspective, my emphasis here on what stands out about Horne's performance reinforces ideas of the body as a site of discreteness, individuality, and integrity, ideas this book has sought to destabilize. But tuning in to differences between dancing bodies is not the same as understanding the body as bounded, autonomous, or even strictly self-referential. Nor does it cancel out the need to create space in our perceptions of star dancing bodies—and all dancing bodies—for the multiplicities and intercorporealities, the reproductive acts of doubling and surrogation, that underwrite them and that they in turn index. To be sure, you can only anticipate a rhythm that you have already learned; you can only play around with movement your body has previously incorporated. Even if we read Horne's moments of asynchrony as refusals of white authority, those refusals are made possible by her familiarity with choreography that could only be acquired through a set of earlier exchanges. Both the moments when Horne aligns her body with Haney's and the moments when she does not bear the traces of unseen rehearsals that involved reproducing movement in relation to another dancer whose body bears traces of still other exchanges. Dancing side by side, Haney and Horne present dancing as a relational act of give-and-take arising out of longer histories of reproduction and embedded in larger circuits of power. Those histories and circuits may not always be visible on screen. But they are there nonetheless, exerting their push and pull on bodies that perhaps always partially index and partially conceal them.

Notes

Acknowledgments

1. Though tracking down that particular lead proved fruitless, I believe the mother in question was Patty DeSautels (1927–1992), who was a stuntwoman and chorus dancer and doubled for Reynolds (most likely in a stunt capacity) in several late 1950s films. See Gene Scott Freese, "Patty deSautels," in *Hollywood Stunt Performers, 1910s–1970s* (Jefferson, NC: McFarland, 2014), 73–74. Chapter 3 addresses the roles Jeanne Coyne and Carol Haney, who danced in for Reynolds and assisted choreographer Gene Kelly, played in shaping the star's corporeality in *Singin' in the Rain* (1952).

Introduction

1. Frank Morriss, "Some Jottings from Hollywood," *Winnipeg Free Press*, August 3, 1940, 4. Perhaps best known for originating several leading roles in Richard Rodgers and Oscar Hammerstein's Broadway musicals in the 1940s and 1950s, Martin also worked in Hollywood, including as the dubbing voice for other stars.
2. See Chapter 1 for the first documented instance of a dance-in that I have uncovered.
3. Interview with Barrie Chase, May 8, 2019, Los Angeles.
4. At times, dance-ins were hired to double for stars on screen as well. Chase, for example, served as Kay Williams's dance double in an opening scene of the 1954 film *The Actress* because Williams was an "awkward" mover. But while movies do not always rely on dance doubles, it is safe to assume that whenever a star performs in a big dance number on screen, a dance-in has been involved. Adrienne L. McLean's *Dying Swans and Madmen: Ballet, the Body, and Narrative Cinema* (New Brunswick, NJ: Rutgers University Press, 2008) cites a number of examples of dance doubles in Hollywood, as does Larry Billman's *Film Choreographers and Dance Directors: An Illustrated Biographical Encyclopedia, with a History and Filmographies,1893 through 1995* (Jefferson, NC: McFarland, 1997). I briefly address the relationship between dance-ins and doubles in Chapter 1.
5. Jackie Stacey, *The Cinematic Life of the Gene* (Durham, NC: Duke University Press, 2010), 258.
6. See, among others, Daniel Bernardi, ed., *Classic Hollywood, Classic Whiteness* (Minneapolis: University of Minnesota Press, 2001); Gwendolyn Audrey Foster, *Performing Whiteness: Postmodern Re/constructions in the Cinema* (Albany: State University of New York Press, 2003); Hernán Vera and Andrew M. Gordon, *Screen Saviors: Hollywood Fictions of Whiteness* (Lanham, MD: Rowman & Littlefield, 2003); Maryann Erigha, *The Hollywood Jim Crow: The Racial Politics of the Movie Industry* (New York: New York University Press, 2019).
7. My use of the term "ecosystem" is inspired by the work of scholars across Black studies, performance studies, and feminist studies who have turned to biological models that destabilize the body as a sovereign entity as a means to resituate embodiment within relational matrices of power. In particular, my thinking has been shaped by the work of Zakiyyah Iman Jackson, *Becoming Human: Matter and Meaning in an Antiblack World* (New York: New York University Press, 2020); Anna Watkins Fisher, *The Play in the System: The Art of Parasitical Resistance* (Durham, NC: Duke University Press, 2020); and Chikako Takeshita, "From Mother/Fetus to Holobiont(s): A Material Feminist Ontology of the Pregnant Body," *Catalyst: Feminism, Theory, Technoscience* 3, no. 1 (2022): 1–28. I discuss their work later in this introduction and/or in subsequent chapters. See also Kate Fortmueller, who proposes that "acting is an ecosystem" in *Below the Stars: How the Labor of Working Actors and Extras Shapes Media Production* (Austin: University of Texas Press, 2021), 5.
8. Miranda J. Banks, "Gender Below-the-Line: Defining Feminist Production Studies," in *Production Studies: Cultural Studies of Media Industries*, ed. Vicki Mayer, Miranda Banks, and John Caldwell (New York: Routledge, 2009), 89.

198 NOTES

9. See also Melissa Phruksachart's use of materialist history to illuminate racial ideologies in "The Many Lives of Mr. Yunioshi: Yellowface and the Queer Buzz of *Breakfast at Tiffany's*," *Camera Obscura: Feminism, Culture, and Media Studies* 32, no. 3 (2017): 93–119.

10. See Jessica Sternfeld and Elizabeth L. Wollman, "After the 'Golden Age,'" in *Histories of the Musical: An Oxford Handbook of the American Musical*, vol. 1, ed. Raymond Knapp, Mitchell Morris, and Stacy Wolf (New York: Oxford University Press, 2018), 177–198, on the "notorious loose[ness]" of the term "Golden Age" with respect to musical theater (177).

11. Bernardi, *Classic Hollywood, Classic Whiteness*.

12. See Patricia Mellencamp, "Spectacle and Spectator: Looking through the American Musical Comedy," *Cine-tracts* 1 (1977): 27–35, on the musical comedy as a "sub-category of classical Hollywood cinema" (28).

13. Bernardi, *Classic Hollywood, Classic Whiteness*, xiv; Harry M. Benshoff and Sean Griffin, *America on Film: Representing Race, Class, Gender, and Sexuality at the Movies* (Hoboken, NJ: Wiley Blackwell, 2021), 35.

14. Arthur Knight, *Disintegrating the Musical: Black Performance and American Musical Film* (Durham, NC: Duke University Press, 2002), 13; Jerome Delameter, *Dance in the Hollywood Musical* (Ann Arbor, MI: UMI Research Press, 1981), 98; Bradley Rogers, *The Song Is You: Musical Theatre and the Politics of Bursting into Song and Dance* (Iowa City: University of Iowa Press, 2020), 1–2; Kirsten Pullen, *Like a Natural Woman: Spectacular Female Performance in Classical Hollywood* (New Brunswick, NJ: Rutgers University Press, 2014), 111. Both Rogers's *The Song Is You* and Stacy Ellen Wolf's "'We'll Always Be Bosom Buddies': Female Duets and the Queering of Broadway Musical Theater," *GLQ: A Journal of Lesbian and Gay Studies* 12, no. 3 (2006): 351–376 offer counterarguments to claims that musicals are fundamentally integrated in form.

15. Benshoff and Griffin, *America on Film*, 35; Knight, *Disintegrating the Musical*, 8. There were also three partially integrated studios, Columbia, Universal, and United Artists, which "did not own their own theaters and had fewer assets with which to produce the lush expensive movies for which the Big 5 were famous." Benshoff and Griffin, *America on Film*, 35.

16. Bernardi, *Classic Hollywood, Classic Whiteness*, xv; Jeanine Basinger, *The Star Machine* (New York: Vintage, 2009), 12.

17. Basinger, *The Star Machine*, 14; Benshoff and Griffin, *America on Film*, 35.

18. Adrienne L. McLean, "Introduction: Stardom in the 1930s," in *Glamour in a Golden Age: Movie Stars of the 1930s*, ed. Adrienne McLean (New Brunswick, NJ: Rutgers University Press, 2011), 1–2.

19. Delameter, *Dance in the Hollywood Musical*, 98.

20. Steven Cohan, "Introduction: Musicals of the Studio Era," in *Hollywood Musicals, The Film Reader*, ed. Steven Cohan (New York: Routledge, 2002), 6.

21. Ibid., 7–10; Steven Cohan, *Incongruous Entertainment: Camp, Cultural Value, and the MGM Musical* (Durham, NC: Duke University Press, 2005), 3.

22. Benshoff and Griffin, *America on Film*, 39; Delameter, *Dance in the Hollywood Musical*, 98. See Amanda Louise McQueen, "After 'the Golden Age': An Industrial History of the Hollywood Musical, 1955–1975" (PhD diss., University of Wisconsin, Madison, 2016), for an account that challenges the standard narrative of the musical's decline in the 1950s.

23. Knight, *Disintegrating the Musical*, 16. See also Sean Griffin, "The Gang's All Here: Generic versus Racial Integration in the 1940s Musical," *Cinema Journal* 42, no. 1 (Fall 2002): 21–45; David Savran, *A Queer Sort of Materialism: Recontextualizing American Theater* (Ann Arbor: University of Michigan Press, 2003).

24. Miriam J. Petty, *Stealing the Show: African American Performers and Audiences in 1930s Hollywood* (Oakland: University of California Press, 2016), 13; Benshoff and Griffin, *America on Film*, 37. See Brynn W. Shiovitz, *Behind the Screen: Tap Dance, Race, and Invisibility during Hollywood's Golden Age* (New York: Oxford University Press, 2023) for a nuanced analysis of the Code's effect on racial representations in Hollywood. See also Erigha, *The Hollywood Jim Crow* on how "the basic structure of Jim Crow remains intact in contemporary U.S. society," including in the movie industry (10).

25. Pamela Grenelle Krayenbuhl, "Dancing Race and Masculinity across Midcentury Screens: The Nicholas Brothers, Gene Kelly, and Elvis Presley on American Film and TV" (PhD diss., Northwestern University, 2017), 11; Delameter, *Dance in the Hollywood Musical*, 79. See also Krayenbuhl's forthcoming book with Oxford University Press, *White Screens, Black Dance: Race and Masculinity in the United States at Midcentury*.

NOTES 199

26. Richard Dyer, *White* (New York: Routledge, 1997), 90; Eva Cherniavsky, *Incorporations: Race, Nation, and the Body Politics of Capital* (Minneapolis: University of Minnesota Press, 2006), 87, 99.
27. Bernardi, *Classic Hollywood, Classic Whiteness*, xv.
28. I address my use of the slash between Asian and American in Chapter 5.
29. Thomas A. Guglielmo and Earl Lewis, "Changing Racial Meanings: Race and Ethnicity in the United States, 1930–1964," in *The Columbia Documentary History of Race and Ethnicity in America*, ed. Ronald H. Bayor (New York: Columbia University Press, 2004), 599–666; Mae M. Ngai, *Impossible Subjects: Illegal Aliens and the Making of Modern America* (Princeton, NJ: Princeton University Press, 2014).
30. Mary L. Dudziak, *Cold War Civil Rights: Race and the Image of American Democracy* (Princeton, NJ: Princeton University Press, 2011), 7.
31. Luis Alvarez, *The Power of the Zoot: Youth Culture and Resistance during World War II* (Berkeley: University of California Press, 2008), 16.
32. Thomas Cripps, *Making Movies Black: The Hollywood Message Movie from World War II to the Civil Rights Era* (New York: Oxford University Press, 1993), 28; Griffin, "The Gang's All Here," 27; Mary Beltrán and Camilla Fojas, "Introduction: Mixed Race in Hollywood Film and Media Culture," in *Mixed Race Hollywood*, ed. Mary Beltrán and Camilla Fojas (New York: New York University Press, 2008), 5.
33. See Alvarez, *The Power of the Zoot*, 155–199, for an analysis of the Los Angeles Zoot Suit Riots "as a multiracial and gendered experience" (156).
34. Grace Kyungwon Hong, *The Ruptures of American Capital: Women of Color Feminism and the Culture of Immigrant Labor* (Minneapolis: University of Minnesota Press, 2006), xiv.
35. Cindy I-Fen Cheng, *Citizens of Asian America: Democracy and Race during the Cold War.* (New York: New York University Press, 2013), 2–3.
36. Hong, *The Ruptures of American Capital*, xvii; Lisa Lowe, *Immigrant Acts: On Asian American Cultural Politics* (Durham, NC: Duke University Press, 1996), 7; Cheng, *Citizens of Asian America*, 6, 3.
37. Matthew Frye Jacobson, *Whiteness of a Different Color* (Cambridge, MA: Harvard University Press, 1999), 95, emphasis in original; Priscilla Peña Ovalle, *Dance and the Hollywood Latina: Race, Sex, and Stardom* (New Brunswick, NJ: Rutgers University Press, 2011), 78; Karen Brodkin, *How Jews Became White Folks and What That Says about Race in America* (New Brunswick, NJ: Rutgers University Press, 1998), 138.
38. Brian Eugenio Herrera, *Latin Numbers: Playing Latino in Twentieth-Century US Popular Performance* (Ann Arbor: University of Michigan Press, 2015), 15.
39. Jacobson, *Whiteness of a Different Color*, 95.
40. Herrera, *Latin Numbers*, 20, 60; Luis Reyes and Peter Rubie, *Hispanics in Hollywood: A Celebration of 100 Years in Film and Television* (Hollywood, CA: Lone Eagle, 2000), 18–22. See also Ovalle, *Dance and the Hollywood Latina*.
41. Michael Rogin, *Blackface, White Noise: Jewish Immigrants in the Hollywood Melting Pot* (Berkeley: University of California Press, 1996), 251; Donald Bogle, *Bright Boulevards, Bold Dreams: The Story of Black Hollywood* (New York: One World, 2005), 212; Petty, *Stealing the Show*, 9; Shiovitz, *Behind the Screen*, 345.
42. Christina Klein, *Cold War Orientalism: Asia in the Middlebrow Imagination, 1945–1961* (Berkeley: University of California Press, 2003), 5, 4.
43. Benshoff and Griffin, *America on Film*, 158; Delia Malia Caparoso Konzett, "Introduction," in *Hollywood at the Intersection of Race and Identity*, ed. Delia Konzett (New Brunswick, NJ: Rutgers University Press, 2020), 13.
44. Benshoff and Griffin, *America on Film*, 39. See also Nicholas Sammond and Chandra Mukerji, "'What You Are . . . I Wouldn't Eat': Ethnicity, Whiteness, and Performing 'the Jew' in Hollywood's Golden Age," in Bernardi, *Classic Hollywood, Classic Whiteness*, 3–30; Griffin, "The Gang's All Here."
45. As Cherniavsky, citing David Bordwell and Kristin Thompson, points out, there are actually tensions within classic Hollywood's idealization of white faces and its pursuit of continuity filming, for the special lighting and filters required to produce the "soft style" risked exposing seams in a film's editing (*Incorporations*, 87).
46. As will become evident, the work of Frantz Fanon and Hortense Spillers has been especially influential on my thinking about the impossibility of approaching embodiment outside of

200 NOTES

racialization, though there is arguably no work in the field of Black studies that does not critique universalized approaches to embodiment.

47. See also Ben Spatz, who writes, "One . . . has no business talking about the body, materiality, or artistic research without engaging in some way with critical race theory, including radically interdisciplinary black studies." Ben Spatz, *Race and the Forms of Knowledge: Technique, Identity, and Place in Artistic Research* (Evanston, IL: Northwestern University Press, 2024), 67.

48. Jane Desmond, "Introduction," in *Meaning in Motion: New Cultural Studies of Dance*, ed. Jane Desmond (Durham, NC: Duke University Press, 1997), 2; Ann Cooper Albright, *Choreographing Difference: The Body and Identity in Contemporary Dance* (Middletown, CT: Wesleyan University Press, 2010), 4, emphasis in original.

49. See also Rudi Laermans, who writes that the human body is "the taken-for-granted medium of dance." Rudi Laermans, "'Dance in General' or Choreographing the Public, Making Assemblages," *Performance Research* 13, no. 1 (2008): 7.

50. See, among others, Randy Martin, *Critical Moves: Dance Studies in Theory and Politics* (Durham, NC: Duke University Press, 1998); Mark Franko, *The Work of Dance: Labor, Movement, and Identity in the 1930s* (Middletown, CT: Wesleyan University Press, 2002); Victoria Fortuna, *Moving Otherwise: Dance, Violence, and Memory in Buenos Aires* (New York: Oxford University Press, 2019); Priya Srinivasan, *Sweating Saris: Indian Dance as Transnational Labor* (Philadelphia: Temple University Press, 2011); Anusha Kedhar, *Flexible Bodies: British South Asian Dancers in an Age of Neoliberalism* (New York: Oxford University Press, 2020); José Luis Reynoso, *Dancing Mestizo Modernisms: Choreographing Postcolonial and Postrevolutionary Mexico* (New York: Oxford University Press, 2023).

51. See, for example, Paul Scolieri, "Global/Mobile: Re-orienting Dance and Migration Studies," *Dance Research Journal* 40, no. 2 (2008): v–xx; Cindy Garcia, *Salsa Crossings: Dancing Latinidad in Los Angeles* (Durham, NC: Duke University Press, 2013); Srinivasan, *Sweating Saris*.

52. VéVé Clark, "Performing the Memory of Difference in Afro-Caribbean Dance: Katherine Dunham's Choreography, 1938–87," in *History and Memory in African-American Culture*, ed. Geneviève Fabre and Robert O'Meally (New York: Oxford University Press, 1994), 188–204; Clare Parfitt, ed., *Cultural Memory and Popular Dance: Dancing to Remember, Dancing to Forget* (London: Palgrave Macmillan, 2021).

53. Celeste Fraser Delgado and José Esteban Muñoz, eds., *Everynight Life: Culture and Dance in Latin/o America* (Durham, NC: Duke University Press, 1997); Kemi Adeyemi, Kareem Khubchandani, and Ramón H. Rivera-Servera, eds., *Queer Nightlife* (Ann Arbor: University of Michigan Press, 2021); Kedhar, *Flexible Bodies*.

54. A partial list of scholarship in this vein would include Marta Savigliano, *Tango and the Political Economy of Passion* (New York: Routledge, 1995); Linda J. Tomko, *Dancing Class: Gender, Ethnicity, and Social Divides in American Dance, 1890–1920* (Bloomington: Indiana University Press, 2000); Brenda Dixon Gottschild, *Digging the Africanist Presence in American Performance: Dance and Other Contexts* (Westport, CT: Greenwood Press, 1996); Susan Manning, *Modern Dance, Negro Dance: Race in Motion* (Minneapolis: University of Minnesota Press, 2004); Thomas F. DeFrantz, *Dancing Revelations: Alvin Ailey's Embodiment of African American Culture* (New York: Oxford University Press, 2004); Jacqueline Shea Murphy, *The People Have Never Stopped Dancing: Native American Modern Dance Histories* (Minneapolis: University of Minnesota Press, 2007); Yutian Wong, *Choreographing Asian America* (Middletown, CT: Wesleyan University Press, 2011); Jens Richard Giersdorf, *The Body of the People: East German Dance since 1945* (Madison: University of Wisconsin Press, 2013); Rachmi Diyah Larasati, *The Dance That Makes You Vanish: Cultural Reconstruction in Post-genocide Indonesia* (Minneapolis: University of Minnesota Press, 2013); Anthony Shay and Barbara Sellers-Young, eds., *The Oxford Handbook of Dance and Ethnicity* (New York: Oxford University Press, 2016); Anurima Banerji, *Dancing Odissi: Paratopic Performances of Gender and State* (Chicago: University of Chicago Press, 2019); Ahalya Satkunaratnam, *Moving Bodies, Navigating Conflict: Practicing Bharata Natyam in Colombo, Sri Lanka* (Middletown, CT: Wesleyan University Press, 2020); Reynoso, *Dancing Mestizo Modernisms*.

55. See Hayden White, *The Content of the Form: Narrative Discourse and Historical Representation* (Baltimore: Johns Hopkins University Press, 1990); Michel Foucault, *Discipline and Punish: The Birth of the Prison* (New York: Pantheon Books, 1977); Judith Butler, *Gender Trouble: Feminism and the Subversion of Identity* (New York: Routledge, 1990); Judith Butler, *Bodies That Matter: On the Discursive Limits of "Sex"* (New York: Routledge, 1993).

NOTES   201

56. Susan Leigh Foster, "Choreographing History," in *Choreographing History*, ed. Susan Leigh Foster (Bloomington: Indiana University Press, 1995), 15; Martin, *Critical Moves*, 156; Naomi Bragin, "Techniques of Back Male Re/dress: Corporeal Drag and Kinesthetic Politics in the Rebirth of Waacking/Punkin,'" *Women & Performance: A Journal of Feminist Theory* 24, no. 1 (2014): 74. See Carrie Noland, *Agency and Embodiment: Performing Gestures/Producing Culture* (Cambridge, MA: Harvard University Press, 2009) for a "theory of agency fully implicated in embodiment" (3).

57. UMass Fine Arts Center, "Bodies at Risk: Emily Johnson and Alice Sheppard," YouTube, March 18, 2021, https://www.youtube.com/watch?v=iYXKvzZGzKU.

58. There are also echoes between Sheppard's critique and queer feminist disability scholar Alison Kafer's challenge to individual and medical models that cast disability "as a problematic characteristic" that resides "in particular bodies and minds." Alison Kafer, *Feminist, Queer, Crip* (Bloomington: Indiana University Press, 2013), 5. My thanks to Clare Croft for bringing this work to my attention.

59. Robin D. G. Kelley, "Black Study, Black Struggle," *Boston Review*, March 1, 2016, http://bostonreview.net/forum/robin-d-g-kelley-black-study-black-struggle.

60. Anaïs Duplan, "A Body That Is Ultra-Body: In Conversation with Fred Moten and Elysia Crampton," *Ploughshares*, July 13, 2016, https://blog.pshares.org/a-body-that-is-ultra-body-in-conversation-with-fred-moten-and-elysia-crampton/. My thanks to Naomi Bragin for originally calling my attention to this interview. In a related vein, Tiffany Lethabo King has called for critical approaches that "impede the normative movement and momentum of the practice of gazing upon, reading, and theorizing 'black bodies.'" Tiffany Lethabo King, "Off Littorality (Shoal 1.0): Black Study off the Shores of 'the Black Body,'" *Propter Nos* 3, no. 1 (2019): 40.

61. In a 2021 online conversation with choreographers nia long and Lela Aisha Jones, Moten repeated that "it's impossible for [him] to talk about the body," but added, "I also know that . . . it should be impossible for y'all . . . as dancers not to." Arts at Bryn Mawr College, "The Porch: A Studio Dialogue with nia love and Fred Moten," March 25, 2021, https://brynmawr.hosted.panopto.com/Panopto/Pages/Viewer.aspx?id=44e4721a-7b03-4f68-83f1-acf2011600ac.

62. André Lepecki, "Introduction: Presence and Body in Dance and Performance Theory," in *Of the Presence of the Body: Essays on Dance and Performance Theory*, ed. André Lepecki (Middletown, CT: Wesleyan University Press, 2004), 7.

63. The reference to "bodily reality" as "not [a] natural or absolute given but . . . a tangible and substantial category of cultural experience" in the 1996 edited volume *Corporealities* encapsulates dance studies' emphasis on the co-constitution of materiality and discourse in the making of bodies. Susan Leigh Foster, "Introduction," in *Corporealities: Dancing Knowledge, Culture and Power*, ed. Susan Leigh Foster (New York: Routledge, 1996), xi. Pressing further on corporeality's literal implications, Melissa Blanco Borelli uses the term "corpo-realize" to denote the body as "a real, living, meaning making entity." Melissa Blanco Borelli, *She Is Cuba: A Genealogy of the Mulata Body* (New York: Oxford University Press, 2015), 30. Rainy Demerson likewise uses the term "corpo-realize" to indicate how one "learns through the body." Rainy Demerson, "Sensing the Stage: Decolonial Readings of African Contemporary Dance," in *African Somaesthetics: Cultures, Feminisms, Politics*, ed. Catherine F. Botha (Leiden: Brill, 2020), 102.

64. While there is an abundance of insightful scholarship on embodiment from scholars outside of dance and performance studies, including scholarship that I draw on in this book, I can't help but notice how many of those insights are derived from analyses of literary texts. Insofar as this book hopes to show the value of grounding our theories of bodies in specific practices in historically specific contexts, I follow the lead of Susan Leigh Foster, whose book *Choreographing Empathy* traces "shifts in the construction of corporeality" in Europe, Britain, and the United States from its earlier incarnation "as a composite of substances" to its coalescence over the course of the sixteenth and seventeenth centuries "as a stilled and singular entity capable of looking out onto the world," to its emergence in the late nineteenth and early twentieth century as a "muscularly dynamic body" capable of expressivity, to a twenty-first-century "cyborgian synthesis of digital and physical matter." Susan Leigh Foster, *Choreographing Empathy: Kinesthesia in Performance* (New York: Routledge, 2010), 175, 125, 178. Rather than chart change over time, *Hollywood Dance-ins* explores one industry's corporeal infrastructure during a particular period in U.S. culture.

65. See, for example, Susan Manning, *Ecstasy and the Demon: The Dances of Mary Wigman* (Berkeley: University of California Press, 1993); Foster, *Choreographing History*; Foster et al.,

202 NOTES

Corporealities; Susan Leigh Foster, "Choreographies of Gender," *Signs: Journal of Women in Culture and Society* 24, no. 1 (1998): 1–33.

66. See, for example, Clare Croft, *Dancers as Diplomats: American Choreography in Cultural Exchange* (New York: Oxford University Press, 2015); Kedhar, *Flexible Bodies.*

67. Anne Anlin Cheng, *Ornamentalism* (New York: Oxford University Press, 2019), 4.

68. Rizvana Bradley, *Anteaesthetics: Black Aesthesis and the Critique of Form* (Stanford: Stanford University Press, 2023), 158.

69. Frantz Fanon, "The Fact of Blackness," in *Black Skin, White Masks,* by Frantz Fanon (New York: Grove Press, 1967), 111.

70. Demerson, "Sensing the Stage," 103.

71. See, for example, Demerson, "Sensing the Stage"; Blanco Borelli, *She Is Cuba;* Tara Aisha Willis, "Stumbling into Place: Seeing Blackness in David Thomson's Choreographies of Ambiguity," *Black Scholar* 46, no. 1 (2016): 4–14. See also Harvey Young, *Embodying Black Experience: Stillness, Critical Memory, and the Black Body* (Ann Arbor: University of Michigan Press, 2010), which explores how "an *idea* of the black body has been and continues to be projected across actually physical bodies" (4, emphasis in original). Young draws on both Fanon and Spillers in demonstrating how racialization produces the "slippage of abstraction into materiality" for Black people living "an objectified existence within the Western world" (7, 4). See also Paul Gilroy, "Exer(or)cising Power: Black Bodies in the Black Public Sphere," in *Dance in the City,* ed. Helen Thomas (London: Palgrave Macmillan, 1997), 21–34.

72. Noland, *Agency and Embodiment,* 201. As Sara Ahmed writes of Fanon's "corporeal schema," "[R]ace does not just interrupt such a schema but structures its mode of operation." Sara Ahmed, *Queer Phenomenology: Orientations, Objects, Others* (Durham, NC: Duke University Press, 2006), 111.

73. Hortense Spillers, "Mama's Baby, Papa's Maybe: An American Grammar Book," *Diacritics* 17, no. 2 (Summer 1987): 67.

74. Ibid., 74, emphasis in original.

75. Ibid., 67.

76. Alexander Ghedi Weheliye, *Habeas Viscus: Racializing Assemblages, Biopolitics, and Black Feminist Theories of the Human* (Durham, NC: Duke University Press, 2014), 39.

77. Jackson, *Becoming Human,* 193.

78. Bradley, *Anteaesthetics,* 86.

79. Weheliye, *Habeas Viscus,* 39; Hershini Bhana Young, *Illegible Will: Coercive Spectacles of Labor in South Africa and the Diaspora* (Durham, NC: Duke University Press, 2017), 9; Spillers, "Mama's Baby, Papa's Maybe," 67. For Denise Ferrera Da Silva, Spillers's flesh constitutes an "ethical device" that invites "speculative" thought, including "the possibility of traversing spatiotemporal boundaries." Denise Ferreira Da Silva, *Unpayable Debt* (London: Sternberg Press, 2022), 35n20, 46.

80. Ashon T. Crawley, *Blackpentecostal Breath: The Aesthetics of Possibility* (New York: Fordham University Press, 2016), 59.

81. Bradley, *Anteaesthetics,* 82, 88.

82. Weheliye, *Habeas Viscus,* 39; Spillers, "Mama's Baby, Papa's Maybe," 74.

83. Spillers, "Mama's Baby, Papa's Maybe," 79, 74, 80.

84. See Barry Brannum's dissertation for a useful review of Black studies approaches to performance that build on Spillers. Barry Brannum, "As the Flesh Moves: Lon Fontaine, Black Dance, and Strategies for Rendering Presence" (PhD diss., University of California, Los Angeles, 2021).

85. Other exceptions include Tayana L. Hardin's "Katherine Dunham's Southland and the Archival Quality of Black Dance," *Black Scholar* 46, no. 1 (2016): 46–53, which draws on both Fanon and Spillers; Jade Power-Sotomayor's "Corporeal Sounding: Listening to Bomba Dance, Listening to puertorriqueñxs," *Performance Matters* 6, no. 2 (2020): 43–59; and Ariel Osterweis's *Body Impossible: Desmond Richardson and the Politics of Virtuosity* (New York: Oxford University Press, 2024), the latter two of which draw on Spillers's theorization of flesh.

86. Jasmine Elizabeth Johnson, "Flesh Dance: Black Women from Behind," in *Futures of Dance Studies,* ed. Susan Manning, Janice Ross, and Rebecca Schneider (Madison: University of Wisconsin Press, 2020), 154–155, 167.

87. Mlondolozi Zondi, "Haunting Gathering: Black Dance and Afro-Pessimism," *ASAP/Journal* 5, no. 2 (May 2020): 258.

88. Brannum, *As the Flesh Moves,* 3, 5, 32.

89. Ibid, 32.

NOTES   203

90. On the concept of slavery's afterlife, see Saidiya Hartman, *Scenes of Subjection: Terror, Slavery, and Self-Making in Nineteenth-Century America* (New York: Oxford University Press, 1997). On the multiple registers of the concept of the wake, see Christina Sharpe, *In the Wake: On Blackness and Being* (Durham, NC: Duke University Press, 2016).

91. Bradley, *Anteaesthetics*, 83.

92. I am thinking especially of Weheliye, *Habeas Viscus*; Crawley, *Blackpentecostal Breath;* Amber Jamilla Musser, *Sensational Flesh: Race, Power, and Masochism* (New York: New York University Press, 2014); Amber Jamilla Musser, *Sensual Excess* (New York: New York University Press, 2018); Kevin Quashie, *Black Aliveness, or a Poetics of Being* (Durham, NC: Duke University Press, 2021).

93. Jennifer C. Nash, "Citational Desires: On Black Feminism's Institutional Longings," *Diacritics* 48, no. 3 (2020): 78.

94. My gratitude to my past and present colleagues in UC Riverside's Department of Dance for the engaging and helpful conversations about how to teach and cite Black critical theory without inviting extraction or practicing a superficial citational politics.

95. My thanks to Stephanie Batiste for her thoughtful engagement with me about the stakes of Spillers in relation to this project.

96. Nash, "Citational Desires," 77.

97. In this regard, my book aligns with Arabella Stanger's *Dancing on Violent Ground: Utopia as Dispossession in Euro-American Theater Dance* (Evanston, IL: Northwestern University Press, 2021), which argues that "it remains acutely important that attention be paid to the histories of subjection, imperial and colonial domination, and white supremacist violence that materially subtend . . . idealisms" in the field of dance (15).

98. Soyica Diggs Colbert, *Theory for Theatre Studies: Bodies* (London: Bloomsbury, 2021), 123. Colbert cites Jane Bennett, *Vibrant Matter: A Political Ecology of Things* (Durham, NC: Duke University Press, 2010); Gayle Salamon, *Assuming a Body: Transgender and Rhetorics of Materiality* (New York: Columbia University Press, 2010); Kim Q. Hall, ed., *Feminist Disability Studies* (Bloomington: Indiana University Press, 2011). Rizvana Bradley insightfully attributes the "bodily turn" in academia to "the minority insurgencies . . . of the last third of the twentieth century" and the resultant "reorganizations of knowledge and power within and beyond the university" (*Anteaesthetics*, 77).

99. Lisa Blackman, *The Body: The Key Concepts*, 2nd edition (Abingdon: Routledge, 2021), 27.

100. Takeshita, "From Mother/Fetus to Holobiont(s)," 4.

101. Margrit Shildrick, *Visceral Prostheses: Somatechnics and Posthuman Embodiment* (London: Bloomsbury, 2022), 11. In a slightly different vein, Gayle Salamon's *Assuming a Body,* which reads theories of transgender embodiment alongside various philosophical accounts, problematizes the presumed contours of the body by foregrounding the discontinuities between one's "felt sense" of the body and its materiality.

102. Rachel C. Lee, *The Exquisite Corpse of Asian America: Biopolitics, Biosociality, and Posthuman Ecologies* (New York: New York University Press, 2014), 30–31.

103. Gilles Deleuze and Félix Guattari, *A Thousand Plateaus: Capitalism and Schizophrenia*, trans. Brian Massumi (Minneapolis: University of Minnesota Press, 1987), 158, 161.

104. Ibid., 160.

105. Elizabeth Grosz, *Volatile Bodies: Toward a Corporeal Feminism* (Bloomington: Indiana Unviersity Press, 1994), 165, 181; Mel Y. Chen, *Animacies: Biopolitics, Racial Mattering, and Queer Affect* (Durham, NC: Duke University Press, 2012), 151; Jasbir K. Puar, *The Right to Maim: Debility, Capacity, Disability* (Durham, NC: Duke University Press, 2017), 184n74. Chen sees agreement between the BwO and neurobiological views "that the systems of the body are in fact interdependent and in constant communicative flux" (*Animacies*, 251n52). Puar cautions against the "romanticized sentimentality" that often attends scholars' approach to the BwO, as well as the tendency to treat it as a metaphor, "whereas Deleuze and Guattari insist on the radical materiality of the BwO" (*The Right to Maim,* 184–185n74). See also Weheliye, *Habeas Viscus*, 49–50, on how Deleuze and Guattari's "privileging of racial hybridity" limits the value of their model for sociopolitical approaches to race.

106. Martin, *Critical Moves*, 110, 210.

107. Halifu Osumare, "Global Breakdancing and the Intercultural Body," *Dance Research Journal* 34, no. 2 (2002): 30–45; Erin Manning, *Politics of Touch: Sense, Movement, Sovereignty* (Minneapolis: University of Minnesota Press, 2007); Srinivasan, *Sweating Saris*; Ben Spatz, *Blue Sky Body: Thresholds for Embodied Research* (New York: Routledge, 2019); Selby Wynn

204 NOTES

Schwartz, *The Bodies of Others: Drag Dances and Their Afterlives* (Ann Arbor: University of Michigan Press, 2019); Rosemarie A. Roberts, *Baring Unbearable Sensualities: Hip Hop Dance, Bodies, Race, and Power* (Middletown, CT: Wesleyan University Press, 2021). See also Jo Hall's notion of "heterocorporealities" in *Boys, Bass and Bother: Popular Dance and Identity in UK Drum 'n' Bass Club Culture* (London: Palgrave Macmillan, 2018).

108. Anurima Banerji, "Dance and the Distributed Body: Odissi, Ritual Practice, and Mahari Performance," *About Performance*, no. 11 (2012): 7–39; Kate Elswit, "Dancing with Coronaspheres: Expanded Breath Bodies and the Politics of Public Movement in the Age of COVID-19," *Cultural Studies* 37, no. 6 (2023): 894–916; Elisabeth Motley, "Crip Aesthetics and a Choreographic Method of Leakiness," *Dance Chronicle* 47, no. 1 (2024): 60.

109. María Regina Firmino-Castillo, "What Ma Lach's Bones Tell Us: Performances of Relational Materiality in Response to Genocide," *Transmotion* 4, no. 2 (2018): 33, 57. There is a growing body of scholarship that engages with human and nonhuman, or human and more-than-human relationships in dance, including from Indigenous perspectives. See Tria Blu Wakpa, "What Native American Dance Does and the Stakes of Ecosomatics," in *Geographies of Us: Ecosomatic Essays and Practice Pages*, ed. Sondra Fraleigh and Shannon Rose Riley (New York: Taylor & Francis, 2024), 36–63; Jacqueline Shea Murphy, *Dancing Indigenous Worlds: Choreographies of Relation* (Minneapolis: University of Minnesota Press, 2023). For scholarship on posthumanist perspectives, see Anna Hilary Bergen, "Dancing Media: The Contagious Movement of Posthuman Bodies (or Towards a Posthuman Theory of Dance" (PhD diss., Concordia University, 2022). On new materialist perspectives, see Vicki Hunter, "Dancing-Walking with Trees," in *Walking Bodies: Papers, Provocations, Actions*, ed. Helen Billinghurst, Claire Hind, and Phil Smith (Dorset: Triarchy Press, 2020), 21–33. For human-animal studies perspectives, see Gabriele Brandstetter, "Human, Animal, Thing," in *Moving (across) Borders: Performing Translation, Intervention, Participation*, ed. Gabrielle Brandstetter and Holger Hartung (Bielefeld: transcript Verlag, 2017), 23–42. For disability theory and queer theory perspectives, see Petra Kuppers, *Eco Soma: Pain and Joy in Speculative Performance Encounters* (Minneapolis: University of Minnesota Press, 2022).

110. José Gil, "Paradoxical Body," trans. André Lepecki, *TDR: The Drama Review* 50 (2006): 28. Erin Manning, *Always More Than One: Individuation's Dance* (Durham, NC: Duke University Press, 2013), 31.

111. Manning, *Always More Than One*, 19; Bradley, *Anteaesthetics*, 83.

112. Firmino-Castillo's "What Ma Lach's Bones Tell Us" is an important example of scholarship that attends to the genocidal effects of clashing views of embodiment. See also Royona Mitra, "Unmaking Contact: Choreographic Touch at the Intersections of Race, Caste, and Gender," *Dance Research Journal* 53, no. 3 (2021): 6–24, for an interrogation and critique of the construction of the body as bounded and "closed" from a non-U.S.-centric perspective.

113. Doran George, *The Natural Body in Somatics Dance Training* (New York: Oxford University Press, 2020).

114. Douglas Rosenberg, *Screendance: Inscribing the Ephemeral Image* (New York: Oxford University Press, 2012), 3, emphasis in original.

115. Douglas Rosenberg, "Introduction," in *The Oxford Handbook of Screendance Studies*, ed. Douglas Rosenberg (New York: Oxford University Press, 2016), 5. That split is reflected in the two Oxford *Handbooks* devoted to dance on screen: Rosenberg's *Oxford Handbook of Screendance Studies*, which tends mostly (though by no means exclusively) to avant-garde examples of screendance, and Melissa Blanco Borelli's *The Oxford Handbook of Dance and the Popular Screen* (New York: Oxford University Press, 2014), which is devoted to mainstream examples of screendance.

116. Sherril Dodds, *Dance on Screen: Genres and Media from Hollywood to Experimental Art* (New York: Palgrave, 2001), 29, 170–171, 174. Echoes of this axiom can be found, for example, in Erin Brannigan's 2010 book *Dancefilm*, in which she maintains that the on-screen performing body "is a body created through the cinematic machinations of light, dust, and duration." Erin Brannigan, *Dancefilm: Choreography and the Moving Image* (New York: Oxford University Press, 2010), 11. A similar refrain can be found in Todd Decker's recent study of dancer Fred Astaire, in which he seeks "to understand as concretely as possible the relationship of Astaire's real dancing body and the studio Hollywood moviemaking machine that captured and repackaged it." Todd R. Decker, *Astaire by Numbers: Time and the Straight White Male Dancer* (New York: Oxford University Press, 2022), 5. By contrast, Priscilla Guy and Alanna Thain's more recent volume *LO: TECH: POP: CULT* asserts that "the question of screendance's

NOTES 205

relation . . . to live performance . . . remains an underexplored field." Priscilla Guy and Alanna Thain, "Introduction," in *LO: TECH: POP: CULT: Screendance Remixed*, by Priscilla Guy and Alanna Thain (London: Routledge, 2024), 4.

117. Rosenberg, *Screendance*, 55.

118. Addie Tsai, "Hybrid Texts, Assembled Bodies: Michel Gondry's Merging of Camera and Dancer in 'Let Forever Be,'" *International Journal of Screendance* 6 (2016), https://doi.org/10.18061/ijsd.v6i0.4892.

119. Bradley, *Anteaesthetics*, 86.

120. See, among others, Stephen Heath, "Dossier Suture: Notes on Suture," *Screen* 18, no. 4 (1977): 48–76; Kaja Silverman, *The Acoustic Mirror: The Female Voice in Psychoanalysis and Cinema* (Bloomington: Indiana University Press, 1988), 10–13.

121. In this regard, I share Selby Schwartz's call to move beyond an assumption that the digitally mediated and the live are necessarily opposed. See Selby Wynn Schwartz, "Light, Shadow, Screendance: Catherine Gallaso's *Bring on the Lumière!*," in Rosenberg, *The Oxford Handbook of Screendance Studies*, 205–224.

122. The concept of indexicality in film is generally traced to the film theorist André Bazin and the semioticians Roland Barthes and Charles Peirce. Helpful overviews of the concept of indexicality can be found in Kara Keeling, "Passing for Human: Bamboozled and Digital Humanism," *Women & Performance: A Journal of Feminist Theory* 15, no. 1 (2005): 237–250; Laura Mulvey, "The Index and the Uncanny: Life and Death in the Photograph," in *Death 24x a Second: Stillness and the Moving Image* (London: Reaktion Books, 2006), 54–66; Mary Ann Doane, "Indexicality: Trace and Sign: Introduction," *differences* 18, no. 1 (2007): 1–6; Mary Ann Doane, "The Indexical and the Concept of Medium Specificity," *differences* 18, no. 1 (2007): 128–152; Margaret Iversen, "Indexicality: A Trauma of Signification," in *Photography, Trace, and Trauma*, by Margaret Iversen (Chicago: University of Chicago Press, 2017), 17–32. In her book *Dancing Machines*, Felicia McCarren draws on indexical theory to assert, "Cinematic images of dance qualify . . . as indices—indexical images linked to their subject through physical proximity." Felicia M. McCarren, *Dancing Machines: Choreographies of the Age of Mechanical Reproduction* (Stanford: Stanford University Press, 2003), 26.

123. Doane, "The Indexical and the Concept of Medium Specificity," 136.

124. Ibid. See also Tsai, "Hybrid Texts, Assembled Bodies"; Joanna Bouldin, "The Body, Animation and the Real: Race, Reality and the Rotoscope in Betty Boop," in *Proceedings of Affective Encounters: Rethinking Embodiment in Feminist Media Studies*, ed. Anu Koivunen and Susanna Paasen (Turku: University of Turku, School of Art, Literature and Music, Media Studies, 2001), 48–54, https://susannapaasonen.files.wordpress.com/2014/11/proceedings.pdf.

125. See, for example, Linda Williams, "Film Bodies: Gender, Genre, and Excess," *Film Quarterly* 44, no. 4 (1991): 2–13; Steven Shaviro, *The Cinematic Body* (Minneapolis: University of Minnesota Press, 1994); Laura U. Marks, *The Skin of the Film: Intercultural Cinema, Embodiment, and the Senses* (Durham, NC: Duke University Press, 2000); Vivian Sobchack, *Carnal Thoughts: Embodiment and Moving Image Culture* (Berkeley: University of California Press, 2004); Niall Richardson, *Transgressive Bodies: Representations in Film and Popular Culture* (New York: Routledge, 2016); Kartik Nair, "Unfinished Bodies: The Sticky Materiality of Prosthetic Effects," *JCMS: Journal of Cinema and Media Studies* 60, no. 3 (2021): 104–128.

126. Adrienne L. McLean, *Being Rita Hayworth: Labor, Identity, and Hollywood Stardom* (New Brunswick, NJ: Rutgers University Press, 2004); Jennifer M. Bean, "Technologies of Early Stardom and the Extraordinary Body," *Camera Obscura* 16, no. 3 (2001): 8–57; Ann Chisholm, "Missing Persons and Bodies of Evidence," *Camera Obscura* 15, no. 1 (2000): 123–161; Cherniavsky, *Incorporations*; Shiovitz, *Behind the Screen*; Krayenbuhl, "Dancing Race and Masculinity"; Usha Iyer, *Dancing Women: Choreographing Corporeal Histories of Hindi Cinema* (New York: Oxford University Press, 2020). See also Sima Belmar, "Behind the Screens: Race, Space, and Place in *Saturday Night Fever*," in Rosenberg, *The Oxford Handbook of Screendance Studies*, 461–479.

127. Iyer, *Dancing Women*, 7.

128. Jane Gaines, *Fire and Desire: Mixed-Race Movies in the Silent Era* (Chicago: University of Chicago Press, 2001), 195–196. See also McCarren, *Dancing Machines*, for a thorough analysis of how dancers have been analogized to "finely tuned machines" (2).

129. On dance's ephemerality, see especially Marcia B. Siegel, *At the Vanishing Point: A Critic Looks at Dance* (New York: Saturday Review Press, 1972); José Esteban Muñoz, "Gesture, Ephemera, and Queer Feeling," in *Dancing Desires: Choreographing Sexualities on and off the Stage*, ed.

206   NOTES

Jane Desmond (Madison: University of Wisconsin Press, 2001), 423–442; Anthea Kraut, *Choreographing Copyright: Race, Gender, and Intellectual Property Rights in American Dance* (New York: Oxford University Press, 2016); Susan Leigh Foster, *Valuing Dance: Commodities and Gifts in Motion* (New York: Oxford University Press, 2019); Harmony Bench, *Perpetual Motion: Dance, Digital Cultures, and the Common* (Minneapolis: University of Minnesota Press, 2020); Rebecca Chaleff, "Economies of Reperformance: Unearthing Racial Capitalism in Dancing at Dusk," *TDR: The Drama Review* 67, no. 1 (2023): 167–185.

130. Mark Franko, ed., *The Oxford Handbook of Dance and Reenactment* (New York: Oxford University Press, 2017). Notably, however, as Anna Pakes observes in that volume, "contemporary theory and practice resist ... the idea that reenactment is a mimetic reproduction of an earlier dance." Anna Pakes, "Reenactment, Dance Identity, and Historical Fictions," in Franko, *Oxford Handbook of Dance and Reenactment*, 91.

131. See, for example, Savigliano, *Tango and the Political Economy of Passion*; Desmond, "Introduction"; Gottschild, *Digging the Africanist Presence*; Shea Murphy, *The People Have Never Stopped Dancing*; Srinivasan, *Sweating Saris*; Reynoso, *Dancing Mestizo Modernisms*; Anusha Kedhar, "It's Time for a Caste Reckoning in Indian 'Classical' Dance," in *Conversations across the Field of Dance Studies: Decolonizing Dance Discourses*, ed. Anurima Banerji and Royona Mitra (Dance Studies Association, 2020), 40: 16–19.

132. Imani Kai Johnson, "Black Culture without Black People: Hip Hop Dance beyond Appropriation Discourse," in *Are You Entertained? Black Popular Culture in the Twenty-First Century*, ed. Simone C. Drake and Dwan K. Henderson (Durham, NC: Duke University Press, 2020), 192.

133. Kraut, *Choreographing Copyright*, 133n22.

134. Randy Martin, for example, writes about the "mimetic economy" in a university modern dance technique course (*Critical Moves*, 162), and Tomie Hahn describes how teachers of the traditional Japanese dance form *nihon buyo* "serve as models for students to follow and emulate." Tomie Hahn, *Sensational Knowledge: Embodying Culture through Japanese Dance* (Middletown, CT: Wesleyan University Press, 2007), 86.

135. Jasmine Elizabeth Johnson, "Casualties," *TDR/The Drama Review* 62, no. 1 (2018): 169.

136. Susan Leigh Foster, "Dancing Bodies," in Desmond, *Meaning in Motion*, 236. See also Royona Mitra, who writes of her training in classical *kathak* dance, "I only knew how to move by moving as much as possible like my gurus, but simultaneously always sensing an unattainable gap between them and myself." Anurima Banerji, Anusha Kedhar, Royona Mitra, Janet O'Shea, and Shanti Pillai, "Postcolonial Pedagogies: Recasting the Guru–Shishya Parampara," *Theatre Topics* 27, no. 3 (November 2017): 223.

137. See Priya Srinivasan's account of second-generation Indian American girls resisting the authority of their guru in a rehearsal setting (*Sweating Saris*, 126–130).

138. Martin, *Critical Moves*, 164–165. See also Anna Beatrice Scott, "Spectacle and Dancing Bodies That Matter: Or, If It Don't Fit, Don't Force It," in Desmond, *Meaning in Motion*, 259–269.

139. Soyica Diggs Colbert, Douglas A. Jones Jr., and Shane Vogel, "Tidying Up after Repetition," in *Race and Performance after Repetition*, ed. Soyica Diggs Colbert, Douglas A. Jones Jr., and Shane Vogel (Durham, NC: Duke University Press, 2020), 6–7.

140. Richard Schechner, *Between Theater and Anthropology* (Philadelphia: University of Pennsylvania Press, 1985), 36.

141. Diggs, Jones, and Vogel, "Tidying Up after Repetition," 7. Notably, Diggs, Jones, and Vogel's volume seeks to decenter the trope of repetition in discussions of performance's relationship to time.

142. As Phelan (in)famously wrote in 1993, "To the degree that performance attempts to enter the economy of reproduction it betrays and lessens the promise of its own ontology." Peggy Phelan, *Unmarked: The Politics of Performance* (New York: Routledge, 1993), 146.

143. Joshua Chambers-Letson, "Performance's Mode of Reproduction I: Searching for Danh Võ's Mother," *Women & Performance: A Journal of Feminist Theory* 26, nos. 2–3 (2016): 126. Chambers-Letson points to performance theorists José Muñoz, Alex Vazquez, Joseph Roach, Diana Taylor, Dwight Conquergood, and Rebecca Schneider as arguing for performance's intrinsic reproductivity.

144. Fred Moten, *In the Break: The Aesthetics of the Black Radical Tradition* (Minneapolis: University of Minnesota Press, 2003), 5, emphasis in original.

145. Joseph Roach, *Cities of the Dead: Circum-Atlantic Performance* (New York: Columbia University Press, 1996), 2.

NOTES   207

146. Diana Taylor, *The Archive and the Repertoire: Performing Cultural Memory in the Americas* (Durham, NC: Duke University Press, 2003), 46.

147. Chambers-Letson, "Performance's Mode of Reproduction I," 126–127.

148. Alys Eve Weinbaum, *Wayward Reproductions: Genealogies of Race and Nation in Transatlantic Modern Thought* (Durham, NC: Duke University Press, 2004), 5, 6.

149. Alys Eve Weinbaum, *The Afterlife of Reproductive Slavery: Biocapitalism and Black Feminism's Philosophy of History* (Durham, NC: Duke University Press, 2019), 8. Weinbaum's argument draws on Toni Morrison's piercing insight that in the United States, the Black slave population was made to serve as "surrogate selves" for white Americans' "meditations on problems of human freedom." Toni Morrison, *Playing in the Dark: Whiteness and the Literary Imagination* (Cambridge, MA: Harvard University Press, 1992), 37.

150. Weinbaum, *The Afterlife of Reproductive Slavery*, 13, emphasis in original.

151. Saidiya Hartman, "The Belly of the World: A Note on Black Women's Labors," *Souls* 18, no. 1 (2016): 167; Sara Clarke Kaplan, *The Black Reproductive: Unfree Labor and Insurgent Motherhood* (Minneapolis: University of Minnesota Press, 2021), 3, 13. See also Jennifer L. Morgan, *Laboring Women: Reproduction and Gender in New World Slavery* (Philadelphia: University of Pennsylvania Press, 2004).

152. Kaplan, *The Black Reproductive*, 15, 16.

153. Hartman, "The Belly of the World," 166.

154. Anthony Slide, *Hollywood Unknowns: A History of Extras, Bit Players, and Stand-ins* (Jackson: University Press of Mississippi, 2012), 8.

155. See Billman, *Film Choreographers and Dance Directors*, 588. AD reports tended to refer to dance-ins as "standins," although they occasionally used the term "understudy." See various reports in the Arthur Freed Papers at the University of Southern California Cinematic Arts Library (hereafter USC).

156. As summarized by the Japanese/American artist and activist Nobuko Miyamoto, who danced in *West Side Story* (1961) as one of the Puerto Rican Sharks' girlfriends under the name Joanne Miya, "The movie business has a caste system, and you become very aware of your station within it. If you are a dancer, you are at the bottom." Nobuko Miyamoto, *Not Yo' Butterfly: My Long Song of Relocation, Race, Love, and Revolution* (Los Angeles: University of California Press, 2021), 74. My thanks to Deborah Wong for bringing Miyamoto's book to my attention.

157. Decker, *Astaire by Numbers*, 14.

158. Email from NBCUniversal, January 10, 2024.

159. John Franceschina, *Hermes Pan: The Man Who Danced with Fred Astaire* (New York: Oxford University Press, 2012).

160. Published oral histories like Donald Knox's *The Magic Factory: How MGM Made An American in Paris* (Westport, CT: Praeger, 1973); Rose Eichenbaum's *Masters of Movement: Portraits of America's Great Choreographers* (Washington, DC: Smithsonian Books, 2007); and Rose Eichenbaum's *The Dancer Within: Intimate Conversations with Great Dancers* (Middletown, CT: Wesleyan University Press, 2013) proved especially useful, as did Earl J. Hess and Pratibha A. Dabholkar's *Singin' in the Rain: The Making of an American Masterpiece* (Lawrence: University Press of Kansas, 2009).

161. My understanding is that Billman was at work on an encyclopedia of dancers in Hollywood at the time of his death, making his loss especially profound.

162. The blog *arts meme* is available at https://artsmeme.com/.

163. See the IMDb listing at https://www.imdb.com/title/tt0039116/fullcredits. Haney's name does not appear on a single page of the AD report for *Ziegfeld Follies*, housed in the Freed Papers at USC.

164. In fact, it is Marie Groscup, not Coyne, who appears alongside Vera-Ellen and Carol Haney in this number. Groscup is misidentified as Coyne in a number of sources, including in Billman, *Film Choreographers and Dance Directors*, 471; Mark Knowles, *The Man Who Made the Jailhouse Rock: Alex Romero, Hollywood Choreographer* (Jefferson, NC: McFarland, 2013), 62; Beth Genné, *Dance Me a Song: Astaire, Balanchine, Kelly, and the American Film Musical* (New York: Oxford University Press, 2018), 211.

165. Marie Bryant is misidentified as "Julie Bryant" in Hal Erickson, *From Radio to the Big Screen: Hollywood Films Featuring Broadcast Personalities and Programs* (Jefferson, NC: McFarland, 2014), 160. See Chapter 2 for a discussion of the misspelling of Bryant's name as Bruant in the AD reports for *On the Town*.

208 NOTES

166. *Newsweek*, "Finklea & Austerlitz, Alias Charisse & Astaire," July 6, 1953, 50; Assistant Director's Reports, *Ziegfeld Follies*, Arthur Freed Papers, USC.

167. It's possible that Becky Varno spelled her name multiple ways. She appears as "Vorno" in Edwin Howard, "Tough Trying to See 'Lady,'" *Memphis Press-Scimitar*, November 9, 1963, 5 and Peter J. Levinson, *Puttin' on the Ritz: Fred Astaire and the Fine Art of Panache, a Biography* (New York: St. Martin's Press, 2015), x, 269–270.

168. This was the case with Patrick Adiarte, who appears in the 1961 film *Flower Drum Song*, the focus of Chapter 5, but who, while delightful to speak with, was not able to remember much about his interactions with Nancy Kwan, the film's star, and had no memory of Becky Varno, Kwan's dance-in. In the case of Finus Jhung, a dancer in *Flower Drum Song* (1961), by contrast, he turned out not to have appeared in the number "Grant Avenue," as I originally believed.

169. Charlene B. Regester, *Black Entertainers in African American Newspaper Articles*, vol. 1: *An Annotated Bibliography of the* Chicago Defender, *the* Afro-American Baltimore, *the* Los Angeles Sentinel *and the* New York Amsterdam News, *1910–1950* (Jefferson, NC: McFarland, 2002); Charlene B. Regester, *Black Entertainers in African American Newspaper Articles*, vol. 2: *Annotated and Indexed Bibliography of the* Pittsburgh Courier *and the* California Eagle, *1914–1950* (Jefferson, NC: McFarland, 2002).

170. Miranda Banks, "Production Studies," *Feminist Media Histories* 4, no. 2 (2018): 157.

171. Foster, "Choreographing History," 4; Manning, *Modern Dance, Negro Dance*, xviii.

172. Gottschild, *Digging the Africanist Presence*; Nadine George-Graves, *The Royalty of Negro Vaudeville: The Whitman Sisters and the Negotiation of Race, Gender and Class in African American Theater, 1900–1940* (New York: St. Martin's Press, 2000), xiii.

173. Srinivasan, *Sweating Saris*, 10.

174. Banks, "Production Studies," 157, 159.

175. Banks, "Gender Below-the-Line," 88–90; Erin Hill, *Never Done: A History of Women's Work in Media Production* (New Brunswick, NJ: Rutgers University Press, 2016), 5. My sincere thanks to Bliss Cua Lim for first pointing me in the direction of feminist production studies and suggesting that my research had something to contribute to this subfield. See also Helen Hanson, "Looking for Lela Simone: *Singin' in the Rain* and Microhistories of Women's Sound Work behind the Scenes and below-the-line in Classical Hollywood Cinema," *Women's History Review* 29, no. 5 (2020): 822–840.

176. Hill, *Never Done*, 11. See also Radha Vatsal, "Reevaluating Footnotes: Women Directors of the Silent Era," in *A Feminist Reader in Early Cinema*, ed. Jennifer M. Bean and Diane Negra (Durham, NC: Duke University Press, 2002), 119–138. Dance-ins might even be considered doubly "below-the-line," since the choreographers they assist continue to occupy "below-the-line" status in Hollywood. See Kristyn Burtt, "It's Time for IMDb to Give Choreographers an Official Category," *Dance Dish Media*, Februay 20, 2019, https://www.dancedishwithkb.com/post/it-s-time-for-imdb-to-give-choreographers-their-own-category#:~:text=For%20cho reographers%2C%20a%20user%20would,that%20have%20no%20specific%20category.

177. George-Graves, *The Royalty of Negro Vaudeville*, xvi.

178. VéVé A. Clark, "The Archaeology of Black Theatre," *Critical Arts* 2, no. 1 (1981): 38.

179. Vernadette Vicuña Gonzalez, *Empire's Mistress, Starring Isabel Rosario Cooper* (Durham, NC: Duke University Press, 2021), 9.

180. Clare Croft, "Not Yet and Elsewhere: Locating Lesbian Identity in Performance Archives, as Performance Archives," *Contemporary Theatre Review* 31, nos. 1–2 (2021): 35.

181. José Esteban Muñoz, "Ephemera as Evidence: Introductory Notes to Queer Acts," *Women and Performance: A Journal of Feminist Theory* 8, no. 2 (1996): 10. See also, among many others, Gayatri Chakravorty Spivak, "The Rani of Sirmur: An Essay in Reading the Archives," *History and Theory* 24, no. 3 (1985): 247–272; Ann Laura Stoler, *Along the Archival Grain: Epistemic Anxieties and Colonial Common Sense* (Princeton, NJ: Princeton University Press, 2009); Anjali Arondekar, *For the Record: On Sexuality and the Colonial Archive in India* (Durham, NC: Duke University Press, 2009).

182. Tavia Nyong'o, "Unburdening Representation," *Black Scholar* 44, no. 2 (2014): 77; Saidiya Hartman, "Venus in Two Acts," *Small Axe: A Caribbean Journal of Criticism* 12, no. 2 (2008): 11. See also Tavia Nyong'o, *Afro-Fabulations: The Queer Drama of Black Life* (New York: New York University Press, 2018); Saidiya Hartman, *Wayward Lives, Beautiful Experiments: Intimate Histories of Riotous Black Girls, Troublesome Women, and Queer Radicals* (New York: W. W. Norton, 2019). Gonzalez also writes about a subject who "eludes authoritative, documentary claims to truth" (*Empire's Mistress*, 11).

NOTES 209

183. Nyong'o, *Afro-Fabulations*, 47. Jayna Brown's *Babylon Girls: Black Women Performers and the Shaping of the Modern* (Durham, NC: Duke University Press, 2008) similarly refuses to offer "a 'recovery' history . . . designed to fill the gaps left in masculinist and/or white womanist theories" (1). See also the double issue of *Feminist Media Histories* on "Speculative Approaches to Media Histories," 8, nos. 2 and 3 (Spring and Summer 2022).

184. Nyong'o, *Afro-Fabulations*, 62.

185. See Chapter 3 for a fuller discussion of the issue of credit in relation to stars and dance-ins.

186. Jane M. Gaines, *Pink-Slipped: What Happened to Women in the Silent Film Industries?* (Champaign: University of Illinois Press, 2018), 14.

187. Ibid., 2–3, emphasis in original.

188. Gaines, *Pink-Slipped*, 3. See Muñoz, "Ephemera as Evidence," and Hill, *Never Done*, 11, on the value of the anecdote in minoritarian and queer histories and in the history of women workers in Hollywood. See Nyong'o, *Afro-Fabulations*, 46–75, on archival opacity.

189. Tina M. Campt, *Listening to Images* (Durham, NC: Duke University Press, 2017), 8.

190. Banks, "Gender Below-the-Line," 87.

191. Hye Jean Chung, *Media Heterotopias: Digital Effects and Material Labor in Global Film Production* (Durham, NC: Duke University Press, 2018), 3, 2, emphasis in original. As my language here suggests, this is a method that also draws on cultural studies approaches to star studies that "resituate the star within the sphere of production." Danae Clark, *Negotiating Hollywood: The Cultural Politics of Actors' Labor* (Minneapolis: University of Minnesota Press, 1995), x. See also McLean, *Being Rita Hayworth*; Emily Carman, *Independent Stardom: Freelance Women in the Hollywood Studio System* (Austin: University of Texas Press, 2015).

192. Richard Dyer, *Heavenly Bodies: Film Stars and Society* (New York: Routledge, 2013), 7; Brannigan, *Dancefilm*, 142. My gratitude to Stephanie Batiste for a thought-provoking conversation about why it's so hard to see back-up dancers on film and video.

193. Juliana Chang asks a similar set of questions about the Asian/American extras in the background of *Flower Drum Song*. Juliana Chang, "I Dreamed I Was Wanted: *Flower Drum Song* and Specters of Modernity," *Camera Obscura: Feminism, Culture, and Media Studies* 29, no. 3 (2014): 172. See Chapter 5 for further discussion.

194. Gottschild, *Digging the Africanist Presence*; Carol J. Clover, "Dancin' in the Rain," *Critical Inquiry* 21, no. 4 (Summer 1995): 722–747; Thomas F. DeFrantz, "Hip-hop in Hollywood: Encounter, Community, Resistance," in Borelli, *The Oxford Handbook of Dance and the Popular Screen*, 113–131; Shiovitz, *Behind the Screen*; Krayenbuhl, "Dancing Race and Masculinity."

195. Clover, "Dancin' in the Rain," 723.

196. José Esteban Muñoz, *The Sense of Brown* (Durham, NC: Duke University Press, 2020).

197. As *Vanity Fair* pointed out in a 2023 podcast, *Flower Drum Song* was nominated for five Oscars but lost to *West Side Story* in every category. Katey Rich, "The Landmark Asian-American Musical That Never Got Its Due," *Little Gold Men* podcast, *Vanity Fair*, May 12, 2023, https://www.vanityfair.com/hollywood/2023/05/awards-insider-litle-gold-men-flower-drum-song.

Chapter 1

1. *Los Angeles Times*, "Dance Stand-in," December 15, 1935, C9.

2. Delameter, *Dance in the Hollywood Musical*, 15.

3. Slide, *Hollywood Unknowns*; Chisholm, "Missing Persons and Bodies of Evidence."

4. Chisholm, "Missing Persons," 126, 127. Both Chisholm and Slide report that the use of stand-ins became routine in the 1930s. A 1938 article in *Collier's* reports that stand-ins originated with Polish silent film actress Pola Negri, who "couldn't stand still long enough for the electricians to spot their lights or the cameramen to focus, so the director, out of sheer necessity, resorted to a dummy for all preliminary work." Grover Jones, "Star Shadows," *Collier's*, April 30, 1938, 46.

5. Chisholm, "Missing Persons," 125, 128, 125.

6. As Chisholm writes, "the pervasiveness of doubling nearly always was shrouded or contained by industry publicity releases" ("Missing Persons," 128).

7. A 1925 article in the *Los Angeles Daily Times* reported that white silent film star Blanche Sweet "never requires the service of a double in scenes where she is called upon to execute difficult solo dances." *Los Angeles Daily Times*, "Blanche Sweet Never Requires Dance Double," June 11, 1925, 11. Billman's *Film Choreographers and Dance Directors* documents the use of dance doubles in place of stars in 1929 (29).

210 NOTES

8. See, for example, Wendy Perron, "Putting the Black Swan Blackout in Context," *Dance Magazine*, March 11, 2011, https://www.dancemagazine.com/putting-the-black-swan-blackout-in-cont ext/#gsc.tab=0; Randy Schmeltzer, "'Black Swan' Blasted for Ballet Cover-Up," *Adweek*, March 30, 2011, https://www.adweek.com/digital/black-swan-blasted-for-ballet-cover-up/. In what was no doubt an effort to avoid a similar controversy, Twentieth Century-Fox was much more transparent about the dance doubling work that American Ballet Theatre's Isabella Boylston did for Jennifer Lawrence in the 2018 film *Red Sparrow*. See Pia Catton, "It's Hard Work Being Jennifer Lawrence's Body Double, Especially for Jennifer Lawrence," *Daily Beast*, March 2, 2018, https://www.thedailybeast.com/its-hard-work-being-jennifer-lawrences-body-double-especia lly-for-jennifer-lawrence.

9. Slide notes that some stand-ins went on to be performers "in their own right" (*Hollywood Unknowns*, 119), and, as will become clear throughout this book, dance-ins routinely appeared on screen as extras and chorus dancers.

10. My sincere thanks to Yumi Pak for encouraging me to dwell on this ambiguity in a much earlier presentation of this research.

11. Franceschina, *Hermes Pan*.

12. Daniel Bernardi, "Introduction: Race and the Hollywood Style," in Bernardi, *Classic Hollywood, Classic Whiteness*, xiv–xv.

13. Larry Billman, *Betty Grable: A Bio-Bibliography* (Westport, CT: Greenwood Press, 1993), xi.

14. See Sean Redmond, "The Whiteness of Stars: Looking at Kate Winslet's Unruly Body," in *Stardom and Celebrity: A Reader*, ed. Sean Redmond and Su Holmes (London: Sage, 2007), 263–74; Dyer, *White*.

15. Toni Morrison, *The Bluest Eye* (1970; New York: Vintage Books, 2007); Ann duCille, "The Shirley Temple of My Familiar," *Transition* 73 (1997): 10–32; James Snead, ed. "Shirley Temple," in *White Screens/Black Images: Hollywood from the Dark Side* (New York: Routledge, 1994), 47–66; Diane Negra, *Off-White Hollywood: American Culture and Ethnic Female Stardom* (New York: Routledge, 2001); Kristen Hatch, *Shirley Temple and the Performance of Girlhood* (New Brunswick, NJ: Rutgers University Press, 2015). DuCille writes, "Like notoriously racist films such as D. W. Griffith's *Birth of a Nation* (1915) and Walt Disney's *Song of the South* (1946), Shirley Temple movies further a patriarchal ideology of white supremacy, an ideology that equates whiteness with beauty and makes true white womanhood a prized domestic ideal" ("The Shirley Temple of My Familiar," 13–14).

16. See Teresa De Lauretis, *Technologies of Gender: Essays on Theory, Film, and Fiction* (Bloomington: Indiana University Press, 1987) on the cinematic apparatus as part of the technology of gender.

17. See Daniel Bernardi, ed., *The Birth of Whiteness: Race and the Emergence of U.S. Cinema* (New Brunswick, NJ: Rutgers University Press, 1996); Bernardi, *Classic Hollywood, Classic Whiteness*; and volume 9 of *International Journal of Screendance*, which is devoted to interrogating the "assumed heteronormative, white space of the screen." Melissa Blanco Borelli and Raquel Monroe, "Editorial: Screening the Skin: Issues of Race and Nation in Screendance." *International Journal of Screendance* 9 (2018): http://dx.doi.org/10.18061/ijsd.v9i0.6451.

18. Dyer, *White*, 83, 122–142.

19. Dan Mainwaring, "Hollywood Nobodies," *Good Housekeeping*, April 1938, 137. A 1938 article in *Collier's* likewise observed that "many stand-ins resemble their stars so much that they can also double for them." Jones, "Star Shadows," 44. This has not always been the case for Black actors, however. Dyer cites an example of a white woman standing in for Cicely Tyson during production of the 1976 film *The Blue Bird*, with disastrous results (*White*, 97). Similarly, in the fall of 2014 the Warner Brothers television show *Gotham* generated controversy when it was discovered that they had employed a white stuntwoman to double for an African American guest star. Engaging in a practice known as "painting down," apparently Hollywood's preferred term for blackface, the stuntwoman had "dark makeup applied to the face, in a hair and makeup test, in advance of two days of filming in New York" before public outrage caused Warner Brothers to hire a Black stuntwoman and apologize for their "error." The Screen Actors Guild–American Federation of Television and Radio Artists (SAG-AFTRA) contract governing stunt doubles states, "When the stunt performer doubles for a role which is identifiable as female and/or black, Hispanic, Asian Pacific or Native American, and the race and/or sex of the double is also identifiable, stunt coordinator shall endeavor to cast qualified persons of the same sex and/or race involved." David Robb, "Plan to Film 'Gotham' Stuntwoman in Blackface Scrapped by Warner

NOTES 211

Bros. TV," *Deadline*, October 9, 2014, http://deadline.com/2014/10/gotham-stunt-woman-blackface-warner-bros-848969/.

20. I have not been able to locate Harper's name in other sources on Temple's career. Biographer Ann Edwards lists Marilyn Granas and Mary Lou Islieb as Temple's stand-ins. Ann Edwards, *Shirley Temple: American Princess* (Guilford, CT: Lyons Press, 2017), 77. So does Slide in *Hollywood Unknowns* (127) and Temple in her autobiography. Shirley Temple Black, *Child Star: An Autobiography* (New York: Warner Books, 1988), 70. It is possible that the *Los Angeles Times* mistakenly identified Granas as Harper. In her autobiography, Temple describes Granas as "someone I vaguely recalled from our ranks at Meglin's" (*Child Star*, 63).

21. Historic Films Stock Footage Archive, "1933 Children Vaudeville Act," accessed June 26, 2018, http://www.historicfilms.com/tapes/53371. According to the *Los Angeles Times*, when Meglin Kiddies founder Ethel Meglin merged her dance studios with two other organizations in 1936, she "presided over what was believed the largest dance organization in the nation—137 schools." Burt A. Folkart, "E. Meglin, 93; 'Meglin Kiddies' Dance Instructor," obituary, *Los Angeles Times*, June 25, 1988, http://articles.latimes.com/1988-06-25/news/mn-4707_1_meglin-kiddies. Judy Garland also got her start at the Meglin Dance Studio. For more on the Meglin Studios, see Edwards, *Shirley Temple*, 28–30; Black, *Child Star*, 1, 5–6.

22. See Redmond, "The Whiteness of Stars." On the ways African American performers have defined and "stolen" stardom on different terms from the white establishment, see Arthur Knight, "Star Dances: African American Constructions of Stardom, 1925–1960," in Bernardi, *Classic Hollywood, Classic Whiteness*, 386–414; Petty, *Stealing the Show*. See also my discussion of Marie Bryant in Chapter 2.

23. Black, *Child Star*, 63. My thanks to an audience member at the Ohio State University, where I presented an earlier version of this research, for asking how child labor laws may have driven the need for Temple's dancing stand-in. On the degree to which child labor laws affected Temple more generally, see Edwards, *Shirley Temple*.

24. Billman, *Film Choreographers and Directors*, 52–53.

25. See Negra, *Off-White Hollywood* for a thoughtful discussion of how the youthful innocence of Temple, along with the white Norwegian figure skater and film star Sonja Henie, "incarnated the body in exuberant, individualist motion" in ways that sharply contrasted the Depression-era backstage film musicals that "prioritized the bodily collective" and, in doing so, "recovered" or "restored" the association of whiteness with "corporeal individualism" (89). As Robin Bernstein points out in her study of the racialization of childhood innocence, Temple engaged in another kind of surrogation via her emulation of Mae West's sonic and gestural repertoire in the 1933 short "Polly Tix in Washington." Robin Bernstein, *Racial Innocence: White Supremacy and the Performance of American Childhood* (New Haven, CT: Yale University Press, 2004), 23.

26. Roach, *Cities of the Dead*, 3, 80, 2, 6.

27. Spillers, "Mama's Baby, Papa's Maybe," 67, emphasis in original.

28. Bradley, *Anteaesthetics*, 46.

29. Cheryl I. Harris, "Whiteness as Property," *Harvard Law Review* 106, no. 8 (June 1993): 1707–1791.

30. Cherniavsky, *Incorporations*, xv, emphasis in original.

31. My thinking here is also inspired by a talk given at UC Riverside on May 16, 2018, by Kara Keeling titled "'I'm a Man Eating Machine': On Digital Media, Corporate Cannibals, and (Im)Proper Bodies," with a response by Grace Kyungwong Hong. The talk was part of the "Undisciplined Encounters: Experimental Dialogues on Critical Ethnic Studies" series.

32. Cherniavsky, *Incorporations*, xxv, 35, 101, 84, 107, 99.

33. Margaret Iverson, *Photography, Trace, and Trauma* (Chicago: University of Chicago Press, 2017), 18.

34. Ibid., 24; Doane, "The Indexical and the Concept of Medium Specificity," 136.

35. Keeling, "Passing for Human," 238, 244.

36. Keeling cites Frantz Fanon's famous discussion of the anxiety he experiences waiting for images of "the Black" to appear on screen, an image that is "radically incommensurate with Fanon's own sense and understanding of" his prefilmic reality (ibid., 244). See Fanon, *Black Skins, White Masks*.

37. As an anonymous reader thoughtfully pointed out, the existence of accounts of dance-ins in the mainstream press (however scant) raises questions about whether white audiences ever cast doubt on white stars' claims to self-referentiality. Like stunt persons who "were something of an open secret" in Hollywood, knowledge of white stars' use of "supplementary"

212   NOTES

bodies was "potentially disruptive" but never actually destabilizing of white stars' presumed indexicality. Jacob Smith, *The Thrill Makers: Celebrity, Masculinity, and Stunt Performance* (Berkeley: University of California Press, 2012), 11–12. This is no doubt in part because, as Jennifer M. Bean has shown, "the media complex of early stardom constructed and promoted the body of its star" as a means of "heighten[ing] the correspondence between image and object" ("Technologies of Early Stardom and the Extraordinary Body," 14, 17). Indeed, that film is so commonly conceived of as an indexical medium suggests the strength of the ideology surrounding it. Outside of scholarship that has called out white stars' debts to Black dancers, any discernible pressure on images of white stars' dancing bodies has come from attempts to attribute stars' corporealities to their (generally male) choreographers. See, for example, Debra Levine, "Jack Cole Made Marilyn Move," *Los Angeles Times*, August 9, 2009, https://www.lati mes.com/entertainment/arts/la-ca-marilyn-monroe9-2009aug09-story.html. Such efforts, I would suggest, displace the star's originality onto the choreographer's, rather than putting pressure on notions of filmic (or corporeal) indexicality more broadly.

38. Brannigan, *Dancefilm*, 142, 145. Brannigan analyzes the idiogests of Ginger Rogers, Rita Hayworth, and Marilyn Monroe. Although she mentions in a footnote that Hayworth began performing as Rita Cansino (149n20), she doesn't otherwise address Hayworth's transformation from Latina to white, nor Rogers's and Monroe's whiteness.

39. Ibid., 142, 143.

40. Anthea Kraut, "'Stealing Steps' and Signature Moves: Embodied Theories of Dance as Intellectual Property," *Theatre Journal* 62, no. 2 (May 2010): 173–189.

41. Billman, *Betty Grable*, xi.

42. Basinger, *The Star Machine*, 518.

43. Billman, *Betty Grable*, xi.

44. Jane Marie Gaines, "The Popular Icon as Commodity and Sign: The Circulation of Betty Grable, 1941–1945" (PhD diss., Northwestern University, 1982), 274.

45. Robert B. Westbrook, "'I Want a Girl, Just Like the Girl That Married Harry James': American Women and the Problem of Political Obligation in World War II," *American Quarterly* 42, no. 4 (December 1990): 596; Tom McGee, *Betty Grable: The Girl with the Million Dollar Legs* (New York: Welcome Rain, 1995), 85; George Lipsitz, *The Possessive Investment in Whiteness: How White People Profit from Identity Politics* (Philadelphia: Temple University Press, 2006), 76; Basinger, *The Star Machine*, 519.

46. Westbrook, "'I Want a Girl,'" 599, 600.

47. Pete Martin, "The World's Most Popular Blonde," *Saturday Evening Post*, April 15, 1950, 26–27+.

48. Basinger, *The Star Machine*, 12, 14.

49. Ibid., 73–100; Dyer, *Heavenly Bodies*, 5.

50. Gaines, "The Popular Icon as Commodity and Sign," 269.

51. Ibid., 278; Lois W. Banner, "The Creature from the Black Lagoon: Marilyn Monroe and Whiteness," *Cinema Journal* 47, no. 4 (Summer 2008): 11.

52. Basinger, *The Star Machine*, 517. Gaines elaborates on the transition from Faye to Grable: "To cement the connection between Alice Faye whom Fox was phasing out and Grable whom they were preparing to replace her, the two were cast as sisters in *Tin Pan Alley* (1941), the film following *Argentine Way*. Grable and Faye had in common singing, dancing, and blondeness" ("The Popular Icon as Commodity and Sign," 276).

53. Gaines, "The Popular Icon as Commodity and Sign," 275.

54. Banks, "Gender Below-the-Line," 87–98.

55. Billman, *Film Choreographers and Directors*, 240.

56. Ibid.; *Tampa Morning Tribune*, "Davis Island Coliseum Ad," December 19, 1925, 18, https://www.newspapers.com/newspage/326989103/. Blue referred to their act as "The Little Blue Sisters." Angie Blue, "Her Divided Heart (Betty Grable)," *Photoplay*, January 1949, 49, 71–72.

57. Blue, "Her Divided Heart."

58. Hermes Pan, David Patrick Columbia, and Kenyon Kramer, "Meeting the Frog Prince," chapter 7 of unpublished memoir of Hermes Pan, 249, undated, John Franceschina papers, UC Riverside Special Collections and Archives. My deepest thanks to John Franceschina for sending me an image of this page from Pan's memoirs before they were relocated to UCR's Special Collections and Archives.

59. Svetlana McLee Grody and Dorothy Daniels Lister, *Conversations with Choreographers* (Portsmouth, NH: Heinemann, 1996), 8; David Patrick Columbia, "The Man Who Danced with Fred Astaire," *Dancing Times*, May–June 1991, 848.

NOTES 213

60. Todd Decker, "Dancing with the Stars: The Story of Hermes Pan," review of *The Man Who Danced with Fred Astaire* by John Franceschina, *Figure in the Carpet* (Center for the Humanities at Washington University in St. Louis) 11, no. 6 (January 2013): 8.

61. Grody and Lister, *Conversations with Choreographers*, 8.

62. Billman, *Film Choreographers and Directors*, 240.

63. Franceschina, *Hermes Pan*, 106, 110; Martin, "The World's Most Popular Blonde."

64. Blue, "Her Divided Heart."

65. Legal memo from Twentieth Century-Fox Film Corporation, signed by George Wasson, assistant secretary, to Hugh L. Ducker, regional head of Stabilization Unit of the Bureau of Internal Revenue, June 28, 1944. An interoffice Twentieth Century-Fox Film Corporation memo dated May 15, 1944, to Robert H. Patton from Harold H. Bow with the subject "Employment Record of Angela T. Blue" indicates that her pay was $55 per week as a dancer and $66 per week as a skater.

66. Billman, *Film Choreographers and Directors*, 241.

67. Legal memo from Twentieth Century-Fox Film Corporation, signed by Lew Schreiber, executive manager, to Loew's Incorporated, June 23, 1948.

68. Pan, for example, was making $750 a week for Fox in 1943 and was loaned to Paramount Studios for $1,000 a week for the film *Blue Skies* in 1945 (Franceschina, *Hermes Pan*, 127, 143–144). Blue's salary for the latter was still $125 a week (Interoffice memo from Lew Schreiber to George Wasson, subject "Angela Blue," May 21, 1945). A contract dated April 13, 1949, in the Fox Archives lists Billy Daniels's salary as $750 per week for work on the film *Wabash Avenue*. Legal memo from Twentieth Century-Fox Film Corporation, signed Lew Schreiber, executive manager, to "Mr. Billy Daniel," April 13, 1949. Billy Daniels shows up in the Fox Archives and other historical records as "Billy Daniel." As archival specialist Helice Koffler relayed to me in an email dated October 20, 2021, Daniels is "the authorized form of the name in the LC name authority file: https://lccn.loc.gov/no93035628." She also speculates that "it's possible he might have used Billy Daniel more often in the 1950s and 60s to differentiate himself from a somewhat popular singer, Billy Daniels, who was more or less a contemporary of his."

69. Twentieth Century-Fox Film Corporation interoffice memo from Frank Tresselt to Mr. F. L. Metzler et al., subject "Angie Blue," June 2, 1944.

70. Legal memo from Twentieth Century-Fox Film Corporation, assistant secretary (no signature) to Hugh L. Ducker, regional head of Stabilization Unit of the Bureau of Internal Revenue, February 19, 1943.

71. Blue, "Her Divided Heart," 49.

72. Dan Georgakas, "The Man behind Fred and Ginger: An Interview with Hermes Pan," *Cinéaste* 12, no. 4 (1983): 27.

73. Franceschina, *Hermes Pan*, 122, 109, 122.

74. John Kobal, *People Will Talk* (New York: Alfred A. Knopf, 1985), 630. Unsurprisingly, McGee's biography of Grable contains a more favorable appraisal of her dancing. McGee writes that Pan recalled Grable as possessing a "'natural and graceful' dancing style" and that Pan considered Grable, along with Rita Hayworth, one of the "two top female dancers on the screen" (*Betty Grable*, 47, 84).

75. Martin, "The World's Most Popular Blonde," 106; Columbia, "The Man Who Danced," 848. On the surface, Grable's own admission of averageness and her treatment like a chorus dancer might seem to compromise the legitimacy of her star status. But film scholar Sean Redmond reminds us that it is the paradoxical simultaneity of extraordinariness and ordinariness, uniqueness and commonness that lies "at the heart of white stardom" ("The Whiteness of Stars," 267). See also Dyer, *White*.

76. In an interview conducted on May 8, 2019, Barrie Chase expressed doubt that Grable was simply imitating Blue, maintaining that Grable had her own way of moving that couldn't be transmitted. (She also described herself as a big fan of Grable.)

77. Columbia, "The Man Who Danced," 848.

78. Mainwaring, "Hollywood Nobodies," 137.

79. In his review of Franceschina's biography of Pan, music scholar Todd Decker notes that the statement about how many of Grable's moves were "simply her 'doing Angie'" "deserves unpacking." For Decker, the statement "reminds the reader of the complicated nature of collaboration in Hollywood and the difficulty of locating creative agency in the studio context" ("Dancing with the Stars," 8). For my purposes, the assertion that Grable was simply "doing

214 NOTES

Angie" presents a more far-reaching challenge to the assumed self-referentiality of white star dancing bodies.

80. One possible candidate for this "itty-bitty walk" is the leg crossing—in which Grable lifts and crosses one knee in front of the other with each step—that she performs at the opening of "Put Your Arms around Me, Honey" in the 1943 film *Coney Island*, which Pan, assisted by Blue, choreographed. See the 3:49 minute mark here: https://www.youtube.com/watch?v=qk5c WNXXdMs, accessed April 30, 2024. A slightly more stylized and contained (perhaps more "itty-bitty"?) version of this walk can be seen near the top of the "I Love a New Yorker" number in the 1950 film *My Blue Heaven*, on which Blue assisted choreographer Billy Daniels. See the 17-second to 24-second mark here: https://www.youtube.com/watch?v=tBp9n_jRH9o, accessed April 30, 2024. See Kraut, *Choreographing Copyright*, 154–155, for a discussion of signature moves and corporeal autography.

81. Blue, "Her Divided Heart," 49, 71.

82. Ibid., 49, 72.

83. Doug Warren, *Betty Grable: The Reluctant Movie Queen*, Kindle edition, Crossroad Press, 2016, ch. 10, LOC 1014–1025.

84. Gaines, "The Popular Icon as Commodity and Sign," 197.

85. *The Telegraph*, "Twentieth Century Fox Archives," December 2, 2007, https://www.telegraph.co.uk/culture/film/3675305/20th-Century-Fox-Archives.html.

86. Redmond, "The Whiteness of Stars," 266, emphasis in original.

87. John Ellis, *Visible Fictions: Cinema: Television: Video*, revised edition (New York, Routledge, 1992), 58.

88. Jones, "Star Shadows."

89. *Coshocton Tribune*, "Greeks' Dancing Wins War, Claim," December 8, 1940, 12.

90. Allen L. Woll, *The Latin Image in American Film* (Los Angeles: UCLA Latin American Center Publications, 1977), 53. See also Herrera, *Latin Numbers*, 18–53.

91. Delia Malia Caparoso Konzett, *Hollywood's Hawaii: Race, Nation, and War* (New Brunswick, NJ: Rutgers University Press, 2017), 3, 10, 67.

92. Franceschina, *Hermes Pan*, 106–107.

93. Herrera, *Latin Numbers*, 20.

94. See Ovalle, *Dance and the Hollywood Latina*, 49–69, on how Miranda's body mediated Blackness for white North American audiences.

95. Franceschina tells us that Pan found it challenging to teach Miranda his "American way of doing the samba," which he choreographed in 4/4 rather than 6/8 time (*Hermes Pan*, 107).

96. On Grable's blackface performances, see Knight, *Disintegrating the Musical*, 85.

97. Blue's friend Pearlie Norton, for example, appears as an uncredited chorus dancer on the IMDb page for *Song of the Islands*. See https://www.imdb.com/title/tt0035361/fullcredits/?ref_= tt_cl_sm, accessed July 6, 2023. Writing about *Song of the Islands*, Franceschina reports, "For the dancing and local-color segments . . . , Pan and his casting department sought twenty-five chorus girls and three hundred Polynesian types. While many of the dancing girls were cast from among the stable of Hermes Pan's dancers, the ethnic types were more difficult to cast, particularly in such large numbers." He also writes that Pan's hula dances "maximized the amount of cellophane available to the prop department" and that "[d]ark wigs were also an endangered commodity since they were made of real hair typically imported from China and Yugoslavia," access to which was cut off by the war (*Hermes Pan*, 118–119). See Konzett's analysis of *Song of the Islands* on 69–71 of *Hollywood's Hawaii*.

98. See, among others, Clover, "Dancin' in the Rain"; Constance Valis Hill, "From Bharata Natyam to Bop: Jack Cole's 'Modern' Jazz Dance," *Dance Research Journal* 33, no. 2 (2001): 29–39; Shiovitz, *Behind the Screen*; Krayenbuhl, "Dancing Race and Masculinity."

99. Jacqueline Najuma Stewart, *Migrating to the Movies: Cinema and Black Urban Modernity* (Berkeley: University of California Press, 2005), 14.

100. In addition to Pan, the list of choreographers with whom Grable worked includes Jack Cole, Billy Daniels, and Busby Berkeley. See McGee, *Betty Grable*; Billman, *Betty Grable*.

101. Columbia, "The Man Who Danced," 759.

102. Gottschild, *Digging the Africanist Presence*.

103. My sincere thanks once again to John Franceschina for his extreme generosity in sharing his Pan materials with me, as well as to Micheline Laski, Pan's niece, for granting me permission to publish Pan's personal photos.

104. Spillers, "Mama's Baby," 65.

NOTES   215

105. Kimberly Wallace-Sanders, *Mammy: A Century of Race, Gender, and Southern Memory* (Ann Arbor: University of Michigan Press, 2008), 3. See also Harryette Mullen's discussion of the "black woman as a conflicted site of the (re)production of whiteness." Harryette Mullen, "Optic White: Blackness and the Production of Whiteness," *Diacritics* 24, nos. 2–3 (Summer–Autumn 1994): 82.

106. Columbia, "The Man Who Danced," 759; Franceschina, *Hermes Pan*, 17. The Columbia piece on Pan actually refers to the "houseboy" who taught Pan dances like the Black Bottom and Charleston as "Tommy," whereas Franceschina and Fantle and Johnson identify Pan's childhood teacher as Sam Clark, Betty's son. David Fantle and Tom Johnson, *Reel to Real: 25 Years of Celebrity Interviews from Vaudeville to Movies to TV* (Oregon, WI: Badger Books, Inc, 2004). Whether "Tommy" was a real name or not, and whether there was more than one Black domestic worker who taught Pan jazz dance, is not clear.

107. Fantle and Johnson, *Reel to Real*, 87, 89. Franceschina's biography of Pan is full of other anecdotes that document the influence of African American aesthetics on his choreography.

108. Gottschild, *Digging the Africanist Presence*, 17.

109. *Ebony*, "Movie Dance Director," 5 (April 1950): 22–26.

110. Janette Prescod, "Marie Bryant," in *Notable Black American Women*, book 2, ed. Jessie Carney Smith (Detroit, MI: Gale Research, 1996), 71–73. See also Bogle, *Bright Boulevards, Bold Dreams*, 240–243.

111. Erskine Johnson, "In Hollywood," *Miami Daily News-Record*, April 5, 1943, 4; *Ebony*, "Movie Dance Director," 22, 25.

112. An online clip of Bryant dancing in "Mr. Beebe" (between the 0:17 and 0:37 marks) is available here: https://www.youtube.com/watch?v=EFyDd8CFLVw, accessed July 10, 2018.

113. *Meet Me after the Show* credits, TCM, accessed July 25, 2023, https://www.tcm.com/tcmdb/title/83194/meet-me-after-the-show#credits. Several sources identify Bryant as an assistant to Jack Cole at Twentieth Century-Fox, though I have not been able to recover any archival documentation of their collaboration. Addressing the friendship between Bryant and Lena Horne, Buckley writes, "Marie had recently left Dunham to become the assistant, at 20th Century Fox, of Jack Cole, the sinuous and charismatic dancer-choreographer whose students included Bob Fosse, Carol Haney, and Gwen Verdon. When you asked Marie what she did for Jack Cole, she said, 'I teach Betty Grable to shake her buns.'" Gail Lumet Buckley, *The Hornes: An American Family* (Milwaukee, WI: Hal Leonard, 2002), 150–151. It is not clear what her source is. Bryant's friend Alan Marston recalled that "Marie intermittently assisted choreographers Hermes Pan and Jack Cole." Alan Marston, "Marie Bryant—She Always Jumped for Joy," *Los Angeles Times Calendar*, October 8, 1978, N4+. In *Bright Boulevards, Bold Dreams*, Donald Bogle also states that Bryant "landed studio jobs, assisting choreographers Billy Daniels and later Jack Cole" (241), though the only citation listed here is the 1950 *Ebony* article I discuss in both this and the next chapter, which does not mention Cole. Debra Levine likewise writes that Bryant was, "for a time, rehearsal assistant to Jack Cole." Debra Levine, "Marie Bryant Put a Bun in Betty Grable's Oven," *arts meme*, January 15, 2012, https://artsmeme.com/2012/01/15/marie-bryant-put-a-bun-in-betty-grables-oven/. In a comment submitted on January 16, 2012, in response to Levine's blog entry, the late film historian Larry Billman writes, "Bryant was invaluable to Jack Cole and everyone she ever worked with. She 'lived' what Jack 'loved.'" Bryant's name does not appear in Glenn Loney's biography of Jack Cole, *Unsung Genius: The Passion of Dancer-Choreographer Jack Cole* (New York: Franklin Watts, 1984), nor in the Jack Cole Papers in the Performing Arts Special Collections at the University of California, Los Angeles, Charles E. Young Research Library.

114. *Ebony*, "Movie Dance Director," 26.

115. The moment occurs around the 18:26 mark in a YouTube version of the film, https://www.youtube.com/watch?v=7-rlj1TiU48, accessed September 19, 2022.

116. *Ebony*, "Movie Dance Director," 26.

117. Gottschild, *The Black Dancing Body*, 148. An anonymous reader wondered whether white audiences were able to detect traces of the Africanist aesthetic in Grable's movement and, if not, whether Bryant might have deliberately coached Grable in a way that coded her movement as Africanist for Black audiences. As my reading of Vera-Ellen in the next chapter suggests, audiences were capable of detecting transformations in white stars' physicality without recognizing them as embodiments of Blackness. I have uncovered no evidence to suggest that Bryant was transmitting moves in such a way as to deliberately conceal their Africanist influences from white audiences. (She openly cited Dunham as one of her mentors.) I'm less

216 NOTES

interested in Bryant's motives than in the complicated power dynamics that governed her behind-the-scenes roles in Hollywood.

118. Billman, *Film Choreographers and Directors*, 241. TCM lists Blue as "Betty Grable's Dance Instructor," Bryant as "Assistant Dance Director," and Daniels as "Dance Director," with an additional "Dances Staged by" Jack Cole. https://www.tcm.com/tcmdb/title/83194/meet-me-after-the-show#credits, accessed July 25, 2023. According to Harrison Carroll, "Behind the Scenes in Hollywood," *Daily Clintonian*, February 2, 1951, 2, Blue assisted Daniels on the "Meet Me after the Show" lead dance number, in which Grable performs a fast-paced tap dance with the Condos Brothers.

119. Personal email from Matthew Yongue, Clip and Still Licensing, Twentieth Century-Fox, October 30, 2018.

120. Franceschina, *Hermes Pan*, 130.

121. In "My Divided Heart," Blue describes the number as an "Apache dance" and "the toughest dance routine Betty ever had," which included being thrown around by Pan "like a rubber ball." Learning in confidence that Grable was pregnant, Blue evidently convinced Pan to modify the choreography.

122. Roach, *Cities of the Dead*, 6, 3.

123. The film in its entirety is available here: https://www.youtube.com/watch?v=7-rlj1TiU48, accessed July 12, 2023. These moments of shared screen time appear at the 44:57, 46:49, and 50:14 marks.

124. Remarkably, in the corollary scene in *Coney Island*, of which *Wabash Avenue* was a remake, Grable acknowledges and thanks her Black maid, played by Black actress Libby Taylor. "Here, Aunt Libby," Grable's character Kate says as she hands Taylor her large boa and Taylor helps her slip on a dress coat. The lack of response from Grable's character Ruby to Bryant's Elsa in *Wabash Avenue* is all the more glaring by contrast. See the 7:33 mark at https://www.yout ube.com/watch?v=juECQJMgJSU and the 50:14 mark at https://www.youtube.com/watch?v= 7-rlj1TiU48. The next chapter explores the misremembering of Bryant more fully.

Chapter 2

1. *On the Town* budget; AD report, *On the Town* files, both at USC.

2. For more on Bryant's career, see Bogle, *Bright Boulevards, Bold Dreams*, 240–243; Prescod, "Marie Bryant," 71–73; "Bryant, Marie, 1917–1978," the biography written by Helice Koffler for the free online resource Social Networks and Archival Context, accessed January 9, 2025, https://snaccooperative.org/view/85321123#biography.

3. An exception is the SNAC biography cited above, which draws on an earlier presentation I gave of the research in this chapter.

4. For a fuller discussion of the film musical's uncanny racial politics, see Anthea Kraut, "Un/funny Business in *On the Town* (1949)," in *Funny Moves: Dance Humor Politics*, ed. Marta E. Savigliano and Hannah Schwadron (New York: Oxford University Press, 2025), 168–190.. I revisit the making of *On the Town*'s "A Day in New York" ballet in Chapter 4.

5. D'Lana Lockett Research Files (S) *MGZMD 279, box 1, folder 5, "Bryant, Marie," Jerome Robbins Dance Division, New York Public Library for the Performing Arts (hereafter NYPL).

6. Charlene B. Regester, *African American Actresses: The Struggle for Visibility, 1900–1960* (Bloomington: Indiana University Press, 2010); Constance Valis Hill, *Brotherhood in Rhythm: The Jazz Tap Dancing of the Nicholas Brothers* (New York: Oxford University Press, 2021); Petty, *Stealing the Show*; Susie Trenka, *Jumping the Color Line: Vernacular Jazz Dance in American Film, 1929–1945* (Bloomington: Indiana University Press, 2021); Shiovitz, *Behind the Screen*; Krayenbuhl, "Dancing Race and Masculinity." See also Fay Jackson, who wrote in 1934 that "there are NO negro motion picture stars" (cited in Knight, "Star Dances," 403).

7. Although uncovering information about Black dance-ins for Black stars has proven challenging, archival materials for Horne's films confirm the use of "standins" for Horne prior to filming. See, for example, the AD reports for *Ziegfeld Follies* housed in the Freed Collection at USC. Notices in the Black press, meanwhile, indicate that Millie Monroe, Maggie Hathaway, Avanelle Harris, Juliette Ball, and Artie Young all served as doubles or stand-ins for Horne at some point. (The press often used "stand-in" and "double" interchangeably.) *Pittsburgh Courier*, "Film Beauty," November 14, 1942, 20; Harry Levett, "Thru Hollywood," *Chicago Defender*, February 20, 1943, 19; Avanelle Harris, "I Tried to Crash the Movies," *Ebony*, August 1946, 5–10. Writing about the Black movie star Dorothy Dandridge, however, Marguerite Rippy suggests that Dandridge was permitted to do her own stunts *because* she was Black. Marguerite

NOTES   217

H. Rippy, "Commodity, Tragedy, Desire: Female Sexuality and Blackness in the Iconography of Dorothy Dandridge," in Bernardi, *Classic Hollywood, Classic Whiteness*, 189.

8. Bogle, *Bright Boulevards, Bold Dreams*, 240–243; Jeanine Basinger, *The Movie Musical* (New York: Knopf, 2019), 573; Levine, "Marie Bryant Put a Bun in Betty Grable's Oven"; Brenda Dixon Gottschild, *Joan Myers Brown and the Audacious Hope of the Black Ballerina: A Biohistory of American Performance* (New York: Palgrave Macmillan, 2012), 293; Trenka, *Jumping the Color Line*, 127; Robert Jackson, *Fade In, Crossroads: A History of the Southern Cinema* (New York: Oxford University Press, 2017), 89–90; Prescod, "Marie Bryant."

9. Dancer Sarita Allen played the role of Marie Bryant. The other Black stars featured were Bessie Smith, Florence Mills, and Mahalia Jackson. See DeFrantz, *Dancing Revelations*, 171–172.

10. In an eerie echo of Bryant's simultaneous presence in and absence from the archive, in the process of trying to acquire high-resolution photographs of images of her in the *Ebony* feature that I discuss at length in this chapter, I confronted libraries that were missing the *Ebony* volume in which she appears, a volume in which the entire feature on Bryant had been ripped out, and a volume in which one of the photographs of her had been ripped out.

11. See Chapter 1, note 123.

12. Erickson, *From Radio to the Big Screen*, 160.

13. Dolores Calvin, "Who Said Brush-Off? That Is What Marie Bryant Got in Pix," *Chicago Defender*, April 29, 1950, n.p.

14. After praising Bryant's singing appearance in *They Live by Night* (1948), Jeanine Basinger bemoans, "Couldn't she have done an encore? Couldn't she have had more to do in other movies?" (*The Movie Musical*, 573).

15. Dale Wasserman, "An Homage to Marie Bryant," letters, *Los Angeles Times*, October 22, 1978, L100 (in response to Alan Marston story).

16. George-Graves, *The Royalty of Negro Vaudeville*, xviii.

17. Nyong'o, *Afro-Fabulations*, 61; Heather Love, *Feeling Backward: Loss and the Politics of Queer History* (Cambridge, MA: Harvard University Press, 2007), 31–52. See also Anjali Arondekar et al., "Queering Archives: A Roundtable Discussion," *Radical History Review* 2015, no. 122 (2015): 211–231.

18. Kara Keeling, *The Witch's Flight: The Cinematic, the Black Femme, and the Image of Common Sense* (Durham, NC: Duke University Press, 2007), 1, 2.

19. See Nyong'o, *Afro-Fabulations*, 46–75, on "archival opacity" and the "enigmatic shape and undecidability of the images that flicker in the darkened room of the cinema" (48).

20. Here I am paraphrasing Tiffany Lethabo King in conversation with Frank Wilderson. In response to Wilderson's remark "Non-Black people cannot fathom the fact that it's their cultural coherence and not their cultural practices that's the problem," King states, "There is so much work that could be done on whiteness and how its coherence requires parasitism in order to survive." Frank B. Wilderson III and Tiffany Lethabo King, "Staying Ready for Black Study," in *Otherwise Worlds: Against Settler Colonialism and Anti-Blackness*, ed. Tiffany Lethabo King, Jenell Navarro, and Andrea Smith (Durham, NC: Duke University Press, 2020), 57.

21. Prescod, "Marie Bryant," 71.

22. Marston, "Marie Bryant." References to Bryant's Hollywood friendships pervade narratives of her career. A partial list of those friendships also includes Betty Grable, Ava Gardner, Lena Horne, Billy Holliday, Norman Granz, Gene Kelly, Billy Daniels, Lena Horne, Katherine Dunham, John Garfield, Dale Wasserman, and Marlon Brando. *Sydney Morning Herald*, "She Taught Dance Routines to the Stars," October 14, 1954, 26; Donald Clarke, *Wishing on the Moon: The Life and Times of Billie Holiday* (Cambridge, MA: Da Capo Press, 2002), 200; email to Lockett, dated July 8, 2000, Lockett files, NYPL.

23. Bogle, *Bright Boulevards*, 240; *Ebony*, "Movie Dance Director," 26.

24. Bogle erroneously reports that Bryant's lessons from Bruce took place in Los Angeles (*Bright Boulevards*, 240). Bryant told *Ebony* that she began taking lessons with Bruce when she was six years old, though it is not entirely clear when her family moved to Chicago (*Ebony*, "Movie Dance Director," 23).

25. See Social Networks and Archival Content, "Bruce, Mary, 1900–1995," accessed January 9, 2025, https://snaccooperative.org/view/85334651#biography ; Clovis E. Semmes, *The Regal Theater and Black Culture* (New York: Palgrave Macmillan, 2006), 34, 85.

26. *Ebony*, "Movie Dance Director," 23.

218 NOTES

27. A 1929 article names Bryant as one of the "one hundred or more kiddies, protégés of Miss Bruce" performing at the Bruce school's annual recital at the Eighth Street Theater. *Chicago Defender*, "Mary Bruce's Dancing Girls Score Big Hit," June 8, 1929, 6.
28. Bogle, *Bright Boulevards*, 240–242.
29. *Ebony*, "Movie Dance Director," 23.
30. Atkins, *Class Act*, 29–30.
31. Social Networks and Archival Content, "Bryant, Marie."
32. The most up-to-date biographical account of Bryant can be found in Social Networks and Archival Content, "Bryant, Marie." The D'Lana Lockett Research Files in the NYPL Performing Arts Library (box 1, folder 5) contain an inevitably partial list of Bryant's club, stage, and screen appearances and known teaching and coaching gigs. For a record of Bryant's appearances with Duke Ellington, see Klaus Stratemann, *Duke Ellington, Day by Day and Film by Film* (Copenhagen: JazzMedia ApS, 1992).
33. *Ebony*, "Movie Dance Director," 22. Dunham began teaching dance in Chicago in 1933. The Dunham School of Dance and Theater in New York was operational from 1944 to 1954. Joanna Dee Das, *Katherine Dunham: Dance and the African Diaspora* (New York: Oxford University Press, 2017), 103.
34. Das, *Katherine Dunham*, 110. A bio for Bryant in a souvenir program for *The Biggest Show of '51*, housed in the Lockett files at the NYPL, reports, "In between her professional appearances Miss Bryant teaches the modern dance at famed Katharine [*sic*] Dunham School." A reprint of a brochure in the volume on Dunham titled *Kaiso!* lists Bryant as teaching "Tap and Boogie" and describes her as the "Dance instructor for Martha Raye, Arlene Judge and others." "Katherine Dunham School of Arts and Research Brochure, 1946–1947," in *Kaiso! Writings by and about Katherine Dunham*, ed. VéVé A. Clark and Sara E. Johnson (Madison: University of Wisconsin Press, 2005), 473.
35. Marston, "Marie Bryant."
36. Wendy Perron, "Syvilla Fort (1917–1975)," blog, October 2, 2020, https://wendyperron.com/syvilla-fort-1917-1975/.
37. Wasserman, "An Homage to Marie Bryant." The substitution of Bryant for Dunham is confirmed in Billy Rower, "Little Shots about Big Shots," *Pittsburgh Courier*, October 3, 1942, 20, Dunham's Data: Katherine Dunham and Digital Methods for Dance Historical Inquiry, https://dunhamsdata.org/. My thanks to Harmony Bench for locating and sharing the Rower article. Rower writes, "Marie Bryant, who so superbly filled Katherine Dunham's spot in the La Fiesta Show, has dropped out for a spell to present her heart-warmer with a little draft exemption," possibly a reference to the birth of her daughter.
38. Wasserman, "An Homage to Marie Bryant"; Marston, "Marie Bryant." Because a soundie (a short musical number) of "Bli Blip" was recorded, footage of Bryant and White can be found on YouTube at https://www.youtube.com/watch?v=r28Gmaji7-g, accessed April 30, 2024. In it, the pair sing a rhythmic scat with exaggerated facial expressions before breaking into a swinging jazz-tap duet, in which Bryant's Africanist angularity, playful looseness, and exquisite bodily control are on vivid display.
39. Bogle, *Bright Boulevards*, 196.
40. An oral history of Black chorus girl, journalist, and political activist Alice Key explains how the proximity of Los Angeles's Cotton Club to Hollywood "allowed the dancers to acquire small parts in Hollywood movies." "An Interview with Alice Key," an oral history conducted by Claytee White, Las Vegas Women in Gaming and Entertainment Oral History Project, University of Nevada, Las Vegas, 1998, vi.
41. Social Networks and Archival Content, "Bryant, Marie." For more on *The Duke Is Tops*, see Knight, *Disintegrating the Musical*, 169–170, 174–189.
42. See Susan Delson, *Soundies and the Changing Image of Black Americans on Screen: One Dime at a Time* (Bloomington: Indiana University Press, 2021).
43. See a clip of Bryant and Bluett on the Lennie Bluett tribute uploaded to YouTube: https://www.youtube.com/watch?v=4ssRtjszWkk, accessed July 18, 2023.
44. Prescod, "Marie Bryant," 72; Social Networks and Archival Content, "Bryant, Marie." The white jazz producer Norman Granz, another of Bryant's friends, with whom she was romantically linked at one point, served as musical advisor on *Jammin' the Blues*. They were reportedly dating when Granz was asked to recruit a singer who could dance to appear in the film. See Ted Hershorn, *Norman Granz: The Man Who Used Jazz for Justice* (Berkeley: University of

NOTES 219

California Press, 2011), 34–35, 37, 41, 67. For further analysis of *Jammin' the Blues*, see Knight, *Disintegrating the Musical*, 195–230.

45. Harry Levette, "This Is Hollywood," *Chicago Defender*, August 23, 1947, quoted in Charlene Regester, *Black Entertainers in African American Newspapers*, vol. 1, 551.

46. Marston, "Marie Bryant."

47. See Erigha's book by the same name, *The Hollywood Jim Crow*. See also Karen Alexander, "Fatal Beauties: Black Women in Hollywood," in *Stardom: Industry of Desire*, ed. Christine Gledhill (New York: Routledge, 1991), 46–57.

48. "Closing the Gap," sound recording, discussion by Acia Gray (as moderator), Jeni Le Gon, and Ernie Smith, recorded 2001, Performing Arts Research Collections, NYPL.

49. Nadine George-Graves, "Identity Politics and Political Will: Jeni LeGon Living in a Great Big Way," in *The Oxford Handbook of Dance and Politics*, ed. Rebekah Kowal, Gerald Siegmund, and Randy Martin (New York: Oxford University Press, 2017), 518.

50. Harris, "I Tried to Crash the Movies."

51. The "we" here was a "steady group of gals the studios called whenever they wanted colored extras, chorus cuties, or dancers." Harris names Alice Keyes (*sic*), Juliette Ball, Lucille O'Daniell, and Vivian Jackson. Ball appeared in *Cabin in the Sky* and *Stormy Weather*, Key in *Stormy Weather*. Jackson evidently appeared only in soundies, and O'Daniell never landed a film job.

52. Horne, whom I discuss further in relation to Bryant later in this chapter as well as in the coda, was permitted to move very little on screen, another manifestation of Hollywood's gendered racism. For more on Horne's on-screen performances, see, among others, Shane Vogel, "Lena Horne's Impersona," *Camera Obscura: Feminism, Culture, and Media Studies* 23, no. 1 (2008): 11–45; Richard Dyer, "Singing Prettily: Lena Horne in Hollywood," in *In the Space of a Song: The Uses of Song in Film*, by Richard Dyer (New York: Routledge, 2013), 114–144; Deborah Paredez, "Lena Horne and Judy Garland: Divas, Desire, and Discipline in the Civil Rights Era," *TDR/The Drama Review* 58, no. 4 (2014): 105–119; Pullen, *Like a Natural Woman*, 94–126.

53. Alan Marston reports that Twentieth Century-Fox signed Bryant to a "multiple contract" as an actress, singer-dancer, and choreographer in the 1940s and that she "intermittently assisted" both Hermes Pan and Jack Cole, though there is no record of her "deal file" in the Fox archives, nor have I been able to find documentation of her work with Pan or Cole (Marston, "Marie Bryant"; email from Matthew Younge, Clip & Licensing Still, Twentieth Century-Fox, October 30, 2018).

54. *Ebony*, "Movie Dance Director," 26.

55. Ibid., 22.

56. Ibid., 25.

57. Ibid.

58. Jackson, *Becoming Human*, 134. Jackson theorizes symbiosis in relation to Octavia Butler's 1984 speculative short story "Bloodchild," in which humans' survival depends on their ability to live in symbiotic relation to alien life. In Jackson's reading of Butler, symbiosis is productive in its emphasis on "the co-constitutive nature of embodied subjectivity and environment" and in its refiguring of embodied agency as interdependent and receptive (132). Yet Jackson also cautions against reading Butler's vision as "an unqualified endorsement of symbiosis," as some critics have claimed (129).

59. Bryant is quoted in Marston's "Marie Bryant" as saying, "Gene Kelly would send dancers to me to learn certain dance movements that only a few black dance teachers know how to teach. Those lessons kept me going many times during my on-again, off-again career."

60. Jackson, *Becoming Human*, 129.

61. See Karen Wallace, "The Redskin and *The Paleface*: Comedy on the Frontier," in Bernardi, *Classic Hollywood, Classic Whiteness*, 111–138.

62. The *Fancy Pants* Press Book housed at the Margaret Herrick Library at the Academy of Motion Picture Arts and Sciences in Beverly Hills, California (hereafter Herrick Library), contains the following: "In addition to having a favorite blonde and a favorite brunette, Bob Hope also has a favorite Indian. His name is Joseph Vitale and he plays a redskin. . . . A veteran character actor, Vitale actually comes from the sidewalks of New York. But he was cast as an Indian in 'The Paleface,' and Hope insisted that he be signed for a similar role in Fancy Pants."

63. See Chapter 1, note 75 on the variation in spellings of choreographer Billy Daniels's name.

220 NOTES

64. *Fancy Pants*, Budgets (Working Papers); *Fancy Pants*, costs (estimated) 1949, both in Herrick Library. That same year, Bryant worked with Daniels and Grant on the film *Love Happy*, and the pay gap was even more striking: budget records list Daniels's salary as $750 for a total of three weeks, Grant's at $173.30 for one week, and Bryant's (listed here as "special dance coach") at $70 for one week. Budget report, *Love Happy*, USC.

65. Fisher, *The Play in the System*, 21, 6. As Fisher notes, her "theory of parasitical resistance draws on a range of critical and aesthetic experiments with the parasite as an ambivalent and nonemancipatory figure of institutional and systemic critique and intervention," including the French philosopher Michel Serres (12).

66. *Ebony*, "Movie Dance Director," 22–23.

67. Bryant's "all that" here no doubt stands in for the full panoply of white people's physical reactions to the appearance of Black people in white spaces, which a Black readership would not need spelled out.

68. See also Stephanie Batiste's important discussion of "African Americans' fluency in dominant cultural forms that glorify nation, celebrate modernity, and emphasize the difference of others." Stephanie Leigh Batiste, *Darkening Mirrors: Imperial Representation in Depression-Era African American Performance* (Durham, NC: Duke University Press, 2012), 4.

69. Rayna Green, "The Pocahontas Perplex: The Image of Indian Women in American Culture," *Massachusetts Review* 16, no. 4 (Autumn 1975): 703.

70. Clara Sue Kidwell, "Indian Women as Cultural Mediators," *Ethnohistory* 39, no. 2 (Spring 1992): 101.

71. Shea Murphy, *The People Have Never Stopped Dancing*, 58. At the same time, Michelle Raheja points out, Pocahontas came to symbolize the "Indigenous whore-traitor," a trope that renders Native women "betrayers of their communities." Michelle H. Raheja, *Reservation Reelism: Redfacing, Visual Sovereignty, and Representations of Native Americans in Film* (Lincoln: University of Nebraska Press, 2010), 49.

72. Batiste, *Darkening Mirrors*, 117.

73. M. Elise Marubbio, *Killing the Indian Woman: Images of Native American Women in Film* (Lexington: University of Kentucky Press, 2006), 33.

74. For more on how "the analytics of anti-Black racism intersect with the analytics of settler colonialism," see especially King, Navarro, and Smith, *Otherwise Worlds*, 5–6.

75. Bryant and Young both performed in the *Sunset Strip Revue*, which ran for several months at the Mayan Theater in Los Angeles in fall 1948. Bryant appeared as a "torchy vocalist and in a torrid dance routine." *Los Angeles Times*, "'Sunset Strip Revue' Again Spotlights Comedian Vernon," November 29, 1948, 23, ProQuest Historical Newspapers, https://www.proquest.com/news/docview/165874559/7CDDA9CAB9FE4CFCPQ/2?accountid=14521&sourcetype=Historical%20Newspapers.

76. What may be part of a camera is partially in view on the left.

77. In 1954, Bryant described the class she taught for movie stars' wives to the *Sydney Morning Herald*: "I taught them body movement and, instead of giving them exercises that seemed like chores, I had them work to drums and Latin records—so they used up a lot more energy than they thought they did." "Gene Kelly's wife, and John Garfield's and Richard Conte's came to the classes," she added ("She Taught Dance Routines to the Stars"). In this same source, Bryant described Gardner as "a pretty earthy person" and explains that "for 'East Side West Side' there was a certain kind of walk she had to do. So I taught her." That scene may have been cut, for Gardner doesn't perform anything in the film that resembles this move.

78. While a fuller examination of the role of gifts in Hollywood's ecosystem is beyond this book's scope, it is worth noting that the handbag was far from the only gift Bryant received from her movie star friends and pupils. Bryant's former neighbor recalled her driving a used black Cadillac limousine that was a gift from "[singer] Kay Starr or [choreographers] Marge and Gower Champion" (email to Lockett, no author listed, dated July 8, 2000, Lockett files, NYPL). Given that Bryant was paid considerably less than officially named dance directors and also less than those directors' white assistants, we may well see the handbag from Grable as an acknowledgment of the inadequacy of Bryant's pay and of Grable's debts to her. See Chapter 3 for a fuller discussion of credit, debt, and reproductive labor.

79. *Ebony*, "Movie Dance Director," 24. Bryant told a reporter, "Paulette Goddard came to slim down and learn some movements for 'Anna Lucasta'—you know, the movie from the original Negro play" (*Sydney Morning Herald*, "She Taught Dance Routines to the Stars," 26).

NOTES 221

80. Kaplan, *The Black Reproductive*, 16. Kaplan defines "the Black reproductive" as "the constellation of national discourses, state policies, and individual practices through which Black reproductive acts, capacities, and labor have been imagined and administered in the United States for some 350 years" (3).

81. *Afro-American*, "White Woman Dances in Black," April 4, 1942, 13. The article also cites Bill Robinson's tutoring of Shirley Temple and Eleanor Powell as evidence of Hollywood's simultaneous dependence on and erasure of Black dance talent. My sincere gratitude to Harmony Bench, who passed along this article clipping to me.

82. Keeling, "Passing for Human," 244.

83. In Bryant's own words: "I've known Gene for so many years. I don't remember when we first met, but it was long before I came out here. I was still in New York then, with Duke" (Marston, "Marie Bryant"). See also Prescod, "Marie Bryant."

84. At various points in her career, Bryant was a resident performer at the Cotton Club in New York and a headliner at the Cotton Club in Los Angeles. See Prescod, "Marie Bryant." A May 1949 article described her as a "stage and nightclub star." *Los Angeles Sentinel*, "'Blues at Midnight' to Be Presented Saturday," May 13, 1948, 23, Proquest Historical Newspapers, https://www.proquest.com/news/docview/562169154/FDBD9049A73D45FEPQ/16?accountid=14521&sourcetype=Historical%20Newspapers. My sincere thanks to Debra Levine for sharing this article with me.

85. AD report, *On The Town*, USC.

86. Earl J. Hess and Pratibha A. Dabholkar, *Gene Kelly: The Making of a Creative Legend* (Lawrence: University Press of Kansas, 2020), 213.

87. Kelly's Mexican American assistant and dance-in Alex Romero played a critical role in developing the "Slaughter" jazz ballet; their relationship is the subject of Chapter 4.

88. As recently as 2018, Hollywood historian Bernard F. Dick asserted that it "ranks among the greatest examples of dance in the American movie musical." Bernard F. Dick, *That Was Entertainment: The Golden Age of the MGM Musical* (Jackson: University of Mississippi Press, 2018), 144.

89. Charles Samuels, "Vera-Ellen Took a Tumble—Yet Her Fall Sent Her Up!," *Motion Picture and Television Magazine*, nos. 83–84 (1952): 57.

90. Gene Kelly interview by Marilyn Hunt, conducted in Beverly Hills, California, on March 10–14, 1975, NYPL.

91. Samuels, "Vera-Ellen Took a Tumble," 57.

92. Email to Lockett, Lockett Files, NYPL.

93. Sherrie Tucker, *Dance Floor Democracy: The Social Geography of Memory at the Hollywood Canteen* (Durham, NC: Duke University Press, 2014), 66. Tucker writes, "In Los Angeles . . . from 1915 through World War II, there was one African American district in Los Angeles, stretching south from downtown along Central Avenue. In 1940, 70 percent of the 63,774 African Americans in Los Angeles lived in the section east of Main Street, then known as the Eastside and now known as South Central Los Angeles" (42). Other good sources on the Central Avenue district in the 1940s are Donald Bogle, *Bright Boulevards*; Clora Bryant et al., eds., *Central Avenue Sounds: Jazz in Los Angeles* (Berkeley: University of California Press, 1998). According to T. Grimes, "By 1950, the number of African Americans in Los Angeles had more than doubled in size to 171,209." "Historic Resources Associated with African Americans in Los Angeles," National Register of Historic Places, Multiple Property Documentation Form, March 17, 2009, accessed July 19, 2021, http://ohp.parks.ca.gov/pages/1067/files/resources%20associated%20with%20african%20american%20in%20la.pdf.

94. Quoted in Tucker, *Dance Floor Democracy*, 75.

95. See Michel de Certeau's *The Practice of Everyday Life*, trans. Steven Randall (Berkeley: University of California Press, 1984) on strategy versus tactics.

96. Debra Levine writes, "Cole's most distinctive and influential training facility . . . was the resident dance ensemble that he ran in Studio 10 at Columbia Pictures. In this rare halcyon moment for dance in Hollywood (circa 1944–48), dancers drew fulltime salaries, rehearsing and performing as members of a bona fide studio department." Debra Levine, "Jack Cole (1911–1974)," *Dance Heritage Coalition* (2012): 5, URL no longer active..

97. Hartman, "The Belly of the World." Hartman cites Tera Hunter, *To 'Joy My Freedom* (Cambridge, MA: Harvard University Press, 1997) and Thavolia Glymph, *Out of the House of Bondage* (Cambridge: Cambridge University Press, 2008).

222 NOTES

98. Hartman, "The Belly of the World," 170. While Bryant hosted pupils and clients in her living room by day, she hosted social gatherings by night. "She would work diligently from Monday through Friday mid-day," her neighbor recalled, and "then she would kick-back as the current expression puts it with a fifth of Courvoissier [sic] Cognac for the week-end. We would bring wine and whatever we wanted and would sit on pillows and talk through the night" (email to Lockett dated July 8, 2000, Lockett files, NYPL). Singer Bobby Short recalled going often to Bryant's house on the Eastside, "after work, late at night, [to] have drinks" (Bogle, *Bright Boulevards*, 242).

99. Samuels, "Vera-Ellen Took a Tumble," 57.

100. *Ebony*, "Movie Dance Director," 23.

101. American School of Dance News, "Marie Bryant: Boogie at the Barre" (Summer 1950), Eugene Loring Papers, UC Irvine Special Collections, box 9, Langson Library, Irvine, California. While a note in the Eugene Loring Papers indicates that the photo was taken by Ira Doud Jr., Barbara Plunk, who worked with Loring in his Hollywood days and took many photos at his American School of Dance, believes that she took the photo. Plunk also identified the studio in the photo as the Garden Court Apartments, which Loring rented on a yearly basis (email from Rita Marks, July 29, 2024). My gratitude to Barbara Plunk for her permission to use the photo, as well as Rita Marks and Jennifer Fisher, who put me in touch with Plunk.

102. Samuels, "Vera-Ellen Took a Tumble," 57.

103. Vera-Ellen, "The Role I Liked Best," *Saturday Evening Post*, November 1951, 107.

104. Samuels, "Vera-Ellen Took a Tumble"; Carla Valderrama, *This Was Hollywood: Forgotten Stars and Stories* (New York: Running, 2020), 196. Valderrama writes, "As a result of 'Slaughter on Tenth Avenue,' Vera was hired for the new Marx Brothers film *Love Happy* (1949). She was then paired with Gene Kelly again for *On the Town* (1949). The success of *On the Town* cemented Vera's status as a movie star, and after she danced with Fred Astaire in *Three Little Words* (1950), MGM signed her to a long-term contract" (196).

105. *The Argus* (Melbourne), "Talk-About," October 11, 1954, 10, http://trove.nla.gov.au/ndp/del/article/23445043.

106. Johnson, "Casualties."

107. A similar thing could be said of Vera-Ellen's performance in *Love Happy* (1949), a backstage musical starring the Marx Brothers, which was her next film role after *Words and Music*. In what seems unlikely to have been a coincidence, Bryant also worked on the film, this time as an AD to Billy Daniels and "special dance coach," presumably to Vera-Ellen (Production Records, *Love Happy*, USC). Vera-Ellen plays Maggie, a ballerina and Harpo's love interest. Early in the film we see her rehearsing ballet work on pointe, but a short while later she performs with a chorus of men dancers dressed in sailor suits in what the film refers to as the "Sadie Thompson number," a reference to a fictional character from a 1921 W. Somerset Maugham story about a prostitute who causes a man's downfall in the South Seas. A three-and-a-half-minute jazz dance, the number is full of slinky walks, hip rolls, and arm-flailing torso pulses, peppered with partner lifts. Two minutes in, the jazzy score is replaced briefly by a pulsing drum beat, which Vera-Ellen responds to with more frenzied movements, as a group of bare-chested men clearly intended to be "natives" join her.

108. Jeanine Basinger is less diplomatic. "[T]he inexplicable Vera-Ellen," she writes. "She couldn't act. She was a mediocre dancer. Her singing had to be dubbed. And she was anorexic. Yet she became a star. Not a big star, admittedly, but still, a star" (*The Star Machine*, 120).

109. Given the praise that was heaped on Vera-Ellen for these performances, it's hard not to think of scholar Koritha Mitchell's incisive analysis of "how often white mediocrity is treated as merit." Koritha Mitchell, "Identifying White Mediocrity and Know-Your-Place Aggression: A Form of Self-Care," *African American Review* 51, no. 4 (2018): 254.

110. Ibid., 257.

111. *Words and Music* filming was completed in fall 1948, while *On the Town* filming was completed in summer 1949. Cynthia Brideson and Sara Brideson, *He's Got Rhythm: The Life and Career of Gene Kelly* (Lexington: University Press of Kentucky, 2017), 210, 229.

112. While surely a coincidence, there is a certain irony in the fact that Bates returned to the MGM set for looping on the same day as Bryant.

113. In a chapter of her book *Native Shoals* that reads the images of Black bodies on a 1757 map of a coastal South Carolina indigo plantation in tandem with the indigo-stained hands depicted in Julie Dash's 1991 film *Daughters of the Dust*, King writes that the forms on the map's landscape are "dynamic, unstable, and therefore opaque Black figures [that] are beyond full knowability

NOTES 223

and containability." Tiffany Lethabo King, *The Black Shoals: Offshore Formations of Black and Native Studies* (Durham, NC: Duke University Press, 2019), 139.

114. Samuels, "Vera-Ellen Took a Tumble," 57.
115. Wasserman, "An Homage to Marie Bryant"; Prescod, "Marie Bryant," 73.
116. See Buckley, *The Hornes*, 150.
117. There was some consensus that Horne was not the greatest dancer. Choreographer Jeni LeGon, for example, told Horne biographer James Gavin, "She moved awkwardly. She was a better singer" (*Stormy Weather*, 107). And a review of Horne's appearance in the 1948 film *Words and Music*, in which she performed "The Lady Is a Tramp," was headlined "Lena Can't Dance but She's Great in Musical." Delores Calvin, *Baltimore Afro-American*, January 15, 1949, 7. See the coda for further discussion of Horne's dancing.
118. Gavin, *Stormy Weather*, 233, 235, 237, 242; Buckley, *The Hornes*, 221, 222; Vogel, "Lena Horne's Impersona," 21.
119. Email to Lockett, July 4, 2000, Lockett files, NYPL.
120. Gavin, *Stormy Weather*, 261.
121. On Graham's Orientalism, see, Victoria Phillips, *Martha Graham's Cold War: The Dance of American Diplomacy* (New York: Oxford University Press, 2020). In the early 1950s, Bryant married the Indian-born John Rajkumar, and according to an article titled "Rajkumari Marie Bryant," he taught her classical Indian dance while she taught him American dances like the Shim Sham Shimmie. The article includes photographs of Bryant posing with her hands forming mudras (clipping, Lockett files, NYPL).
122. Al Freeman, "It's Colossal Job to Set Up TV Network Show from Resort Hotel," *Las Vegas Review Journal*, September 29, 1957, 21–22. My thanks to librarian Stacey Fott at the Special Collections and Archives, University of Nevada, Las Vegas, for her assistance locating this article.
123. Maria Cole (as Mrs. Nat King Cole), "Why I Am Returning to Show Business," *Ebony* 21 (January 1966): 45–52.
124. Ibid., 48.
125. Bob Lucas, "Las Vegas Triumph Sets Maria Cole on New Career," *Los Angeles Sentinel*, December 8, 1966, A1, ProQuest Historical Newspapers, https://www.proquest.com/news/docview/564803789/1C446B4C3D9B4DC1PQ/133?accountid=14521&sourcetype=Historical%20Newspapers. My thanks to Debra Levine for this article.
126. Bryant also "polished" acts for the Black jazz singer Abbey Lincoln and the white vocalist Kay Thomas. Dom Cerulli, "The Arrival of Abbey," *Downbeat*, June 12, 1958, 19. Bryant died of cancer in Los Angeles in 1978 at the age of fifty-nine.
127. See Brannum, *As the Flesh Moves* on "polish" at Motown's "finishing school" in the 1960s.
128. See Amber Jamilla Musser, "Surface-Becoming: Lyle Ashton Harris and Brown Jouissance," *Women & Performance: A Journal of Feminist Theory* 28, no. 1 (2018): 34–45; Musser, *Sensual Excess*, 2. In both the essay and the book, Musser proposes a theory of embodiment for Black and brown femmes that emerges from thinking through fleshiness and sensual ways of knowing.
129. See Jennifer Nash on the concern a number of Black feminist scholars have expressed "with the material labor Black women perform in institutionalizing Black feminist studies—labor which ... quite often kills Black women academics" ("Citational Desires," 77).

Chapter 3

1. Clover, "Dancin' in the Rain," 723, 742, 737.
2. Clover ("Dancin' in the Rain," 724) cites Rudy Behlmer's assertion that Gene Kelly post-dubbed all of Reynolds's tap sounds for the "Good Morning" number; Rudy Behlmer, *America's Favorite Movies: Behind the Scenes* (New York: Frederick Ungar, 1982), 267. But *Singin' in the Rain* production records housed in the Arthur Freed Collection at USC indicate that Carol Haney recorded some of the tap sounds for "Good Morning." The recording notes for production of the musical number "You Were Meant for Me," in which Reynolds and Kelly dance together, read, "Taps (Carol alone) leather shoes."
3. Peter Wollen, *Singin' in the Rain* (London: British Film Institute, 1992), 57. See also Cohan, *Incongruous Entertainment*, 186–187. On the gender politics of authenticity in the film, see Cohan, *Incongruous Entertainment*, 194; Stephen Prock, "Music, Gender and the Politics of Performance in *Singin' in the Rain*," *Colby Quarterly* 36, no. 4 (December 2000): 295–318.

224 NOTES

4. Coyne's marriage to Donen lasted from 1948 to 1951. She was married to Kelly from 1960 until her death in 1973.

5. In addition to scholarship cited throughout this essay, the vast literature on *Singin' in the Rain* includes Silverman, *The Acoustic Mirror*, 45–47, 57; Ruth Johnston, "Technologically Produced Forms of Drag in *Singin' in the Rain* and *Radio Days*," *Quarterly Review of Film and Video* 21, no. 2 (2004): 119–129; Janice La Pointe-Crump, "The Dancer, Dance, and Viewer Dialogues," *Interdisciplinary Humanities* 21, no. 1 (Spring 2004): 62–77; Beth Genné, "Dancin' in the Rain: Gene Kelly's Musical Films," in *Envisioning Dance on Film and Video,* ed. Judy Mitoma, Elizabeth Zimmer, and Dale Ann Stieber (New York: Routledge, 2003), 71–77; Jane Feuer, "*Singin' in the Rain*: Winking at the Audience," in *Film Analysis: A Norton Reader,* ed. Jeffrey Geiger and R. L. Rutsky (New York: W. W. Norton, 2005), 440–456; Steven Cohan, "Case Study: Interpreting *Singin' in the Rain*," in *Reinventing Film Studies,* ed. Christine Gledhill and Linda Williams (New York: Oxford University Press, 2000), 53–75; Peter N. Chumo, "Dance, Flexibility, and the Renewal of Genre in *Singin' in the Rain*," *Cinema Journal* 36, no. 1 (1996): 39–54. See also Hanson, "Looking for Lela Simone," which analyzes the technical labor of Lela Simone in the production of sound for the film's title number.

6. As such, this essay departs from Jane Feuer's contention that, "[a]side from providing amusing anecdotes, the knowledge that . . . Debbie Reynolds did not know how to dance before this film might be construed not just as irrelevant to an interpretation of the film but as a positive hindrance to reading the film" ("*Singin' in the Rain*," 496).

7. Steven Harney and Fred Moten, *The Undercommons: Fugitive Planning and Black Study* (New York: Minor Compositions, 2013), 63.

8. David Graeber, *Debt, the First 5,000 Years* (New York: Melville, 2011), 4–5; Miranda Joseph, *Debt to Society: Accounting for Life under Capitalism* (Minneapolis: University of Minnesota Press, 2014), ix. See also Maurizio Lazzarato, *The Making of the Indebted Man: An Essay on the Neoliberal Condition*, trans. Joshua David Jordan (Los Angeles: Semiotext(e), 2012).

9. Paula Chakravartty and Denise Ferreira da Silva, "Accumulation, Dispossession, and Debt: The Racial Logic of Global Capitalism—An Introduction," *American Quarterly* 64, no. 3 (September 2012): 361–385. Da Silva's 2022 book *Unpayable Debt* offers a far-reaching critique of "the racial dialectic [that] renders . . . 'subprime' borrowers the owners of a debt that is not theirs to pay in the same way it renders the murdered unarmed black person responsible for their killing" (155).

10. Fred Moten, "The Subprime and the Beautiful," *African Identities* 11, no. 2 (2013): 237–245.

11. Stephen M. Best, *The Fugitive's Properties: Law and the Poetics of Possession* (Chicago: University of Chicago Press, 2004); Hartman, *Scenes of Subjection*, 130–134.

12. Amaryah Shaye, "Blackness and Value; Part 2: On Whiteness as Credit," *Women in Theology*, blog, February 11, 2015, https://womenintheology.org/2015/02/11/blackness-and-value-part-2-on-whiteness-as-credit/.

13. Eula Biss, "White Debt," *New York Times Magazine*, December 2, 2015, https://www.nytimes.com/2015/12/06/magazine/white-debt.html?_r=1.

14. Harney and Moten, *The Undercommons*, 61.

15. Foster, *Valuing Dance*, 18.

16. Noland, *Agency and Embodiment*, 13.

17. Clover, "Dancin' in the Rain," 727–728, emphasis in original. See also Kraut, *Choreographing Copyright*, 127–164.

18. See, among others, Gottschild, *Digging the Africanist Presence in American Performance*; Manning, *Modern Dance, Negro Dance*; Shea Murphy, *The People Have Never Stopped Dancing*; Srinivasan, *Sweating Saris*; Sally Banes, *Dancing Women: Female Bodies on Stage* (New York: Routledge, 1998); Carrie Gaiser Casey, "Ballet's Feminisms: Genealogy and Gender in Twentieth-Century American Ballet History" (PhD diss., University of California, Berkeley, 2009).

19. See this book's introduction for a fuller discussion of "the body" as a racial project.

20. Dodds, *Dance on Screen*, 1.

21. Hess and Dabholkar, *Singin' in the Rain*, 48, 50.

22. Behlmer, *America's Favorite Movies*, 260.

23. John Mariani, "Come on with the Rain," *Film Comment* 14, no. 3 (May–June 1978): 9.

24. Prock, "Music, Gender and the Politics of Performance," 295. Hess and Dabholkar also identify Mayer as the "moving force" behind Reynolds's selection, part of the studio's "policy of grooming young talent for star status" (*Singin' in the Rain*, 48, 50, 52). Gene Kelly insisted that the idea that Mayer "foisted" Reynolds on him was "patently untrue" and noted that Mayer was not even the

NOTES 225

head of MGM at the time *Singin' in the Rain* was made. He resigned in August 1951 (Fantle and Johnson, *Reel to Real*, 71).

25. Sumiko Higashi, *Stars, Fans, and Consumption in the 1950s: Reading Photoplay* (New York: Palgrave, 2014), 47.

26. Debbie Reynolds with David Patrick Columbia, *Debbie: My Life* (New York: William Morrow, 1988), 87.

27. *Singin' in the Rain* AD reports, USC.

28. Hess and Dabholkar, *Singin' in the Rain*, 73.

29. See, for example, Rudy Behlmer's commentary on the 2002 DVD version of the film. *Singin' in the Rain* (1952), Warner Home Video.

30. See, among others, Tony Thomas, *That's Dancing!* (New York: Harry N. Abrams, 1984), 46; Debbie Reynolds and Dorian Hannaway, *Unsinkable: A Memoir* (New York: HarperCollins, 2013), 206.

31. Joseph, *Debt to Society*, x.

32. One exception to this marginalization of Haney and Coyne in Reynolds's transformation is the assertion by Kelly's widow, Patricia Ward Kelly, "I think [dance assistants] Carol Haney and Jeannie Coyne, working with her day in and day out in a lot of the rehearsals, helped her to advance." Daniel Bubbeo, "Gene Kelly's Widow Chats about Her Late Husband and *Singin' in the Rain*," *Newsday*, July 11, 2012, https://www.newsday.com/entertainment/movies/gene-kelly-s-widow-patricia-chats-about-her-late-husband-and-singin-in-the-rain-1.3832472.

33. Reynolds and Columbia, *Debbie*, 92; Reynolds and Hannaway, *Unsinkable*, 206.

34. Chambers-Letson, "Performance's Mode of Reproduction I," 126, 140.

35. Ibid., 141.

36. Janet O'Shea, "Roots/Routes of Dance Studies," in *The Routledge Dance Studies Reader*, 2nd edition, ed. Alexandra Carter and Janet O'Shea (New York: Routledge, 2010), 11.

37. Manning, *Modern Dance, Negro Dance*, xi, xx–xxi.

38. Casey, "Ballet's Feminisms," 7.

39. See, for example, Erin Hill's study of "women's work" in Hollywood in *Never Done*. My thanks to Kristen Hatch for bringing this text to my attention.

40. Roach, *Cities of the Dead*, 25.

41. Chambers-Letson, "Performance's Mode of Reproduction I," 141.

42. See Weinbaum, *Wayward Reproductions* on the different racial implications of competing ideas of genealogy: "the idea of 'pure' genealogy (that which is based upon the repression of interracial reproduction) . . . [and] as a form of critical genealogy (that which apprehends the ruse of racial 'purity,' and thus the uncomfortable things selectively repressed by would-be white nationals)" (42). See also Rebecca Chaleff, "Choreographic Legacies: (DIS) Embodied Assemblages of Queer and Colonial Histories" (PhD diss., Stanford University, 2017).

43. Hill, *Never Done*. Rosalyn Diprose also notes the tendency to forget "the gifts of women while memorializing those of men" in *Corporeal Generosity: On Giving with Nietzsche, Merleau-Ponty, and Levinas* (Albany: State University of New York Press, 2002), 10.

44. My thanks to Bliss Cua Lim for pointing this out to me.

45. Weinbaum, *The Afterlife of Reproductive Slavery*, 18–25, 7, 31. Weinbaum specifically cites Black feminist critics like Toni Morrison and Dorothy Roberts and Black legal scholars like Anita L. Allen and Patricia J. Williams.

46. *Singin' in the Rain* Budget, USC.

47. Haney herself had considerable experience as a dance-in. Her obituary notes, "She once said she had danced miles as a stand-in for VeraEllen [*sic*]." *New York Times*, "Carol Haney, 'Pajama Game' Dancer, Dies at 39," May 12, 1964, 37.

48. Stephen Watts, "On Arranging Terpsichore for the Camera Eye," *New York Times*, September 14, 1952, 5.

49. Lowell Redelings, "The Hollywood Scene," *Hollywood Citizen-News*, September 13, 1954; Gene Kelly Biography File, Herrick Library.

50. AD report, *Singin' in the Rain*, USC. Production records indicate that Alma Maison was Reynolds's stand-in.

51. Johnson, "Casualties," 169.

52. Reynolds and Columbia, *Debbie*, 87–88.

53. Reynolds and Hannaway, *Unsinkable*, 206; Peter Fitzgerald, *What a Glorious Feeling: The Making of* "Singin' in the Rain," DVD, Turner Entertainment/Warner Home Video/Fitzfilm, 2002.

54. See, for example, Johnston, "Technologically Produced Forms of Drag."

226 NOTES

55. Among other flaws, this genealogy overlooks Katherine Dunham's role in the formation of jazz dance. See Saroya Corbett, "Katherine Dunham's Mark on Jazz Dance," in *Jazz Dance: A History of the Roots and Branches*, ed. Lindsay Guarino and Wendy Oliver (Gainesville: University Press of Florida, 2014), 89–96.

56. On Cole, see Loney, *Unsung Genius*; Hill, "From Bharata Natyam to Bop"; Levine, "Jack Cole"; Adrienne McLean, "The Thousand Ways There Are to Move: Camp and Oriental Dance in the Hollywood Musicals of Jack Cole," in *Visions of the East: Orientalism in Film*, ed. Matthew Bernstein and Gaylyn Studlar (New Brunswick, NJ: Rutgers University Press, 1997), 130–157; Rohini Acharya and Eric Kaufman, "Turns of 'Fate': Jack Cole, Jazz and Bharata Natyam in Diasporic Translation," *Studies in Musical Theatre* 13, no. 1 (March 2019): 9–21.

57. Lisa Jo Sagolla, "Carol Haney," *American National Biography*, February 2000, https://doi.org/10.1093/anb/9780198606697.article.1800523.

58. Clover, "Dancin' in the Rain," 742.

59. As others have noted, *Singin' in the Rain* also repurposed songs that were written in the 1920s. See Clover, "Dancin' in the Rain," 724; Jane Feuer, *The Hollywood Musical*, 2nd edition (Bloomington: Indiana University Press, 1993), 51.

60. See Cohan, *Incongruous Entertainment*, 190–191, on the gendered drag in "Good Morning."

61. Like Jack Cole, Gene Kelly trained in Spanish dancing with Paco Cansino (also known as Angel Cansino). See Brideson and Brideson, *He's Got Rhythm*, 46.

62. Production records refer to these sections as "Hula—Spanish—Charleston," box 23, folder 1, "Musical Numbers for 'Singin' in the Rain,'" USC.

63. Brown, *Babylon Girls*, 3.

64. Knox, *The Magic Factory*, 135–136. In her memoir, Leslie Caron describes the rehearsal process with Haney and Coyne as follows: "Because I was trained in classical ballet, I kept reverting to the formal movements automatically. Hour after hour the two girls, Jeannie and Carol, had to restrain me, saying, 'Bend your knees, Leslie! Keep your feet forward! Forget your second position! Loosen up your arms!' I kept trying to copy Carol Haney, who danced with powerful, voluptuous grace." Leslie Caron, *Thank Heaven: A Memoir* (New York: Viking, 2009), 62.

65. She also appears as one of the "Do Do Dee Oh" singing girls (on the viewer's far right) in the "Beautiful Girls" montage.

66. Here I follow the lead of Brenda Dixon Gottschild, not only in her delineation of Africanist aesthetics but also in her method of comparing two different dancers' embodiments of the same posture, which she does compellingly by juxtaposing photographs of Russian-born ballet choreographer George Balanchine alongside African American dancer Arthur Mitchell in one image and European-born dancer Violette Verdy in another. See Gottschild, *Digging the Africanist Presence*.

67. *Singin' in the Rain* DVD.

68. Clive Hirschhorn, *Gene Kelly: A Biography* (New York: St. Martin's Press, 1984), 190.

69. Reynolds and Columbia, *Debbie*, 96.

70. Elaine K. Ginsberg, "Introduction: The Politics of Passing," in *Passing and the Fictions of Identity*, ed. Elaine K. Ginsberg (Durham, NC: Duke University Press, 1996), 3.

71. McLean, *Being Rita Hayworth*, 33. On how "stardom is like a masquerade," see also Sabrina Qiong Yu, "Performing Stardom: Star Studies in Transformation and Expansion," in *Revisiting Star Studies: Cultures, Themes and Methods*, ed. Sabrina Qiong Yu and Guy Austin (Edinburgh: Edinburgh University Press, 2017), 3.

72. Ginsberg, "Introduction," 2–3.

73. Mullen, "Optic White," 72.

74. Diprose, *Corporeal Generosity*, 8; Roach, *Cities of the Dead*, 6.

75. Shaye, "Blackness and Value."

76. Clover, "Dancin' in the Rain," 725.

77. Bonnie Honig reports that it is actually Reynolds's uncredited vocal double Betty Noyes who we hear in the curtain scene, but according to Hess and Dabholkar, Reynolds's solo version of "Singin' in the Rain" was one of three recordings of her voice that the film used. Bonnie Honig, "Epistemology of the Curtain: Sex, Sound, and Solidarity in *Singin' in the Rain* and *Sorry to Bother You*," *Cultural Critique* 121, no. 1 (2023): 24n10; Hess and Dabholkar, *Singin' in the Rain*, 145.

NOTES   227

78. As Kaja Silverman writes, the "specter of sexual heterogeneity is . . . raised only so that it can be exorcised" (*The Acoustic Mirror*, 47). For queer readings of Lina Lamont, see Cohan, *Incongruous Entertainment*, 242; Honig, "Epistemology of the Curtain."

79. Honig, "Epistemology of the Curtain," 1–2.

80. See Cohan, *Incongruous Entertainment*, 241; Alan Nadel, *Demographic Angst: Cultural Narratives and American Films of the 1950s* (New Brunswick, NJ: Rutgers University Press, 2017), 31–56. See also Martin Roth, who writes that Lamont is "the only center of negative energy" in *Singin' in the Rain*. Martin Roth, "Pulling the Plug on Lina Lamont," *Jump Cut* 35 (1990): 59–65.

81. Clover, "Dancin' in the Rain," 744.

82. Ibid., 724.

83. See note 2 in this chapter.

84. La Pointe-Crump, "The Dancer, Dance, and Viewer Dialogues," 71.

85. The Library of Congress only gives the date the photograph was added to *Look*'s library, not the date it was taken. See https://www.loc.gov/pictures/item/2021681227/, accessed March 18, 2024. The rehearsal photograph never actually appeared in *Look*. The only shot taken by Terrell during that assignment that ran was one of Kelly, solo, in a March 11, 1952, issue. Email correspondence with Jonathan Eaker, reference librarian, Prints & Photographs Division Library of Congress, August 9, 2023.

86. For analyses of the tension between artifice and authenticity in "You Were Meant for Me," see Cohan, "Case Study"; Feuer, "*Singin' in the Rain*"; Johnston, "Technologically Produced Forms of Drag."

87. Cohan, "Case Study," 57.

88. See the introduction and Chapter 1 for more on indexicality.

89. Cohan, *Incongruous Entertainment*, 241, 237; Pamela L. Caughie, "Audible Identities: Passing and Sound Technologies," *Humanities Research* 16, no. 1 (2010): 102; Rogin, *Blackface, White Noise*, 205.

90. Rogin, *Blackface, White Noise*, 205.

91. Cohan, *Incongruous Entertainment*, 237; Stephen R. Duncan, "Not Just Born Yesterday: Judy Holliday, the Red Scare, and the (Mis-)Uses of Hollywood's Blonde Bombshell Image," in *Smart Chicks on Screen: Representing Women's Intellect in Film and Television*, ed. Laura Mattoon D'Amore (New York: Rowman & Littlefield, 2014), 14.

92. See, especially, Jacobson, *Whiteness of a Different Color*; Brodkin, *How Jews Became White Folks*.

93. Higashi, *Stars, Fans, and Consumption in the 1950s*, 47.

94. Rogin, *Blackface, White Noise*, 205.

95. Karen McNally, *The Stardom Film: Creating the Hollywood Fairy Tale* (New York: Columbia University Press, 2021), 41. See also Andrew Buchman, "Developing the Screenplay for *Singin' in the Rain* (1952)," in *The Oxford Handbook of the Hollywood Musical*, ed. Dominic Broomfield-McHugh (New York: Oxford University Press, 2022), 307–324.

96. Rogin, *Blackface, White Noise*, 225.

97. Haney's embodiment of white femininity, however, was deemed not ideal enough for her to appear on film in the role of the temptress in the film's extended "Broadway Melody" number. According to Mariani, Kelly intended to cast Haney in the role eventually played by Cyd Charisse, but producer Freed "did not consider [Haney] beautiful enough for the part." Haney instead served as Charisse's dance-in (Mariani, "Come on with the Rain," 12; Hess and Dabholkar, *Singin' in the Rain*, 158).

98. Ella Shohat, "Ethnicities-in-Relation: Toward a Multicultural Reading of American Cinema," in *Unspeakable Images: Ethnicity and the American Cinema*, ed. Lester Friedman (Champaign: University of Illinois Press, 1991), 223, emphasis in original.

99. See Honig, "Epistemology of the Curtain" for a discussion of other curtain scenes in *Singin' in the Rain*.

100. Clover, "Dancin' in the Rain," 724.

101. Rita Moreno, *Rita Moreno: A Memoir* (New York: Celebra, 2013), 52–56, 64; Judy Kinberg, dir., "Rita Moreno, Jerome Robbins: Something to Dance About," American Masters Digital Archive (WNET), December 12, 2006, https://www.pbs.org/wnet/americanmasters/archive/interview/rita-moreno/.

102. Ovalle, *Dance and the Hollywood Latina*, 105.

228 NOTES

103. *Singin' in the Rain* scripts, USC. The former song was cut completely; the latter was later reduced to part of a montage (Hess and Dabholkar, *Singin' in the Rain*, 70–71, 101).

104. Academy of Motion Picture Arts and Sciences, "*Singin' in the Rain*," Collection Highlights, accessed January 23, 2025, https://www.oscars.org/collection-highlights/singin-rain?.

105. *Singin' in the Rain*, AD report, USC. In addition, a Filipino actor, referred to only as "Philippino" in looping notes housed in the USC archives, plays a servant who directs Reynolds's character to the proper entrance for performers at the party at producer R. F. Simpson's house.

106. Fred Russell, "Gossip of the Rialto," *Bridgeport Post*, February 4, 1968, 57, https://newspaper archive.com/bridgeport-post-feb-04-1968-p-57/.

107. For more on Carmelita Maracci, see Jennifer Dunning, "Carmelita Maracci, a Ballet Instructor and Choreographer," *New York Times*, August 3, 1987, D11, https://www.nytimes.com/1987/08/03/obituaries/carmelita-maracci-a-ballet-instructor-and-choreographer.html. Along with Lester Horton, Maracci was one of only a few white teachers to admit Black students into her West Coast dance classes. Yaël Tamar Lewin, *Night's Dancer: The Life of Janet Collins* (Middletown, CT: Wesleyan University Press, 2015), 96.

108. See also Ovalle, *Dance and the Hollywood Latina* on Spanish dancing's link to racial mobility.

109. Herrera, *Latin Numbers*, 60.

110. Ibid. In a related manner, Adrienne McLean argues that an "ambivalence" between ethnic specificity and American unmarkedness was a "constant" feature of the stardom of Rita Hayworth, who was born Margarita Cansino (*Being Rita Hayworth*, 36).

111. Jon Alpert and Matthew O'Neill, dirs., "The Latin Explosion: A New America," HBO, 2015; Moreno, *Rita Moreno*, 96.

112. Ovalle, *Dance and the Hollywood Latina*, 106. Moreno's recollections at the fiftieth-anniversary celebration complicate this assessment somewhat. Moreno reports that Kelly initially wanted to give her the "Colleen Moore kind of hairdo" that ended up on the dark-haired Cyd Charisse, and that the red wig was brought in when Moreno refused to have her hair bobbed, reportedly telling Kelly, "Cutting hair is not the custom in Puerto Rico." Academy of Motion Picture Arts and Sciences, "*Singin' in the Rain*," Collection Highlights, https://www.oscars.org/collection-highlights/singin-rain?fid=42051; Moreno, *Rita Moreno*, 96.

113. Patricia Mellencamp, "Making History: Julie Dash," *Frontiers: A Journal of Women Studies* 15, no. 1 (1994): 85.

114. Mary C. Beltrán, *Latina/o Stars in U.S. Eyes: The Making and Meanings of Film and TV Stardom* (Urbana: University of Illinois Press, 2009), 70–71; Reyes and Rubie, "Rita Moreno," in *Hispanics in Hollywood*, 520.

115. Mariani, "Come on with the Rain," 10.

116. Quoted in Beltrán, *Latina/o Stars in U.S. Eyes*, 65.

117. Ibid., 65, 63.

118. Moreno, *Rita Moreno*, 98.

Chapter 4

1. *Newsweek*, "Finklea & Austerlitz," 49–50.

2. Ibid, 50.

3. Billman, *Film Choreographers and Dance Directors*, 294–296. In an oral history conducted by dance scholar Heather Castillo, the ensemble dancer Roy Fitzell recalled Denise, who he worked with when she served as Charisse's dance-in on the 1957 film *Silk Stockings*, as a "wonderful dancer" and a "very strong ballet dancer." As Charisse's dance-in, Fitzell explained, Denise "would learn things and teach it to Cyd, as it happened in motion pictures," as well as rehearse choreography with the ensemble while Charisse was elsewhere on set—so much so that Fitzell had only one rehearsal with Charisse for the number "The Red Blues" prior to filming. Heather Castillo, "'Nice Work If You Could Get It': Dancing Ensembles in the Golden Age of Movie Musicals, 1940–1965" (MFA thesis, University of California, Irvine, 2009).

4. Knowles, *The Man Who Made the Jailhouse Rock*; Mary Roark, "Alex Romero, 94, Choreographer for Elvis in 'Jailhouse Rock," *Los Angeles Times*, September 18, 2007, B9.

5. Knowles, *The Man Who Made the Jailhouse Rock*, 55–56; Franceschina, *Hermes Pan*, 154–155.

6. Franceschina, *Hermes Pan*, 187, 279n4.

7. Knowles, *The Man Who Made the Jailhouse Rock*, 61.

8. Ibid., 77.

9. Ibid., 70.

10. Ibid., 111–113.

NOTES 229

11. In general, production records list Romero as assistant dance director. As I hope is clear by now, assistant dance directors frequently if not always danced in for stars during rehearsals. Knowles does explicitly identify Romero as a dance-in for Kelly on *Take Me Out to the Ballgame*, choreographed by Busby Berkeley (ibid., 58). Writing for *Dance Magazine*, Viola Hegyi Swisher also describes Romero as a dance-in for Kelly for the 1967 televised movie *Jack and the Beanstalk*. Viola Hegyi Swisher, "Gene and Jack and the Beanstalk," *Dance Magazine* 41, no. 2 (February 1967): 52–53. And Gene Kelly's widow identifies Romero as Kelly's dance-in on *That's Entertainment II* (1976). Patricia Ward Kelly, Facebook post, October 7, 2017, https://www.facebook.com/photo.php?fbid=10159537747250061&set=p.10159537747250061&type=3&theater.

12. Knowles, *The Man Who Made the Jailhouse Rock*, 171n5, 50; Tim Dirks, "AFI's Greatest Movie Musicals," AMC Filmsite, accessed January 23, 2025, https://www.filmsite.org/afi25musicals.html. As Knowles points out, it is practically impossible to identify with any certainty all of the films on which Romero worked, given how regularly he was asked to assist on an isolated film number (*The Man Who Made the Jailhouse Rock*, 4–5).

13. Krayenbuhl, "Dancing Race and Masculinity," 18–19; Cohan, *Incongruous Entertainment*, 150. See also Gene Kelly, "Dancing: A Man's Game," *Omnibus*, hosted by Alistair Cooke, produced by Robert Saudak, NBC, December 21, 1958; Clover, "Dancin' in the Rain"; David Anthony Gerstner, "Dancer from the Dance: Gene Kelly, Television, and the Beauty of Movement," *Velvet Light Trap*, no. 49 (Spring 2002), https://link.gale.com/apps/doc/A92589215/LitRC?u=ucri verside&sid=LitRC&xid=fe8c2665. Romero's dancing also raised suspicions about his masculinity, as Knowles conveys when he shares Romero's recollection that Elvis Presley once called him "one of those sissy boys" (*The Man Who Made the Jailhouse Rock*, 186n1).

14. Muñoz, *The Sense of Brown*, 33.

15. Eve Kosofsky Sedgwick, *Between Men: English Literature and Male Homosocial Desire* (1985; New York: Columbia University Press, 2016).

16. Clare Croft, "Introduction," in *Queer Dance: Meanings and Makings*, ed. Clare Croft (New York: Oxford University Press, 2017), 2, 6; Muñoz, *The Sense of Brown*, 33, 32.

17. See, for example, Cohan, *Incongruous Entertainment*; Alexander Doty, *Making Things Perfectly Queer* (Minneapolis: University of Minnesota Press, 1993); Wolf, "'We'll Always Be Bosom Buddies.'"

18. José Esteban Muñoz, "Race, Sex, and the Incommensurate: Gary Fisher with Eve Kosofsky Sedgwick," in *Queer Futures: Reconsidering Ethics, Activism, and the Political*, ed. Elahe Haschemi Yekani, Eveline Kilian, and Beatrice Michaelis (New York: Routledge, 2013), 113.

19. Kelly, Facebook post. The same post quotes Gene Kelly as saying that Hoctor was "the first female dance-in a male star ever had," though AD reports for *Singin' in the Rain* make it seem likely that Carol Haney often danced in for Kelly, if not in an official capacity. See Chapter 3.

20. Gene Kelly, Transcript of interview by Marilyn Hunt, 1975, *MGZMT 5-234, Jerome Robbins Dance Division, NYPL.

21. Knowles, *The Man Who Made the Jailhouse Rock*, 50–51.

22. Ibid., 51. In a 1994 interview for *Interview* magazine, Kelly was asked how he "would go about choreographing a dance" like "Slaughter." He replied, "We started out doing a Bolshoi thing, with a lot of magnificent lifts. I had a great assistant, Alex Romero, and we took turns lifting Vera-Ellen; she was great at that. Finally, we saw that we had some high spots but we had lost our story. So we threw out practically all of them and went into the story of the girl vamping the guy, and the bad guy coming in trying to get the girl and shooting her. It was interesting to do and less trouble than doing a thing where you start with an idea in your head." Gene Kelly, "And Now, the Real Kicker . . . ," interview with Graham Fuller, *Interview*, May 1994, 110–114, quote 112. Together, the various accounts of "Slaughter"'s creation underscore the sheer amount of time Romero, Kelly, and Vera-Ellen must have spent testing out different choreographic possibilities.

23. Knowles, *The Man Who Made the Jailhouse Rock*, 38–49.

24. Foster, "Dancing Bodies," 237, 240, 237–238, 238. See also Tomie Hahn's assertion, "The process of looking [in the transmission of dance from teacher to student] is inextricably bound to social structures and issues of desire" (*Sensational Knowledge*, 86).

25. Sedgwick, *Between Men*, 24. See also José Muñoz, *Disidentifications: Queers of Color and the Performance of Politics* (Minneapolis: University of Minnesota Press, 1999) for a model of subject formation that allows for "desire's coterminous relationship with identification" (13).

26. See also Angela K. Ahlgren, "Futari Tomo: A Queer Duet for Taiko," in Croft, *Queer Dance*, esp. 236–237, on the queer longing that can accompany wanting to move like an/other.

230 NOTES

27. The shift from Broadway to film also entailed a "racial retrenchment," as Carol Oja writes in her book about *On the Town*: whereas the Broadway version was notable for its racially integrated cast, which included the Japanese American Sono Osato as Ivy Smith and six African American chorus members, the film cast the white Vera-Ellen as Ivy and eliminated background players of color, save for the nightclub scenes in which Bryant appears. Carol J. Oja, *Bernstein Meets Broadway: Collaborative Art in a Time of War* (New York: Oxford University Press, 2014), 113. I address this racial retrenchment more directly in "Un/funny Business in *On the Town* (1949)."
28. Finding Aid to the Jon Brenneis Photograph Archive, Bancroft Library Staff, Bancroft Library, University of California, Berkeley.
29. While these negatives are filed in a Jon Brenneis Photograph Archive folder dated July 1949, other sources establish that Bernstein traveled to Los Angeles in early June 1949 and that filming of "A Day in New York" was completed on July 2. See Geoffrey Holden Block, *A Fine Romance: Adapting Broadway to Hollywood in the Studio System Era* (New York: Oxford University Press, 2023), 84–85.
30. AD reports, USC, for *On the Town* list "Lee Sneddon" instead of "Lee Scott."
31. Kelly, Transcript of interview by Hunt, NYPL.
32. See also Hermes Pan's characterization of Angie Blue as "putty-like," as discussed in Chapter 1.
33. Robyn Wiegman, "Eve's Triangles, or Queer Studies beside Itself," *differences* 26, no. 1 (2015): 58.
34. Sedgwick, *Between Men*, 16, 49; Wiegman, "Eve's Triangles," 58–59.
35. Wiegman, "Eve's Triangles," 59.
36. Sedgwick, *Between Men*, 25; Wiegman, "Eve's Triangles," 59.
37. Block, *A Fine Romance*, 87; Hess and Dabholkar, *Gene Kelly*, 229.
38. Hess and Dabholkar, *Gene Kelly*, 229.
39. Quoted in Shiovitz, *Behind the Screen*, 356. In effect from the 1930s to 1960s, the Production Code, also known as the Hays Code, was a moralistic set of guidelines designed to produce self-censorship by the major movie studios. See Block, *A Fine Romance*, 79–80, on the Code and the policing of the "Prehistoric Man" lyrics in *On the Town*. Hess and Dabholkar include an anecdote about how Kelly tried to outwit Code enforcers through charm during rehearsals for *An American in Paris* (*Gene Kelly*, 245–246). See Shiovitz, *Behind the Screen* for an analysis of how the Code served to disguise the perpetuation of blackface minstrelsy conventions.
40. Cohan, *Incongruous Entertainment*, 150–151.
41. Ibid., 193.
42. Ibid., 165.
43. Ibid., 188.
44. There is some discrepancy about whether Romero was replacing Sinatra or Munshin in "A Day in New York." In his biography of Romero, Knowles states plainly that Romero was doubling for Sinatra (*The Man Who Made the Jailhouse Rock*, 62). In his discussion of *On the Town*, Geoffrey Block seems to confirm this fact, remarking that Romero "bears a familial resemblance to Sinatra." But Block also misidentifies Romero as the dancer on the left and misidentifies Lee Scott (calling him Gene Scott) as the dancer on the right. In point of fact, in the sequence Block is writing about (the opening of "A Day in New York"), Romero is on the viewer's right, and Scott is on the viewer's left, and, at least to my eye, it is Scott who bears the stronger resemblance to Sinatra (Block, *A Fine Romance*, 86). According to Knowles, Romero suggested Scott to Kelly when Kelly asked for suggestions for "another guy about your size that can do this stuff" (quoted in Knowles, *The Man Who Made the Jailhouse Rock*, 62). Lee Scott (sometimes Lee Sneddon), in addition to studying ballet and tap, also trained with Jack Cole. He later became a choreographer for film, television, and nightclub acts (Billman, *Film Choreographers and Dance Directors*, 485).
45. Genne, *Dance Me a Song*, 211.
46. Groscup is misidentified as Jeanne Coyne in several sources, including ibid., 211.
47. This speculation is based on the *On the Town* AD reports at USC, which list the "rehearsal unit" for the dream ballet, originally titled "Lonely Town," as Vera-Ellen, Carol Haney, Marie Grosscup [*sic*], Gene Freedley, and Lee Sneddon. Lee Scott went by Lee Sneddon at times.
48. *On the Town* production records at USC also list Haney as a dance-in for Ann Miller.
49. Cohan, *Incongruous Entertainment*, 189.
50. Eichenbaum, "The Assistant," in *Masters of Movement*, 166.
51. I borrow the term "machinic practice" from Karen Tongson's analysis of karaoke as "an activity founded fundamentally on repetition." Karen Tongson, "Karaoke, Queer Theory, Queer

Performance," in *The Oxford Handbook of Music and Queerness*, ed. Fred Everett Maus and Sheila Whiteley (New York: Oxford University Press, 2022), 211, 213.

52. Harmony Bench, "Virtual Embodiment and the Materiality of Images," *Extensions: The Journal of Embodied Technology* 1 (2004). [Manuscript from author via personal communication, June 20, 2019.]

53. Eichenbaum, "The Assistant," 166.

54. Chisholm, "Missing Persons," 128, 125.

55. Rebecca Schneider, "Hello Dolly Well Hello Dolly: The Double and Its Theatre," in *Performance and Psychoanalysis*, ed. Adrian Kear and Patrick Campbell (New York: Routledge, 2001), 96, emphasis in original.

56. Ibid., 98. In her work on debates about reproduction in both cinema and genetic engineering, feminist film theorist Jackie Stacey likewise points to the "gendered history" of "mimetic dynamics" and the "traditionally feminized place of one who performs the image for the other" (*Cinematic Life of the Gene*, 104, 120).

57. Eichenbaum, "The Assistant," 166. Romero also tells Eichenbaum that Fred Astaire acknowledged his reliance on Romero to Arthur Freed, suggesting that this anxiety around authorship and originality was not monolithic (166).

58. Eve Kosofsky Sedgwick, *Epistemology of the Closet*, updated with a new preface (Berkeley: University of California Press, 2007), 3.

59. Honig, "Epistemology of the Curtain," 3.

60. Ibid, 2, 6.

61. Schneider, "Hello Dolly," 98.

62. Knowles, *The Man Who Made the Jailhouse Rock*, 86. For example, Knowles's biography includes an account of Romero "mimicking" Ginger Rogers's part "for her to follow" before "switch[ing] over to Astaire's part beside her" in the making of the 1949 *Barkleys of Broadway* and of learning and teaching both Mitzi Gaynor and Gene Kelly their parts in Jack Cole's choreography for *Les Girls* (55–56, 94).

63. Stacey, *Cinematic Life of the Gene*, 136. See also Jonathan Flatley's discussion of Andy Warhol's project of "likeness," which "made space for Warhol to conceive of attraction, affection and attachment without relying on the homo/hetero opposition so central to modern ideas of sexual identity and desire." Jonathan Flatley, *Like Andy Warhol* (Chicago: University of Chicago Press, 2017), 14. My thanks to Rebecca Chaleff for calling Flatley's text to my attention. Richard Meyer's analysis of "Warhol's clones" is also pertinent here. Meyer writes, "When a movie still of Elvis Presley seeks itself through Warholian repetition, it discovers a homoeroticism that its original Hollywood context could not acknowledge." Richard Meyer, "Warhol's Clones," *Yale Journal of Criticism* 7 (1994): 96. We might also see the dance-in as a site of homoerotically charged repetition, although a repetition that precedes rather than succeeds the "original Hollywood context," once again disrupting the chronology of original and copy.

64. Quoted in Rebecca Schneider, "Solo Solo Solo," in *After Criticism: New Responses to Art and Performance*, ed. Gavin Butt (Malden, MA: Blackwell, 2005), 26.

65. See also Homi Bhabha, "Of Mimicry and Man: The Ambivalence of Colonial Discourse," *October* 28 (1984): 125–133; Michael Taussig, *Mimesis and Alterity: A Particular History of the Senses* (New York: Routledge, 2018) on the racial dynamics of mimesis.

66. Clara E. Rodríguez, "Counting Latinos in the US Census," in *How the United States Racializes Latinos*, ed. José A. Cobas, Jorge Duany, and Joe R. Feagin (New York: Routledge, 2015), 40.

67. Alvarez, *The Power of the Zoot*, 16.

68. George J. Sánchez, *Becoming Mexican American: Ethnicity, Culture and Identity in Chicano Los Angeles, 1900–1945* (New York: Oxford University Press, 1993), 267.

69. Reyes and Rubie, *Hispanics in Hollywood*, 18–22; Herrera, *Latin Numbers*, 60.

70. Knowles, *The Man Who Made the Jailhouse Rock*, 10–11.

71. There is some ambiguity regarding Romero's birth year and birth location. Knowles reports that it is not clear if he was born in Monterrey, Mexico, or San Antonio, Texas, and not certain which year (*The Man Who Made the Jailhouse Rock*, 163–164n9). Romero told interviewer Rose Eichenbaum both that he was born in Mexico in 1913 and, in the same paragraph, that his mother was pregnant with him when they fled Mexico and he was born in San Antonio (*Masters of Movement*, 165). Billman reports that he was born in San Antonio in 1913 (*Film Choreographers and Directors*, 470).

232 NOTES

72. Eichenbaum, *Masters of Movement*, 165; Knowles, *The Man Who Made the Jailhouse Rock*, 7–15. According to Knowles, the Quiroga family lived at 3861 Second Avenue in Los Angeles in what today is part of Leimert Park (14). Though I have not been able to locate the family in any census records, it seems likely that Romero would have been counted as "Mexican" in 1930, and "white" but culturally Latino in 1940 and 1950 by virtue of his mother tongue and surname.

73. Knowles, *The Man Who Made the Jailhouse Rock*, 16; Roy Clark, "Alex Romero Compares Hollywood and Broadway," *Dance Magazine* 36 (1962): 45.

74. Billman, *Film Choreographers and Directors*, 471.

75. Anthony Macías, *Mexican American Mojo: Popular Music, Dance, and Urban Culture in Los Angeles, 1935–1968* (Durham, NC: Duke University Press, 2008), 11.

76. Knowles, *The Man Who Made the Jailhouse Rock*, 15, 43–44, 168n9, 173n14, 24–26.

77. Eichenbaum, *Masters of Movement*, 165–66.

78. Clark, "Alex Romero Compares Hollywood and Broadway," 45.

79. Knowles, *The Man Who Made the Jailhouse Rock*, 190n9. As such, Romero's career might bear similarities with that of the postwar light-skinned Mexican singer Andy Russell, about whom Paloma Martinez-Cruz writes, "With an Anglicized name, light complexion, and a sonically White performance profile, Russell serves as a counterpoint to radical Latino performance because he did not cut what might be described as an 'oppositional' path to the top of the charts." But, she maintains, "his serenely cheerful, bilingual self-representation" and his emphasis on his "Americanness" should not be equated with an assimilationist stance. Paloma Martinez-Cruz, "Unfixing the Race: Midcentury Sonic Latinidad in the Shadow of Hollywood," *Latino Studies* 14 (2016): 159.

80. Knowles, *The Man Who Made the Jailhouse Rock*, 95–96. As Anna Lvovsky documents, "The policing of so-called sexual deviance was part of a long tradition of morals regulations in the United States, pursued in the mid-twentieth century against a backdrop of heightened suspicions of sexual nonconformity as a threat to both public safety and national security." Anna Lvovsky, *Vice Patrol: Cops, Courts, and the Struggle over Urban Gay Life before Stonewall* (Chicago: University of Chicago Press, 2021), 7

81. See Roberto A. Mónico, "Los Angeles and William H. Parker: Race, Vice, and Police during the Red Scare" (PhD diss., University of Colorado at Boulder, 2022) on the restructuring of the LAPD in 1950 under Chief Willliam H. Parker and the ensuing "hyper-policing" of African Americans and Mexican descended Angelenos, as well as of gay men.

82. Alvarez, *Power of the Zoot*, 25–26; Macías, *Mexican American Mojo*, 135. Macías observes, "Even though Mexican Americans were relatively freer to move about a wider range of the city than African Americans were, doing so exposed them to further police discrimination" (95).

83. Herrera, *Latin Numbers*, 16.

84. On the privilege of being read as "unmarked" in dance, see Manning, *Modern Dance, Negro Dance*. Notably, Romero's nonethnic appearance in *On the Town* contrasts with the racialized and exoticized Latin dancers at the Club Sambacabaña, one of three nightclubs that the film's leads visit in quick succession (and the only locations where people of color seem to reside in the movie's diegetic New York). Although most of the Sambacabaña dancers are white-appearing, at least one has darker skin, as do the backing musicians. The AD's log for *On the Town* indicates a pause in filming the Sambacabaña scene to "fix body makeup on dancers" (USC). Between the Sambacabaña dancers and Romero, Latinas/os in *On the Town* thus exemplify the oscillation "between the normalcy of whiteness and the exoticism of blackness" that Priscilla Ovalle identifies as the "ambiguously racialized space" occupied by Latinas in Hollywood (*Dance and the Hollywood Latina*, 7).

85. Knowles, *The Man Who Made the Jailhouse Rock*, 42–45.

86. Manning, *Modern Dance, Negro Dance*, 10, 118.

87. Barrie Chase interview, May 8, 2019, Los Angeles.

88. Herrera, *Latin Numbers*, 60.

89. Note the consonance with other musical numbers deploying racist Native American tropes, such as "Home Cooking" in *Fancy Pants* (1950), discussed in Chapter 2.

90. Herrera, *Latin Numbers*, 60.

91. Krayenbuhl, "Dancing Race and Masculinity," 296, 126, 124.

92. Here I invoke Homi Bhabha's terms for the ambivalence of the colonized subject, who mimics but can never achieve the whiteness of the colonizer ("Of Mimicry and Man," 132). As I have been suggesting throughout, the relational schema of the dance-in required mimicry in two directions. In fact, as Krayenbuhl points out, Kelly darkened his skin for his role in *The Pirate*

NOTES 233

(1948), which was "likely a purposeful means of marking Kelly's character as 'Latin,' since he claims to come from Madrid" ("Dancing Race and Masculinity," 151–152). Romero and Kelly began working together after Kelly's appearance in *The Pirate*.

93. Clover, "Dancin' in the Rain," 738.

94. Eric Lott, *Love and Theft: Blackface Minstrelsy and the American Middle Class* (New York: Oxford University Press, 1993); Gottschild, *Digging the Africanist Presence*.

95. Herrera, *Latin Numbers*, 59.

96. Jill Dolan, *Utopia in Performance: Finding Hope at the Theater* (Ann Arbor: University of Michigan Press, 2010), 55, 87.

97. Muñoz, "Race, Sex, and the Incommensurate," 104, 110, 108, 111, 113, 112. My reading of Muñoz is informed and enriched by Joshua Chambers-Letson, *After the Party: A Manifesto for Queer of Color Life* (New York: New York University Press, 2018).

98. Eichenbaum, *Masters of Movement*, 166.

99. My thanks to Clare Croft for underscoring the importance of intimacy as a facet of the queer relations between dance-in and star.

100. Sedgwick points to love as one of psychoanalyst Melanie Klein's names for the reparative process, a practice not of suspicion but of "extracting sustenance from the objects of a culture—even of a culture whose avowed desire has been not to sustain them." Eve Kosofsky Sedgwick "Paranoid Reading and Reparative Reading, or You're So Paranoid, You Probably Think This Essay Is about You," in Eve Kosofsky Sedgwick, *Touching Feeling: Affect, Pedagogy, Performativity* (Durham, NC: Duke University Press, 2003), 150–151. Muñoz writes, "Love for Klein is . . . not just a romantic abstraction; it is . . . a kind of striving for belonging that does not ignore the various obstacles that the subject must overcome to achieve the most provisional belonging." José Esteban Muñoz, "Feeling Brown, Feeling Down: Latina Affect, the Performativity of Race, and the Depressive Position," *Signs: Journal of Women in Culture and Society* 31, no. 3 (2006): 683. This more complex love seems fitting for Romero, whose assertion of acceptance and forgiveness comes even as he recounts the story about Kelly's imposed closet. He "loved the man," but he was mindful of the incommensurability between them.

101. Knowles, *The Man Who Made the Jailhouse Rock*, 187n6.

102. Ibid., 188n6.

103. Billman, *Film Directors and Choreographers*, 476.

104. Clark, "Alex Romero Compares Hollywood and Broadway."

105. Ibid. Romero, Ruiz, also worked together on Vincente Minelli's 1962 film *The Four Horsemen of the Apocalypse*. Knowles writes, "Alex especially enjoyed working with Yvette Mimieux, whose father was French and whose mother was Mexican. Mimieux spoke fluent Spanish, and Alex and she had long conversations together during rehearsals" (*The Man Who Made the Jailhouse Rock*, 192n25).

106. Deborah Paredez, *Selenidad: Selena, Latinos, and the Performance of Memory* (Durham, NC: Duke University Press, 2009), 131.

Chapter 5

1. As I explain a little later in this chapter, I follow other Asian Americanists in using the slash between "Asian" and "American" to signal the complicated racialization of Asian diasporic subjects within and vis-à-vis the United States.

2. See Bruce A. McConachie, "The 'Oriental' Musicals of Rodgers and Hammerstein and the U.S. War in Southeast Asia," *Theatre Journal* 46 (1994) 385–398. Sean Metzger describes *Flower Drum Song* as "the pinnacle of the Chinese/American musical in the twentieth century at a historical moment when the genre had obtained widespread popularity on the domestic cultural scene." Sean Metzger, *Chinese Looks: Fashion, Performance, Race* (Bloomington: Indiana University Press, 2014), 181.

3. Larry Glenn, "'Flower Drum Song' Reprised Close to Home," *New York Times*, April 30, 1961, X9.

4. The use of the word "Caucasian" was rare in contemporaneous coverage of *Flower Drum Song*, even in reviews of the Broadway musical, in which the white Larry Blyden played a Chinese nightclub owner in yellowface. See, for example, Walter Kerr, "First Night Report: 'Flower Drum Song,'" *New York Herald Tribune*, December 2, 1958, 29; Brooks Atkinson, "'Flower Drum' Song Opens at St. James," *New York Times*, December 2, 1958, 44; Kenneth Tynan, "Tiny Chinese Minds," *New Yorker*, December 13, 1958, 104, 106.

234 NOTES

5. Ahmed, *Queer Phenomenology*, 161. I draw on Ahmed's theory of racialization as an operation that "orientates bodies in specific directions" throughout this chapter (111). My early thinking about Kwan was shaped by my participation in a 2018 American Society for Theatre Research Working Group titled "Between Orientalism and Orientation: Rethinking Arousal through East Asian Performance," led by Tara Rodman, Soo Ryon Yoon, and Kayla Ji Hyon Yuh.

6. See Dyer, *White* (especially 21), and Edward W. Said's *Orientalism* (1978; New York: Random House, 1994) on constructions of whiteness and Orientalism, respectively. *Flower Drum Song* did employ an Asian/American stand-in for Kwan, a woman named Esther Lee Johnson, who was clear about the direction in which cross-racial surrogation could take place: "I mean a Caucasian can portray as an Oriental but an Oriental can't, you know, do things like for a Caucasian." "Esther Lee Johnson: Actress and Hollywood Extra," PBS SoCal, June 30, 2010, https://www.kcet.org/shows/departures/esther-lee-johnson-actress-hollywood-extra.

7. Chang-Hee Kim, "Asian Performance on the Stage of American Empire in *Flower Drum Song*," *Cultural Critique* 85 (Fall 2013): 25.

8. Ibid., 30.

9. Anne Anlin Cheng, *The Melancholy of Race: Psychoanalysis, Assimilation, and Hidden Grief* (New York: Oxford University Press, 2000), 46, emphasis in original.

10. Klein, *Cold War Orientalism*, 236, 240.

11. Jennifer Leah Chan, "Transgressive Babymaking: Narratives of Reproduction and the Asian American Subject" (PhD diss., New York University, 2007), 124.

12. Kim, "Asian Performance," 27. For Kim, this narrative ending, in which Low is married off to the nightclub owner Sammy Fong, serves to "castrate" Kwan's character's "internalized desire to become a universal woman, by Western standards" (27).

13. Levinson, *Puttin' on the Ritz*, 269; Franceschina, *Hermes Pan*, 229. Angie Blue's last credit as Pan's assistant came in 1957 on the MGM film *Silk Stockings* (Billman, *Film Choreographers and Dance Directors*, 241).

14. Levinson, *Puttin' on the Ritz*, 269.

15. Howard, "Tough Trying to See 'Lady,'" 5.

16. Mainwaring, "Hollywood Nobodies," 137.

17. Interview with Barrie Chase, May 8, 2019, Los Angeles; Levinson, *Puttin' on the Ritz*, 269.

18. A 1959 article recorded Varno's height at 5'4" and contemporaneous reports list Kwan as 5'2". "Girl Dancers in Fred Astaire Show Watch Own Figures, Too," *Decatur Sunday Herald and Review*, November 1, 1959, 52; Jon Whitcomb, "A New Suzie Wong," *Cosmopolitan* 148 (June 1960): 12; Bill Davidson, "China Doll," *McCall's*, February 1962, 168. Whether by happenstance or at Kwan's request, Varno danced in for Kwan a second time, when Kwan appeared as a guest on a December 13, 1961, *Bob Hope Special*, in which she performed a jazzy number choreographed by Nick Castle. A "Presstime News" update in *Dance Magazine* reports that "Nick Castle, assisted by Jim Huntley, choreographed for Nancy Kwan, with Becky Varno as dance-in, on a recent Bob Hope TV show." "Presstime News," *Dance Magazine* 36, no. 1 (January 1962): 6. Kwan appears in both a comedy sketch and a dance number on the episode. My thanks to Jim Hardy, audiovisual archivist of Bob Hope Enterprises, for lending me a copy of the show for research purposes.

19. I discuss the concept and politics of indexicality more fully below, as well as in this book's introduction and Chapter 1.

20. See, among others, Knight, "Star Dances"; Regester, *African American Actresses*; Petty, *Stealing the Show*; Erigha, *The Hollywood Jim Crow*.

21. Kim, "Asian Performance," 25.

22. My use of "panethnic" is indebted to Anthony Ocampo, discussed below. On Asian American panethnicity more generally, see Yến Lê Espiritu, *Asian American Panethnicity: Bridging Institutions and Identities* (Philadelphia: Temple University Press, 1992).

23. Heidi Kim, "'Flower Drum Song,' Whitewashing, and Operation Wetback: A Message from 1961," *Los Angeles Review of Books*, September 22, 2016, https://lareviewofbooks.org/article/flower-drum-song-whitewashing-operation-wetback-message-1961/.

24. As Heidi Kim points out, in 1959 there were "five Asian-themed plays on Broadway" (ibid.).

25. Cheng, *Melancholy of Race*, 32.

26. Said's influential concept of Orientalism encapsulates how Western constructions of the East as feminized, exotic, and backward have justified centuries of European imperialism in the Middle East. See Said, *Orientalism*.

27. Klein, *Cold War Orientalism*, 5.

NOTES 235

28. McConachie, "The 'Oriental' Musicals of Rodgers and Hammerstein," 385–386, 398.
29. Klein, *Cold War Orientalism*, 225.
30. Josephine Lee, *Performing Asian America: Race and Ethnicity on the Contemporary Stage* (Philadelphia: Temple University Press, 1998), 2–3.
31. Kim, "Asian Performance on the Stage of American Empire," 2.
32. Ibid.
33. Lowe, *Immigrant Acts*; Shelley Sang-Hee Lee, *A New History of Asian America* (New York: Taylor & Francis, 2014), 259.
34. Wong, *Choreographing Asian America*, 15, 17; Robert G. Lee, *Orientals: Asian Americans in Popular Culture* (Philadelphia: Temple University Press, 1999), 10.
35. Kim, "Asian Performance on the Stage of American Empire," 7.
36. Ibid., 25. See also Sheng-mei Ma, "Rodgers and Hammerstein's 'Chopsticks' Musicals," *Literature/Film Quarterly* 31, no. 1 (2003): 17–26.
37. Lowe, *Immigrant Acts*, 5, 8.
38. Karen Shimakawa, *National Abjection: The Asian American Body Onstage* (Durham, NC: Duke University Press, 2002), 3.
39. Yutian Wong, "Introduction: Issues in Asian American Dance Studies," in *Contemporary Directions in Asian American Dance*, ed. Yutian Wong (Madison: University of Wisconsin Press, 2016), 3; Ju Yon Kim, *The Racial Mundane: Asian American Performance and the Embodied Everyday* (New York: New York University Press, 2015), 189, emphasis in original.
40. David Palumbo-Liu, *Asian/American: Historical Crossings of a Racial Frontier* (Stanford: Stanford University Press, 1999), 1.
41. Metzger, *Chinese Looks*, 9.
42. Mila Zuo, *Vulgar Beauty: Acting Chinese in the Global Sensorium* (Durham, NC: Duke University Press, 2022), 6.
43. See Jennifer Ann Ho, *Racial Ambiguity in Asian American Culture* (New Brunswick, NJ: Rutgers University Press, 2015); Yutian Wong, "Artistic Utopias: Michio Ito and the Trope of the International," in *Worlding Dance*, ed. Susan Leigh Foster (London: Palgrave Macmillan, 2009), 144–162.
44. Pete Martin, "Backstage with Nancy Kwan," *Saturday Evening Post*, February 10, 1962, 45.
45. While I have not been able to verify unequivocally that the woman adjusting Kwan's stole in this photograph is Varno, my estimation is based on the fact that Varno was Pan's primary female assistant on the film and on the resemblance between the woman in the photo and Varno's identification of herself as the dancer who does a kick over Fred Astaire's head in the "Night Train" number in *Another Evening with Fred Astaire*. Levinson, *Puttin' on the Ritz*, 269; *Another Evening with Fred Astaire*, Ava Productions, Inc., produced and directed by Bud Yorkin, November 4, 1959, UCLA Film & Television Archive. Hermes Pan biographer John Franceschina echoed my belief that it is Varno in the photo. Email correspondence, January 29, 2018.
46. Henry Koster, dir., *Flower Drum Song*, Universal Studios Home Entertainment, DVD, 2006.
47. Doane, "The Indexical and the Concept of Medium Specificity," 132, 136.
48. Julian Hanich, "Reflecting on Reflections: Cinema's Complex Mirror Shots," in *Indefinite Visions: Cinema and the Attractions of Uncertainty*, ed. Martine Beugnet, Allan Cameron, and Arild Fetveit (Edinburgh: Edinburgh University Press, 2017), 140; Christian Metz, "Mirrors" (1991), in *Impersonal Enunciation, or the Place of Film* (New York: Columbia University Press, 2016), 60.
49. Metz, "Mirrors," 61, 62.
50. There are two places in "I Enjoy Being a Girl" where these splices are readily detectable: around the 36:45 and 38:08 marks.
51. Hanich, "Reflecting on Reflections," 149.
52. *Flower Drum Song*'s cinematographer Russell Metty received an Academy Award nomination for his work on the film. Choreographer Hermes Pan staged breaks in indexicality in two prior numbers: in Fred Astaire's "Bojangles of Harlem" number in *Swing Time* (1936), in which Astaire's three silhouettes begin dancing out of synch with him, and in the televised special *Astaire Time* (1960), in which Astaire dances with the white twins Jane and Ruth Earl, who appear to be mirror reflections of one another until only the "reflection" does a double turn. See Franceschina, *Hermes Pan*, 80–81, 228. Franceschina's description of how the break was achieved in "Bojangles of Harlem" is helpful. RKO's camera-effects specialist Vernon Walker, Franceschina writes, explained, "All you do is get Astaire in front of a screen and photograph

236 NOTES

his shadows first. Then we take those shadows and make a split screen, and then we photograph Astaire doing the same routine in front of them" (81).

53. Koster, *Flower Drum Song*. For an interesting discussion of the indexical status of flies that accidentally end up on film or photograph, see Peter Geimer, "Image as Trace: Speculations about an Undead Paradigm," *differences* 18, no. 1 (2007): 7–28.

54. In their readings of *Flower Drum Song*, both Anne Cheng and Christina Klein assign weight to the play of mirrors in "I Enjoy Being a Girl," although they arrive at different conclusions about its implications. For Klein, the moment when Kwan's body produces three separate reflections is a "quasi-surreal" one that presents Linda Low as "the epitome of the assimilated, Americanized, Asian woman" insofar as she is no different "from any other Hollywood bombshell—Marilyn Monroe or Doris Day could perform this number without any real changes" (*Cold War Orientalism*, 237). Cheng also compares Kwan's performance in "I Enjoy Being a Girl" to Marilyn Monroe's scene in front of a three-way mirror in *How I Married a Millionaire* (1953) but finds that Kwan maintains a "remoteness from the [white female] norm of beauty" and that the filmic pleasure Kwan as Low takes in her reflections may "be less about 'being a girl' than about transforming the abject state of being a (racialized) girl into celebrated materiality" (*Melancholy of Race*, 54–55, 57). When Cheng turns her attention to the conditions of production for "I Enjoy Being a Girl," however, she arrives at a different assessment. Reading a production still of Kwan on set performing under the gaze of producer Ross Hunter and other crew members (not unlike Figure 5.2), Cheng concludes, "Linda might be enjoying the view of herself, but what Kwan the performer (with her voice dubbed over) saw was not herself but the watchful eyes of the camera and her producer" (57–58). My reading departs from Cheng's in that I see more continuity than discontinuity between the indexical uncertainty on display in "I Enjoy Being a Girl" and the indexical uncertainty surrounding the reproduction and status of Kwan's corporeality. Rather than arguing for or against Kwan's agency in this scene or throughout the film, I'm interested in how the acts of reproduction that shaped her corporeality and its image(s) did and did not cohere, and how and when that (in)coherence registered in racial terms. Stepping "outside of the frame," as Cheng suggests (58), I imagine that Kwan the actor-dancer may have seen not only the eyes of the white production team (including Pan's and Varno's) gazing at her but also a reflection of her own corporeal history, both the sediments that were part of its conditions of arrival and the orientations it acquired through her exchanges on *Flower Drum Song*.

55. Koster, *Flower Drum Song*; Richard Cromelin, "B. J. Baker, 74; Backed Top Singers of '50s, '60s," *Los Angeles Times*, April 13, 2002, https://www.latimes.com/archives/la-xpm-2002-apr-13-me-baker13-story.html.

56. Marni Nixon with Stephen Cole, *I Could Have Sung All Night: My Story* (New York: Billboard Books, 2006), 91–92.

57. Nina Sun Eidsheim, *The Race of Sound: Listening, Timbre, and Vocality in African American Music* (Durham, NC: Duke University Press, 2019), 23; Nixon, *I Could Have Sung*, 92. Nixon's description also bears some striking similarities to the mirroring process that Alex Romero describes as characteristic of his work as a choreographic assistant, as discussed in the previous chapter.

58. See Kathryn Kalinak, "Classical Hollywood, 1928–1946," in *Sound: Dialogue, Music, and Effects*, ed. Kathryn Kalinak (New Brunswick, NJ: Rutgers University Press, 2015), 37–58, on techniques of sound recording in classical Hollywood film. See Nathan Platte, "Postwar Hollywood, 1947–1967," in Kalinak, *Sound*, 64 on how the adoption of magnetic tape in the postwar years "simplified both production and postproduction."

59. Shiovitz, *Behind the Screen*, 13. The manipulation of sound to shape visual perception is what Shiovitz terms "the sonic guise."

60. Silverman, *The Acoustic Mirror*, 47, 46.

61. Koster, *Flower Drum Song*. In a 2014 Q&A following a screening of *Flower Drum Song* at the Monterey Park Bruggemeyer Library, film historian Foster Hirsch echoes Redman's assessment almost exactly: "Her voice sounds like it could come from you, which is good." Nick Goto, "*Flower Drum Song* Screening, Q&A with Nancy Kwan," Monterey Park Bruggemeyer Library, YouTube, July 26, 2014, https://www.youtube.com/watch?v=R0Q2RPd-Pug.

62. *Flower Drum Song* clipping file, Herrick Library.

63. In the *Los Angeles Times*, Philip K. Scheuer deemed Kwan "delectable" and "able to carry a tune, if nothing more," and listed "I Enjoy Being a Girl" as her "cleverest number." Philip K. Scheuer, "'Flower Drum Song' Bright as Yule Tinsel," *Los Angeles Times*, December 3, 1961, A3. This was echoed by John L. Scott, writing in the same paper, who described "I Enjoy Being a Girl"

as "immensely clever." John L. Scott, "'Flower Drum Song' Opulent and Tuneful," *Los Angeles Times*, December 22, 1961, 21. In the *Pacific Citizen*, Larry Tajiri judged "I Enjoy Being a Girl" particularly "effective." Larry Tajiri, "Oriental Kick Leaves Broadway," *Pacific Citizen*, November 24, 1961, 3.

64. Jennifer Lynn Stoever, *The Sonic Color Line: Race and the Cultural Politics of Listening* (New York: New York University Press, 2016).

65. Lewis, *Flower Drum Songs*, 107.

66. William A. Everett, "Performing Whiteness through the First-Generation American Immigrant Experience from Viennese Nights to Pitch Perfect," in *The Oxford Handbook of the Hollywood Musical*, ed. Dominic McHugh (New York: Oxford University Press, 2022), 158.

67. Here I draw on and adapt Nina Sun Eidsheim's deployment of Mendi Obadike's concept of "acousmatic blackness." Eidsheim writes that the "acousmatic question is the audile technique, or the measuring tape, used to determine the degree to which blackness is present" (*The Race of Sound*, 7). See also Matthew D. Morrison's *Blacksound: Making Race and Popular Music in the United States* (Oakland: University of California Press, 2024).

68. David H. Lewis, *Flower Drum Songs: The Story of Two Musicals* (Jefferson, NC: McFarland, 2006), 105.

69. Cheng, *Melancholy of Race*, 52.

70. Martin, "Backstage with Nancy Kwan," 45.

71. Hedda Hopper, "The Best of Two Worlds Merge in Nancy Kwan," *Hartford Courant*, March 22, 1964, 11F, ProQuest Historical Newspapers. https://www.proquest.com/docview/548339174/EA15ABAB0FD14B7DPQ/1?accountid=14521&sourcetype=Historical%20Newspapers.

72. Cheng, *The Melancholy of Race*, 45. On the technology of yellowface, see Esther Kim Lee, *Made-up Asians: Yellowface during the Exclusion Era* (Ann Arbor: University of Michigan Press, 2022). The film also continued to employ yellowface in the case of African American actress Juanita Hill and, as I discuss below, in that of several chorus dancers.

73. My thanks to Stephen Sohn for suggesting this line of argument. See also Hye Seung Chung, *Hollywood Asian: Philip Ahn and the Politics of Cross-ethnic Performance* (Philadelphia: Temple University Press, 2006) on "Oriental masquerade" as a strategy deployed by Asian/American actors in Hollywood.

74. See, for example, Yutian Wong's discussion of how the racialized mind/body division on which the "model minority" myth hinges effectively "disembodies Asian American subjects" (*Choreographing Asian America*, 14); Ju Yun Kim's discussion of how Asian/American racial formation is sustained through an "ambiguous relationship" between Asian/American bodies and everyday behaviors—behaviors that are "enacted *by* the body, but may or may not be *of* the body" (*The Racial Mundane*, 3, emphasis in original); and Rachel C. Lee's discussion of "the designation 'Asian American' as a fictional (discursive) construct [that is] only ambivalently, incoherently, or 'problematically' linked to the biological body" (*The Exquisite Corpse of Asian America*, 8).

75. See this book's introduction for further discussion of Fanon and Spillers, as well as Rizvana Bradley's critique of Cheng's approach to them.

76. Anne Anlin Cheng, "Ornamentalism: A Feminist Theory for the Yellow Woman," *Critical Inquiry* 44 (Spring 2018): 416.

77. Ibid., 433, 416. Cheng explains elsewhere, "In the late eighties, Kwan acted as spokesperson for a moisturizer called Pearl Cream," which "contained a whitening product and promised to give its users flawless 'porcelain skin'" (176n18).

78. Bill B. Davidson, "China Doll," *McCall's*, February 1962, 86–87, 168–170. A *Los Angeles Times* review of *Flower Drum Song* also described Kwan as "a China doll with lots of talent." Scott, "'Flower Drum Song' Opulent and Tuneful," 10. The power of a racial imaginary that positions Asian women as ornaments may also help explain what I have been describing as Kwan's indexical instability. Writing about the vessels in the Metropolitan Museum of Art's 2015 exhibition "China: Through the Looking Glass," Cheng states that they "short circuit[ed]" projecting human interiority because "all the empty containers . . . are already wholly occupied by emptiness" ("Ornamentalism," 435). Following Cheng's logic, Kwan too may have short-circuited the operation of indexicality, breaking any sense of "causal connection" between (filmic) representation and (corporeal) referent (Hanich, "Reflecting on Reflections," 140). If Kwan's corporeality was constituted *as* surface, that is, how could her screen image index any corporeal fullness, any organic depth? Under this light, the mirrors that project multiply adorned versions of Kwan in "I Enjoy Being a Girl," as well as critiques of the superficiality of her performance, may be evidence of a racial logic that figures Kwan's body as ornament.

238 NOTES

79. Ahmed, *Queer Phenomenology*, 143.
80. Davidson, "China Doll," 168.
81. Brian Jamieson, dir., *To Whom It May Concern: Ka Shen's Journey*, Redwind Productions, DVD, 2009; Lydia Joel, "Three Points of View," *Dance Magazine* 35, no. 11 (November, 1961): 40–41; Davidson, "China Doll," 170; Whitcomb, "A New Suzie Wong."
82. Richard Rodgers, "The Mosaic That Is Called 'Flower Drum,'" *Los Angeles Times*, November 5, 1961, A9; Susan King, "Nancy Kwan Looks Back on an All-Asian 'Groundbreaking' Film," *Los Angeles Times*, January 25, 2002, http://articles.latimes.com/2002/jan/25/entertainment/et-kingside25; Koster, *Flower Drum Song*; Jamieson, *To Whom It May Concern*; Joel, "Three Points of View," 40.
83. See Sally Ann Ness, "The Inscription of Gesture: Inward Migrations in Dance," in *Migrations of Gesture*, ed. Carrie Noland and Sally Ann Ness (Minneapolis: University of Minnesota Press, 2008), 1–30.
84. Lynn Tornabene, "Lunch Date with Nancy Kwan," *Cosmopolitan* 153, no. 5 (November 1962): 14.
85. On the "habitus," see Pierre Bourdieu, *The Logic of Practice* (Stanford: Stanford University Press, 1990).
86. As Kwan tells us on the *Flower Drum Song* DVD commentary, Pan was well aware of Kwan's ballet background when they began working together (Koster, *Flower Drum Song*).
87. Ahmed, *Queer Phenomenology*, 126.
88. In "Choreographing 'One Country, Two Systems': Dance and Politics in (Post) Colonial Hong Kong" (PhD diss., University of California, Los Angeles, 2021), Ellen Virginia Proctor Gerdes writes that, in colonial Hong Kong, "ballet studios emerged for Hong Kong elite" (21).
89. Ahmed, *Queer Phenomenology*, 143.
90. Whitcomb, "A New Suzie Wong," 10.
91. See, among others, Joann Kealiinohomoku, "An Anthropologist Looks at Ballet as a Form of Ethnic Dance," *Impulse* 20 (1970): 24–33; Gottschild, *Digging the Africanist Presence*; Stanger, *Dancing on Violent Ground*. Gerdes writes, "Before dance professionalization in Hong Kong in the 1980s, Western dance forms—social forms, folk forms, and ballet—reflected British cultural colonialism and the civilizing mission of Western imperialism" ("Choreographing 'One Country, Two Systems,'" 20).
92. See Adesola Akinleye's edited volume *(Re:) Claiming Ballet* (Bristol: Intellect Books, 2021) for essays that address "the common misconception that ballet is owned and populated by mainstream Whiteness" (1).
93. Ahmed, *Queer Phenomenology*, 135.
94. Martin, "Backstage with Nancy Kwan," 45; Davidson, "China Doll," 86.
95. See Claire Jean Kim, "The Racial Triangulation of Asian Americans," *Politics & Society* 27, no. 1 (1999): 107. See also Shannon Steen, *Racial Geometries of the Black Atlantic, Asian Pacific, and American Theatre* (New York: Palgrave Macmillan, 2010) and Josephine Lee, *Oriental, Black, and White: The Formation of Racial Habits in American Theater* (Chapel Hill: University of North Carolina Press, 2022) on the history of intertwined Black and Asian racial tropes in U.S. performance practices, as well as grace shinhae jun, "Asian American Liminality," in *The Oxford Handbook of Hip Hop Studies*, ed. Mary Fogarty and Imani Kai Johnson (New York: Oxford University Press, 2022), 280–291.
96. SanSan Kwan, "Performing a Geography of Asian America: The Chop Suey Circuit," *TDR: The Drama Review* 55, no. 1 (Spring 2011): 130.
97. Ibid., 127.
98. *Des Moines Register*, "A Square Dance in 'Flower Drum,'" April 30, 1961, 120, https://www.newspapers.com/image/128705478.
99. Pan also choreographed a jazz-infused dream ballet for *Flower Drum Song*, "Love Look Away," in which the Japanese/American Jack Cole–trained dancer Reiko Sato and the Hawaiian-born Korean/American ballet dancer Finis Jhung both performed.
100. My estimation is based on Glenn's description of the set, where the "delightful bit of inspired nonsense" took place as a "make-believe garden," and his reference to the presence of Juanita Hall, Miyoshi Umeki, James Shigeta, Benson Fong, and "the other Asian and Eurasian principals of the picture." This matches the setting and actors involved in "Chop Suey" and "You Be the Rock" (only the latter of which Kwan had a role in) (Glenn, "'Flower Drum Song' Reprised," 9).

NOTES   239

101. "You Be the Rock" starts around the 1:04 mark in the film.
102. Jon Whitcomb, "Producer with the Midas Touch," *Cosmopolitan* 151 (December 1961): 12. Lisa Jo Sagolla describes the Slop as a "distinctive '50s rock 'n' roll dance that originated in the African-American community," in which men would "put their hands in their pockets and yank up their pants legs as if showing off their shoes or this footwork," and that it was performed "independently, without touching your partner." Lisa Jo Sagolla, *Rock 'n' Roll Dances of the 1950s* (Santa Barbara, CA: Greenwood Press, 2011), 69. This does not quite match the dance between Adiarte and Kwan; the two clasp hands, and Adiarte does not hike up his pants. Whether this was a misrecognition on Whitcomb's part or the Slop had more variations than what Sagolla describes, it is safe to say the rock 'n' roll step they are performing was an African American-derived dance.
103. Cheng, *Melancholy of Race*, 47.
104. Palumbo-Liu, *Asian/America*, 161. Palumbo-Liu contrasts the dance between Low and Adiarte with the historical "repertoire of American dance" that unfolds in "Chop Suey." For Palumbo-Liu, the latter suggests Asian/Americans' "mastery of American cultural forms" and the "alienation of white America from these forms" (162). Still, he argues, both dance scenes produce "a safely sequestered vision of Asian America," devoid of any interracial encounters (162).
105. Gottschild, *Digging the Africanist Presence*.
106. Born in Manilla in 1943 to a Filipino father and a Spanish ballet dancer mother, Adiarte moved with his family to New York City when he was one or two years old. At seven, he was cast as one of the royal children in the Broadway production of *The King and I*, the first in Rodgers and Hammerstein's "Orientalist" trilogy, choreographed by Robbins. Adiarte performed in and toured with the production for three years. Sometime during the run of the show, he began learning tap dance from Paul Draper, an influential white tap artist who studied with African American tap and jazz dance choreographer Buddy Bradley. Draper was known for combining tap dance with ballet, Spanish dance, and modern dance. At around age twelve, Adiarte started taking ballet classes with the Russian ballet mistress Madame Pereyaslavec at the American Ballet Theatre School, and shortly after, he began studying jazz dance with the Italian American Luigi (Eugene Louis Faccuito), sometimes credited as the "father" of American jazz dancing. In 1956, Adiarte played the crown prince in the film version of *The King and I*, and two years later Kelly cast him as Wang San in the Broadway production of *Flower Drum Song*, choreographed by Haney; this is the same role he would play in the 1961 film. In 1958, he tap danced alongside Kelly in *Dancing, a Man's Game with Gene Kelly*. Adiarte went on to dance in the 1965 television variety show *Hullaballoo*, and, in the early 1970s he had acting roles in television shows including *The Brady Bunch* and *M*A*S*H*. Edwin Denby, quoted in Hill, *Tap Dance America*, 190; Marshall Stearns and Jean Stearns, *Jazz Dance: The Story of American Vernacular Dance* (New York: Schirmer Books, 1968), 161; Lewis, *Flower Drum Songs*, 38–39; Joel, "Three Points of View," 41; Norma McClain Stoop, "American Musical Dancer/Choreographer: Patrick Adiarte: 'Art Is Aggressive,'" *Dance Magazine*, February 1978, 54–57; Cynthia Lowry, "Patrick Adiarte's Face, Frame TV Standouts," *Sioux City Journal*, November 28, 1965, 39; Michelle Keating, "He Put His 'Stamp' on ACT Musical," *Tucson Citizen*, June 29, 1978, 21; Margalit Fox, "Eugene Faccuito, 90, Creator of Jazz Dance Style, Is Dead," *New York Times*, April 12, 2015, 22. As late as 2019, Adiarte was still teaching dance at the Hollywood Dance Center. In an October 2023 phone interview, he recalled all of his dance teachers fondly; described Nancy Kwan as "a ballet dancer first," who was "very good"; affirmed that Hermes Pan "choreographed around you," creating "steps that would highlight what you looked good in," but did not recall any of Pan's assistants on *Flower Drum Song*. Phone interview with Patrick Adiarte, October 17, 2023.
107. Gottschild, *Digging the Africanist Presence*, 8, 16–18. While Pan, of course, was officially the choreographer of these sequences, as Adiarte relayed on multiple occasions, Pan "didn't give [Adiarte] stuff" but let him "fool around" to see what he could do and then "choreographed around" him. Lewis, *Flower Drum Songs*, 102; Joel, "Three Points of View, 41.
108. Whitcomb, "Producer with the Midas Touch," 12.
109. I have not been able to determine where Adiarte was teaching when Kwan took classes with him. According to an oral history with Margaret Graham Hills, Adiarte taught jazz at Stanley Holden's dance studio in Los Angeles, which appears to have opened around 1971. Margaret Graham Hills, interviewed by Genie Guerard, "Tending the Flame Oral History Transcript, 1997–1998: Teaching Classical Ballet in Three Continents," Oral History Program, University

240 NOTES

of California, Los Angeles, 2000. Adiarte later taught at Santa Monica College and at the Harkness Ballet (Keating, "He Put His 'Stamp' on ACT Musical," 21).

110. Anthony Christian Ocampo, *The Latinos of Asia: How Filipino Americans Break the Rules of Race* (Stanford: Stanford University Press, 2016), 4.

111. See a number of the essays in Lindsay Guarino and Wendy Oliver, eds., *Jazz Dance: A History of the Roots and Branches* (Gainesville: University Press of Florida, 2014); Julio Agustin, "From Mu-Cha-Cha to Ay-Ay-Ay! A Critical Explication of the Use of 'Latin' Dance Styles and the Absence of Latinx Creatives in the Broadway Musical," *Theatre Topics* 31, no. 1 (2021): 43–54; Khadifa Wong, dir., *Uprooted: The Journey of Jazz Dance*, Good Docs, DVD, 2020.

112. While the U.S. colonization of the Philippines, which began in 1898 during the Spanish-American War, formally ended with its recognition of Philippine independence in 1946, Ocampo writes that the U.S. government has "maintained a neocolonial influence by way of its continued military, economic, and cultural presence in the country" (*Latinos of Asia*, 15).

113. Stoop, "American Musical Dancer/Choreographer," 55; Keating, "He Put His 'Stamp' on ACT Musical," 21.

114. Ocampo, *The Latinos of Asia*, 19.

115. As Sarita See has written, Filipinos have been "[w]idely regarded as consummate mimics both in Asia and Asian America" in ways that frame them as "a simultaneously inassimilable and assimilable vestige of American imperialism." Sarita Echavez See, *The Filipino Primitive: Accumulation and Resistance in the American Museum* (New York: New York University Press, 2017), 143; Sarita Echavez See, *Decolonized Eye: Filipino American Art and Performance* (Minneapolis: University of Minnesota Press, 2009), xi; . See also Lucy Mae San Pablo Burns, *Puro Arte: Filipinos on the Stages of Empire* (New York: New York University Press, 2012), 49–74; Lorenzo J. Perillo, *Choreographing in Color: Filipinos, Hip-hop, and the Cultural Politics of Euphemism* (New York: Oxford University Press, 2020), 6. See Perillo on the much longer history of "AfroFilipino formations" (*Choreographing in Color*, especially 4, 11).

116. Lowry, "Patrick Adiarte's Face, Frame TV Standouts," 39. In this regard, Adiarte might be seen as a descendant of the Filipino men whose "dazzling steps" and "splendid dancing" in American taxi dance halls in the 1920s and 1930s, as Burns has shown, figured them as "at once desirable and racialized" and, via the discourse of exceptionalism, "work[ed] to contain and domesticate the unwieldy colonized Filipino body" (*Puro Arte*, 54, 50, 58, 65). More immediately, Adiarte's early career overlaps with that of the Rocky Fellers, a Filipino American rock 'n' roll family act that performed on television variety shows in the late 1950s and early 1960s and whose brown Filipino bodies, as Melissa Phruksachart observes, mediated the consumption of Black culture for white American Cold War audiences. Melissa Phruksachart, "The Rocky Fellers: Doo-Wop's 'Little Brown Brothers.'" Pop Conference, Museum of Pop, Seattle, April 2018. My gratitude to Melissa for sending me a copy of this paper. I have been complicit in mobilizing the trope of exceptionalism with respect to Adiarte when I have excitedly talked up the skill he displays in *Flower Drum Song*.

117. Franceschina, *Hermes Pan*, 231.

118. As Juliana Chang writes, the ensemble numbers in *Flower Drum Song*, including "Grant Avenue," "ease our relentless gaze on individual female icons" and the "spectacularization of femininity" and provide sources of identification for contemporary Asian American audiences, even as they feel "uncanny, strange, and spectral" in their anonymity and unknown backstories ("I Dreamed I Was Wanted," 172).

119. Ibid., 173–174.

120. Koster, *Flower Drum Song*.

121. Kwan recalled six weeks of rehearsal (King, "Nancy Kwan Looks Back on an All-Asian 'Groundbreaking' Film," F2). Franceschina writes that Pan worked "on the creation and teaching of the dance numbers . . . from February 1961 well into May, assisted by Jimmy Huntley . . . Becky Varno . . . and his constant companion, Gino Malerba" (*Hermes Pan*, 229). AD reports for Universal films, if they still exist, are not accessible to researchers, at least at the time of this writing.

122. Koster, *Flower Drum Song*.

123. Delameter, *Dance in the Hollywood Musical*, 107. A contemporaneous review of *Flower Drum Song* in the *Hollywood Reporter* praised Pan's choreography in "Grant Avenue" for being "indigenous to the locale and rising out of the pavements" (quoted in Franceschina, *Hermes Pan*, 233). As Hess and Dabholkar write in their biography of Kelly, "Although Gene talked with Carol Haney about the choreography early on, he left her alone to work out the numbers,"

though they add, "True to her tutelage under Kelly, Haney pulled movements from virtually every dance style imaginable" (*Gene Kelly*, 314).

124. The only extant footage of Haney's choreography in *Flower Drum Song* I have been able to find is the performance of several numbers on the *Ed Sullivan Show* in 1958, posted to YouTube, accessed April 5, 2024, https://www.youtube.com/watch?v=jkYQaNHl2K8.

125. Finis Jhung, *Ballet for Life: A Pictorial Memoir* (New York: Ballet Dynamics, 2017), 66. Baayork Lee, who also performed in the Broadway production (but not in the film), likewise described Haney's choreography as possessing the "Jack Cole kind of smooth aggressiveness" (cited in Lewis, *Flower Drum Songs*, 56).

126. Ma, "Chopsticks Musicals," 23.

127. Ibid.

128. *Variety*, "Flower Drum Song" review, November 8, 1961, 3.

129. A similarly Orientalizing and blatantly racist gesture was evidently part of Haney's choreography for "Chop Suey." Recalling Haney's "endless tinkering" with that number, Broadway dancer Wonci Lui described as "offensive" a move in which dancers were instructed ".Put your fingers up!" (cited in Lewis, *Flower Drum Songs*, 56). Nobuko Miyamoto, who also danced in the Broadway production of *Flower Drum Song*, likewise remembered "Haney's satirical choreography" for "Chop Suey" as a combination of "the cha-cha-cha with the stereotypical Chinese hand movement of chop-chop, poking our index fingers in the air" (*Not Yo' Butterfly*, 68).

130. As Adrienne McLean writes in "The Thousand Ways There Are to Move," "American dance is profoundly marked by Cole's Orientalist practices, assumptions, and input, just as it is by African, Latin, Spanish, and other ethnic dance forms" (70).

131. Chang, "I Dreamed I Was Wanted," 172, 155.

132. Rodgers, "The Mosaic That Is Called 'Flower Drum,'" A9. A 1958 article in *Time* magazine told a similar story about the search for Broadway cast members. *Time,* "The Girls *on Grant Avenue,*" December 22, 1958, 42.

133. Joel, "Three Perspectives," 40.

134. Lewis, *Flower Drum Songs*, 44. Though the 1944 cabaret tax and the end of World War II dealt serious blows to the "golden era" of the Chinese American nightclub industry, Forbidden City did not shut its doors until 1970, and throughout the 1950s the club "still put crack entertainers" who sang English and "dazzled with pizzazz and snappy footwork" "before a discriminating public." Arthur Dong, *Forbidden City, USA: Chinatown Nightclubs, 1936–1970* (Los Angeles: DeepFocus Productions, 2014), 30, 34, 35; Lewis, *Flower Drum Songs*, 44.

135. Lewis, *Flower Drum Songs*, 44; Dong, *Forbidden City*, 74, 76.

136. Lewis, *Flower Drum Songs*, 44.

137. Dong, *Forbidden City*, 147; Lewis, *Flower Drum Songs*, 44. Born Dorothy Takahashi, the Japanese/American Toy used Chinese billing to evade internment during World War II (Kwan, "Chop Suey Circuit," 130). See also Lloyd Shearer, "Hollywood Comes to Bessie Loo for Oriental Beauties," *Oakland Tribune*, January 15, 1961, 69–70, on the casting agent Bessie Loo, who provided Asian/American extras for the major Hollywood studios.

138. Dong, *Forbidden City*, 147; Rodgers, "The Mosaic That Is Called 'Flower Drum,'" A9.

139. IMDb lists these chorus dancers as "Dancer (uncredited)" without indicating which number they appeared in. Most of those listed appear to have only the *Flower Drum Song* credit. See https://www.imdb.com/title/tt0054885/fullcredits/?ref_=tt_cl_sm, accessed November 28, 2023.

140. Billman, *Film Choreographers and Dance Directors*, 297.

141. Finis Jhung, private Facebook message, November 18, 2018.

142. A number of those listed on IMDb as uncredited dancers have Japanese surnames, such as Alice Nishimura, Keiko Kamitsuka, and Teruku Suzuki. One of the background dancers in the film, who was likely also in "Grant Avenue," was Irene Tsu, who was born in Shanghai, fled to Hong Kong during the communist takeover, and emigrated to the United States in the mid-1950s. Like Kwan, she trained in ballet, and the two became friends when Tsu was cast in *The World of Suzie Wong*. See Tom Lisanti, "Irene Tsu," in *Fantasy Femmes of Sixties Cinema: Interviews with Twenty Actresses from Biker, Beach, and Elvis Movies* (Jefferson, NC: McFarland, 2015), 158–169; Irene Tsu, *A Water Color Dream: The Many Lives of Irene Tsu*, ed. Jim Martyka (Orlando, FL: BearManor Media, 2020), 33, 35. Asian/American women chorus dancers also appear in *Flower Drum Song* in "Fan Tan Fanny" and "Gliding through My Memories."

143. Chang, "I Dreamed I Was Wanted," 174.

144. Phruksachart, "The Many Lives of Mr. Yunioshi," 109.

242 NOTES

145. Cheng, "Ornamentalism," 444; Lee, *The Exquisite Corpse of Asian America*, 30.
146. My thanks to Brynn Shiovitz for alerting me to this photo's existence.
147. *Los Angeles Mirror*, "Nancy Kwan Now 'Little Deer,'" Mar. 4, 1961, 2.
148. Franceschina, *Hermes Pan*, 232. See Chang, "I Dreamed I Was Wanted," 161–169 for a description and compelling reading of "Sunday" as a "fantasy of domestic modernity [that] collapses when [Low and Fong] are confronted with . . . the archetypal coupling of the cowboy and Indian that embodies the historical violence and trauma of settler colonialism" (163).
149. Following *Flower Drum Song*, Kwan was cast in film roles that racialized her as Italian and English Tahitian. As she shares on the *Flower Drum Song* DVD commentary, producer Ray Stark wanted her to "get away from playing Asians."
150. Within the film, Asian/American racial status is also imagined through the figure of the Mexican "wetback," a term the character Mei Li, whose illegal immigration contrasts Linda Low's, encounters when watching late-night television. See Kim, "'Flower Drum Song,'" on the musical's deployment of "comparative racialization," and Chang, "I Dreamed I Was Wanted," for an insightful discussion of how the film rehearses Asian/Americans' oscillation "between racial outsiders to the nation and exemplary national or neoliberal citizens used to discipline other racial subjects" (177).
151. Chang, "I Dreamed I Was Wanted," 169.
152. Raheja, *Reservation Reelism*, 102, 104.
153. Ibid., 109.
154. Ibid., 107.

Coda

1. The clip is available on YouTube, accessed November 6, 2018, https://www.youtube.com/watch?v=MCkpbsB8xzM&list=RDMCkpbsB8xzM&index=1. YouTube misdates the clip to 1963. The correct date can be found in David M. Inman, *Television Variety Shows: Histories and Episode Guides to 57 Programs* (Jefferson, NC: McFarland, 2006), 233. Horne's version of "Deed I Do," released on MGM's record label, was one of her hits in the late 1940s (Gavin, *Stormy Weather*, 212).
2. J. Don Schlaerth, "A Story-Telling Delight on the Way," *Buffalo News*, October 16, 1962, 5.
3. Chung, *Media Heterotopias*, 2.
4. As Jane Feuer has written, however, the framing of a dance number as a rehearsal is a common trope in Hollywood musicals. Jane Feuer, "Hollywood Musicals: Mass Art as Folk Art," *Jump Cut* 23 (1980): 23–25.
5. According to Malcolm Macfarlane and Ken Crossland's *Perry Como: A Biography and Complete Career Record* (Jefferson, NC: McFarland, 2012), the regulars on Como's show during the 1962–1963 season included the Mitchell Ayres Orchestra and the Ray Charles Singers, Peter Gennaro and his dancers, Don Adams, Sandy Stewart, Jack Duffy, and Kaye Ballard, and announcer Frank Gallop (222).
6. See that opening on YouTube, accessed February 29, 2024, https://www.youtube.com/watch?v=xliuM_DI894&t=140s.
7. The African American dancers Leonard Reed and Willie Bryant are often considered the creators of the Shim Sham. On the origin of the dance and its name, see Mark Knowles, *Tap Roots: The Early History of Tap Dancing* (Jefferson, NC: McFarland, 2002), 238–239n39.
8. Gennaro was Como's choreographer between 1960 and 1963 (Billman, *Film Choreographers and Dance Directors*, 333–335).
9. In her autobiography, Horne emphasizes the influence that members of *Jamaica*'s dance ensemble, including a young Alvin Ailey, had on her. "When we worked together," she writes, "I had the sensation of being a part of their bodies, that we were almost physically touching one another." (Lena Horne and Richard Schickel, *Lena* (Garden City, NJ: Doubleday, 1965), 260;
10. Marston, "Marie Bryant."
11. *Variety*, "Marie Bryant," obituary, June 7, 1978, 91.
12. *New York Times*, "Carol Haney, 'Pajama Game' Dancer, Dies at 39," 37.
13. Lena Horne, Gene Kelly, Vera-Ellen, Alex Romero, and Marie Bryant were each also involved in *Words and Music* (1948): Horne sang "Lady and the Tramp," Vera-Ellen and Kelly danced together in "Slaughter on Tenth Avenue," and Romero and Bryant assisted Kelly and Vera-Ellen off-screen.

NOTES 243

14. Barry Keith Grant, *The Hollywood Film Musical* (Hoboken, NJ: John Wiley & Sons, 2012), 24. See also Matthew Kennedy, *Roadshow! The Fall of Film Musicals in the 1960s* (New York: Oxford University Press, 2014).

15. Benshoff and Griffin, *America on Film*, 39.

16. Billman, *Film Choreographers and Dance Directors*, 241.

17. Marie Bryant clipping, George P. Johnson Negro Film Collection (Collection 1042), UCLA Library Special Collections, Charles E. Young Research Library, University of California, Los Angeles.

18. Knowles, *The Man Who Made the Jailhouse Rock*, 96.

19. *Dance Magazine*, "Presstime News," 6.

20. As Pamela Krayenbuhl points out, "Both film and dance scholars have overlooked midcentury dance stars' televisual dances," which "usually occurred in the context of variety shows" ("Dancing Race and Masculinity," 24). Her work is a corrective. See also Julie Malnig, *Dancing Black, Dancing White: Rock'n'Roll, Race, and Youth Culture of the 1950s and Early 1960s* (New York: Oxford University Press, 2023) on televised teen dance shows in the post–World War II era.

21. Swisher, "Gene and Jack and the Beanstalk," 52.

22. See Cohan, *Incongruous Entertainment*, on homosociality and anxieties around masculinity in midcentury Hollywood musicals, as well as Ramsay Burt, *The Male Dancer: Bodies, Spectacle, Sexualities* (1995; New York: Routledge, 2022) and several of the essays in Jane Desmond, ed., *Dancing Desires: Choreographing Sexualities on and off the Stage* (Madison: University of Wisconsin Press, 2001).

23. Those gowns can be seen in the clip available on YouTube, accessed April 22, 2024, https://www.youtube.com/watch?v=xliuM_DI894&t=2s.

24. Clare Croft writes, "No single entity marks something as queer dance, but rather it is how [multiple and at times competing] textures press on the world and against one another that opens the possibility for dance to be queer" ("Introduction," 1).

25. Wolf, "'We'll Always Be Bosom Buddies,'" 352, 353, 354, 358.

26. Paredez, "Lena Horne and Judy Garland," 108, 114, 117.

27. Horne and Schickel, *Lena*, 275–276; Paredez, "Lena Horne and Judy Garland," 109. See also Gavin, *Stormy Weather*, 318. Certainly, Horne had expressed her rage in public before. In an infamous "unscheduled performance" at a Beverly Hills restaurant in 1960, for example, Horne threw an ashtray at a white man who insulted her with a racial slur, an incident that garnered appreciative mail from Black fans (Horne and Schickel, *Lena*, 272–273).

28. Paredez, "Lena Horne and Judy Garland," 110. See Vogel, "Lena Horne's Impersona."

29. Paredez, "Lena Horne and Judy Garland," 107–108.

30. Gavin, *Stormy Weather*, 339. In one of her prior appearances on Como's show, he touched Horne's arm on-air, generating a slew of angry letters (Gavin, *Stormy Weather*, 279–280).

31. Horne and Schickel, *Lena*, 135. Richard Dyer writes, "To be pedantic, there are no numbers in any of her films in which Horne is positioned against a column." Yet, he goes on, "the fact that the image of her thus, draped and pinned, is so insistent in the memory, including it seems Horne's own, suggests that if not literally true, it is metaphorically so." Richard Dyer, *In the Space of a Song: The Uses of Song in Film* (New York: Routledge, 2012), 125.

32. Wolf, "'We'll Always Be Bosom Buddies,'" 365.

33. For further discussion of debates about the origins of tap dance and the problems with standard narratives of tap dance as an Afro-Irish fusion, see Sonja Thomas, "Black Soundwork, Knowledge Production, and the 'Debate' over Tap Dance Origins," *Resonance: The Journal of Sound and Culture* 1, no. 4 (2020): 412–421.

34. Johnson, "Casualties."

35. Thomas F. DeFrantz, "What Is Black Dance? What Can It Do?," in *Thinking through Theatre and Performance*, ed. Maaike Bleeker, Adrian Kear, Joe Kelleher, and Heike Roms (London: Bloomsbury, 2019), 87; Gottschild, *Digging the Africanist Presence*, 16–17.

36. See Tina Campt's body of work on "the practice of refusal as an extension of the range of creative responses black communities have marshaled in the face of racialized dispossession" (*Listening to Images*, 10).

Bibliography

Secondary Sources

Acharya, Rohini, and Eric Kaufman. "Turns of 'Fate': Jack Cole, Jazz and Bharata Natyam in Diasporic Translation." *Studies in Musical Theatre* 13, no. 1 (March 2019): 9–21.

Adeyemi, Kemi, Kareem Khubchandani, and Ramón H. Rivera-Servera, eds. *Queer Nightlife*. Ann Arbor: University of Michigan Press, 2021.

Agustin, Julio. "From Mu-Cha-Cha to Ay-Ay-Ay! A Critical Explication of the Use of 'Latin' Dance Styles and the Absence of Latinx Creatives in the Broadway Musical." *Theatre Topics* 31, no. 1 (2021): 43–54.

Ahlgren, Angela K. "Futari Tomo: A Queer Duet for Taiko." In *Queer Dance: Meanings and Makings*, edited by Clare Croft, 229–242. New York: Oxford University Press, 2017.

Ahmed, Sara. *Queer Phenomenology: Orientations, Objects, Others*. Durham, NC: Duke University Press, 2006.

Akinleye, Adesola, ed. *(Re:) Claiming Ballet*. Bristol: Intellect Books, 2021.

Albright, Ann Cooper. *Choreographing Difference: The Body and Identity in Contemporary Dance*. Middletown, CT: Wesleyan University Press, 2010.

Alexander, Karen. "Fatal Beauties: Black Women in Hollywood." In *Stardom: Industry of Desire*, edited by Christine Gledhill, 46–57. New York: Routledge, 1991.

Alvarez, Luis. *The Power of the Zoot: Youth Culture and Resistance during World War II*. Berkeley: University of California Press, 2008.

Arondekar, Anjali. *For the Record: On Sexuality and the Colonial Archive in India*. Durham, NC: Duke University Press, 2009.

Arondekar, Anjali, Ann Cvetkovich, Christina B. Hanhardt, Regina Kunzel, Tavia Nyong'o, Juana María Rodríguez, Susan Stryker, Daniel Marshall, Kevin P. Murphy, and Zeb Tortorici. "Queering Archives: A Roundtable Discussion." *Radical History Review* 2015, no. 122 (2015): 211–231.

Arts at Bryn Mawr College. "The Porch: A Studio Dialogue with nia love and Fred Moten." March 25, 2021. https://brynmawr.hosted.panopto.com/Panopto/Pages/Viewer.aspx?id=44e4721a-7b03-4f68-83f1-acf2011600ac.

Banerji, Anurima. "Dance and the Distributed Body: Odissi, Ritual Practice, and Mahari Performance." *About Performance* (Sydney Centre for Performance Studies), no. 11 (2012): 7–39.

Banerji, Anurima. *Dancing Odissi: Paratopic Performances of Gender and State*. Chicago: University of Chicago Press, 2019.

Banerji, Anurima, Anusha Kedhar, Royona Mitra, Janet O'Shea, and Shanti Pillai. "Postcolonial Pedagogies: Recasting the Guru–Shishya Parampara." *Theatre Topics* 27, no. 3 (November 2017): 221–230.

Banes, Sally. *Dancing Women: Female Bodies on Stage*. New York: Routledge, 1998.

Banks, Miranda J. "Gender Below-the-Line: Defining Feminist Production Studies." In *Production Studies: Cultural Studies of Media Industries*, edited by Vicki Mayer, Miranda Banks, and John Caldwell, 87–98. New York: Routledge, 2009.

Banks, Miranda J. "Production Studies." *Feminist Media Histories* 4, no. 2 (2018): 157–161.

Banner, Lois W. "The Creature from the Black Lagoon: Marilyn Monroe and Whiteness." *Cinema Journal* 47, no. 4 (Summer 2008): 4–29.

Basinger, Jeanine. *The Movie Musical*. New York: Knopf, 2019.

246 BIBLIOGRAPHY

Basinger, Jeanine. *The Star Machine*. New York: Vintage, 2009.

Batiste, Stephanie Leigh. *Darkening Mirrors: Imperial Representation in Depression-Era African American Performance*. Durham, NC: Duke University Press, 2012.

Bean, Jennifer M. "Technologies of Early Stardom and the Extraordinary Body." *Camera Obscura* 16, no. 3 (2001): 8–57.

Behlmer, Rudy. *America's Favorite Movies: Behind the Scenes*. New York: Frederick Ungar, 1982.

Belmar, Sima. "Behind the Screens: Race, Space, and Place in *Saturday Night Fever*." In *The Oxford Handbook of Screendance Studies*, edited by Douglas Rosenberg, 461–79. New York: Oxford University Press, 2016.

Beltrán, Mary C. *Latina/o Stars in U.S. Eyes: The Making and Meanings of Film and TV Stardom*. Urbana: University of Illinois Press, 2009.

Beltrán, Mary C., and Camilla Fojas. "Introduction: Mixed Race in Hollywood Film and Media Culture." In *Mixed Race Hollywood*, edited by Mary Beltrán and Camilla Fojas, 1–20. New York: New York University Press, 2008.

Bench, Harmony. *Perpetual Motion: Dance, Digital Cultures, and the Common*. Minneapolis: University of Minnesota Press, 2020.

Bench, Harmony. "Virtual Embodiment and the Materiality of Images." *Extensions: The Journal of Embodied Technology* 1 (2004). [Manuscript from author via personal communication, June 20, 2019.]

Benshoff, Harry M., and Sean Griffin. *America on Film: Representing Race, Class, Gender, and Sexuality at the Movies*. Hoboken, NJ: Wiley Blackwell, 2021.

Bergen, Anna Hilary. "Dancing Media: The Contagious Movement of Posthuman Bodies (or Towards a Posthuman Theory of Dance." PhD diss., Concordia University, 2022.

Bernardi, Daniel, ed. *The Birth of Whiteness: Race and the Emergence of U.S. Cinema*. New Brunswick, NJ: Rutgers University Press, 1996.

Bernardi, Daniel. *Classic Hollywood, Classic Whiteness*. Minneapolis: University of Minnesota Press, 2001.

Bernstein, Robin. *Racial Innocence: White Supremacy and the Performance of American Childhood*. New Haven, CT: Yale University Press, 2004.

Best, Stephen M. *The Fugitive's Properties: Law and the Poetics of Possession*. Chicago: University of Chicago Press, 2004.

Bhabha, Homi. "Of Mimicry and Man: The Ambivalence of Colonial Discourse." *October* 28 (1984): 125–133.

Billman, Larry. *Betty Grable: A Bio-Bibliography*. Westport, CT: Greenwood Press, 1993.

Billman, Larry. *Film Choreographers and Dance Directors: An Illustrated Biographical Encyclopedia, with a History and Filmographies,1893 through 1995*. Jefferson, NC: McFarland, 1997.

Biss, Eula. "White Debt." *New York Times Magazine*, December 2, 2015. https://www.nytimes.com/2015/12/06/magazine/white-debt.html?_r=1.

Blackman, Lisa. *The Body: The Key Concepts*. 2nd edition. Abingdon: Routledge, 2021.

Block, Geoffrey Holden. *A Fine Romance: Adapting Broadway to Hollywood in the Studio System Era*. New York: Oxford University Press, 2023.

Bogle, Donald. *Bright Boulevards, Bold Dreams: The Story of Black Hollywood*. New York: One World, 2005.

Bogle, Donald. *Lena Horne: Goddess Reclaimed*. Philadelphia: Running Press, 2023.

Borelli, Melissa Blanco, ed. *The Oxford Handbook of Dance and the Popular Screen*. New York: Oxford University Press, 2014.

Borelli, Melissa Blanco. *She Is Cuba: A Genealogy of the Mulata Body*. New York: Oxford University Press, 2015.

Borelli, Melissa Blanco, and Raquel Monroe. "Editorial: Screening the Skin: Issues of Race and Nation in Screendance." *International Journal of Screendance* 9 (2018). http://dx.doi.org/10.18061/ijsd.v9i0.6451.

BIBLIOGRAPHY 247

Bouldin, Joanna. "The Body, Animation and the Real: Race, Reality and the Rotoscope in Betty Boop." In *Proceedings of Affective Encounters: Rethinking Embodiment in Feminist Media Studies*, edited by Anu Koivunen and Susanna Paasen, 48–54. Turku: University of Turku, School of Art, Literature and Music, Media Studies, 2001. https://susannapaasonen.files. wordpress.com/2014/11/proceedings.pdf.

Bourdieu, Pierre. *The Logic of Practice*. Stanford: Stanford University Press, 1990.

Bradley, Rizvana. *Anteaesthetics: Black Aesthesis and the Critique of Form*. Stanford: Stanford University Press, 2023.

Bragin, Naomi. "Techniques of Back Male Re/dress: Corporeal Drag and Kinesthetic Politics in the Rebirth of Waacking/Punkin." *Women & Performance: A Journal of Feminist Theory* 24, no. 1 (2014): 61–78.

Brandstetter, Gabriele. "Human, Animal, Thing." In *Moving (across) Borders: Performing Translation, Intervention, Participation*, edited by Gabrielle Brandstetter and Holger Hartung, 23–42. Bielefeld: Transcript Verlag, 2017.

Brannigan, Erin. *Dancefilm: Choreography and the Moving Image.* New York: Oxford University Press, 2010.

Brannum, Barry. "As the Flesh Moves: Lon Fontaine, Black Dance, and Strategies for Rendering Presence." PhD diss., University of California, Los Angeles, 2021.

Brideson, Cynthia, and Sara Brideson. *He's Got Rhythm: The Life and Career of Gene Kelly*. Lexington: University Press of Kentucky, 2017.

Brodkin, Karen. *How Jews Became White Folks and What That Says about Race in America*. New Brunswick, NJ: Rutgers University Press, 1998.

Brown, Jayna. *Babylon Girls: Black Women Performers and the Shaping of the Modern*. Durham, NC: Duke University Press, 2008.

Bryant, Clora, Buddy Collette, William Green, Steven Isoardi, Jack Kelson, Horace Tapscott, Gerald Wilson, and Marl Young, eds. *Central Avenue Sounds: Jazz in Los Angeles*. Berkeley: University of California Press, 1998.

Buchman, Andrew. "Developing the Screenplay for *Singin' in the Rain* (1952)." In *The Oxford Handbook of the Hollywood Musical*, edited by Dominic Broomfield-McHugh, 307–324. New York: Oxford University Press, 2022.

Buckley, Gail Lumet. *The Hornes: An American Family*. Milwaukee, WI: Hal Leonard, 2002.

Burns, Lucy Mae San Pablo. *Puro Arte: Filipinos on the Stages of Empire*. New York: New York University Press, 2012.

Burt, Ramsay. *The Male Dancer: Bodies, Spectacle, Sexualities*. 1995; New York: Routledge, 2022.

Burtt, Kristyn. "It's Time for IMDb to Give Choreographers an Official Category." *Dance Dish Media*, February 20, 2019. https://www.dancedishwithkb.com/post/it-s-time-for-imdb-to-give-choreographers-their-own-category#:~:text=For%20choreographers%2C%20a%20user%20would,that%20have%20no%20specific%20category.

Butler, Judith. *Bodies That Matter: On the Discursive Limits of "Sex."* New York: Routledge, 1993.

Butler, Judith. *Gender Trouble: Feminism and the Subversion of Identity*. New York: Routledge, 1990.

Campt, Tina M. *Listening to Images*. Durham, NC: Duke University Press, 2017.

Carman, Emily. *Independent Stardom: Freelance Women in the Hollywood Studio System*. Austin: University of Texas Press, 2015.

Caron, Leslie. *Thank Heaven: A Memoir*. New York: Viking, 2009.

Casey, Carrie Gaiser. "Ballet's Feminisms: Genealogy and Gender in Twentieth-Century American Ballet History." PhD diss., University of California, Berkeley, 2009.

Castillo, Heather. "'Nice Work If You Could Get It': Dancing Ensembles in the Golden Age of Movie Musicals, 1940–1965." MFA thesis, University of California, Irvine, 2009.

Caughie, Pamela L. "Audible Identities: Passing and Sound Technologies." *Humanities Research* 16, no. 1 (2010): 91–109.

Chakravartty, Paula, and Denise Ferreira da Silva. "Accumulation, Dispossession, and Debt: The Racial Logic of Global Capitalism—An Introduction." *American Quarterly* 64, no. 3 (September 2012): 361–385.

248 BIBLIOGRAPHY

Chaleff, Rebecca. "Choreographic Legacies:(DIS) Embodied Assemblages of Queer and Colonial Histories." PhD diss. Stanford University, 2017.

Chaleff, Rebecca. "Economies of Reperformance: Unearthing Racial Capitalism in Dancing at Dusk." *TDR: The Drama Review* 67, no. 1 (2023): 167–185.

Chambers-Letson, Joshua. *After the Party: A Manifesto for Queer of Color Life.* New York: New York University Press, 2018.

Chambers-Letson, Joshua. "Performance's Mode of Reproduction I: Searching for Danh Võ's Mother." *Women & Performance: A Journal of Feminist Theory* 26, nos. 2–3 (2016): 122–145.

Chan, Jennifer Leah. "Transgressive Babymaking: Narratives of Reproduction and the Asian American Subject." PhD diss., New York University, 2007.

Chang, Juliana. "I Dreamed I Was Wanted: *Flower Drum Song* and Specters of Modernity." *Camera Obscura: Feminism, Culture, and Media Studies* 29, no. 3 (2014): 149–183.

Chen, Mel Y. *Animacies: Biopolitics, Racial Mattering, and Queer Affect.* Durham, NC: Duke University Press, 2012.

Cheng, Anne Anlin. *The Melancholy of Race: Psychoanalysis, Assimilation, and Hidden Grief.* New York: Oxford University Press, 2000.

Cheng, Anne Anlin. *Ornamentalism.* New York: Oxford University Press, 2019.

Cheng, Anne Anlin. "Ornamentalism: A Feminist Theory for the Yellow Woman." *Critical Inquiry* 44 (Spring 2018): 415–446.

Cheng, Cindy I-Fen. *Citizens of Asian America: Democracy and Race during the Cold War.* New York: New York University Press, 2013.

Cherniavsky, Eva. *Incorporations: Race, Nation, and the Body Politics of Capital.* Minneapolis: University of Minnesota Press, 2006.

Chisholm, Ann. "Missing Persons and Bodies of Evidence." *Camera Obscura* 15, no. 1 (2000): 123–161.

Chumo, Peter N. "Dance, Flexibility, and the Renewal of Genre in *Singin' in the Rain.*" *Cinema Journal* 36, no. 1 (1996): 39–54.

Chung, Hye Jean. *Media Heterotopias: Digital Effects and Material Labor in Global Film Production.* Durham, NC: Duke University Press, 2018.

Chung, Hye Seung. *Hollywood Asian: Philip Ahn and the Politics of Cross-ethnic Performance.* Philadelphia: Temple University Press, 2006.

Clark, Danae. *Negotiating Hollywood: The Cultural Politics of Actors' Labor.* Minneapolis: University of Minnesota Press, 1995.

Clark, VéVé A. "The Archaeology of Black Theatre." *Critical Arts* 2, no. 1 (1981): 34–50.

Clark, VéVé A. "Performing the Memory of Difference in Afro-Caribbean Dance: Katherine Dunham's Choreography, 1938–87." In *History and Memory in African-American Culture*, edited by Geneviève Fabre and Robert O'Meally, 188–204. New York: Oxford University Press, 1994.

Clark, VéVé A., and Sara E. Johnson, eds. *Kaiso! Writings by and about Katherine Dunham.* Madison: University of Wisconsin Press, 2005.

Clarke, Donald. *Wishing on the Moon: The Life and Times of Billie Holiday.* Cambridge, MA: Da Capo Press, 2002.

Clover, Carol J. "Dancin' in the Rain." *Critical Inquiry* 21, no. 4 (Summer 1995): 722–747.

Cohan, Steven. "Case Study: Interpreting *Singin' in the Rain.*" In *Reinventing Film Studies*, edited by Christine Gledhill and Linda Williams, 53–75. New York: Oxford University Press, 2000.

Cohan, Steven. *Incongruous Entertainment: Camp, Cultural Value, and the MGM Musical.* Durham, NC: Duke University Press, 2005.

Cohan, Steven. "Introduction: Musicals of the Studio Era." In *Hollywood Musicals, the Film Reader*, edited by Steven Cohan, 1–15. New York: Routledge, 2002.

Colbert, Soyica Diggs. *Theory for Theatre Studies: Bodies.* London: Bloomsbury, 2021.

Colbert, Soyica Diggs, Douglas A. Jones Jr., and Shane Vogel. "Tidying Up after Repetition." In *Race and Performance after Repetition*, edited by Soyica Diggs Colbert, Douglas A. Jones Jr., and Shane Vogel, 1–26. Durham, NC: Duke University Press, 2020.

BIBLIOGRAPHY 249

Corbett, Saroya. "Katherine Dunham's Mark on Jazz Dance." In *Jazz Dance: A History of the Roots and Branches*, edited by Lindsay Guarino and Wendy Oliver, 89–96. Gainesville: University Press of Florida, 2014.

Crawley, Ashon T. *Blackpentecostal Breath: The Aesthetics of Possibility*. New York: Fordham University Press, 2016.

Cripps, Thomas. *Making Movies Black: The Hollywood Message Movie from World War II to the Civil Rights Era*. New York: Oxford University Press, 1993.

Croft, Clare. *Dancers as Diplomats: American Choreography in Cultural Exchange*. New York: Oxford University Press, 2015.

Croft, Clare. "Introduction." In *Queer Dance: Meanings and Makings*, edited by Clare Croft, 1–33. New York: Oxford University Press, 2017.

Croft, Clare. "Not Yet and Elsewhere: Locating Lesbian Identity in Performance Archives, as Performance Archives." *Contemporary Theatre Review* 31, nos. 1–2 (2021): 34–50.

Das, Joanna Dee. *Katherine Dunham: Dance and the African Diaspora*. New York: Oxford University Press, 2017.

de Certeau, Michel. *The Practice of Everyday Life*. Translated by Steven Randall. Berkeley: University of California Press, 1984.

Decker, Todd R. *Astaire by Numbers: Time and the Straight White Male Dancer*. New York: Oxford University Press, 2022.

Decker, Todd R. "Dancing with the Stars: The Story of Hermes Pan." Review of *The Man Who Danced with Fred Astaire* by John Franceschina. *Figure in the Carpet* (Center for the Humanities at Washington University in St. Louis) 11, no. 6 (January 2013): 6–8.

DeFrantz, Thomas F. *Dancing Revelations: Alvin Ailey's Embodiment of African American Culture*. New York: Oxford University Press, 2004.

DeFrantz, Thomas F. "Hip-hop in Hollywood: Encounter, Community, Resistance." In *The Oxford Handbook of Dance and the Popular Screen*, edited by Melissa Blanco Borelli, 113–131. New York: Oxford University Press, 2014.

DeFrantz, Thomas F. "What Is Black Dance? What Can It Do?" In *Thinking through Theatre and Performance*, edited by Maaike Bleeker, Adrian Kear, Joe Kelleher, and Heike Roms, 87–99. London: Bloomsbury, 2019.

Delameter, Jerome. *Dance in the Hollywood Musical*. Ann Arbor, MI: UMI Research Press, 1981.

De Lauretis, Teresa. *Technologies of Gender: Essays on Theory, Film, and Fiction*. Bloomington: Indiana University Press, 1987.

Deleuze, Gilles, and Félix Guattari. *A Thousand Plateaus: Capitalism and Schizophrenia*. Translated by Brian Massumi. Minneapolis: University of Minnesota Press, 1987.

Delgado, Celeste Fraser, and José Esteban Muñoz, eds. *Everynight Life: Culture and Dance in Latin/o America*. Durham, NC: Duke University Press, 1997.

Delson, Susan. *Soundies and the Changing Image of Black Americans on Screen: One Dime at a Time*. Bloomington: Indiana University Press, 2021.

Demerson, Rainy. "Sensing the Stage: Decolonial Readings of African Contemporary Dance." In *African Somaesthetics: Cultures, Feminisms, Politics*, ed. Catherine F. Botha, 95–119. Leiden: Brill, 2020.

Desmond, Jane, ed. *Dancing Desires: Choreographing Sexualities on and off the Stage*. Madison: University of Wisconsin Press, 2001.

Desmond, Jane. "Introduction." In *Meaning in Motion: New Cultural Studies of Dance*, edited by Jane Desmond, 1–25. Durham, NC: Duke University Press, 1997.

Dick, Bernard F. *That Was Entertainment: The Golden Age of the MGM Musical*. Jackson: University of Mississippi Press, 2018.

Diprose, Rosalyn. *Corporeal Generosity: On Giving with Nietzsche, Merleau-Ponty, and Levinas*. Albany: State University of New York Press, 2002.

Dirks, Tim. "AFI's Greatest Movie Musicals." AMC Filmsite, accessed January 23, 2025. https://www.filmsite.org/afi25musicals.html.

250 BIBLIOGRAPHY

Doane, Mary Ann. "The Indexical and the Concept of Medium Specificity." *differences* 18, no. 1 (2007): 128–152.

Doane, Mary Ann. "Indexicality: Trace and Sign: Introduction." *differences* 18, no. 1 (2007): 1–6.

Dodds, Sherril. *Dance on Screen: Genres and Media from Hollywood to Experimental Art.* New York: Palgrave, 2001.

Dolan, Jill. *Utopia in Performance: Finding Hope at the Theater.* Ann Arbor: University of Michigan Press, 2010.

Dong, Arthur. *Forbidden City, USA: Chinatown Nightclubs, 1936–1970.* Los Angeles: DeepFocus Productions, 2014.

Doty, Alexander. *Making Things Perfectly Queer.* Minneapolis: University of Minnesota Press, 1993.

duCille, Ann. "The Shirley Temple of My Familiar." *Transition* 73 (1997): 10–32.

Dudziak, Mary L. *Cold War Civil Rights: Race and the Image of American Democracy.* Princeton, NJ: Princeton University Press, 2011.

Duncan, Stephen R. "Not Just Born Yesterday: Judy Holliday, the Red Scare, and the (Mis-) Uses of Hollywood's Blonde Bombshell Image." In *Smart Chicks on Screen: Representing Women's Intellect in Film and Television*, edited by Laura Mattoon D'Amore, 9–28. New York: Rowman & Littlefield, 2014.

Duplan, Anaïs. "A Body That Is Ultra-Body: In Conversation with Fred Moten and Elysia Crampton." *Ploughshares*, July 13, 2016. https://blog.pshares.org/a-body-that-is-ultra-body-in-conversation-with-fred-moten-and-elysia-crampton/.

Dyer, Richard. *Heavenly Bodies: Film Stars and Society.* New York: Routledge, 2013.

Dyer, Richard. *In the Space of a Song: The Uses of Song in Film.* New York: Routledge, 2012.

Dyer, Richard. "Singing Prettily: Lena Horne in Hollywood." In *In the Space of a Song: The Uses of Song in Film*, by Richard Dyer, 114–144. New York: Routledge, 2013.

Dyer, Richard. *White.* New York: Routledge, 1997.

Edwards, Ann. *Shirley Temple: American Princess.* Guilford, CT: Lyons Press, 2017.

Eichenbaum, Rose. *The Dancer Within: Intimate Conversations with Great Dancers.* Middletown, CT: Wesleyan University Press, 2013.

Eichenbaum, Rose. *Masters of Movement: Portraits of America's Great Choreographers.* Washington, DC: Smithsonian Books, 2007.

Eidsheim, Nina Sun. *The Race of Sound: Listening, Timbre, and Vocality in African American Music.* Durham, NC: Duke University Press, 2019.

Ellis, John. *Visible Fictions: Cinema: Television: Video.* Revised edition. New York: Routledge, 1992.

Elswit, Kate. "Dancing with Coronaspheres: Expanded Breath Bodies and the Politics of Public Movement in the Age of COVID-19." *Cultural Studies* 37, no. 6 (2023): 894–916.

Erickson, Hal. *From Radio to the Big Screen: Hollywood Films Featuring Broadcast Personalities and Programs.* Jefferson, NC: McFarland, 2014.

Erigha, Maryann. *The Hollywood Jim Crow: The Racial Politics of the Movie Industry.* New York: New York University Press, 2019.

Espiritu, Yến Lê. *Asian American Panethnicity: Bridging Institutions and Identities.* Philadelphia: Temple University Press, 1992.

Everett, William A. "Performing Whiteness through the First-Generation American Immigrant Experience from Viennese Nights to Pitch Perfect." In *The Oxford Handbook of the Hollywood Musical*, edited by Dominic McHugh, 142–166. New York: Oxford University Press, 2022.

Fanon, Frantz. "The Fact of Blackness." In *Black Skin, White Masks*, by Frantz Fanon, 109–140. New York: Grove Press, 1967.

Fantle, David, and Tom Johnson. *Reel to Real: 25 Years of Celebrity Interviews from Vaudeville to Movies to TV.* Oregon, WI: Badger Books, 2004.

Ferreira Da Silva, Denise. *Unpayable Debt.* London: Sternberg Press, 2022.

BIBLIOGRAPHY 251

Feuer, Jane. *The Hollywood Musical*. 2nd edition. Bloomington: Indiana University Press, 1993.

Feuer, Jane. "Hollywood Musicals: Mass Art as Folk Art." *Jump Cut* 23 (1980): 23–25.

Feuer, Jane. "*Singin' in the Rain*: Winking at the Audience." In *Film Analysis: A Norton Reader*, edited by Jeffrey Geiger and R. L. Rutsky, 440–456. New York: W. W. Norton, 2005.

Field, Allison Nadia, ed. "Speculative Approaches to Media Histories." Special issue, *Feminist Media Histories* 8, nos. 2–3 (Spring–Summer 2022).

Firmino-Castillo, María Regina. "What Ma Lach's Bones Tell Us: Performances of Relational Materiality in Response to Genocide." *Transmotion* 4, no. 2 (2018): 31–62.

Fisher, Anna Watkins. *The Play in the System: The Art of Parasitical Resistance*. Durham, NC: Duke University Press, 2020.

Fitzgerald, Peter. *What a Glorious Feeling: The Making of* "Singin' in the Rain." DVD, Turner Entertainment/Warner Home Video/Fitzfilm, 2002.

Flatley, Jonathan. *Like Andy Warhol*. Chicago: University of Chicago Press, 2017.

Fortmueller, Kate. *Below the Stars: How the Labor of Working Actors and Extras Shapes Media Production*. Austin: University of Texas Press, 2021.

Fortuna, Victoria. *Moving Otherwise: Dance, Violence, and Memory in Buenos Aires*. New York: Oxford University Press, 2019.

Foster, Gwendolyn Audrey. *Performing Whiteness: Postmodern Re/constructions in the Cinema*. Albany: State University of New York Press, 2003.

Foster, Susan Leigh. "Choreographies of Gender." *Signs: Journal of Women in Culture and Society* 24, no. 1 (1998): 1–33.

Foster, Susan Leigh. *Choreographing Empathy: Kinesthesia in Performance*. New York: Routledge, 2010.

Foster, Susan Leigh. "Choreographing History." In *Choreographing History*, edited by Susan Leigh Foster, 3–21. Bloomington: Indiana University Press, 1995.

Foster, Susan Leigh. "Dancing Bodies." In *Meaning in Motion: New Cultural Studies of Dance*, edited by Jane Desmond, 235–258. Durham, NC: Duke University Press, 1997.

Foster, Susan Leigh. "Introduction." In *Corporealities: Dancing Knowledge, Culture and Power*, edited by Susan Leigh Foster, xi–xvii. New York: Routledge, 1996.

Foster, Susan Leigh. *Valuing Dance: Commodities and Gifts in Motion*. New York: Oxford University Press, 2019.

Foucault, Michel. *Discipline and Punish: The Birth of the Prison*. New York: Pantheon Books, 1977.

Franceschina, John. *Hermes Pan: The Man Who Danced with Fred Astaire*. New York: Oxford University Press, 2012.

Franko, Mark, ed., *The Oxford Handbook of Dance and Reenactment*. New York: Oxford University Press, 2017.

Franko, Mark. *The Work of Dance: Labor, Movement, and Identity in the 1930s*. Middletown, CT: Wesleyan University Press, 2002.

Freese, Gene Scott. *Hollywood Stunt Performers, 1910s–1970s*. Jefferson, NC: McFarland, 2014.

Gaines, Jane M. *Fire and Desire: Mixed-Race Movies in the Silent Era*. Chicago: University of Chicago Press, 2001.

Gaines, Jane M. *Pink-Slipped: What Happened to Women in the Silent Film Industries?* Champaign: University of Illinois Press, 2018.

Gaines, Jane M. "The Popular Icon as Commodity and Sign: The Circulation of Betty Grable, 1941–1945." PhD diss., Northwestern University, 1982.

Garcia, Cindy. *Salsa Crossings: Dancing Latinidad in Los Angeles*. Durham, NC: Duke University Press, 2013.

Gavin, James. *Stormy Weather: The Life of Lena Horne*. New York: Atria Books, 2009.

Geimer, Peter. "Image as Trace: Speculations about an Undead Paradigm." *differences* 18, no. 1 (2007): 7–28.

Genné, Beth. *Dance Me a Song: Astaire, Balanchine, Kelly, and the American Film Musical*. New York: Oxford University Press, 2018.

252 BIBLIOGRAPHY

Genné, Beth. "Dancin' in the Rain: Gene Kelly's Musical Films." In *Envisioning Dance on Film and Video*, edited by Judy Mitoma, Elizabeth Zimmer, and Dale Ann Stieber, 71–77. New York: Routledge, 2003.

George, Doran. *The Natural Body in Somatics Dance Training*. New York: Oxford University Press, 2020.

George-Graves, Nadine. "Identity Politics and Political Will: Jeni LeGon Living in a Great Big Way." In *The Oxford Handbook of Dance and Politics*, edited by Rebekah Kowal, Gerald Siegmund, and Randy Martin, 511–534. New York: Oxford University Press, 2017.

George-Graves, Nadine. *The Royalty of Negro Vaudeville: The Whitman Sisters and the Negotiation of Race, Gender and Class in African American Theater, 1900–1940*. New York: St. Martin's Press, 2000.

Gerdes, Ellen Virginia Proctor. "Choreographing 'One Country, Two Systems': Dance and Politics in (Post) Colonial Hong Kong." PhD diss., University of California, Los Angeles, 2021.

Gerstner, David Anthony. "Dancer from the Dance: Gene Kelly, Television, and the Beauty of Movement," *Velvet Light Trap*, no. 49 (Spring 2002). https://link.gale.com/apps/doc/A92589215/LitRC?u=ucriverside&sid=LitRC&xid=fe8c2665.

Giersdorf, Jens Richard. *The Body of the People: East German Dance since 1945*. Madison: University of Wisconsin Press, 2013.

Gil, José. "Paradoxical Body." Translated by André Lepecki. *TDR: The Drama Review* 50 (2006): 21–35.

Gilroy, Paul. "Exer(or)cising Power: Black Bodies in the Black Public Sphere." In *Dance in the City*, edited by Helen Thomas, 21–34. London: Palgrave Macmillan, 1997.

Ginsberg, Elaine K. "Introduction: The Politics of Passing." In *Passing and the Fictions of Identity*, edited by Elaine K. Ginsberg, 1–18. Durham, NC: Duke University Press, 1996.

Glymph, Thavolia. *Out of the House of Bondage*. Cambridge: Cambridge University Press, 2008.

Gonzalez, Vernadette Vicuña. *Empire's Mistress, Starring Isabel Rosario Cooper*. Durham, NC: Duke University Press, 2021.

Gottschild, Brenda Dixon. *Digging the Africanist Presence in American Performance: Dance and Other Contexts*. Westport, CT: Greenwood Press, 1996.

Gottschild, Brenda Dixon. *Joan Myers Brown and the Audacious Hope of the Black Ballerina: A Biohistory of American Performance*. New York: Palgrave Macmillan, 2012.

Graeber, David. *Debt, the First 5,000 Years*. New York: Melville, 2011.

Grant, Barry Keith. *The Hollywood Film Musical*. Hoboken, NJ: John Wiley & Sons, 2012.

Green, Rayna. "The Pocahontas Perplex: The Image of Indian Women in American Culture." *Massachusetts Review* 16, no. 4 (Autumn 1975): 698–714.

Griffin, Sean. "The Gang's All Here: Generic versus Racial Integration in the 1940s Musical." *Cinema Journal* 42, no. 1 (Fall 2002): 21–45.

Grody, Svetlana McLee, and Dorothy Daniels Lister. *Conversations with Choreographers*. Portsmouth, NH: Heinemann, 1996.

Grosz, Elizabeth. *Volatile Bodies: Toward a Corporeal Feminism*. Bloomington: Indiana Unviersity Press, 1994.

Guarino, Lindsay, and Wendy Oliver, eds. *Jazz Dance: A History of the Roots and Branches*. Gainesville: University Press of Florida, 2014.

Guglielmo, Thomas A., and Earl Lewis. "Changing Racial Meanings: Race and Ethnicity in the United States, 1930–1964." In *The Columbia Documentary History of Race and Ethnicity in America*, edited by Ronald H. Bayor, 599–666. New York: Columbia University Press, 2004.

Guy, Priscilla, and Alanna Thain, eds. *LO: TECH: POP: CULT: Screendance Remixed*. London: Routledge, 2024.

Hahn, Tomie. *Sensational Knowledge: Embodying Culture through Japanese Dance*. Middletown, CT: Wesleyan University Press, 2007.

BIBLIOGRAPHY 253

Hall, Jo. *Boys, Bass and Bother: Popular Dance and Identity in UK Drum 'n' Bass Club Culture.* London: Palgrave Macmillan, 2018.

Hanich, Julian. "Reflecting on Reflections: Cinema's Complex Mirror Shots." In *Indefinite Visions: Cinema and the Attractions of Uncertainty*, edited by Martine Beugnet, Allan Cameron, and Arild Fetveit, 131–156. Edinburgh: Edinburgh University Press, 2017.

Hanson, Helen. "Looking for Lela Simone: *Singin' in the Rain* and Microhistories of Women's Sound Work behind the Scenes and below-the-line in Classical Hollywood Cinema." *Women's History Review* 29, no. 5 (2020): 822–840.

Hardin, Tayana L. "Katherine Dunham's Southland and the Archival Quality of Black Dance." *Black Scholar* 46, no. 1 (2016): 46–53.

Harney, Steven, and Fred Moten. *The Undercommons: Fugitive Planning and Black Study.* New York: Minor Compositions, 2013.

Harris, Cheryl I. "Whiteness as Property." *Harvard Law Review* 106, no. 8 (June 1993): 1707–1791.

Hartman, Saidiya. "The Belly of the World: A Note on Black Women's Labors." *Souls* 18, no. 1 (2016): 166–173.

Hartman, Saidiya. *Scenes of Subjection: Terror, Slavery, and Self-Making in Nineteenth-Century America.* New York: Oxford University Press, 1997.

Hartman, Saidiya. "Venus in Two Acts." *Small Axe: A Caribbean Journal of Criticism* 12, no. 2 (2008): 1–14.

Hartman, Saidiya. *Wayward Lives, Beautiful Experiments: Intimate Histories of Riotous Black Girls, Troublesome Women, and Queer Radicals.* New York: W. W. Norton, 2019.

Hatch, Kristen. *Shirley Temple and the Performance of Girlhood.* New Brunswick, NJ: Rutgers University Press, 2015.

Heath, Stephen. "Dossier Suture: Notes on Suture." *Screen* 18, no. 4 (1977): 48–76.

Herrera, Brian Eugenio. *Latin Numbers: Playing Latino in Twentieth-Century US Popular Performance.* Ann Arbor: University of Michigan Press, 2015.

Hershorn, Ted. *Norman Granz: The Man Who Used Jazz for Justice.* Berkeley: University of California Press, 2011.

Hess, Earl J., and Pratibha A. Dabholkar. *Gene Kelly: The Making of a Creative Legend.* Lawrence: University Press of Kansas, 2020.

Hess, Earl J., and Pratibha A. Dabholkar. *Singin' in the Rain: The Making of an American Masterpiece.* Lawrence: University Press of Kansas, 2009.

Higashi, Sumiko. *Stars, Fans, and Consumption in the 1950s: Reading Photoplay.* New York: Palgrave, 2014.

Hill, Constance Valis. *Brotherhood in Rhythm: The Jazz Tap Dancing of the Nicholas Brothers.* New York: Oxford University Press, 2021.

Hill, Constance Valis. "From Bharata Natyam to Bop: Jack Cole's 'Modern' Jazz Dance." *Dance Research Journal* 33, no. 2 (2001): 29–39.

Hill, Erin. *Never Done: A History of Women's Work in Media Production.* New Brunswick, NJ: Rutgers University Press, 2016.

Hirschhorn, Clive. *Gene Kelly: A Biography.* New York: St. Martin's Press, 1984.

Ho, Jennifer Ann. *Racial Ambiguity in Asian American Culture.* New Brunswick, NJ: Rutgers University Press, 2015.

Hong, Grace Kyungwon. *The Ruptures of American Capital: Women of Color Feminism and the Culture of Immigrant Labor.* Minneapolis: University of Minnesota Press, 2006.

Honig, Bonnie. "Epistemology of the Curtain: Sex, Sound, and Solidarity in *Singin' in the Rain* and *Sorry to Bother You*." *Cultural Critique* 121, no. 1 (2023): 1–41.

Hunter, Tera. *To 'Joy My Freedom.* Cambridge, MA: Harvard University Press, 1997.

Hunter, Vicki. "Dancing-Walking with Trees." In *Walking Bodies: Papers, Provocations, Actions*, edited by Helen Billinghurst, Claire Hind, and Phil Smith, 21–33. Dorset: Triarchy Press, 2020.

254 BIBLIOGRAPHY

Inman, David M. *Television Variety Shows: Histories and Episode Guides to 57 Programs*. Jefferson, NC: McFarland, 2006.

Iversen, Margaret. *Photography, Trace, and Trauma*. Chicago: University of Chicago Press, 2017.

Iyer, Usha. *Dancing Women: Choreographing Corporeal Histories of Hindi Cinema*. New York: Oxford University Press, 2020.

Jackson, Robert. *Fade in, Crossroads: A History of the Southern Cinema*. New York: Oxford University Press, 2017.

Jackson, Zakiyyah Iman. *Becoming Human: Matter and Meaning in an Antiblack World*. New York: New York University Press, 2020.

Jacobson, Matthew Frye. *Whiteness of a Different Color*. Cambridge, MA: Harvard University Press, 1999.

Johnson, Imani Kai. "Black Culture without Black People: Hip Hop Dance beyond Appropriation Discourse." In *Are You Entertained? Black Popular Culture in the Twenty-First Century*, edited by Simone C. Drake and Dwan K. Henderson, 191–206. Durham, NC: Duke University Press, 2020.

Johnson, Jasmine Elizabeth. "Casualties." *TDR/The Drama Review* 62, no. 1 (2018): 169–171.

Johnson, Jasmine Elizabeth. "Flesh Dance: Black Women from Behind." In *Futures of Dance Studies*, edited by Susan Manning, Janice Ross, and Rebecca Schneider, 154–169. Madison: University of Wisconsin Press, 2020.

Johnston, Ruth. "Technologically Produced Forms of Drag in *Singin' in the Rain* and *Radio Days*." *Quarterly Review of Film and Video* 21, no. 2 (2004): 119–129.

Joseph, Miranda. *Debt to Society: Accounting for Life under Capitalism*. Minneapolis: University of Minnesota Press, 2014.

jun, grace shinhae. "Asian American Liminality." In *The Oxford Handbook of Hip Hop Studies*, edited by Mary Fogarty and Imani Kai Johnson, 280–291. New York: Oxford University Press, 2022.

Kafer, Alison. *Feminist, Queer, Crip*. Bloomington: Indiana University Press, 2013.

Kalinak, Kathryn. "Classical Hollywood, 1928–1946." In *Sound: Dialogue, Music, and Effects*, edited by Kathryn Kalinak, 37–58. New Brunswick, NJ: Rutgers University Press, 2015.

Kaplan, Sara Clarke. *The Black Reproductive: Unfree Labor and Insurgent Motherhood*. Minneapolis: University of Minnesota Press, 2021.

Kealiinohomoku, Joann. "An Anthropologist Looks at Ballet as a Form of Ethnic Dance." *Impulse* 20 (1970): 24–33.

Kedhar, Anusha. *Flexible Bodies: British South Asian Dancers in an Age of Neoliberalism*. New York: Oxford University Press, 2020.

Kedhar, Anusha. "It's Time for a Caste Reckoning in Indian 'Classical' Dance.'" In *Conversations across the Field of Dance Studies: Decolonizing Dance Discourses*, edited by Anurima Banerji and Royona Mitra, 40: 16–19. Dance Studies Association, 2020.

Keeling, Kara. "Passing for Human: Bamboozled and Digital Humanism." *Women & Performance: A Journal of Feminist Theory* 15, no. 1 (2005): 237–250.

Keeling, Kara. *The Witch's Flight: The Cinematic, the Black Femme, and the Image of Common Sense*. Durham, NC: Duke University Press, 2007.

Kelley, Robin D. G. "Black Study, Black Struggle." *Boston Review*, March 1, 2016. http://bostonreview.net/forum/robin-d-g-kelley-black-study-black-struggle.

Kennedy, Matthew. *Roadshow! The Fall of Film Musicals in the 1960s*. New York: Oxford University Press, 2014.

Kidwell, Clara Sue. "Indian Women as Cultural Mediators." *Ethnohistory* 39, no. 2 (Spring 1992): 97–107.

Kim, Chang-Hee. "Asian Performance on the Stage of American Empire in *Flower Drum Song*." *Cultural Critique* 85 (Fall 2013): 1–37.

Kim, Claire Jean. "The Racial Triangulation of Asian Americans." *Politics & Society* 27, no. 1 (1999): 105–138.

BIBLIOGRAPHY   255

Kim, Heidi. "'Flower Drum Song,' Whitewashing, and Operation Wetback: A Message from 1961." *Los Angeles Review of Books*, September 22, 2016. https://lareviewofbooks.org/arti cle/flower-drum-song-whitewashing-operation-wetback-message-1961/.

Kim, Ju Yon. *The Racial Mundane: Asian American Performance and the Embodied Everyday*. New York: New York University Press, 2015.

King, Tiffany Lethabo. *The Black Shoals: Offshore Formations of Black and Native Studies*. Durham, NC: Duke University Press, 2019.

King, Tiffany Lethabo. "Off Littorality (Shoal 1.0): Black Study off the Shores of 'the Black Body.'" *Propter Nos* 3, no. 1 (2019): 40–50.

King, Tiffany Lethabo, Jenell Navarro, and Andrea Smith, eds. *Otherwise Worlds: Against Settler Colonialism and Anti-Blackness*. Durham, NC: Duke University Press, 2020.

Klein, Christina. *Cold War Orientalism: Asia in the Middlebrow Imagination, 1945–1961*. Berkeley: University of California Press, 2003.

Knight, Arthur. *Disintegrating the Musical: Black Performance and American Musical Film*. Durham, NC: Duke University Press, 2002.

Knight, Arthur. "Star Dances: African American Constructions of Stardom, 1925–1960." In *Classic Hollywood, Classic Whiteness*, edited by Daniel Bernardi, 386–414. Minneapolis: University of Minnesota Press, 2001.

Knowles, Mark. *The Man Who Made the Jailhouse Rock: Alex Romero, Hollywood Choreographer*. Jefferson, NC: McFarland, 2013.

Knowles, Mark. *Tap Roots: The Early History of Tap Dancing*. Jefferson, NC: McFarland, 2002.

Knox, Donald. *The Magic Factory: How MGM Made An American in Paris*. Westport, CT: Praeger, 1973.

Kobal, John. *People Will Talk*. New York: Alfred A. Knopf, 1985.

Koffler, Helice. "Bryant, Marie, 1917–1978." Social Networks and Archival Context. Accessed January 10, 2025. https://snaccooperative.org/view/85321123#biography.

Konzett, Delia Malia Caparoso. *Hollywood's Hawaii: Race, Nation, and War*. New Brunswick, NJ: Rutgers University Press, 2017.

Konzett, Delia Malia Caparoso. "Introduction." In *Hollywood at the Intersection of Race and Identity*, edited by Delia Konzett, 1–18. New Brunswick, NJ: Rutgers University Press, 2020.

Kraut, Anthea. *Choreographing Copyright: Race, Gender, and Intellectual Property Rights in American Dance*. New York: Oxford University Press, 2016.

Kraut, Anthea. "'Stealing Steps' and Signature Moves: Embodied Theories of Dance as Intellectual Property." *Theatre Journal* 62, no. 2 (May 2010): 173–189.

Kraut, Anthea. "Un/funny Business in *On the Town* (1949)." In *Funny Moves: Dance Humor Politics*, edited by Marta E. Savigliano and Hannah Schwadron, 168–190. New York: Oxford University Press, 2025.

Krayenbuhl, Pamela Grenelle. "Dancing Race and Masculinity across Midcentury Screens: The Nicholas Brothers, Gene Kelly, and Elvis Presley on American Film and TV." PhD diss., Northwestern University, 2017.

Kuppers, Petra. *Eco Soma: Pain and Joy in Speculative Performance Encounters*. Minneapolis: University of Minnesota Press, 2022.

Kwan, SanSan. "Performing a Geography of Asian America: The Chop Suey Circuit." *TDR: The Drama Review* 55, no. 1 (Spring 2011): 120–136.

Laermans, Rudi. "'Dance in General' or Choreographing the Public, Making Assemblages." *Performance Research* 13, no. 1 (2008): 7–14.

La Pointe-Crump, Janice. "The Dancer, Dance, and Viewer Dialogues." *Interdisciplinary Humanities* 21, no. 1 (Spring 2004): 62–77.

Larasati, Rachmi Diyah. *The Dance That Makes You Vanish: Cultural Reconstruction in Post-genocide Indonesia*. Minneapolis: University of Minnesota Press, 2013.

Lazzarato, Maurizio. *The Making of the Indebted Man: An Essay on the Neoliberal Condition*. Translated by Joshua David Jordan. Los Angeles: Semiotext(e), 2012.

256 BIBLIOGRAPHY

Lee, Esther Kim. *Made-up Asians: Yellowface during the Exclusion Era*. Ann Arbor: University of Michigan Press, 2022.

Lee, Josephine. *Oriental, Black, and White: The Formation of Racial Habits in American Theater*. Chapel Hill: University of North Carolina Press, 2022.

Lee, Josephine. *Performing Asian America: Race and Ethnicity on the Contemporary Stage*. Philadelphia: Temple University Press, 1998.

Lee, Rachel C. *The Exquisite Corpse of Asian America: Biopolitics, Biosociality, and Posthuman Ecologies*. New York: New York University Press, 2014.

Lee, Robert G. *Orientals: Asian Americans in Popular Culture*. Philadelphia: Temple University Press, 1999.

Lee, Shelley Sang-Hee. *A New History of Asian America*. New York: Taylor & Francis, 2014.

Lepecki, André. "Introduction: Presence and Body in Dance and Performance Theory." In *Of the Presence of the Body: Essays on Dance and Performance Theory*, edited by André Lepecki, 1–9. Middletown, CT: Wesleyan University Press, 2004.

Levine, Debra. "Jack Cole (1911–1974)." *Dance Heritage Coalition* (2012): 5. URL no longer active.

Levine, Debra. "Jack Cole Made Marilyn Move." *Los Angeles Times*, August 9, 2009. https://www.latimes.com/entertainment/arts/la-ca-marilyn-monroe9-2009aug09-story.html.

Levinson, Peter J. *Puttin' on the Ritz: Fred Astaire and the Fine Art of Panache. A Biography*. New York: St. Martin's Press, 2015.

Lewin, Yaël Tamar. *Night's Dancer: The Life of Janet Collins*. Middletown, CT: Wesleyan University Press, 2015.

Lewis, David H. *Flower Drum Songs: The Story of Two Musicals*. Jefferson, NC: McFarland, 2006.

Lipsitz, George. *The Possessive Investment in Whiteness: How White People Profit from Identity Politics*. Philadelphia: Temple University Press, 2006.

Lisanti, Tom. "Irene Tsu." In *Fantasy Femmes of Sixties Cinema: Interviews with Twenty Actresses from Biker, Beach, and Elvis Movies*, 158–169. Jefferson, NC: McFarland, 2015.

Loney, Glenn. *Unsung Genius: The Passion of Dancer-Choreographer Jack Cole*. New York: Franklin Watts, 1984.

Lott, Eric. *Love and Theft: Blackface Minstrelsy and the American Middle Class*. New York: Oxford University Press, 1993.

Love, Heather. *Feeling Backward: Loss and the Politics of Queer History*. Cambridge, MA: Harvard University Press, 2007.

Lowe, Lisa. *Immigrant Acts: On Asian American Cultural Politics*. Durham, NC: Duke University Press, 1996.

Lvovsky, Anna. *Vice Patrol: Cops, Courts, and the Struggle over Urban Gay Life before Stonewall*. Chicago: University of Chicago Press, 2021.

Ma, Sheng-mei. "Rodgers and Hammerstein's 'Chopsticks' Musicals." *Literature/Film Quarterly* 31, no. 1 (2003): 17–26.

Macfarlane, Malcolm, and Ken Crossland. *Perry Como: A Biography and Complete Career Record*. Jefferson, NC: McFarland, 2012.

Macías, Anthony. *Mexican American Mojo: Popular Music, Dance, and Urban Culture in Los Angeles, 1935–1968*. Durham, NC: Duke University Press, 2008.

Malnig, Julie. *Dancing Black, Dancing White: Rock'n'Roll, Race, and Youth Culture of the 1950s and Early 1960s*. New York: Oxford University Press, 2023.

Manning, Erin. *Always More Than One: Individuation's Dance*. Durham, NC: Duke University Press, 2013.

Manning, Erin. *Politics of Touch: Sense, Movement, Sovereignty*. Minneapolis: University of Minnesota Press, 2007.

Manning, Susan. *Ecstasy and the Demon: The Dances of Mary Wigman*. Berkeley: University of California Press, 1993.

Manning, Susan. *Modern Dance, Negro Dance: Race in Motion*. Minneapolis: University of Minnesota Press, 2004.

BIBLIOGRAPHY 257

Marks, Laura U. *The Skin of the Film: Intercultural Cinema, Embodiment, and the Senses.* Durham, NC: Duke University Press, 2000.

Martin, Randy. *Critical Moves: Dance Studies in Theory and Politics.* Durham, NC: Duke University Press, 1998.

Marubbio, M. Elise. *Killing the Indian Woman: Images of Native American Women in Film.* Lexington: University of Kentucky Press, 2006.

McCarren, Felicia M. *Dancing Machines: Choreographies of the Age of Mechanical Reproduction.* Stanford: Stanford University Press, 2003.

McConachie, Bruce A. "The 'Oriental' Musicals of Rodgers and Hammerstein and the U.S. War in Southeast Asia." *Theatre Journal* 46 (1994): 385–398.

McGee, Tom. *Betty Grable: The Girl with the Million Dollar Legs.* New York: Welcome Rain, 1995.

McLean, Adrienne L. *Being Rita Hayworth: Labor, Identity, and Hollywood Stardom.* New Brunswick, NJ: Rutgers University Press, 2004.

McLean, Adrienne L. *Dying Swans and Madmen: Ballet, the Body, and Narrative Cinema.* New Brunswick, NJ: Rutgers University Press, 2008.

McLean, Adrienne L. "Introduction: Stardom in the 1930s." In *Glamour in a Golden Age: Movie Stars of the 1930s,* edited by Adrienne McLean, 1–17. New Brunswick, NJ: Rutgers University Press, 2011.

McLean, Adrienne L. "The Thousand Ways There Are to Move: Camp and Oriental Dance in the Hollywood Musicals of Jack Cole." In *Visions of the East: Orientalism in Film,* edited by Matthew Bernstein and Gaylyn Studlar, 130–157. New Brunswick, NJ: Rutgers University Press, 1997.

McNally, Karen. *The Stardom Film: Creating the Hollywood Fairy Tale.* New York: Columbia University Press, 2021.

McQueen, Amanda Louise. "After 'the Golden Age': An Industrial History of the Hollywood Musical, 1955–1975." PhD diss., University of Wisconsin, Madison, 2016.

Mellencamp, Patricia. "Making History: Julie Dash." *Frontiers: A Journal of Women Studies* 15, no. 1 (1994): 76–101.

Mellencamp, Patricia. "Spectacle and Spectator: Looking through the American Musical Comedy." *Cine-tracts* 1 (1977): 27–35.

Metz, Christian. "Mirrors" (1991). In *Impersonal Enunciation, or the Place of Film,* 60–63. New York: Columbia University Press, 2016.

Metzger, Sean. *Chinese Looks: Fashion, Performance, Race.* Bloomington: Indiana University Press, 2014.

Meyer, Richard. "Warhol's Clones." *Yale Journal of Criticism* 7 (1994): 79–109.

Mitchell, Koritha. "Identifying White Mediocrity and Know-Your-Place Aggression: A Form of Self-Care." *African American Review* 51, no. 4 (2018): 253–262.

Mitra, Royona. "Unmaking Contact: Choreographic Touch at the Intersections of Race, Caste, and Gender." *Dance Research Journal* 53, no. 3 (2021): 6–24.

Mónico, Roberto A. "Los Angeles and William H. Parker: Race, Vice, and Police during the Red Scare." PhD diss., University of Colorado at Boulder, 2022.

Morgan, Jennifer L. *Laboring Women: Reproduction and Gender in New World Slavery.* Philadelphia: University of Pennsylvania Press, 2004.

Morrison, Matthew D. *Blacksound: Making Race and Popular Music in the United States.* Oakland: University of California Press, 2024.

Morrison, Toni. *The Bluest Eye.* 1970; New York: Vintage Books, 2007.

Morrison, Toni. *Playing in the Dark: Whiteness and the Literary Imagination.* Cambridge, MA: Harvard University Press, 1992.

Moten, Fred. *In the Break: The Aesthetics of the Black Radical Tradition.* Minneapolis: University of Minnesota Press, 2003.

Moten, Fred. "The Subprime and the Beautiful." *African Identities* 11, no. 2 (2013): 237–245.

BIBLIOGRAPHY

Motley, Elisabeth. "Crip Aesthetics and a Choreographic Method of Leakiness." *Dance Chronicle* 47, no. 1 (2024): 55–76.

Mullen, Haryette. "Optic White: Blackness and the Production of Whiteness." *Diacritics* 24, nos. 2–3 (Summer–Autumn 1994): 71–89.

Mulvey, Laura. "The Index and the Uncanny: Life and Death in the Photograph." In *Death 24x a Second: Stillness and the Moving Image*, 54–66. London: Reaktion Books, 2006.

Muñoz, José Esteban. *Disidentifications: Queers of Color and the Performance of Politics.* Minneapolis: University of Minnesota Press, 1999.

Muñoz, José Esteban. "Ephemera as Evidence: Introductory Notes to Queer Acts." *Women and Performance: A Journal of Feminist Theory* 8, no. 2 (1996): 5–16.

Muñoz, José Esteban. "Feeling Brown, Feeling Down: Latina Affect, the Performativity of Race, and the Depressive Position." *Signs: Journal of Women in Culture and Society* 31, no. 3 (2006): 675–688.

Muñoz, José Esteban. "Gesture, Ephemera, and Queer Feeling." In *Dancing Desires: Choreographing Sexualities on and off the Stage*, edited by Jane Desmond, 423–442. Madison: University of Wisconsin Press, 2001.

Muñoz, José Esteban. "Race, Sex, and the Incommensurate: Gary Fisher with Eve Kosofsky Sedgwick." In *Queer Futures: Reconsidering Ethics, Activism, and the Political*, edited by Elahe Haschemi Yekani, Eveline Kilian, and Beatrice Michaelis, 103–116. New York: Routledge, 2013.

Muñoz, José Esteban. *The Sense of Brown.* Durham, NC: Duke University Press, 2020.

Musser, Amber Jamilla. *Sensational Flesh: Race, Power, and Masochism.* New York: New York University Press, 2014.

Musser, Amber Jamilla. *Sensual Excess.* New York: New York University Press, 2018.

Musser, Amber Jamilla. "Surface-Becoming: Lyle Ashton Harris and Brown Jouissance." *Women & Performance: A Journal of Feminist Theory* 28, no. 1 (2018): 34–45.

Nadel, Alan. *Demographic Angst: Cultural Narratives and American Films of the 1950s.* New Brunswick, NJ: Rutgers University Press, 2017.

Nair, Kartik. "Unfinished Bodies: The Sticky Materiality of Prosthetic Effects." *JCMS: Journal of Cinema and Media Studies* 60, no. 3 (2021): 104–128.

Nash, Jennifer C. "Citational Desires: On Black Feminism's Institutional Longings." *Diacritics* 48, no. 3 (2020): 76–91.

Negra, Diane. *Off-White Hollywood: American Culture and Ethnic Female Stardom.* New York: Routledge, 2001.

Ness, Sally Ann. "The Inscription of Gesture: Inward Migrations in Dance." In *Migrations of Gesture*, edited by Carrie Noland and Sally Ann Ness, 1–30. Minneapolis: University of Minnesota Press, 2008.

Ngai, Mae M. *Impossible Subjects: Illegal Aliens and the Making of Modern America.* Princeton, NJ: Princeton University Press, 2014.

Noland, Carrie. *Agency and Embodiment: Performing Gestures/Producing Culture.* Cambridge, MA: Harvard University Press, 2009.

Nyong'o, Tavia. *Afro-Fabulations: The Queer Drama of Black Life.* New York: New York University Press, 2018.

Nyong'o, Tavia. "Unburdening Representation." *Black Scholar* 44, no. 2 (2014): 70–80.

Ocampo, Anthony Christian. *The Latinos of Asia: How Filipino Americans Break the Rules of Race.* Stanford: Stanford University Press, 2016.

Oja, Carol J. *Bernstein Meets Broadway: Collaborative Art in a Time of War.* New York: Oxford University Press, 2014.

O'Shea, Janet. "Roots/Routes of Dance Studies." In *The Routledge Dance Studies Reader*, 2nd edition, edited by Alexandra Carter and Janet O'Shea, 1–16. New York: Routledge, 2010.

Osterweis, Ariel. *Body Impossible: Desmond Richardson and the Politics of Virtuosity.* New York: Oxford University Press, 2024.

Osumare, Halifu. "Global Breakdancing and the Intercultural Body." *Dance Research Journal* 34, no. 2 (2002): 30–45.

BIBLIOGRAPHY 259

Ovalle, Priscilla Peña. *Dance and the Hollywood Latina: Race, Sex, and Stardom*. New Brunswick, NJ: Rutgers University Press, 2011.

Palumbo-Liu, David. *Asian/American: Historical Crossings of a Racial Frontier*. Stanford: Stanford University Press, 1999.

Paredez, Deborah. "Lena Horne and Judy Garland: Divas, Desire, and Discipline in the Civil Rights Era." *TDR/The Drama Review* 58, no. 4 (2014): 105–119.

Paredez, Deborah. *Selenidad: Selena, Latinos, and the Performance of Memory*. Durham, NC: Duke University Press, 2009.

Parfitt, Clare, ed. *Cultural Memory and Popular Dance: Dancing to Remember, Dancing to Forget*. London: Palgrave Macmillan, 2021.

Perillo, Lorenzo J. *Choreographing in Color: Filipinos, Hip-hop, and the Cultural Politics of Euphemism*. New York: Oxford University Press, 2020.

Perron, Wendy. "Putting the Black Swan Blackout in Context." *Dance Magazine*, March 11, 2011. https://www.dancemagazine.com/putting-the-black-swan-blackout-in-context/#gsc.tab=0.

Perron, Wendy. "Syvilla Fort (1917–1975)." Blog. October 3, 2020. https://wendyperron.com/syvilla-fort-1917-1975/.

Petty, Miriam J. *Stealing the Show: African American Performers and Audiences in 1930s Hollywood*. Oakland: University of California Press, 2016.

Phelan, Peggy. *Unmarked: The Politics of Performance*. New York: Routledge, 1993.

Phillips, Victoria. *Martha Graham's Cold War: The Dance of American Diplomacy*. New York: Oxford University Press, 2020.

Phruksachart, Melissa. "The Many Lives of Mr. Yunioshi: Yellowface and the Queer Buzz of *Breakfast at Tiffany's*." *Camera Obscura: Feminism, Culture, and Media Studies* 32, no. 3 (2017): 93–119.

Platte, Nathan. "Postwar Hollywood, 1947–1967." In *Sound: Dialogue, Music, and Effects*, edited by Kathryn Kalinak, 59–82. New Brunswick, NJ: Rutgers University Press, 2015.

Power-Sotomayor, Jade. "Corporeal Sounding: Listening to Bomba Dance, Listening to puertorriqueñxs." *Performance Matters* 6, no. 2 (2020): 43–59.

Prescod, Janette. "Marie Bryant." In *Notable Black American Women*, book 2, edited by Jessie Carney Smith, 71–73. Detroit, MI: Gale Research, 1996.

Prock, Stephen. "Music, Gender and the Politics of Performance in *Singin' in the Rain*." *Colby Quarterly* 36, no. 4 (December 2000): 295–318.

Puar, Jasbir K. *The Right to Maim: Debility, Capacity, Disability*. Durham, NC: Duke University Press, 2017.

Pullen, Kirsten. *Like a Natural Woman: Spectacular Female Performance in Classical Hollywood*. New Brunswick, NJ: Rutgers University Press, 2014.

Quashie, Kevin. *Black Aliveness, or a Poetics of Being*. Durham, NC: Duke University Press, 2021.

Raheja, Michelle H. *Reservation Reelism: Redfacing, Visual Sovereignty, and Representations of Native Americans in Film*. Lincoln: University of Nebraska Press, 2010.

Redmond, Sean. "The Whiteness of Stars: Looking at Kate Winslet's Unruly Body." In *Stardom and Celebrity: A Reader*, edited by Sean Redmond and Su Holmes, 263–274. London: Sage, 2007.

Regester, Charlene B. *African American Actresses: The Struggle for Visibility, 1900–1960*. Bloomington: Indiana University Press, 2010.

Regester, Charlene B. *Black Entertainers in African American Newspaper Articles*. Vol. 1: *An Annotated Bibliography of the* Chicago Defender, *the* Afro-American Baltimore, *the* Los Angeles Sentinel *and the* New York Amsterdam News, *1910–1950*. Jefferson, NC: McFarland, 2002.

Regester, Charlene B. *Black Entertainers in African American Newspaper Articles*. Vol. 2: *Annotated and Indexed Bibliography of the* Pittsburgh Courier *and the* California Eagle, *1914–1950*. Jefferson, NC: McFarland, 2002.

260 BIBLIOGRAPHY

Reyes, Luis, and Peter Rubie. *Hispanics in Hollywood: A Celebration of 100 Years in Film and Television.* Hollywood, CA: Lone Eagle, 2000.

Reynoso, José Luis. *Dancing Mestizo Modernisms: Choreographing Postcolonial and Postrevolutionary Mexico.* New York: Oxford University Press, 2023.

Rich, Katey. "The Landmark Asian-American Musical That Never Got Its Due." *Little Gold Men* podcast, *Vanity Fair*, May 12, 2023. https://www.vanityfair.com/hollywood/2023/05/awards-insider-litle-gold-men-flower-drum-song.

Richardson, Niall. *Transgressive Bodies: Representations in Film and Popular Culture.* New York: Routledge, 2016.

Rippy, Marguerite H. "Commodity, Tragedy, Desire: Female Sexuality and Blackness in the Iconography of Dorothy Dandridge." In *Classic Hollywood, Classic Whiteness*, edited by Daniel Bernardi, 178–209. Minneapolis: University of Minnesota Press, 2001.

Roach, Joseph. *Cities of the Dead: Circum-Atlantic Performance.* New York: Columbia University Press, 1996.

Roberts, Rosemarie A. *Baring Unbearable Sensualities: Hip Hop Dance, Bodies, Race, and Power.* Middletown, CT: Wesleyan University Press, 2021.

Rodríguez, Clara E. "Counting Latinos in the US Census." In *How the United States Racializes Latinos*, edited by José A. Cobas, Jorge Duany, and Joe R. Feagin, 37–53. New York: Routledge, 2015.

Rogers, Bradley. *The Song Is You: Musical Theatre and the Politics of Bursting into Song and Dance.* Iowa City: University of Iowa Press, 2020.

Rogin, Michael. *Blackface, White Noise: Jewish Immigrants in the Hollywood Melting Pot.* Berkeley: University of California Press, 1996.

Rosenberg, Douglas, ed. *The Oxford Handbook of Screendance Studies.* New York: Oxford University Press, 2016.

Rosenberg, Douglas. *Screendance: Inscribing the Ephemeral Image.* New York: Oxford University Press, 2012.

Roth, Martin. "Pulling the Plug on Lina Lamont." *Jump Cut* 35 (1990): 59–65.

Sagolla, Lisa Jo. "Carol Haney." *American National Biography.* February 2000. https://doi.org/10.1093/anb/9780198606697.article.1800523.

Sagolla, Lisa Jo. *Rock 'n' Roll Dances of the 1950s.* Santa Barbara, CA: Greenwood Press, 2011.

Said, Edward W. *Orientalism.* 1978; New York: Random House, 1994.

Salamon, Gayle. *Assuming a Body: Transgender and Rhetorics of Materiality.* New York: Columbia University Press, 2010.

Sánchez, George J. *Becoming Mexican American: Ethnicity, Culture and Identity in Chicano Los Angeles, 1900–1945.* New York: Oxford University Press, 1993.

Satkunaratnam, Ahalya. *Moving Bodies, Navigating Conflict: Practicing Bharata Natyam in Colombo, Sri Lanka.* Middletown, CT: Wesleyan University Press, 2020.

Savigliano, Marta. *Tango and the Political Economy of Passion.* New York: Routledge, 1995.

Savran, David. *A Queer Sort of Materialism: Recontextualizing American Theater.* Ann Arbor: University of Michigan Press, 2003.

Schechner, Richard. *Between Theater and Anthropology.* Philadelphia: University of Pennsylvania Press, 1985.

Schneider, Rebecca. "Hello Dolly Well Hello Dolly: The Double and Its Theatre." In *Performance and Psychoanalysis*, edited by Adrian Kear and Patrick Campbell, 94–114. New York: Routledge, 2001.

Schneider, Rebecca. "Solo Solo Solo." In *After Criticism: New Responses to Art and Performance*, edited by Gavin Butt, 23–47. Malden, MA: Blackwell, 2005.

Schwartz, Selby Wynn. *The Bodies of Others: Drag Dances and Their Afterlives.* Ann Arbor: University of Michigan Press, 2019.

Schwartz, Selby Wynn. "Light, Shadow, Screendance: Catherine Gallaso's *Bring on the Lumière!*" In *The Oxford Handbook of Screendance Studies*, edited by Douglas Rosenberg, 205–224. New York: Oxford University Press, 2016.

BIBLIOGRAPHY 261

Scolieri, Paul. "Global/Mobile: Re-orienting Dance and Migration Studies." *Dance Research Journal* 40, no. 2 (2008): v–xx.

Scott, Anna Beatrice. "Spectacle and Dancing Bodies That Matter: Or, If It Don't Fit, Don't Force It." In *Meaning in Motion: New Cultural Studies of Dance*, edited by Jane Desmond, 259–269. Durham, NC: Duke University Press, 1997.

Sedgwick, Eve Kosofsky. *Between Men: English Literature and Male Homosocial Desire*. 1985; New York: Columbia University Press, 2016.

Sedgwick, Eve Kosofsky. *Epistemology of the Closet*. Updated with a new preface. Berkeley: University of California Press, 2007.

Sedgwick, Eve Kosofsky. "Paranoid Reading and Reparative Reading, or You're So Paranoid, You Probably Think This Essay Is about You." In *Touching Feeling: Affect, Pedagogy, Performativity*, 123–152. Durham, NC: Duke University Press, 2003.

See, Sarita Echavez. *Decolonized Eye: Filipino American Art and Performance*. Minneapolis: University of Minnesota Press, 2009.

See, Sarita Echavez. *The Filipino Primitive: Accumulation and Resistance in the American Museum*. New York: New York University Press, 2017.

Semmes, Clovis E. *The Regal Theater and Black Culture*. New York: Palgrave Macmillan, 2006.

Sharpe, Christina. *In the Wake: On Blackness and Being*. Durham, NC: Duke University Press, 2016.

Shaviro, Steven. *The Cinematic Body*. Minneapolis: University of Minnesota Press, 1994.

Shay, Anthony, and Barbara Sellers-Young, eds. *The Oxford Handbook of Dance and Ethnicity*. New York: Oxford University Press, 2016.

Shaye, Amaryah. "Blackness and Value; Part 2: On Whiteness as Credit." *Women in Theology*, blog, February 11, 2015. https://womenintheology.org/2015/02/11/blackness-and-value-part-2-on-whiteness-as-credit/.

Shea Murphy, Jacqueline. *Dancing Indigenous Worlds: Choreographies of Relation*. Minneapolis: University of Minnesota Press, 2023.

Shea Murphy, Jacqueline. *The People Have Never Stopped Dancing: Native American Modern Dance Histories*. Minneapolis: University of Minnesota Press, 2007.

Shildrick, Margrit. *Visceral Prostheses: Somatechnics and Posthuman Embodiment*. London: Bloomsbury, 2022.

Shimakawa, Karen. *National Abjection: The Asian American Body Onstage*. Durham, NC: Duke University Press, 2002.

Shiovitz, Brynn W. *Behind the Screen: Tap Dance, Race, and Invisibility during Hollywood's Golden Age*. New York: Oxford University Press, 2023.

Shohat, Ella. "Ethnicities-in-Relation: Toward a Multicultural Reading of American Cinema." In *Unspeakable Images: Ethnicity and the American Cinema*, edited by Lester Friedman, 215–250. Champaign: University of Illinois Press, 1991.

Siegel, Marcia B. *At the Vanishing Point: A Critic Looks at Dance*. New York: Saturday Review Press, 1972.

Silverman, Kaja. *The Acoustic Mirror: The Female Voice in Psychoanalysis and Cinema*. Bloomington: Indiana University Press, 1988.

Slide, Anthony. *Hollywood Unknowns: A History of Extras, Bit Players, and Stand-Ins*. Jackson: University Press of Mississippi, 2012.

Smith, Jacob. *The Thrill Makers: Celebrity, Masculinity, and Stunt Performance*. Berkeley: University of California Press, 2012.

Snead, James. "Shirley Temple." In *White Screens/Black Images: Hollywood from the Dark Side*, 47–66. New York: Routledge, 1994.

Sobchack, Vivian. *Carnal Thoughts: Embodiment and Moving Image Culture*. Berkeley: University of California Press, 2004.

Social Networks and Archival Content. "Bruce, Mary, 1900–1995." Accessed January 9, 2025. https://snaccooperative.org/view/85334651#biography.

Spatz, Ben. *Blue Sky Body: Thresholds for Embodied Research*. New York: Routledge, 2019.

262 BIBLIOGRAPHY

Spatz, Ben. *Race and the Forms of Knowledge: Technique, Identity, and Place in Artistic Research.* Evanston, IL: Northwestern University Press, 2024.

Spillers, Hortense. "Mama's Baby, Papa's Maybe: An American Grammar Book." *Diacritics* 17, no. 2 (Summer 1987): 64–81.

Spivak, Gayatri Chakravorty. "The Rani of Sirmur: An Essay in Reading the Archives." *History and Theory* 24, no. 3 (1985): 247–272.

Srinivasan, Priya. *Sweating Saris: Indian Dance as Transnational Labor.* Philadelphia: Temple University Press, 2011.

Stacey, Jackie. *The Cinematic Life of the Gene.* Durham, NC: Duke University Press, 2010.

Stanger, Arabella. *Dancing on Violent Ground: Utopia as Dispossession in Euro-American Theater Dance.* Evanston, IL: Northwestern University Press, 2021.

Stearns, Marshall, and Jean Stearns. *Jazz Dance: The Story of American Vernacular Dance.* New York: Schirmer Books, 1968.

Steen, Shannon. *Racial Geometries of the Black Atlantic, Asian Pacific, and American Theatre.* New York: Palgrave Macmillan, 2010.

Sternfeld, Jessica, and Elizabeth L. Wollman. "After the 'Golden Age.'" In *Histories of the Musical: An Oxford Handbook of the American Musical*, vol. 1, edited by Raymond Knapp, Mitchell Morris, and Stacy Wolf, 177–198. New York: Oxford University Press, 2018.

Stewart, Jacqueline Najuma. *Migrating to the Movies: Cinema and Black Urban Modernity.* Berkeley: University of California Press, 2005.

Stoever, Jennifer Lynn. *The Sonic Color Line: Race and the Cultural Politics of Listening.* New York: New York University Press, 2016.

Stoler, Ann Laura. *Along the Archival Grain: Epistemic Anxieties and Colonial Common Sense.* Princeton, NJ: Princeton University Press, 2009.

Stratemann, Klaus. *Duke Ellington, Day by Day and Film by Film.* Copenhagen: JazzMedia ApS, 1992.

Takeshita, Chikako. "From Mother/Fetus to Holobiont(s): A Material Feminist Ontology of the Pregnant Body." *Catalyst: Feminism, Theory, Technoscience* 3, no. 1 (2022): 1–28.

Taussig, Michael. *Mimesis and Alterity: A Particular History of the Senses.* New York: Routledge, 2018.

Taylor, Diana. *The Archive and the Repertoire: Performing Cultural Memory in the Americas.* Durham, NC: Duke University Press, 2003.

Thomas, Sonja. "Black Soundwork, Knowledge Production, and the 'Debate' over Tap Dance Origins." *Resonance: The Journal of Sound and Culture* 1, no. 4 (2020): 412–421.

Thomas, Tony. *That's Dancing!* New York: Harry N. Abrams, 1984.

Tomko, Linda J. *Dancing Class: Gender, Ethnicity, and Social Divides in American Dance, 1890–1920.* Bloomington: Indiana University Press, 2000.

Tongson, Karen. "Karaoke, Queer Theory, Queer Performance." In *The Oxford Handbook of Music and Queerness*, edited by Fred Everett Maus and Sheila Whiteley, 211–226. New York: Oxford University Press, 2022.

Trenka, Susie. *Jumping the Color Line: Vernacular Jazz Dance in American Film, 1929–1945.* Bloomington: Indiana University Press, 2021.

Tsai, Addie. "Hybrid Texts, Assembled Bodies: Michel Gondry's Merging of Camera and Dancer in 'Let Forever Be.'" *International Journal of Screendance* 6 (2016). https://doi.org/10.18061/ijsd.v6i0.4892.

Tucker, Sherrie. *Dance Floor Democracy: The Social Geography of Memory at the Hollywood Canteen.* Durham, NC: Duke University Press, 2014.

UMass Fine Arts Center. "Bodies at Risk: Emily Johnson and Alice Sheppard." YouTube, March 18, 2021. https://www.youtube.com/watch?v=iYXKvzZGzKU.

Valderrama, Carla. *This Was Hollywood: Forgotten Stars and Stories.* New York: Running, 2020.

Vatsal, Radha. "Reevaluating Footnotes: Women Directors of the Silent Era." In *A Feminist Reader in Early Cinema*, edited by Jennifer M. Bean and Diane Negra, 119–138. Durham, NC: Duke University Press, 2002.

BIBLIOGRAPHY 263

Vera, Hernán, and Andrew M. Gordon. *Screen Saviors: Hollywood Fictions of Whiteness.* Lanham, MD: Rowman & Littlefield, 2003.

Vogel, Shane. "Lena Horne's Impersona." *Camera Obscura: Feminism, Culture, and Media Studies* 23, no. 1 (2008): 11–45.

Wakpa, Tria Blu. "What Native American Dance Does and the Stakes of Ecosomatics." In *Geographies of Us: Ecosomatic Essays and Practice Pages,* edited by Sondra Fraleigh and Shannon Rose Riley, 36–63. New York: Taylor & Francis, 2024.

Wallace, Karen. "The Redskin and *The Paleface*: Comedy on the Frontier." In *Classic Hollywood, Classic Whiteness,* edited by Daniel Bernardi, 111–138. Minneapolis: University of Minnesota Press, 2001.

Wallace-Sanders, Kimberly. *Mammy: A Century of Race, Gender, and Southern Memory.* Ann Arbor: University of Michigan Press, 2008.

Warren, Doug. *Betty Grable: The Reluctant Movie Queen.* Kindle edition. Crossroad Press, 2016.

Weheliye, Alexander Ghedi. *Habeas Viscus: Racializing Assemblages, Biopolitics, and Black Feminist Theories of the Human.* Durham, NC: Duke University Press, 2014.

Weinbaum, Alys Eve. *The Afterlife of Reproductive Slavery: Biocapitalism and Black Feminism's Philosophy of History.* Durham, NC: Duke University Press, 2019.

Weinbaum, Alys Eve. *Wayward Reproductions: Genealogies of Race and Nation in Transatlantic Modern Thought.* Durham, NC: Duke University Press, 2004.

Westbrook, Robert B. "'I Want a Girl, Just Like the Girl That Married Harry James': American Women and the Problem of Political Obligation in World War II." *American Quarterly* 42, no. 4 (December 1990): 587–614.

White, Hayden. *The Content of the Form: Narrative Discourse and Historical Representation.* Baltimore: Johns Hopkins University Press, 1990.

Wiegman, Robyn. "Eve's Triangles, or Queer Studies beside Itself." *differences* 26, no. 1 (2015): 48–73.

Wilderson, Frank B., III, and Tiffany Lethabo King. "Staying Ready for Black Study." In *Otherwise Worlds: Against Settler Colonialism and Anti-Blackness,* edited by Tiffany Lethabo King, Jenell Navarro, and Andrea Smith, 52–74. Durham, NC: Duke University Press, 2020.

Williams, Linda. "Film Bodies: Gender, Genre, and Excess." *Film Quarterly* 44, no. 4 (1991): 2–13.

Willis, Tara Aisha. "Stumbling into Place: Seeing Blackness in David Thomson's Choreographies of Ambiguity." *Black Scholar* 46, no. 1 (2016): 4–14.

Wolf, Stacy Ellen. "'We'll Always Be Bosom Buddies': Female Duets and the Queering of Broadway Musical Theater." *GLQ: A Journal of Lesbian and Gay Studies* 12, no. 3 (2006): 351–376.

Woll, Allen L. *The Latin Image in American Film.* Los Angeles: UCLA Latin American Center, 1977.

Wollen, Peter. *Singin' in the Rain.* London: British Film Institute, 1992.

Wong, Yutian. "Artistic Utopias: Michio Ito and the Trope of the International." In *Worlding Dance,* edited by Susan Leigh Foster, 144–162. London: Palgrave Macmillan, 2009.

Wong, Yutian. *Choreographing Asian America.* Middletown, CT: Wesleyan University Press, 2011.

Wong, Yutian. "Introduction: Issues in Asian American Dance Studies." In *Contemporary Directions in Asian American Dance,* edited by Yutian Wong, 3–26. Madison: University of Wisconsin Press, 2016.

Young, Harvey. *Embodying Black Experience: Stillness, Critical Memory, and the Black Body.* Ann Arbor: University of Michigan Press, 2010.

Young, Hershini Bhana. *Illegible Will: Coercive Spectacles of Labor in South Africa and the Diaspora.* Durham, NC: Duke University Press, 2017.

Yu, Sabrina Qiong. "Performing Stardom: Star Studies in Transformation and Expansion." In *Revisiting Star Studies: Cultures, Themes and Methods,* edited by Sabrina Qiong Yu and Guy Austin, 1–22. Edinburgh: Edinburgh University Press, 2017.

264 BIBLIOGRAPHY

Zondi, Mlondolozi. "Haunting Gathering: Black Dance and Afro-Pessimism." *ASAP/Journal* 5, no. 2 (May 2020): 256–266.

Zuo, Mila. *Vulgar Beauty: Acting Chinese in the Global Sensorium*. Durham, NC: Duke University Press, 2022.

Archival Sources

Afro-American. "White Woman Dances in Black." April 4, 1942, 13.

The Argus (Melbourne). "Talk-About." October 11, 1954, 10. http://trove.nla.gov.au/ndp/del/article/23445043.

Atkinson, Brooks. "'Flower Drum' Song Opens at St. James." *New York Times*, December 2, 1958, 44.

Black, Shirley Temple. *Child Star: An Autobiography*. New York: Warner Books, 1988.

Blue, Angie. "Her Divided Heart (Betty Grable)." *Photoplay*, January 1949, 49, 71–72.

Bubbeo, Daniel. "Gene Kelly's Widow Chats about Her Late Husband and *Singin' in the Rain*." *Newsday*, July 11, 2012. https://www.newsday.com/entertainment/movies/gene-kelly-s-widow-patricia-chats-about-her-late-husband-and-singin-in-the-rain-l23258.

Calvin, Dolores. "Lena Can't Dance but She's Great in Musical." *Baltimore Afro-American*, January 15, 1949, 7.

Calvin, Dolores. "Who Said Brush-Off? That Is What Marie Bryant Got in Pix." *Chicago Defender*, April 29, 1950, n.p.

Carroll, Harrison. "Behind the Scenes in Hollywood." *Daily Clintonian*, February 2, 1951, 2.

Catton, Pia. "It's Hard Work Being Jennifer Lawrence's Body Double, Especially for Jennifer Lawrence." *Daily Beast*, March 2, 2018. https://www.thedailybeast.com/its-hard-work-being-jennifer-lawrences-body-double-especially-for-jennifer-lawrence.

Cerulli, Dom. "The Arrival of Abbey." *Downbeat*, June 12, 1958, 19.

Chicago Defender. "Mary Bruce's Dancing Girls Score Big Hit." June 8, 1929, 6.

Clark, Roy. "Alex Romero Compares Hollywood and Broadway." *Dance Magazine* 36 (January 1962): 42–45.

Cole, Maria (as Mrs. Nat King Cole)."Why I Am Returning to Show Business." *Ebony* 21 (January 1966): 45–52.

Columbia, David Patrick. "The Man Who Danced with Fred Astaire." *Dancing Times*, May–June 1991, 759, 848–850.

Coshocton Tribune. "Greeks' Dancing Wins War, Claim." December 8, 1940, 12.

Cromelin, Richard "B. J. Baker, 74; Backed Top Singers of '50s, '60s." *Los Angeles Times*, April 13, 2002. https://www.latimes.com/archives/la-xpm-2002-apr-13-me-baker13-story.html.

Dance Magazine. "Presstime News." 36, no. 1 (January 1962): 6.

Davidson, Bill. "China Doll." *McCall's*, February 1962, 86–87, 168–170.

Decatur Sunday Herald and Review. "Girl Dancers in Fred Astaire Show Watch Own Figures, Too." November 1, 1959, 52.

Des Moines Register. "A Square Dance in 'Flower Drum.'" April 30, 1961, 120. https://www.newspapers.com/image/128705478.

Dunning, Jennifer. "Carmelita Maracci, A Ballet Instructor and Choreographer." *New York Times*, August 3, 1987, D11. https://www.nytimes.com/1987/08/03/obituaries/carmelita-maracci-a-ballet-instructor-and-choreographer.html.

Ebony. "Movie Dance Director." 5 (April 1950): 22–26.

Folkart, Burt A. "E. Meglin, 93; 'Meglin Kiddies' Dance Instructor." Obituary. *Los Angeles Times*, June 25, 1988. http://articles.latimes.com/1988-06-25/news/mn-4707_1_meglin-kiddies.

Fox, Margalit. "Eugene Faccuito, 90, Creator of Jazz Dance Style, Is Dead." *New York Times*, April 12, 2015, 22.

Freeman, Al. "It's Colossal Job to Set Up TV Network Show from Resort Hotel." *Las Vegas Review Journal*, September 29, 1957, 21–22.

Georgakas, Dan. "The Man behind Fred and Ginger: An Interview with Hermes Pan." *Cinéaste* 12, no. 4 (1983): 26–29.

BIBLIOGRAPHY 265

Glenn, Larry. "'Flower Drum Song' Reprised Close to Home." *New York Times*, April 30, 1961, Section X, 9.

Harris, Avanelle. "I Tried to Crash the Movies." *Ebony*, August 1946, 5–10.

Hopper, Hedda. "The Best of Two Worlds Merge in Nancy Kwan." *Hartford Courant*, March 22, 1964, 11F. ProQuest Historical Newspapers. https://www.proquest.com/docview/548339174/EA15ABAB0FD14B7DPQ/1?accountid=14521&sourcetype=Historical%20Newspapers.

Horne, Lena, and Richard Schickel. *Lena*. Garden City, NY: Doubleday, 1965.

Howard, Edwin. "Tough Trying to See 'Lady.'" *Memphis Press-Scimitar*, November 9, 1963, 5.

Jhung, Finis. *Ballet for Life: A Pictorial Memoir*. New York: Ballet Dynamics, 2017.

Joel, Lydia. "Three Points of View." *Dance Magazine* 35, no. 11 (November 1961): 40–41.

Johnson, Erskine. "In Hollywood." *Miami Daily News-Record*, April 5, 1943, 4.

Jones, Grover. "Star Shadows." *Collier's*, April 30, 1938, 43–46.

Keating, Michelle. "He Put His 'Stamp' on ACT Musical." *Tucson Citizen*, June 29, 1978, 21.

Kelly, Gene. "And Now, the Real Kicker..." Interview with Graham Fuller. *Interview Magazine*, May 1994, 110–114.

Kerr, Walter. "First Night Report: 'Flower Drum Song.'" *New York Herald Tribune*, December 2, 1958, 29.

Kinberg, Judy, dir. "Rita Moreno, Jerome Robbins: Something to Dance About." American Masters Digital Archive (WNET). December 12, 2006. https://www.pbs.org/wnet/americanmasters/archive/interview/rita-moreno/.

King, Susan. "Nancy Kwan Looks Back on an All-Asian 'Groundbreaking' Film." *Los Angeles Times*, January 25, 2002. http://articles.latimes.com/2002/jan/25/entertainment/et-kingside25.

Levett, Harry. "Thru Hollywood." *Chicago Defender*, February 20, 1943, 19.

Los Angeles Daily Times. "Blanche Sweet Never Requires Dance Double." June 11, 1925, 11.

Los Angeles Mirror. "Nancy Kwan Now 'Little Deer.'" March 4, 1961, 2.

Los Angeles Sentinel. "'Blues at Midnight' to Be Presented Saturday." May 13, 1948, 23. Proquest Historical Newspapers. https://www.proquest.com/news/docview/562169154/FDBD9049A73D45FEPQ/16?accountid=14521&sourcetype=Historical%20Newspapers.

Los Angeles Times. "Dance Stand-in." December 15, 1935, C9.

Los Angeles Times. "'Sunset Strip Revue' Again Spotlights Comedian Vernon." November 29, 1948, 23. ProQuest Historical Newspapers. https://www.proquest.com/news/docview/165874559/7CDDA9CAB9FE4CFCPQ/2?accountid=14521&sourcetype=Historical%20Newspapers.

Lowry, Cynthia. "Patrick Adiarte's Face, Frame TV Standouts." *Sioux City Journal*, November 28, 1965, 39.

Lucas, Bob. "Las Vegas Triumph Sets Maria Cole on New Career." *Los Angeles Sentinel*, December 8, 1966, A1. ProQuest Historical Newspapers. https://www.proquest.com/news/docview/564803789/1C446B4C3D9B4DC1PQ/133?accountid=14521&sourcetype=Historical%20Newspapers.

Mainwaring, Dan. "Hollywood Nobodies." *Good Housekeeping*, April 1938, 40–41+.

Marston, Alan. "Marie Bryant—She Always Jumped for Joy." *Los Angeles Times Calendar*, October 8, 1978, N4+.

Martin, Pete. "Backstage with Nancy Kwan." *Saturday Evening Post*, February 10, 1962, 45.

Miyamoto, Nobuko. *Not Yo' Butterfly: My Long Song of Relocation, Race, Love, and Revolution*. Los Angeles: University of California Press, 2021.

Moreno, Rita. *Rita Moreno: A Memoir*. New York: Celebra, 2013.

Morriss, Frank. "Some Jottings from Hollywood." *Winnipeg Free Press*, August 3, 1940, 5.

Newsweek. "Finklea & Austerlitz, Alias Charisse & Astaire." July 6, 1953, 48–50.

New York Times. "Carol Haney, 'Pajama Game' Dancer, Dies at 39." May 12, 1964, 37.

Nixon, Marni, with Stephen Cole. *I Could Have Sung All Night: My Story*. New York: Billboard Books, 2006.

266   BIBLIOGRAPHY

Pittsburgh Courier. "Film Beauty." November 14, 1942, 20.

Redelings, Lowell. "The Hollywood Scene." *Hollywood Citizen-News*, September 13, 1954.

Reynolds, Debbie, with David Patrick Columbia. *Debbie: My Life*. New York: William Morrow, 1988.

Reynolds, Debbie, and Dorian Hannaway. *Unsinkable: A Memoir*. New York: HarperCollins, 2013.

Roark, Mary. "Alex Romero, 94, Choreographer for Elvis in 'Jailhouse Rock.'" *Los Angeles Times*, September 18, 2007, B9.

Robb, David. "Plan to Film 'Gotham' Stuntwoman in Blackface Scrapped by Warner Bros. TV." *Deadline*, October 9, 2014. http://deadline.com/2014/10/gotham-stunt-woman-blackface-warner-bros-848969/.

Rodgers, Richard. "The Mosaic That Is Called 'Flower Drum.'" *Los Angeles Times*, November 5, 1961, A9.

Rower, Billy. "Little Shots about Big Shots." *Pittsburgh Courier*, October 3, 1942, 20. Dunham's Data: Katherine Dunham and Digital Methods for Dance Historical Inquiry. https://dunhamsdata.org/.

Russell, Fred. "Gossip of the Rialto." *Bridgeport Post*, February 4, 1968, 57. https://newspaperarchive.com/bridgeport-post-feb-04-1968-p-57/.

Samuels, Charles. "Vera-Ellen Took a Tumble—Yet Her Fall Sent Her Up!" *Motion Picture and Television Magazine*, nos. 83–84 (1952): 30–31, 57.

Scheuer, Philip K. "'Flower Drum Song' Bright as Yule Tinsel." *Los Angeles Times*, December 3, 1961, A3.

Schlaerth, J. Don. "A Story-telling Delight on the Way." *Buffalo News*, October 16, 1962, 5.

Schmeltzer, Randy. "'Black Swan' Blasted for Ballet Cover-Up." *Adweek*, March 30, 2011. https://www.adweek.com/digital/black-swan-blasted-for-ballet-cover-up/.

Shearer, Lloyd. "Hollywood Comes to Bessie Loo for Oriental Beauties." *Oakland Tribune*, January 15, 1961, 69–70.

Stoop, Norma McClain. "American Musical Dancer/Choreographer: Patrick Adiarte: 'Art Is Aggressive.'" *Dance Magazine*, February 1978, 54–57.

Swisher, Viola Hegyi. "Gene and Jack and the Beanstalk." *Dance Magazine* 41, no. 2 (February 1967): 52–53.

Sydney Morning Herald. "She Taught Dance Routines to the Stars." October 14, 1954, 26.

Tajiri, Larry. "Oriental Kick Leaves Broadway." *Pacific Citizen*, November 24, 1961, 3.

Tampa Morning Tribune. "Davis Island Coliseum Ad." December 19, 1925, 18. https://www.newspapers.com/newspage/326989103/.

The Telegraph. "Twentieth Century Fox Archives." December 2, 2007. https://www.telegraph.co.uk/culture/film/3675305/20th-Century-Fox-Archives.html.

Time. "The Girls on Grant Avenue." December 22, 1958, 42.

Tornabene, Lynn. "Lunch Date with Nancy Kwan." *Cosmopolitan* 153, no. 5 (November 1962): 14.

Tsu, Irene. *A Water Color Dream: The Many Lives of Irene Tsu*. Edited by Jim Martyka. Orlando, FL: BearManor Media, 2020.

Tynan, Kenneth. "Tiny Chinese Minds." *New Yorker*, December 13, 1958, 104, 106.

Vera-Ellen. "The Role I Liked Best." *Saturday Evening Post*, November 1951, 107.

Wasserman, Dale. "An Homage to Marie Bryant." Letters. *Los Angeles Times,* October 22, 1978, L100.

Watts, Stephen. "On Arranging Terpsichore for the Camera Eye." *New York Times*, September 14, 1952, 5.

Whitcomb, Jon. "A New Suzie Wong." *Cosmopolitan* 148 (June 1960): 10–13.

Whitcomb, Jon. "Producer with the Midas Touch." *Cosmopolitan* 151 (December 1961): 10–13.

Index

For the benefit of digital users, indexed terms that span two pages (e.g., 52–53) may, on occasion, appear on only one of those pages.

Figures are indicated by an italic *f* following the page number.

Adiarte, Patrick, 174–78, 189–90, 208n.168
  and Nancy Kwan, 33, 160, 174–78,
    175*f*, 189–90
  See also Flower Drum Song
African Americans, 6–7, 8, 26, 173
  and antiblackness, 161
  and Charleston, 111–12, 174–75
  and dance, 55–58, 71, 99, 100, 110–11, 121–
    22, 130, 150, 152–53
  and *Flower Drum Song*, 176–78, 180–
    81, 193–94
  and Juanita Hall, 175–76
  and Lena Horne, 33
  and Los Angeles, 91, 150
  and Marie Bryant, 2–3, 14–15, 30–31,
    36, 58, 71
  and *Singin' in the Rain*, 102, 111
  and slavery, 55–58
  and white appropriation, 130, 152–
    53, 193–94
  See also antiblackness; Black studies
Africanist aesthetics, 59–61, 173, 180–
  81, 194–95
Africanist dance, 8, 112–14, 173–74, 175–76
  and Betty Grable, 58
  and Brenda Dixon Gottschild, 55, 101–
    2, 175–76
  and Gene Kelly, 129, 152
  and jazz dance, 33, 129
  and Marie Bryant, 90, 94
  and Patrick Adiarte, 33
Ahmed, Sara, 156–57, 171
Ailey, Alvin, 68
Alton, Robert, 92–93, 132, 150–51
American Ballet Theater, 35. *See also* ballet
An American in Paris (1951), 32–33, 112–13,
  129, 150–51
antiblackness, 9, 17
appropriation, 14–15, 21, 40–41, 130, 152–53,
  173–74, 180–81, 193–94

Asian/American(s), 52–53, 161, 162, 170–71,
  173–74, 179–81
  and anti-immigration laws, 6–7, 161
  and anti-miscegenation law, 6–7
  and assimilation, 161–62
  and *Flower Drum Song*, 4, 33, 156–61, 174,
    178, 181–83, 193–94
  as "model minorities," 161, 162
  and Orientalism, 173–74
  and racialization, 15
  studies, 33
  See also Nancy Kwan
Astaire, Fred, 44–46, 55–58, 67, 190
  and Alex Romero, 127, 128
  and Barry Chase, 1, 158
  and biographer Peter Levinson, 157–58
  and Ginger Rogers, 5–6, 44, 47, 181–82
  in *The Band Wagon*, 127
  in *The Barkleys of Broadway*, 128
  in *The Gay Divorcee*, 44–46
Atkins, Cholly, 72

Bailey, Pearl, 67, 95
Baker, B. J., 167–69, 172, 178–79
Baker, Jack, 127–28
Baker, Josephine, 71
Balanchine, George, 90, 107
ballet, 105, 123–24, 127–28, 178
  and Alex Romero, 127–28, 129, 134–35, 141–
    42, 150–51, 153–54
  and Betty Grable, 47–48
  and Carol Haney, 105–6, 109
  and *Flower Drum Song*, 33, 171, 172, 183–84
  and George Balanchine, 107
  and histories of, 107
  and Katherine Dunham, 72, 107
  and Marie Bryant, 66, 71–72, 88, 93*f*
  and Nancy Kwan, 33, 165, 171–73,
    174, 183–84
  and *On the Town*, 25–26, 66, 109, 141–42

268 INDEX

ballet (*cont.*)
    and Patrick Adiarte, 175–77
    and Rita Moreno, 122
    See also American Ballet Theater; Royal
        Ballet Academy
The Band Wagon (1953), 127, 128
Banerji, Anurima, 16–17
Banks, Miranda, 26–27
Barbier, Larry, 60*f*, 76–79, 77*f*, 79*f*, 80*f*, 81*f*, 82*f*,
    83*f*, 84*f*
Barthes, Roland, 50–51
Basinger, Jeanine, 68
Bates, Florence, 66, 94
Bean, Jennifer, 20, 211–12n.37
Behlmer, Rudy, 105, 114
Beltrán, Mary, 124–26
Bench, Harmony, 145
Berkeley, Busby, 5–6
Bernardi, Daniel, 38
Bernstein, Leonard, 134–35, 138–39, 140*f*
Billman, Larry, 25, 39, 43, 46, 153–54
Biss, Eula, 103–4
Black dance, 13–14, 30, 100, 193–94
    scholars, 11, 69
Black feminist studies/scholars, 12, 13–16, 23–
    24, 27, 40–41, 69–70, 108
Black theater, 27, 72–73
blackface, 8, 38–39, 52–54, 121, 152
Blackman, Lisa, 15–16
Blackness, 11–12, 14, 40, 42, 64, 89, 152,
    173, 175–76
    and appropriations of, 152–53, 193–94
    See also antiblackness
Blue, Angie, 38, 46–48, 49–51, 49*f*, 59, 62,
    64, 190–91
    and *The Barkleys of Broadway*, 128
    and "Blue Sisters," 44, 45*f*
    as dance-in for Betty Grable, 2, 20–22, 30–31,
        36–37, 44–46, 48, 53–55, 62–63, 190
    and early life of, 44
    and Hermes Pan, 2, 36, 44–46, 47–48, 51–52,
        53, 54–55, 59, 62–63, 62*f*, 128, 190
    and John Franceschina, 25, 36–37, 47–48
    and Marie Bryant, 36, 61–62
    and *Pin-Up Girl*, 62–63
    and salary, 46–47
    and *That Night in Rio*, 53, 54*f*
Bluett, Lennie, 73–74
bodily turn, 15–18
Bogle, Donald, 67–68, 71
Bradley, Rizvana, 11, 12–13, 17–18, 40
Brannigan, Erin, 42–43
Brannum, Barry, 13–14

Brenneis, Jon, 134–35, 136*f*, 137*f*, 139*f*, 140*f*,
    143, 144*f*
Brown, Michael, 9–10
brownface, 52–53, 128
Bruce, Mary, 71–72
Bruce, Virginia, 89
Bryant, Marie, 2–3, 73–76, 77*f*, 78*f*, 79*f*, 81*f*, 84*f*,
    85, 86–99, 150, 190–91
    and Alvin Ailey, 68
    and Angie Blue, 36–37, 61–62
    and Betty Grable, 30–31, 36–38, 58–65,
        63*f*, 76–79
    and Billy Daniels, 58–61, 60*f*, 84–85
    and Bob Hope, 67, 79–81, 83*f*, 84–85, 183–84
    in *Carolina Blues*, 73–74, 74*f*
    and death of, 69
    and Debbie Reynolds, 21–22
    and Duke Ellington, 58, 67–72
    and early life of, 71–73
    and Eugene Loring's American School of
        Dance, 92, 93*f*
    and "finishing," 96–98
    and Gene Kelly, 76–84, 82*f*, 87–88
    and Hollywood racism, 31, 70–71, 75, 85–86
    and home of, 91
    in *Jump for Joy*, 72–73, 73*f*
    and Katherine Dunham, 72, 94
    and Lena Horne, 31, 33, 67, 95–96, 189–90,
        193, 194–95
    and marginalization of, 67–68, 76–79
    and Maria Cole, 67, 96, 97*f*
    and Marlon Brando, 72
    and misidentification/misspelling of name,
        25–26, 66, 69
    and *Nat King Cole Television Show*, 190
    in *On the Town*, 31, 66, 67*f*, 67, 79*f*, 90, 94,
        128, 134–35
    and parasitism, 14–15, 91, 135–36
    as "Pocahontas," 86, 183–85
    and professional debut, 72
    and reproductive labor, 14–15, 25–26,
        31, 66–99
    and remembering of, 64, 68–71
    and segregation, 61–62
    and Vera-Ellen, 31, 67, 70–71, 76–79, 80*f*, 87–
        88, 89–95, 131–32, 135–36, 189–90
    and visibility of, 70
    and *Wabash Avenue*, 69–70, 88, 89
Bubbles, John, 111
Butler, Judith, 9, 22

Calvin, Dolores, 69–70, 89
del Campo, Rudy, 123–24, 182

INDEX

Cansino, Paco, 110–11, 122, 149
capitalism, 8, 11, 12, 23–25, 103–4
Carolina Blues (1944), 58, 73–74, 74*f*
Casey, Carrie Gaiser, 107
Castle, Nick, 58, 76–81, 84*f*
Caughie, Pamela, 120–21
celluloid, 19–20, 42, 166–67
Chakravartty, Paula, 103–4
Chambers-Letson, Joshua, 23, 106–7
Chan, Jennifer, 157
Chang, Julianna, 178, 181, 182, 185
Charisse, Cyd, 67, 76–79, 78*f*, 88, 127, 128, 227n.97
Charleston, 111–14, 113*f*, 122–23, 174–75
Chase, Barrie, 1, 25, 150–51, 158
Cheng, Ann Anlin, 11, 157, 170–71, 174–75, 180–81, 183
Cherniavsky, Eva, 20, 40–41, 64–65
Chicago, 69, 71–72, 75
Chinese Exclusion Act, 161. *See also* Asian Americans
Chisholm, Ann, 20, 34–35
chorus dancer(s), 2–3, 52–54, 66, 78*f*, 123–24, 182
　Angie Blue, 2, 44
　as anonymous, 178–85
　and dance-ins, 29–30
　Debbie Reynolds, 100–1
　Jeanne Coyne, 113–14, 113*f*
　Marie Bryant, 72
　and Nancy Kwan, 178, 179–80, 181
　Patricia (Pat) Denise, 128, 181
Chung, Hye Jean, 29
cinematography/ers, 1, 5, 6, 29–30, 38–39, 40–41, 131, 166–67
Clark, Sam, 55–58, 57*f*
Clark, VéVé, 27
Clover, Carol, 30, 100–1, 102, 111–12, 115–16, 118–19, 130, 152
Cody, Iron Eyes, 183–84, 184*f*, 185
Cohan, Steven, 120–21, 141–42
Colbert, Soyica, 15–16
Cold War, 7, 160–61
　Orientalism, 160–62
Cole, Jack, 91, 111–12, 122
　and Alex Romero, 127–28, 132–33, 134, 142, 147–48, 149, 150–51, 189–90
　and Barrie Chase, 150–51
　and Billy Daniels, 58–59
　as "father" of jazz dance, 110–11
　and Hermes Pan, 189–90
　and Jeanne Coyne, 110–12
　and Marie Bryant, 69

and Patricia (Pat) Denise, 127–28
and style of, 129, 178–79, 180–81, 193–94
Cole, Maria, 67, 96, 97*f*
Coney Island, 50, 53–54, 59–61
corporeal signature, 42–43
corporeality, 10–11, 17, 18–19, 42–43, 133–34, 135–36
　and Asian/American, 33, 160–61
　and Asian women, 11
　and Betty Grable, 30–31, 36, 50, 58, 62
　and Debbie Reynolds, 111, 115–16, 119, 121–22
　and film studies, 20
　and Gene Kelly, 33
　and Nancy Kwan, 163–64, 167, 169, 170–72, 173, 174, 177–78, 183
　off-screen, 35
　and race, 13, 14, 40, 104, 170–71
　and reproduction, 13, 20
　and surrogates, 22–23, 27–28
　and Vera-Ellen, 92, 94, 135–36
　as white/and whiteness, 36, 64–65, 89–90
Coyne, Jeanne, 102, 107–10, 111–14, 115–16, 117–18, 190–91
　and Carol Haney, 102, 105–6, 107–9, 128
　as dance-in, 32, 190
　and Debbie Reynolds, 2, 21–22, 32, 102–3, 105–6
　and Gene Kelly, 101–2, 101*f*, 131–32, 190
　and miscrediting of, 25–26
　and reproductive labor, 106
　and Rita Moreno, 102–3, 126
　and *Singin' in the Rain*, 2, 101*f*, 102–3, 113*f*, 117*f*, 119
　and whiteness, 120–22
craft labor, 3–4
Crawley, Ashon, 12–13
creative labor, 29
credit, 25–26, 27–28, 103–4, 107, 115, 146, 152–53
　and Hollywood's corporeal ecosystem, 3–4
　and Marie Bryant, 69, 94–95
　and *Singin' in the Rain*, 32, 100, 102–3, 104, 106, 119, 125–26. *See also* debt
Cuban/Afro-Cuban, 7, 92, 150

Dabholkar, Pratibha, 105–6, 139
dance-in, 1, 2–3, 14–15, 47, 64–65, 127–55, 181
　and Alex Romero, 4, 32–33, 128–30, 146–48, 152–53
　and Angie Blue, 2, 20–22, 25, 30–31, 36–37, 44, 46, 47, 50, 51–52, 53–54, 190
　and archives, 24, 26, 27–28

270   INDEX

dance-in (*cont.*)
  and Becky Varno, 33, 157–58, 178–79, 190
  and Carol Haney, 2, 33, 186, 190–91
  and doubling, 145
  and film, 18–19
  and Gene Kelly, 131
  and indexicality, 19–20
  and Jeanne Coyne, 2, 32, 101–2, 108–10,
    112–13, 190
  and Jeni LeGon, 193
  and labor, 8, 24, 194–95
  and Lena Horne, 186, 190–91, 193
  and Marie Bryant, 31, 67–68
  and Patricia (Pat) Denise, 128
  and queerness, 129–30, 143
  and racialization of, 156–57
  and Shirley Temple, 30–31, 38, 39–40
  and surrogation, 22–24, 40, 41, 109
  and whiteness, 4, 38, 54–55, 58, 157–58
dance studies, 1–2, 4–5, 9, 11, 26–27
  and appropriation, 21
  and Black studies, 14–15
  and the body, 9–11, 13–14, 16–17
  and Hortense Spillers, 11, 14
  and reproduction, 21
  and screendance studies, 18–19
  and white women, 102
Daniels, Billy, 46, 58–61, 60*f*, 61*f*, 76–79,
  78*f*, 84–85
debt, 103–4, 116–22. *See also* credit
DeFrantz, Thomas, 30
Delameter, Jerome, 5–6, 178–79
Deleuze, Gilles, 16–17, 70
Denise, Patricia (Pat), 127–28
Devoe, Irene, 1
Diggs, Soyica, 22
digital media, 18–19, 42, 85
disability studies, 15–16
Doane, Mary Ann, 19–20, 42, 64
Dodds, Sherril, 18–19
Donen, Stanley, 101–2, 101*f*, 131–32, 134–35
Donohue, Jack, 39
Duncan, Isadora, 107
Dunham, Katherine, 89, 90, 107
  and Marie Bryant, 58, 72, 76–79, 88, 92, 94
Dyer, Richard, 38–39, 40–41

Easterlea, Rob, 50
Ebony, 75–76, 80*f*, 84–85, 91–92
  and Maria Cole, 96
  and Marie Bryant feature, 31, 58–61, 60*f*, 70–
    71, 76, 77*f*, 78*f*, 86–87, 88–90
Ebsen, Buddy, 39

Eichenbaum, Rose, 143–45, 146, 150, 153
Ellington, Duke, 58, 68, 72–73, 88, 90
Ellis, John, 50–51
Elswit, Kate, 16–17
embodiment, 15–16, 130, 145, 154–55
  as Asian/American, 170–71, 183
  as "dual," 96–98
  and Franz Fanon, 11–15, 170–71
  and Hortense Spillers, 11–15, 170–71
  and Nancy Kwan, 170–71, 173–74, 183
  and Patrick Adiarte, 33
  and privilege, 38–41, 64–65
  as racial, 4–5, 9, 11–15, 170–71
  and Shirley Temple, 30–31
  as white/and whiteness, 4–5, 9, 40–41
environmental studies, 15–16
ephemerality, 21
Erigha, Maryann, 75
Everett, William, 169
Evers, Medgar, 192–93

Fair Labor Standards Act, 39
Fancy Pants (1950), 79–81, 84–85, 185
Fanon, Frantz, 11–15, 170–71
Faye, Alice, 44, 53
Felix, Seymour, 46
femininity, 96–98, 147–48, 157, 163–64, 170–
  71, 178, 192–93
  as white, 30–31, 38, 121, 124–25, 172–73, 177
Ferreira da Silva, Denise, 103–4
Filipinos, 6–7, 84 , –124, 162, 176–77, 182. *See
  also* Adiarte, Patrick
finishing, 96–98
Firmino-Castillo, María Regina, 16–17
Fisher, Anna Watkins, 85, 91
Fisher, Gary, 152–53
Flatt, Ernie, 105–6, 110, 115
Flower Drum Song (1961), 4, 29–30, 156, 164,
  174, 175–77, 181–82, 183–85
  and Asian immigrants, 161–62
  and Becky Varno, 25–26, 157–58, 163–64,
    163*f*, 167
  and Carol Haney, 189–90, 193–94
  and Chinatown, 180–81
  and "Chop Suey" ensemble, 174–75
  and corporeality of Nancy Kwan, 172, 173
  and dancers in, 180–81
  and Finis Jhung, 178–79
  and Hermes Pan, 157–58, 163*f*, 167, 172
  and indexical instability of Nancy Kwan,
    158–60, 162
  and racial ambivalence of Nancy
    Kwan, 170–71

and rise of Nancy Kwan, 158–60, 171
and scholarly attention to, 160–61
and *The World of Suzie Wong*, 158–60, 170
See also Kwan, Nancy; Varno, Becky
Fontaine, Joan, 46
Fontaine, Len, 13–14
Fort, Syvilla, 72
Foster, Susan, 104, 133–34
Foucault, Michel, 9, 29
Franceschina, John, 25, 36–37, 47–48, 51–52, 55
Freedley, Eugene, 143
Fuller, Loïe, 107

Gaines, Jane, 20–21, 28–29, 44, 50
Gallop, Frank, 188–89, 190–91
Garbo, Greta, 35
Gardner, Ava, 67, 81*f*, 87–88
Garland, Judy, 150–51, 192–93
Gavin, James, 95
The Gay Divorcee (1934), 44–46, 47–48
Gaynor, Mitzi, 67
Gennaro, Peter, 72
    Dancers, 188–89
Genne, Beth, 142
Georgakas, Dan, 47
George, Doran, 17
George-Graves, Nadine, 27, 75
Gil, José, 16–17
Ginsberg, Elaine, 115
Girard, René, 136–37
Glenn, Larry, 156–58, 174–75
Goddard, Paulette, 67, 76–79, 78*f*, 88, 89–90
Gottschild, Brenda Dixon, 30, 55, 68, 113–
    14, 175–76
Grable, Betty, 45*f*, 78*f*
    and Angie Blue, 2, 20–21, 30–31, 36–37, 44–
        46, 47–48, 49–52, 49*f*, 62–64, 190–91
    and Hermes Pan, 46, 47–48, 50
    and Marie Bryant, 30–31, 58–61, 60*f*, 63–64,
        66–68, 76–79, 88, 95
    and *Moon over Miami*, 48
    and pin-up image, 2, 36, 37*f*, 43, 50–51, 58
    and rise of, 44
    and surrogation, 30–31, 34–65
    and Twentieth Century-Fox, 6, 44, 46, 49–50
    and *Wabash Avenue*, 59–61, 60*f*, 63*f*, 88
    and whiteness, 34–65
    See also Blue, Angie; Bryant, Marie
Graeber, David, 103–4
Graham, Martha, 95, 107
Grant, Frances, 84–85
Groscup, Marie, 142, 207n.164
Guattari, Félix, 16–17, 70

Hagen, Jean, 100, 118*f*, 119–22, 123*f*
Hall, Juanita, 175–76
Haney, Carol, 25–26, 107–13, 115–16, 117*f*,
    119–21, 126, 142–43
    and Debbie Reynolds, 21–22, 32, 101–3,
        105–6, 190–91
    and Gene Kelly, 128, 131–32
    and Jack Cole, 128, 178–79, 180–81
    and Jeanne Coyne, 2, 105–6, 121–22, 190–91
    and labor, 102–3, 107–8
    and Lena Horne, 186–87, 187*f*, 188–95
    and *On the Town*, 128, 144*f*
    and Patrick Adiarte, 175–76
    and *Singin' in the Rain*, 2, 101–2, 101*f*,
        106, 117–18
    See also Coyne, Jeanne
Harlow, Jean, 44
Harney, Stefano, 102, 104
Harper, Marilyn, 34, 35–36, 38–39
Harris, Avanelle, 75–76
Harris, Cheryl, 40–41
Hart, Lorenz, 90
Hartman, Saidiya, 23–24, 27
Hawai'i/Hawaiian, 52–53, 111–12, 112*f*, 182
Hayworth, Rita, 110–11, 149, 150–51
Hepburn, Audrey, 157–58, 167–68
Hepburn, Katharine, 72–73
Herrera, Brian, 53, 124, 125–26, 150–51
Hess, Earl, 105–6, 139
Hill, Constance Valis, 67–68
Hip Hop, 13–14
Hirschhorn, Clive, 114
Holliday, Judy, 120–21
Hollywood, 36–37, 69, 73–74, 134–35, 189–90
    and Alex Romero, 130, 149–50, 154–55
    and Alex Ruiz, 153–54
    and Asian/America, 156, 181
    and Betty Grable, 44, 66
    and Billy Daniels, 60*f*
    and Black press, 89
    and body doubling, 34–35
    and choreographers, 44–46, 128–29
    and continuity, 5, 38
    and corporeal ecosystem of, 17–18, 184–85
    and corporeal exchanges, 158
    and credit and debt, 107
    and dance, 14–15, 58
    and dance-ins, 2–3, 8, 17–18, 23–24, 34,
        42–43, 186
    and dancing bodies, 33, 42–43
    and displacement of dancers of color, 36
    and film industry, 20
    and film production, 24–25

272   INDEX

Hollywood (*cont.*)
  and film sets, 156, 157–58
  and Golden Age of, 5
  and integration, 5, 6
  and Jewish Americans, 121
  and Jim Crow, 75
  and labor, 107
  and Latin America, 52–53, 148–49
  and Lena Horne, 31, 75–76, 91, 186–87
  and Marie Bryant, 2–3, 31, 61–62, 66–68, 69–71, 72, 79–81, 84–86, 87–88, 91, 96
  and midcentury musicals, 4, 6, 25, 30, 34, 54–55, 67–68
  and Nancy Kwan, 167, 169, 171, 173
  and Patricia (Pat) Denise, 127–28
  and racial politics of, 8, 86, 186–87
  and Red Scare, 8
  and Rita Moreno, 124–26
  and segregation, 6
  and television, 190
  and "unknowns," 34
  and white corporeality, 64–65
  and white female body, 40–41
  and whiteness, 3–4, 5, 6, 8, 38, 42–43, 52–53, 130, 158–60, 181
Hollywood Production Code, 6, 34–35, 141
Honig, Bonnie, 116–17
Hope, Bob, 67, 76–86, 81*f*, 183–84, 190
Horne, Lena, 73–74, 75–76, 195
  and *Broadway Rhythm*, 66, 193
  and Carol Haney, 33, 186–87, 187*f*, 188–95
  and Judy Garland, 192–93
  and Marie Bryant, 31, 33, 58, 67, 91, 95, 96, 189–90, 193
  and nightclub career, 95–96
Hunt, Marilyn, 131–32, 135–36
Hunter, Ross, 156–57

immigration, 7, 161
  laws, 6–7, 160–61, 178
indexicality, 19–20, 30–31, 34–65, 163–67, 183–84
  and digital media, 42
  and *Flower Drum Song*, 166–67, 168–69, 170
  and politics of, 35
intercorporeality, 83–84. *See also* corporeality
Ireland, John, 78*f*, 88
Iverson, Margaret, 41–42, 64
Iyer, Usha, 20

Jackson, Robert, 68
Jackson, Zakkiyah Iman, 12–13, 83–84

jazz (dance), 115–16, 121–22, 142, 176–77, 178–79, 180–81
Jewish Americans, 7, 120–21
Jhung, Finis, 178–79, 208n.168
Johnson, Emily, 9–10
Johnson, Imani Kai, 21
Johnson, Jasmine, 13–14, 21–22, 93–94, 110
Jones, Douglas, 22
Joseph, Miranda, 106
Jump for Joy (1941), 72–73, 73*f*, 88

Kaplan, Sarah Clarke, 23–24, 88–89
Keeling, Kara, 42–43, 64, 70, 89
Kelley, Robin D. G., 9–10
Kelly, Gene, 4, 20–21, 178–79, 180–81
  and Alex Romero, 2, 32–33, 128–33, 134–36, 138–39, 140*f*, 142–43, 145–48, 151–54, 158, 191
  and biographer Clive Hirschhorn, 114
  and biographers Earl Hess and Pratibha Dabholkar, 139–41
  and Black dance traditions, 100, 111
  and Carol Haney, 33, 109–10, 128, 131–32, 142–43, 186
  and Cyd Charisse, 127
  and Debbie Reynolds, 100–1, 102–3, 105–6, 109–10, 111, 114–15, 120*f*
  and Donald O'Connor, 100–1, 105, 110, 111–12, 112*f*, 115
  and *Flower Drum Song*, 156, 181–82, 189–90
  and heteronormative masculinity, 4, 131–32, 141–42
  and Jeanne Coyne, 101–2, 109–10, 131–32, 190
  and *Les Girls*, 150
  and Marie Bryant, 31, 58, 66, 76–84, 82*f*, 89–90, 91–92, 94–95, 189–90
  and Metro-Goldwyn Mayer (MGM), 131–32, 134–35, 136*f*, 141–42, 150
  and *On the Town*, 134–35, 136*f*, 142, 150–51
  and Paco Cansino, 122
  and Patricia Ward Kelly, 131
  and Patrick Adiarte, 175–76
  and Rita Moreno, 122–23, 124–25
  and Robert Alton, 92–93
  and *Singin' in the Rain*, 2, 101*f*, 105–6, 112–13, 112*f*, 116–18, 117*f*, 119
  and Vera-Ellen, 31, 90, 91–93, 135–36, 138–39, 139*f*, 140*f*, 141, 189–90
  and *Words and Music*, 31, 32–33, 87–88, 89–90, 131–32, 137*f*, 138*f*
  See also Romero, Alex; *Singin' in the Rain*
Kerr, Deborah, 167–68

INDEX 273

Kidd, Michael 127
Kidwell, Clara Sue, 86
Kim, Chang-Hee, 157, 161
Kim, Claire Jean, 173
Kim, Ju Yon, 162
King, Tiffany Lethabo, 94–95
Klein, Christina, 157, 160–61
Knight, Arthur, 6
Knowles, Mark, 127–28, 129, 132, 149–50, 153–54
Knox, Donald, 112–13
Konzett, Delia Malia Caparoso, 52–53
Koster, Henry, 156
Krayenbuhl, Pamela, 20, 30, 67–68, 128–29, 130
Kwan, Nancy, 4, 156–57, 159f, 167–68, 174, 179f, 184–85
   and Anne Cheng, 183
   and Becky Varno, 25–26, 33, 67–68, 158, 163–64, 181, 190–91
   and B. J. Baker, 167, 168, 169
   and chorus dancers, 178, 179–80, 181
   and corporeality of, 171–72, 183
   and early life of, 158–60, 171
   and Flower Drum Song, 33, 161–62, 163–64, 165, 166f, 167, 171, 174, 178–80, 183–84
   and Hermes Pan, 178–79
   and heteronormative femininity, 157
   and indexical instability, 33, 158–60, 166–67, 168–69, 183
   and Iron Eyes Cody, 183–84, 185
   and Jose de Vega, 182
   and panethnicity, 158–60, 176–78
   and Patrick Adiarte, 174–78, 175f, 189–90
   and racial ambiguity, 162, 172–73, 185
   and screen image of, 170
   and whiteness, 157, 160
Kwan, SanSan, 173–74

LaFarge, Antoinette, 148
La Meri, 110–11
Lane, Sarah, 35
Latin America(n), 8, 52–53, 148–49, 173–74, 176–77
Latinx, 6–7, 15, 52–53, 124, 148–49, 150–51, 176–77
   dancers, 3–4, 182
   See also Romero, Alex
Lee, C. Y., 156
Lee, Josephine, 161
Lee, Rachel C., 15–16, 183
LeGon, Jeni, 75, 193, 194–95
Levine, Debra, 25, 68
Lewis, David, 169, 181–82

Lindy Hop, 72
Lockett, D'Lana, 99
Lopez, Shirley, 123–24
Loring, Eugene, 58, 73f, 92, 127–28, 158
Los Angeles, 24–25, 73–74, 183–84
   and Alex Romero, 149, 150
   and Jump for Joy, 72–73, 73f
   and Lena Horne, 95
   and Marie Bryant, 58–59, 72, 79–81, 90, 92, 96
   and Meglin's Kiddies, 38–39
   and zoot suit riots, 6–7, 148–49
   See also Hollywood
Los Angeles Times, 34, 35–36, 38, 69, 181–82
Love, Heather, 69–70
Lowe, Lisa, 162

Macias, Anthony, 149–50
Manning, Erin, 16–17
Manning, Susan, 150–51
Maracci, Carmelita, 123–24
Mariani, John, 124–25
Marston, Alan, 71, 72–73, 75
Martin, Mary, 1
Martin, Randy, 16–17
masculinity, 4, 129–30, 141–42, 146, 147–48, 152, 154–55
Mast, Gerald, 141–42
McConachie, Bruce, 160–61
McLean, Adrienne, 20
McNally, Karen, 121
media studies, 26–27, 29
Meglins Kiddies, 34, 38–39
Mellencamp, Patricia, 124–25
Metro-Goldwyn-Mayer (MGM), 5, 127–28, 134–35, 141–42
   and Alex Romero, 131–32, 150, 153–54
   and Angie Blue, 44–46
   and Annie Get Your Gun, 150–51
   and Arthur Freed unit, 24–25
   and Debbie Reynolds, 105–6, 107–8
   and Jean Harlow, 44
   and Jeni LeGon, 75, 193
   and Lena Horne, 75–76
   and Marie Bryant, 67, 91
   and musicals, 5–6
   and On the Town, 66, 67, 92, 136f
   and Rita Moreno, 122, 124–25
   and Vera-Ellen, 80f, 91, 92
   and Words and Music, 89–90
Metzger, Sean, 162
Mexican Americans, 6–7, 32–33, 148–50, 152–53, 182. See also ; Latinx; Romero, Alex

274 INDEX

Miller, Ann, 73–74, 142, 150–51
Mimieux, Yvette, 153–54, 154f, 155f
minstrelsy, 8, 53–54, 150–51
Miranda, Carmen, 5–6, 53
Mitchard, Millard, 116–17
modern dance, 17, 110–11, 123–24, 142, 150–51
    and history of, 107
    and Katherine Dunham, 72
    and Martha Graham, 95, 107
    and Rita Moreno, 122
Monroe, Marilyn, 44
Moon over Miami (1941), 46, 48
Moreno, Rita, 32, 102–3, 122–26, 123f, 128, 148–49
Moten, Fred, 9–10, 102, 104
Motley, Elisabeth, 16–17
Moynihan Report, 12
Muñoz, Jose, 129–30, 152–53
Munshin, Jules, 134–35, 142
Musser, Amber, 96–98

Nash, Jennifer C., 14–15
National Association for the Advancement of Colored People (NAACP), 8
neoliberalism, 85, 103–4
Ness, Sally Ann, 171–72
New York City, 120–21, 123–24, 134–35, 137f, 138–39, 142
    and "A Day in New York" ballet, 25–26, 130, 134–35, 136f, 138–39, 138f, 141–42, 144f, 150–51
    and Jack Cole, 110–11
    and Lena Horne, 95
    and Marie Bryant, 72, 90
    and New York Public Library, 99, 131–32, 159f
Nicholas Brothers, 100, 111
Nicholas, Harold, 58, 73–74, 74f
Nixon, Marni, 167–68
Noland, Carrie, 104
Norton, Pearlie May, 51–52, 53
Noyes, Betty, 115–16, 119
Nyong'o, Tavia, 27–28, 69–70

Ocampo, Anthony, 176–77
O'Connor, Donald, 102–3, 105–6
    and Debbie Reynolds, 100–2, 105, 110, 114–16
    and *Singin' in the Rain*, 100, 101f, 111–12, 112f, 115–17, 141–42
On the Town (1949), 66, 134–35
    and "A Day in New York" ballet, 25–26, 130, 134–35, 136f, 138–39, 138f, 141–42, 144f, 150–51

and Alex Romero, 32–33, 128, 129, 150–51, 189–90
and Carol Haney, 109, 189–90
and Marie Bryant, 31, 66, 67, 67f, 90, 94, 128, 134–36
and Vera-Ellen, 90, 92–93, 135–36
Orientalism, 84–85, 95, 110–11, 170–71, 179–81
    and Cold War, 160–62
Ossorio, Robert, 123–24
Osumare, Halifu, 16–17
Ovalle, Priscilla, 124–25

The Paleface (1948), 84–85, 185
Palumbo-Liu, David, 162, 175–76
Pan, Hermes, 47–48, 52, 54–58, 56f–57f, 62f, 156–57, 189–90
    and Alex Romero, 128
    and Angie Blue, 2, 36, 44–46, 50, 53, 59, 62–63, 128
    and Becky Varno, 50, 157–58, 178–79
    and Betty Grable, 46, 59
    and *Flower Drum Song*, 157–58, 163–64, 163f, 167, 174–75, 181–82, 184–85
    and *The Gay Divorcee*, 44–46
    and jazz dance, 55–58, 180–81
    and John Franceschina, 25, 36–37, 51–52
    and Nancy Kwan, 172
    and *Pin-Up Girl*, 62–63
    and surrogation, 58
    and *That Night in Rio*, 53
panethnicity, 156–57, 174–78, 234n.22
Paramount, 5–6
parasitism (artistic), 14–15, 31, 66–99, 135–36
Paredez, Deborah, 153–54, 192–93
Peirce, Charles Sanders, 41–42, 166–67
performance studies, 1–2, 9, 13–14, 26–27, 85, 106–7, 146
    and reproduction, 21, 22
    and surrogation, 22–23, 40
    and whiteness, 38
performance theory, 23, 106–8
Perron, Wendy, 72
Perry Como's Kraft Music Hall, 186, 187f, 188, 193–94
Petty, Miriam, 67–68
Phelan, Peggy, 22
photography, 50, 73–74, 76–79, 134–35, 143–45, 166–67
Photoplay, 46, 48, 49–50, 49f
Pin-Up Girl, 62–63, 62f
Polowney, Frank, 50
Powell, Eleanor, 75

INDEX   275

Prescod, Janette, 71
Presley, Elvis, 127–28, 153–54
Primus, Pearl, 107
Puerto Ricans, 7, 32, 102–3, 122, 123–24, 123*f*, 148–49, 182. *See also* Moreno, Rita

queer/queerness, 129–30, 143, 191–92
    and Alex Romero, 32–33, 127–55, 191
    and dance-ins, 154–55
queer scholarship, 15–16, 27, 69–70, 134, 191–92

racial capitalism, 23–24
Raheja, Michelle, 185
Red Scare, 8. *See also* Cold War
Redman, Nick, 167–68, 169
Redmond, Sean, 50–51, 88–89
Regester, Charlene, 26, 67–68
reproductive labor, 1–33, 106–14, 115–16, 128–29
    and Angie Blue, 30–31
    as Black, 14–15, 31, 70–71, 86, 88–90
    and Carol Haney, 102, 106, 107–8
    and choreography, 2–3
    and dance-in, 3, 8, 18–19, 29, 67–68, 128–29, 143
    and gender, 23–24, 29, 102–3
    and Jeanne Coyne, 102, 106, 107–8
    and Marie Bryant, 30–31, 66–99
    and Sadiya Hartman, 23–24
    and *Singin' in the Rain*, 32, 100–26
    and surrogacy, 23
    and white hegemony, 108
    and white stardom, 2–3, 89–90
Reynolds, Debbie, 112–13, 122, 123*f*
    and Alex Romero, 128
    and Carol Haney, 2, 32, 33, 101–2, 105–6, 107–8, 109–10, 115–16, 117–18, 190–91
    and debt, 102–3, 106, 115, 120–21
    and Donald O'Connor, 114–15
    and Ernie Flatt, 105–6
    and Gene Kelly, 105, 111, 114–15, 119, 120*f*
    Jeanne Coyne, 33, 101–2, 105–6, 107–8, 109–10, 115–16, 118–19, 190–91
    and Marie Bryant, 67
    and reproductive labor, 106–8, 126
    and Rita Moreno, 125–26
    and *Singin' in the Rain*, 2, 100–3, 105–6, 111–12, 112*f*, 113*f*, 114, 116–18, 117*f*, 118*f*, 141–42
    and whiteness, 105, 121–22
RKO, 5–6, 44–46, 80*f*, 86
Roach, Joseph, 22–23, 40, 62–63, 107–8

Robbins, Jerome, 99, 175–76
Roberts, Rosemary, 16–17
Robinson, Bill "Bojangles," 100, 111
Rodgers and Hammerstein, 156–57
    and *The King and I* (1951), 160–61
    See also Rodgers, Richard
Rodgers, Richard, 90, 181–82
Rodríguez, Clara E., 148–49
Rogers, Ginger, 5–6, 44, 47, 181–82
Rogin, Michael, 38–39, 120–21
Romero, Alex, 4, 128–29, 131–43, 136*f*, 137*f*, 138*f*
    and Alex Ruiz, 153–54, 154*f*, 155*f*
    and ballet, 127–28, 129, 134–35, 141–42, 150–51, 153–54
    and biography by Mark Knowles, 129, 132, 149
    and Carol Haney, 128, 189–90
    and dance-in, 4, 32–33, 128–30, 146–48, 152–53
    and Debbie Reynolds, 128
    and *The Eddie Fisher Show*, 190
    and Fred Astaire, 127, 128
    and Gene Kelly, 2, 20–21, 32–33, 67–68, 129–33, 134–36, 138–39, 140*f*, 142–43, 145–48, 151–54, 158, 191
    and Hermes Pan, 128
    and Jack Cole, 127–28, 132–33, 134, 142, 147–48, 149, 150–51, 189–90
    and Latino heritage, 149
    and Los Angeles, 149, 150
    and Metro-Goldwyn Mayer (MGM), 131–32, 150, 153–54
    and misspelling of name, 127–28
    and *On the Town*, 32–33, 128, 129, 150–51, 189–90
    and Patricia (Pat) Denise, 128
    and queer/queerness, 32–33, 127–55, 191
    and *Singin' in the Rain*, 128
    and tap, 127–28, 129, 150
    and Vera-Ellen, 134–36, 138–39, 139*f*, 140*f*, 153–54
    and whiteness, 150–52
    and *Words and Music*, 32–33, 129, 131–32, 135
Rosenberg, Douglas, 18–19
Rubin, Gayle, 136–37
Ruiz, Alex, 153–54, 154*f*, 155*f*

Sage, Sally, 48
Said, Edward, 160–61
Samuels, Charles, 90–93
San Francisco, 72, 153–54, 156, 173–74, 178, 181–82, 184–85

276 INDEX

Schechner, Richard, 22
Schneider, Rebecca, 146, 148
Schwartz, Selby, 16–17
Scott, Lee, 135, 142–43
Sedgwick, Eve, 116–17, 129–30, 136–39, 143,
  146–48, 154–55
segregation, 6–7, 61–62, 91, 148–49
sexuality, 130, 156–57, 158–60
  and Betty Grable, 50
  and Marie Bryant, 91–92
  studies, 15–16
Shawn, Ted, 110–11
Shaye, Amaryah, 103–4, 115
Sheppard, Alice, 9–10
Shildrik, Margrit, 15–16
Shimakawa, Karen, 162
Shiovitz, Brynn, 20, 30, 67–68
Shohat, Ella, 121–22
Sinatra, Frank, 134–35, 142
Singin' in the Rain (1963), 101*f*, 113*f*,
  117*f*, 120–21
  and African American dance, 111–12, 112*f*
  and Alex Romero, 128
  and Carol Clover, 100, 102, 111–12, 115–16
  and Carol Haney and Jeanne Coyne, 2, 101–
  2, 108–9, 111
  and credit and debt, 32, 100–26
  and Cyd Charisse, 127
  and Debbie Reynolds, 101–3, 105, 106–7,
  114, 116–17, 141–42
  and Gene Kelly, 111, 141–42, 152, 190
  and Jewish screenwriters, 120–21
  and labor, 106–7, 110, 111, 125–26
  and Patricia (Pat) Denise, 128
  and Rita Moreno, 32, 102–3, 123–25, 126
  and Rudy del Campo, 182
  See also Kelly, Gene; Reynolds, Debbie
slavery, 12, 13–14, 23–24, 108
Slide, Anthony, 24
somatics, 11–12, 17
Spatz, Ben, 16–17
Spillers, Hortense, 11–15, 23–24, 40–41,
  55, 170–71
Srinivasan, Priya, 16–17
Stark, Ray, 162, 170, 171
St. Denis, Ruth, 107, 110–11
surrogation, 23–24, 38–41, 58–59, 109, 170,
  183–84, 195
  and Betty Grable, 30–31, 34–65
  and Joseph Roach, 22–23, 62–63, 107–8
  and performance theories, 22
  and reproduction, 58
  and reproductive labor, 108, 143

and *Singin' in the Rain*, 32, 116–17
and slavery, 108
and U.S. racial formations, 55
and whiteness, 41, 53–54, 108
See also Roach, Joseph

Takeshita, Chikako, 15–16
tap, 38–39, 55–58, 75, 99, 119, 188, 193–94
  and Alex Romero, 127–28, 129, 150
  and Alex Ruiz, 153–54
  and Betty Grable, 47–48
  and Black dancers, 100, 111
  and Debbie Reynolds, 105–6
  and Marie Bryant, 71–72
  and Nancy Kwan, 176–77
  and Patrick Adiarte, 175–76
  and Rita Moreno, 122
  Singin' in the Rain, 100, 111–12
Taylor, Diana, 22–23
Temple, Shirley, 30–31, 34, 35–36, 38–40, 47–48
Terrell, Maurice, 117–18, 117*f*, 119
That Night in Rio (1941), 53, 54*f*
That's Entertainment Part III (1976), 131, 150–51
They Live by Night (1948), 66, 75, 80*f*
Toy, Dorothy, 181–82
transgender studies, 15–16
Trenka, Susie, 67–68
Tsai, Addie, 18–19
Twentieth Century-Fox, 5–6, 24–25, 46, 50,
  51–52, 59–61, 190
Tygett, Jack, 182

University of Southern California Cinematic
  Arts Library, 24–25, 66, 105–6

Varno, Becky, 164, 165, 167, 172, 174–75, 178–
  79, 180–81, 190–91
  and Barrie Chase, 158
  as dance-in, 33, 67–68, 157–58
  and Hermes Pan, 157–58, 163–64, 163*f*
  and misspelling of name of, 25–26
  and Nancy Kwan, 158, 163–64, 163*f*
  See also Flower Drum Song; Kwan, Nancy
Vera-Ellen, 88, 89–95
  and Alex Romero, 134–36, 138–39, 139*f*,
  140*f*, 153–54
  and Carol Haney, 143
  and Gene Kelly, 131–32, 135–36, 138–39,
  138*f*, 141, 153–54
  and Marie Bryant, 31, 67, 70–71, 76–79, 80*f*,
  89–94, 189–90
  and *On the Town*, 66, 94, 134–36
  and *Words and Music*, 87–88, 90, 131–32

INDEX 277

Vitale, Joseph, 84–85, 185
Vogel, Shane, 22
de Vorak, Geraldine, 35

Wabash Avenue (1950), 216n.124
  and Angie Blue, 61–62
  and Betty Grable, 58–61, 60f, 61f, 63–64,
    63f, 88
  and Marie Bryant, 58–59, 60f, 63–64, 63f, 66,
    69–70, 88, 89
Wallace-Sanders, Kimberly, 55–58
Warner Brothers, 5–6, 24–25, 157–58
Warren, Doug, 50
Wasserman, Dale, 69–70, 72–73
Watts, Stephen, 109
Weheliye, Alexander, 12–13
Weinbaum, Alys, 23–24, 108
West Side Story (1961), 32, 33, 122, 123–24, 182
Westbrook, Robert, 43
Whitcomb, Jon, 174–75, 176–77
white privilege, 3, 8, 115
white supremacy, 8, 14, 17, 40–41, 86
white womanhood/femininity, 36, 38, 43, 88–
    89, 121, 172–73, 177. *See also* Grable, Betty
whiteness, 9, 30–31, 34–65, 86, 94, 156–57
  and Alex Romero, 150–52
  and "Americanness," 175–76
  and Angie Blue, 51–52, 64
  and Asianness, 160, 173
  and ballet, 172–73
  and Betty Grable, 38, 43–44, 50–52, 64
  and Black reproductive labor, 88–89
  and the body, 15
  and choreographers, 4
  and credit, 103–4
  and Debbie Reynolds, 32, 121–22
  and debts, 116–22
  as ethnic, 116–22
  and expansion of, 7, 32, 121
  and film, 6, 38–39, 50–51
  and formations of, 32, 86, 102–3, 120–21
  and Hollywood, 3–4, 5, 38, 158–60, 181

  and Lena Horne, 194–95
  and Nancy Kwan, 157, 158–60, 169–70, 172–
    73, 183, 185
  as a photograph, 50–51, 88–89
  and privilege, 40–41, 103–4, 150, 183
  and reproduction of, 39, 44, 53–54, 108, 130
  and Shirley Temple, 38
  and *Singin' in the Rain*, 123–24, 125–26
  and stratifications within, 125–26
  and surrogation, 38–41, 53–54
Wiegman, Robyn, 136–37
Wing, Paul, 181–82
Wolf, Stacy, 191–92
Wollen, Peter, 100–1
The Wonderful World of the Brothers Grimm
    (1962), 153–54, 154f, 155f
Wong, Yutian, 162
Wood, Natalie, 167–68
Words and Music (1948), 89–90, 135, 141–42,
    222n.111
  and Alex Romero, 32–33, 129, 131–32, 135
  and Cyd Charisse, 88
  and Marie Bryant, 31, 79–81, 80f, 87–88,
    90, 131–32
The World of Suzie Wong (1961), 158–60, 170,
    241n.142
World War II, 52–53, 149
  and Asian/America, 164
  and Betty Grable, 36, 43
  and internment of Japanese Americans
  and racial structures in the U.S., 6–7
  and whiteness, 121, 150–51

yellowface, 52–53, 170, 175–76, 182
Young, Genii, 76–79, 87
Young, Hershini Bhana, 12–13
Young, Lester, 73–74

Ziegfeld Follies (1945), 25–26, 66
Zondi, Mlondolozi, 13–14
Zoot Suit Riots, 6–7, 148–49
Zuo, Mila, 162